A TYNESIDE HERITAGE

PETER S. CHAPMAN

A TYNESIDE HERITAGE

SOUTH SHIELDS, COUNTY DURHAM AND THE CHAPMAN FAMILY, 1811–1963

The History Press

For my family

First published 2021

The History Press
97 St George's Place, Cheltenham,
Gloucestershire, GL50 3QB
www.thehistorypress.co.uk

© Peter S. Chapman, 2021

Front cover: 'Mouth of the Tyne', © Christine Westerback

The right of Peter S. Chapman to be identified as the Author
of this work has been asserted in accordance with the
Copyright, Designs and Patents Act 1988.

British Library Cataloguing in Publication Data.
A catalogue record for this book is available from the British Library.

ISBN 978 0 7509 9626 6

Typesetting and origination by Typo•glyphix
Printed and bound in Europe by Imak

CONTENTS

PREFACE

Memories of my grandparents' house, *Undercliff* in Cleadon, where I was born in 1944, have remained vivid throughout my adult life. In the dining room were ancestral portraits, in the drawing room a display cabinet with my grandfather's medals and decorations, and upstairs in my grandmother's sewing room a long shelf in the mahogany bookcase full of scrapbooks, recording family events over three decades from the 1930s. Some newspaper articles took the reader back to early nineteenth-century Tyneside. I became fascinated by this historical collection.

Seven years ago I was invited by the South Shields Local History Group to give a lecture on the lives of my grandparents, Sir Robert and Lady Chapman, and the contribution they had made to the local community from the 1920s to the early '60s. Inspired by this invitation I got to work reading each scrapbook page and sifting through family archives meticulously preserved by my elder brother, Sir David, and his wife, Marika.

By the time the lecture had taken place, the idea for the book was born. I would push back its historical start date to the beginning of the nineteenth century, the family link being my great-great-grandfather Robert Chapman, who had been born in 1811, and the focus would be on the changing fortunes of South Shields, Tyneside and County Durham, brought into sharp relief through the lives of the Chapman family over 150 years, ending with my grandfather's death in 1963.

The book involved extensive and enjoyable research on topics ranging from shipbuilding and coal exporting to political and economic developments and leisure activities, all affected dramatically by two world wars.

Numerous librarians, archivists and museum staff members have given me the benefit of their knowledge and expertise. Catrin Galt, Community Librarian, Family History and Heritage, at South Tyneside Libraries, has answered numerous queries, provided ideas for images from the council's exceptional historic collection and allowed me to access a wide range of unpublished documents. Anne Sharp, former Local History Librarian, and Caroline Barnsley, former Senior Library and Information Assistant, have both been very supportive.

Assistance from Adam Bell, Assistant Keeper, Social History at the South Shields Museum & Art Gallery, from Ruth Sheret at the Philip Robinson Library of Newcastle University, from Julie Biddlescombe-Brown formerly at Durham University's Palace Green Library and from Kay Easson and her colleagues at the Lit & Phil Library in Newcastle has all been much appreciated.

Research reports and documents provided by Tyne & Wear Archives in Newcastle have filled in many gaps. Assistance from Durham County Records Office, the National Archives, the National Library of Scotland, Historic Environment Scotland, the Imperial War Museum, Bridgeman Images, RIBA Collections, Stirling Council, the British Red Cross Society, St John Ambulance, the Institute of Chartered Accountants in England and Wales, D.C. Thomson & Co. Ltd, Clarion Housing Group (successor to the Sutton Dwellings Trust), Hew Stevenson and Owen P. Elton, Head of Mathematics at Marlborough College, is gratefully acknowledged. Staff at the London Library have, as ever, been unfailingly helpful and I give special thanks to Amanda Stebbings, Head of Member Services, for research assistance and permission to photograph images from books and journals in the library's collection.

Ian Whitehead, former Keeper of Maritime History at the Discovery Museum in Newcastle upon Tyne, has been an invaluable source of information and research on shipping generally, and on Tyne rowing in the nineteenth century. I also happily acknowledge a debt of gratitude to Len Barnett, Alan Johnson, the late Richard E. Keys, Norman L. Middlemiss, Dave Waller and Christine Westerback.

On the First World War I benefited from research and assistance provided by Chris Baker, David Wardrop, Patrick Brennan and Mary Ingham (who also helped with Second World War research). Lt Col Peter Winton, Commanding Officer 101st (Northumbrian) Regiment, Royal Artillery, kindly arranged access to regimental memorabilia at the

Napier Armoury in Gateshead through his colleagues Capt. Jim Foster and Lorraine Dent, RAWO.

The education of family members in the nineteenth century was a fruitful topic, and I acknowledge with gratitude help from Oliver Edwards, Archivist of the Royal Grammar School in Newcastle, Mrs Rachel Roberts, College Archivist of Cheltenham Ladies' College, Jane Claydon, Archivist of St Leonards School in St Andrews, and Mike Todd for information on the South Shields Boys' High School. Assistance from Graham Allen, Chairman of South Shields and Westoe Rugby Football Club, and from Phil McGowan of the Rugby Football Union was much appreciated.

Throughout the book's long gestation period I have benefited from the strong support of the South Shields Local History Group and particularly of its Honorary President, Dorothy Fleet. Her exceptional knowledge of South Shields was generously shared with me, and no request was too much trouble. Her SSLHG colleagues Janis Blower (Patron), Alan Newham (Chairman), Jean Stokes (Vice-Chair), Jim Mulholland and Jim Smith have all been enthusiastic and helpful. Information from Pauline Shawyer and Heather Thomas on family members was also much appreciated.

Friends and family have kept me going. Julia Carnwath kindly made available detailed information on the Armstrongs, who were great friends of my family. My own close friend the late Professor Michael Dickson CBE generously left me a legacy to help fund research and development costs. My brother David, sister Elizabeth Levy and cousin Caroline Steane have provided encouragement, information and some splendid images.

Laurie Danaher has typed every draft and redraft, every caption and credit, with good humour and meticulous attention to detail. I know how fortunate I have been to have had her professional help and expertise from the very beginning.

My wife, Joan, has been a star. Unwavering in her support for the project, she has helped me with its structure, given constructive criticism on early drafts, taken camera shots of family portraits and documents, set up digital files for nearly 200 images, and somehow found the energy to spur me on if I seemed to be flagging. Our children Christopher, Vicky, Katherine and Rachel have been loyal supporters from the start, wisely taking the long view on a publication timescale.

In the event, once the manuscript and images were with The History Press, Nicola Guy (Commissioning Editor, Local History) and Juanita Zoe Hall (Managing Editor) facilitated a smooth passage to publication, despite Covid-19 obstacles. I am very grateful to them and to my indexer, Joanna Luke, for their professional help and encouragement.

INTRODUCTION

Migration in England was not always from north to south. The Chapman family had lived for four generations in Upleatham in the Yorkshire parish of Guisborough, before William Chapman ('Yeoman otherwise butcher'), born in 1747, moved to Elwick in the parish of Hart in what was still called the County Palatine of Durham, reflecting the jurisdictive powers formerly exercised by its bishops. His son, Robert Chapman, born in 1782 at Hart, moved further north to South Shields at the mouth of the River Tyne and became a mariner and shipwright, marrying Elizabeth Cleugh of Westoe.

This account of 150 years of the Chapman family in South Shields and County Durham begins with the life of his son, Robert Chapman, JP, who was born in 1811 and died in 1894. It continues with his son, Henry Chapman, JP, FCA (1850–1936), and ends with his grandson, Col Sir Robert Chapman, Bt (1880–1963).

South Shields was transformed out of all recognition during Robert Chapman's nineteenth-century life, as the coal trade, industry and shipbuilding boomed. This heady expansion, and later severe contraction, of the economy formed the backcloth to the business and public service endeavours of the Chapman family for a century and a half.

PART 1

SOUTH SHIELDS AND THE TYNE

Perchance a person South of York
May, whilst having varied talk,
(But not of fair Elysian fields)
Have heard of such a place as Shields.
Matthew Stainton, 1868[1]

1

THE TRANSFORMATION BEGINS

Robert Chapman's life spanned most of the nineteenth century. Born in 1811 during the Napoleonic Wars, he would see profound social and economic changes before his death in 1894. At the time of his birth in South Shields on the south bank of the River Tyne where it meets the North Sea – then called the German Ocean – the town's population had started to increase dramatically. From small beginnings of 11,000 at the time of the first national census in 1801, there was a 40 per cent increase by 1811, and by the end of the century the population had risen to 100,000.

In the early years of the nineteenth century, South Shields was largely concentrated along the river, with small communities to the south in the nearby agricultural villages of Westoe and Harton. Its architectural pride and joy was the eighteenth-century Town Hall. Affectionately known as the 'Pepper Box', it was situated prominently in the middle of the Market Place, which was 'chiefly occupied by private houses and the residences and offices of professional men'.[1]

They were fortunate enough to be comparatively well housed. However, for the vast majority of the population, living conditions ranged from the fairly primitive to the absolutely appalling. There was no gas or electricity supply and therefore no street lighting, little or no paving, no sewerage or efficient drainage system, and water supply was totally inadequate both in distribution – mostly by water carts – and in quality. This situation was both typical of expanding industrial towns and cities throughout Britain, and also disastrous for public health. To ameliorate conditions would require a strong economy, new municipal powers, and resolute political will.

1855 Ordnance Survey map of South Shields, published in 1862, by which time the population

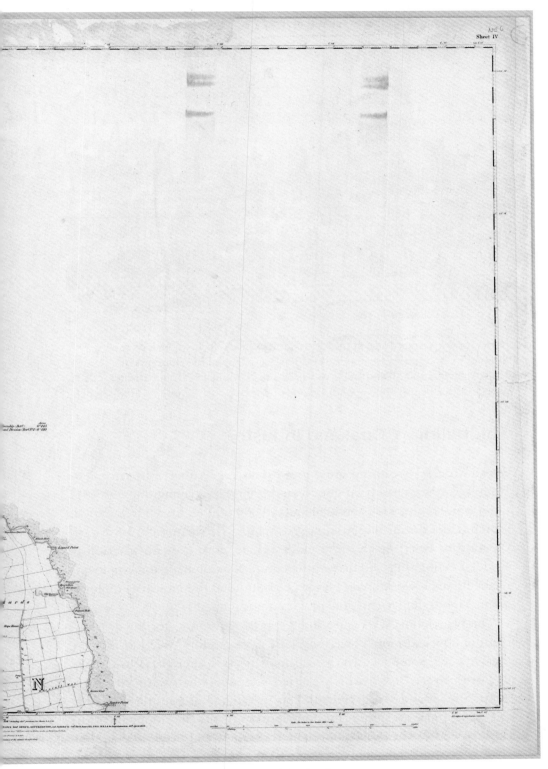

was around 35,000. (National Library of Scotland)

Town Hall and Market Place, South Shields

Sketch of the Market Place in the 1850s, showing the Old Town Hall of 1768, St Hilda's Church (*c.* 1764), St Hilda's Colliery (1825) and the chimneys of R. & W. Swinburn & Co.'s plate glass works. The Town Hall was affectionately known as the 'Pepper Box'. (South Tyneside Libraries)

Shipbuilding, Coal and Industry

South Shields' economy grew rapidly during Robert's lifetime. The Napoleonic Wars had been good years for building sailing ships: by 1811 there were some 500 vessels totalling 100,000 tons registered to the town, which had a dozen shipbuilding yards and a larger number of docks.[2] Operations were mostly on a modest scale, with the construction of wooden sailing ships requiring little complex equipment and employing relatively small workforces. Nevertheless, in total the industry employed around 1,000 shipwrights, one of whom was Robert's father.

The Napoleonic Wars had also been productive years for the development of new and more powerful vessels. A year before Waterloo, in 1814, the Tyne celebrated its own first steamboat called, appropriately enough, the *Tyne Steam Packet*, which carried passengers between Newcastle, South Shields and North Shields. This new mode of transport would in due course make a significant contribution to the development of the river, especially since road communications between Newcastle and the coast were – and remained for another half century – exceptionally poor.

The town clerk of South Shields, Thomas Salmon, recognised the revolutionary significance of the steamer's maiden journey on 19 May 1814, recalling that 'Being Ascension Day, it joined the procession of barges and boats, and was a great novelty. I was one of the multitude of wondering spectators, who witnessed its performances from Newcastle Bridge.'[3] As it turned out, the passenger service was not a commercial success, and a new owner, Joseph Price from Gateshead, renamed her *Perseverance* a few years later and turned her very successfully into the first steam tug on the river.

The French may have been decisively defeated in 1815, but the immediate result was economic depression and distress, exacerbated by a currency panic. The Army reduced its numbers, and the Royal Navy reduced the size of its fleet, discharging seamen for whom there was no alternative employment. As Hodgson put it, 'an immense body of seamen were thrown idle',[4] resulting in bitter strikes throughout the North East. In what were known as the 'two Shields' (North and South, reflecting the towns' Tyneside locations), there were around 7,000 seamen and their demands were for increased wages and manning levels. Their strike committee was well organised and maintained strict discipline. Pickets prevented nearly all ships from sailing, and seamen who tried to set sail were taken out and paraded through the streets with 'faces blackened and jackets turned'.[5]

Perseverance towing the brig *Friends' Adventure* up river to Newcastle. Built in 1814, she became the first steam tug on the Tyne. Painting (formally entitled *Seascape*) by the American mariner and artist Frank Wildes Thompson (1836–1905). (Laing Art Gallery, Newcastle upon Tyne. © Tyne & Wear Archives & Museums/ Bridgeman Images)

The ship owners appealed successfully for help from the Navy and the military. Cavalry were sent from Newcastle; a troop of dragoons was stationed on the Bank Top and marines on the sands; 600 special constables were sworn in; and two sloops of war stood by. The odds were stacked very heavily against the seamen, and in the event the strike collapsed in October 1815, just a month after it had started. Some 200 affected ships then put to sea. Nevertheless, three months later in January 1816, between 300 and 400 sailing vessels were still 'laid up in Shields Harbour and unrigged owing to the badness of trade'.[6]

Economic conditions gradually improved, the new technology of steam started to spread widely, and expanding shipyards created jobs for unemployed seamen. In South Shields, Thomas Dunn Marshall had successfully developed steam tugs and in 1839 his yard launched the North East's first iron ship, the *Star*. He then launched the SS *Bedlington*, an innovative iron-built, twin-screw train ferry, designed to carry loaded coal trucks in her hold. Although she was a commercial failure, the technological advance was significant, and in 1845 he built two iron-screw steamers (*Hengist* and *Horsa*) for owners in Bremen, followed by commissions for Hamburg owners, 'the Germans thus showing their facility for assimilating new ideas quicker than their British competitors'.[7]

In 1844 there was another important technical innovation on the Tyne. John Coutts had built at his Walker shipyard, upstream on the north bank, a small sailing vessel of 271 tons, the *Q.E.D.* She was subsequently fitted with auxiliary engines made by Messrs Hawthorn at their Newcastle engine works. *Q.E.D.* (an abbreviation of the Latin *Quod erat demonstrandum*, or 'what it was necessary to prove') was not only a pioneering screw-propelled vessel, but, most importantly, she was the first ship to be built with a double bottom, enabling her to take in water to act as a ballast without spoiling the cargo holds. This was revolutionary, since the typical practice at the time was to use chalk as a ballast when empty vessels were returning to their home ports after delivering their cargoes. The banks of the Tyne were disfigured by huge heaps of chalk ballast. South Shields was no exception, with The Bents Ballast Hills alone covering an area of 30 acres.

By 1848 there were thirty-six shipbuilding yards on the Tyne, with steam power poised to replace sail in the decades ahead. Nevertheless, at this mid-century point, over 90 per cent of all vessels were sailing ships, and they continued to be built on a very substantial scale. When Robert

Chalk ballast unloaded from sailing ships at Cookson's Quay was transported by railway to The Bents, whose unsightly ballast hills covered some 30 acres. In the background can be seen Tynemouth Priory. (South Tyneside Libraries)

Chapman became a ship owner in 1854, it was a sailing ship in which he invested. Its fortunes, and those of the mercantile sailing fleet as a whole, will be explored in the next chapter.

The growth of Tyne shipbuilding in the first half of the nineteenth century was despite, rather than because of, the state of the river. South Shields and neighbouring downstream ports suffered from what can best be described as the curse of Newcastle, which through 'ancient chartered privileges' controlled the whole river, from its mouth to the west of the city. Newcastle had been an irresponsible conservator, and:

> In fact the Tyne was a treacherous and inconvenient port with no defences at the entrance against gales which frequently strewed the Black Midden rocks with wrecks, and with a channel beset by shoals and obstructions. During the first half of the nineteenth century Newcastle took over £1 million in dues from shipping which used the port, but only about a third of that amount was spent in maintaining or improving the harbour.[8]

The brig *Margaret* at the mouth of the Tyne painted by the South Shields seafarer-turned-artist John Scott in 1849, when over 90 per cent of all vessels were still sailing ships. (South Shields Museum and Art Gallery. © Tyne & Wear Archives & Museums/Bridgeman Images)

This hugely disadvantageous situation – which had undoubtedly held back development in South Shields – started to be ameliorated in 1848, and was finally resolved in the early 1850s.

It was coal that fuelled the growth of the Tyne's shipbuilding industry and economy. The increase in coal mining during the first half of the nineteenth century was by far the most important of all the industrial activities on Tyneside. It profited greatly from the existence of a ready market, especially in London, and from the ship-borne route to it. Transportation to ports was facilitated by the use of new waggon ways, while the increased use of steam power for pumping enabled deeper seams to be reached.[9] New and deeper pits included the Templetown Pit, named after its owner Simon Temple, at the eastern end of Jarrow Slake in 1810, and the St Hilda's pit in South Shields itself, owned by J. and R.W. Brandling, in 1822. Output almost doubled between 1831, when annual shipments from the Tyne were 2.2 million tons, to the early 1850s when they were around 4 million tons. Most of the coal continued to go to London, but exports responded to strongly increasing demand and started to be significant from 1831, when

dues were reduced. They were abolished in 1845 for British-owned colliers (coal-carrying vessels). This export trade from the Tyne amounted to
161,000 tons in 1831 (7.3 per cent of total shipments), increasing sixfold to
over 1 million tons in 1845 (30.6 per cent of all shipments).

Employment conditions and labour relations were woeful. In 1825 a
Miners' Union was formed, its publication, *A Voice from the Coal Mine*,
heavily critical of poor ventilation and of the annual bond system
with its low wages and potential for fines ('a kind of legalised temporary serfdom').[10] A few years later the Union was incorporated into the
Association of Colliers on the Rivers Tyne and Wear, which soon had
some 4,000 members. In 1831 there was a miners' strike, one of the key
demands being a reduction in the punishingly long hours worked by
boys from the age of 6 upwards. The colliery owners finally agreed that
in future boys should not work for more than twelve hours a day.

Then, in June 1839, disaster struck. There was a terrible explosion at
St Hilda's Pit, close to the town centre of South Shields, in which fifty
men and boys died.[11] The town clerk at the time, Thomas Salmon, recalled

DROPS AT WALLSEND.

Thomas Hair's sketch of coal 'drops' at Wallsend on the north bank of the Tyne in the
early 1840s, when booming coal exports reached 1 million tons a year. (T.H. Hair
and M. Ross, *A Series of Views of the Collieries in the Counties of Northumberland and
Durham* [London, 1844])

St Hilda's Pit in the centre of South Shields, sketched by Thomas Hair, was the scene
of a terrible explosion in 1839 that killed fifty men and boys. (T.H. Hair and
M. Ross, *A Series of Views of the Collieries in the Counties of Northumberland and
Durham* [London, 1844])

the tragedy: 'Never shall I forget … the harrowing spectacle that presented
itself at the mouth of Saint Hilda Pit, when on that day, so sad and melan-
choly in the annals of our borough, one scorched and blackened corpse
after another was brought to bank, amidst the wailings and lamentations of
surrounding relatives.'[12]

The town, in a state of shock, was determined to prevent a repeat of
this terrible tragedy. A local Committee for the Prevention of Accidents in
Mines was formed at a public meeting. Chaired by the Borough's Member
of Parliament, Robert Ingham, its members were leading residents, notably James Mather, a wine and spirits merchant, and an active Radical
in politics. The committee's hard-hitting report of 1842 was produced
by Mather himself. It called for sweeping changes in mining operations,
including mandatory improved ventilation systems, an end to employing children under 11 years old, and for the appointment of Inspectors
of Mines. The report, which became famous in Britain and abroad, was
considered by a House of Lords Committee in 1849 (by which time a
new Pitman's Union had been formed and the great miners' strike of 1844
had taken place), and by a Parliamentary Committee in 1852. Almost all
of its recommendations were adopted in the subsequent Mines Act and
internationally it became a textbook of best practice. The grateful miners

of Northumberland and Durham presented a silver cup to James Mather in recognition of his outstanding achievements.

The increased output from the coalfields facilitated the growth of a wide variety of coal-using industries on Tyneside and in South Shields itself, notably the chemical industry and glass-making, which expanded dramatically after the 1820s. By mid-century, Tyneside's chemical manufacturers employed 50 per cent (3,067) of the national total of 6,326 in the industry, and consumed nearly 250,000 tons of coal a year. They produced about a third of the national supply of alkali and two-thirds of the national output of crystal soda.[13] In South Shields the largest chemical firm was Cookson & Cuthbert, which used the Leblanc process (named after a French chemist) for the manufacture of alkali. Unfortunately this process involved pumping into the atmosphere large quantities of highly noxious hydrochloric acid gas. A number of private prosecutions were brought against the company in the late 1830s and early '40s, notably by a local farmer who complained – successfully – about damage to his crops. As further prosecutions were launched, the company received support not only from its 700 employees, but also from a large number of local working men in marches and public meetings. A resolution was passed opposing the prosecutors, whose proceedings 'would sacrifice an enormous extent of valuable property and deprive several thousands of their helpless countrymen of bread'.[14] Jobs that caused pollution were better than no jobs at all.

However, the proprietors of Cookson's had had enough, and, as they had threatened, they closed their plant in 1843. Fortunately for the workers, it was purchased in the following year by James Stevenson of Glasgow, and renamed the Jarrow Chemical Works. His son was James Cochran Stevenson, who would make an exceptionally important contribution to public life in South Shields. He ran the company successfully for several decades and oversaw a major restructuring as competitive pressures intensified in the 1880s. Unfortunately those pressures proved terminal. The company's interests were transferred in 1891 to the United Alkali Company, which closed down the South Shields works the following year.[15] By the end of the century the Tyneside chemical industry was a mere shadow of its former self.

Cookson's business interests had not been confined to the chemical industry. They had been glass-makers since the eighteenth century, and by the 1830s Cookson & Co.'s Works had become the biggest glass-making enterprise in the country. It remained in pole position after its sale in 1845 to a new company, R.W. Swinburne & Co., which shared with a Birmingham company an enormous order for the rolled plate glass required for the Great Exhibition at Crystal Palace in 1850, where the company obtained a prize medal for its innovative craftsmanship. However, the following decades would also see glass-making in South Shields in gradual, and then final, decline.

The Railways Arrive

The glass-making, chemical and coal industries benefited enormously from the transport revolution in the first half of the nineteenth century, the Stockton and Darlington Railway of 1825 being 'the first clear demonstration of the commercial transformation which could be produced by the construction of a railway'.[16] The benefits were two-fold. First, local transportation costs were reduced by as much as two-thirds compared to road transport, and, even more importantly, the new railway lines provided cost-effective access to the lucrative 'sea-sale' markets for coal from the mines of inland South Durham. Before the advent of the railways, it cost less to move a ton of coal from Newcastle to London by sea than to move it 19 miles overland from Bishop Auckland in south Durham to Stockton.

For its part, South Shields was an early beneficiary, becoming the terminus for the new Stanhope & Tyne Railway, which opened in 1834. Like other early railways, it drew on experience of the technology of the colliery waggon ways. When it was first completed, 'it combined every form of motive power then known. Ten and a half miles were worked by horses, nine and a quarter miles by locomotives; there were three miles of self-acting inclined plane and no less than eleven miles which were worked by fixed haulage engines.'[17]

The development of railways to South Shields and other Tyne ports enabled coal to be loaded directly into colliers' holds from 'drops' or 'staithes' (waterside depots equipped with staging and shoots for loading vessels). This gradually and painfully led to the demise of keelmen, who had previously transferred coal from shore to colliers in their small boats or keels. Strikes – sometimes long and bitter – could not halt the technological advance. The Stanhope & Tyne brought another benefit: it gave South

Shields the first Tyneside public railway, carrying passengers to Vigo, near Washington, and thence by coach to Durham. More importantly, passengers could, by 1840, travel by rail from South Shields to Gateshead, on the Brandling Junction line. This involved changing trains at Brockley Whins to join the railway company's main line from Sunderland to Gateshead, but the service was rather spasmodic: 'loud were the complaints of the long delays involved by waiting at the junction'.[18] Facilities for passengers were basic, as was noted in a review fifty years later:

> The first-class carriages were not so good by any means as the main line third-class of today; the second-class were uncushioned and comfortless; the third-class simply open waggons. A journey to London (in the early 1840s) was a fearful undertaking. To accomplish it by Parliamentary train you had to leave South Shields about five o'clock in the morning,[19]

arriving in London twelve hours later. Fortunately, in 1844 the improved rail route from Tyneside to London was completed, the inaugural journey taking just under seven hours from Euston to Gateshead.[20]

Municipal Developments

While trade, industry and transportation were expanding rapidly, local government was still in an embryonic state. Indeed its forerunner, the Select Vestry (whose responsibilities included the administration of the Poor Law, policing, the provision of medical relief, and the assessment and collection of the rates), could not cope with the scale of the town's expansion. An important step in extending municipal powers was taken in 1828. A 'Bill for paving, lighting, watching [policing], cleaning, regulating and improving the town of South Shields, and its neighbourhood' was approved at a public meeting in the Town Hall and subsequently by Parliament. The resulting Act set up an Improvement Commission for defined areas of the townships of South Shields and Westoe. The Commissioners first met in July 1829 and although their rating powers were limited, they introduced a regular system of 'scavenging' (refuse collection), and a programme of repairing roads, which were generally in a 'filthy condition', not least because houses were undrained. By arrangement with the Select Vestry, 'paupers' (men receiving financial assistance, or 'relief', under the Poor Laws) were employed as 'scavengers', street sweepers and general labourers.

It is hard to imagine now just how dark, filthy and unhealthy towns like South Shields were in this period. The Commissioners started what was to be the very slow and long process of providing adequate street lighting. Gas lamps were provided for the first time in 1829 – twenty of them. Fifteen years later there were still only 178. As for public health, epidemics were regular life-taking visitors. After the arrival of the terrible and prolonged cholera epidemic of 1831, South Shields formed an ad hoc 'Board of Health' to try to prevent its spread. Meanwhile, 'January 11, 1832 was observed as a fast day. All business was suspended, all shops closed, and services of intercession were held in St Hild's and the various chapels that the cholera scourge might be stayed.'[21]

The year 1832 did, however, bring excellent news for the town's political health. This was the landmark year in which Earl Grey's famous Reform Bill, despite its earlier rejection by the House of Lords, received the Royal Assent as the Representation of the People Act. It established

Robert Ingham, MP, QC, became South Shields' first Member of Parliament in 1832 following the enactment of the 'Reform Bill'. A Liberal, he represented the borough at Westminster with distinction for twenty-five years. (South Tyneside Libraries)

a new parliamentary Borough for South Shields (including Westoe), for which the town had petitioned Westminster two years earlier. Even though the restrictive electoral qualifications meant that only around 3 per cent of the 1832 population of 19,000 residents were eligible to vote, the fact that the town would have its own representative in London would bring significant benefits over the following two decades. The town's first MP was Robert Ingham, QC (1793–1875), born in Newcastle upon Tyne. He was a 'Whig or Moderate Liberal' lawyer who had become Recorder at Berwick before the 1832 South Shields election, having 'taken a very active part in promoting the enfranchisement of the town'.[22]

Parliamentary activity affecting South Shields continued apace in the 1830s. Following a Royal Commission on the Poor Laws (the national system of parish 'relief', or assistance, to the destitute originally introduced in 1601 in the reign of Queen Elizabeth I), the Poor Law Amendment Act of 1834 reached the statute book. This important Act set up, at national level, the Poor Law Commission, which would become the Poor Law Board in 1847, and eventually the Local Government Board in 1871, as the responsibilities of local government continued to expand. Under the 1834 Act, South Shields, Westoe, Whitburn, Harton, Boldon and the townships of Hedworth, Monkton and Jarrow were combined to form the South Shields Poor Law Union, administered by a Board of Guardians drawn from the participating townships. The South Shields Union had twenty-five guardians (eighteen of whom came from South Shields and Westoe). In addition all county magistrates residing in the Union's area automatically became members. The first Chairman of the Union was an ex-officio member, the magistrate Richard Shortridge. He was a glass manufacturer, 'perhaps the wealthiest man in South Shields', and 'a commercial man of the richest integrity'.[23] He remained chairman until 1854, and died thirty years later, leaving generous legacies to twenty-one charities.

The 1834 Act enshrined the Royal Commission's recommended principle of 'less eligibility', namely that the pauper's 'situation on the whole shall not be made really or apparently so eligible as the situation of the independent labourer of the lowest class'. That is to say, financial assistance ('relief') to paupers should not exceed the wages of the poorest labourers. In South Shields, two-thirds of those receiving relief were the widows and children of seamen – a mariner's life was extremely dangerous – and in 1839 the Union considered that as many as 'one person in ten in the township of South Shields was a pauper', in other words eligible for 'relief'.[24]

The responsibilities of the Poor Law Guardians were extended by a new registration role under the 1836 Births and Deaths Registration Act. To carry out their increased duties, the Board appointed a clerk, a treasurer, an auditor, two relieving officers, three rate collectors, three medical officers, two registrars and a superintendent registrar. The Board also decided to build a new workhouse for the Union, purchasing land on the eastern corner of Ocean Road and Park Terrace from Robert Ingham, MP. It was completed in 1838 and could house 260 inmates.

Meanwhile, the first half of the nineteenth century also saw a spectacular growth in the number of friendly societies and savings banks, a legal framework having been provided by Parliament. These philanthropic or not for profit organisations were supported by the active encouragement and financial assistance of the richer sections of society. South Shields was no exception. One important example of a new friendly society was the South Shields Master Mariners' Asylum and Annuity Society, established in 1839. The originators of the idea of providing 'an Asylum and Annuities for aged members, their widows and orphans' met at the Seamen's Hall

Dr Thomas Winterbottom (1776–1859), medical practitioner and exceptionally generous philanthropist who founded South Shields' Marine School and was the leading benefactor of the Master Mariners' Asylum and Annuity Society, whose Mariners' Cottages still stand. (South Tyneside Libraries)

in Fowler Street in January 1839. All sixteen of them were Ship Masters, supported by James Young, a prominent ship owner, and Dr Thomas M. Winterbottom, who had already provided funding for a new Marine School,[25] and who would become an exceptionally generous benefactor to numerous other good causes in the town.

The Lord Bishop of Durham became the patron of the new Society, whose rules and regulations were approved at a general meeting on 15 February, attended by 'officers or major contributors', including Robert Chapman. In addition to the proposed distribution of annuities to the beneficiaries – and, with the huge number of sailing ships that sank in storms and rough seas, there was sadly no shortage of widows and orphans – in 1843 the Society commenced the task of building the 'asylum' (alms-houses) in the form of linked cottages. They became known as Mariners' Cottages, Dr Winterbottom providing generous funding including for a library, a wash-house and proper drainage. Between 1843 and 1862, when the scheme was completed, thirty-nine cottages were built, one of which would later be occupied by Robert Chapman's sister-in-law, Ann Isabella Robson. The cottages still stand today.

Even the most generous philanthropists could only fund the reduc-tion of insanitary nuisances such as 'noxious effluvium from cesspools' on a very small scale indeed. So, given the enormous increase in the urban population of England and Wales in the first half of the nineteenth cen-tury, accompanied by frequent outbreaks of cholera and other epidemic diseases, it is not surprising that health and sanitary conditions became a national issue. In 1843 Sir Robert Peel's Government appointed a Royal Commission to 'inquire into the health of large towns and populous dis-tricts'. A South Shields committee was formed, and its 1844 report painted a depressing picture, all too typical of towns and cities of the period:

In the older parts of the town the houses were two or three stories high, many of them back to back, and closely built in narrow streets and alleys along the bank of the river. In other parts of the town the houses were chiefly single cottages of two or three rooms. The number of fami-lies in each house varied from one to seventeen, the average number of persons to each room being three and three-fourths. The tenement houses were always badly ventilated, almost always destitute of necessary conveniences, and their condition 'had led to the formation amongst the poorer classes of habits not only disgusting and unwholesome but inconsistent with a high tone of morals'. The supply of water to the poor was inadequate, and the provision of cheap public baths urgently necessary. There were some sewers and drains, but the arrangements for under drainage were very defective, and the house drains, where they existed, were not properly cleansed, and frequently choked with refuse. The nuisances most strongly complained of were the smoke from the glassworks and manufactories, the exhalations from the alkali-works, the overcrowded condition of St. Hild's Churchyard, and the want of suitable slaughterhouses. The report alleged that the worst-conditioned part of the town was the district including Commercial Road, Johnson's Hill, Carpenter Street, Nile Street, Dockwray Bank, Cone Street, Academy Hill, Pleasant Place, etc., with a population of 2302, where the death-rate was 37.3 per thousand, or 14.9 above the average.[26]

An 1894/95 map of South Shields, published in 1898, by which time the population was approaching 100,000. Note that the 'German Ocean' had not finally been supplanted by the 'North Sea'. (National Library of Scotland)

to grow. It reached 28,974 in 1851, almost doubling in the forty years since Robert Chapman was born in 1811, when the total population was 15,165. Given the dreadful performance and unresponsiveness of the old South Shields Water Company, the new council took decisive action in 1851, inviting the efficient Sunderland Water Company to extend its system to South Shields. Agreement was reached and an enabling Bill introduced into Parliament in 1851. Terms were agreed for buying out the waterworks of the South Shields Water Company, and the Bill was enacted as the Sunderland and South Shields Water Act, 1852. Its area of supply was extended not only to the Borough of South Shields itself, but also to the parish of Jarrow, and the townships of Harton, Cleadon and Whitburn.

The Sunderland and South Shields Water Company moved forward with commendable speed. It sank an additional well at Fulwell in 1852, creating a new steam-powered water pumping station. From it, water was pumped to a reservoir on Fulwell Bank, with distributing mains then laid to South Shields and Jarrow. The new supply was turned on in South Shields early in 1855, a transforming event for quality of life, or as Thomas Salmon put it, 'the invaluable blessing of a copious and wholesome supply of pure and uncontaminated water'.[7] In the same year, the company raised finance for an additional main at Westoe and for the purchase of 4 acres of land for the

The steam-powered pumping station on Cleadon Hill, built by the Sunderland and South Shields Water Company in 1862. Designed by Thomas Hawksley in the Italianate style, its detached chimney disguised as a campanile became a striking landmark. (South Tyneside Libraries)

sinking of a new well and the erection of a new steam-powered pumping station and reservoir on Cleadon Hill. Work started immediately, and the new pumping station, completed in 1862, was an architectural gem. It was designed by Thomas Hawksley in the Italianate style, with its detached chimney disguised as a campanile, and set in pleasantly landscaped grounds. Its prominent position on the western edge of the hill created an important and still enduring landmark. By 1864 the Cleadon well was providing 250,000 gallons per day. Even so, demand was increasing so quickly – especially from Charles Palmer's expanding Shipbuilding & Iron Company works at Jarrow – that a further well was sunk in the same year, at Ryhope, to ensure that a sufficient supply would be available.

The council's next step was to promote an Improvement Bill in Parliament in 1852. This was a successful initiative, the South Shields Improvement Act reaching the statute book in 1853. The entire borough became an 'improvement area' and the council was constituted as the local Board of Health. It also received significant additional powers: to purchase land for street improvements and for a new cemetery; to compulsorily acquire the Town Hall, and the markets, fairs and tolls that belonged to the Dean and

Charles Palmer's rapidly expanding Iron Shipbuilding Co.'s works at Jarrow eventually covered 100 acres with a river frontage of ¾ mile and a labour force of 7,500. (South Tyneside Libraries)

In addition to launching almost a million tons of shipping, Charles Palmer's company had a graving dock where ships such as *Batoum* (pictured) were repaired. (South Tyneside Libraries)

Chapter of Durham Cathedral; and to borrow money to carry out the newly authorised activities. The council was also empowered to set up committees to oversee its wide new range of activities and duties. It duly formed a Watch Committee, Town Improvement Committee, Baths and Wash-houses Committee, Health Committee and Sanitary Committee. Progress continued to be made at a brisk pace. In 1854 baths and wash-houses in John Street and Cuthbert Street were erected, with, as the town clerk Thomas Salmon put it, 'a kind consideration for the comforts of the working classes'.[8]

The year 1855 was another milestone. The council duly acquired from the Dean and Chapter of Durham Cathedral the Town Hall and its market and related rights after an amicable negotiation. This was an important outcome, particularly since the Dean and Chapter still owned most of the land in South Shields, which they let on 21-year leases, and over whose renewal terms there had been bitter disputes. Indeed, Thomas Salmon described Church Leasehold Tenure as 'that incubus, which has been such a bar to our advancement!'[9] The council proceeded to adapt the small Town Hall for use as a council chamber and limited municipal offices. It would be another fifty years before a new and very splendid Town Hall was built.

In the 1850s, baths and wash-houses were built in Derby Street (pictured) and elsewhere in the town as 'a kind consideration for the comforts of the working classes'. (South Tyneside Libraries)

In 1855 the borough council acquired the Old Town Hall and its market rights from the Dean and Chapter of Durham Cathedral. Fairground attractions enlivened the scene later in the century. (South Tyneside Libraries)

Also in 1855, the South Shields and Westoe Burial Board, set up a year earlier, acquired 16 acres of Robert Ingham's leasehold land, midway between Westoe Lane and the sea, as a site for the very badly needed new cemetery:

> No time was lost in laying out the site, two chapels in the decorated Gothic style being erected, with a circular plot of ground between them, the latter intended as a sort of local Pantheon for the interment of towns-men who had rendered conspicuous service to their fellow-citizens, the first interment in this reserved plot being, appropriately enough, that of Dr. Winterbottom[10] (the much loved benefactor of numerous good causes, who died in 1859).

Robert had been taking a keen interest in these important municipal developments, and in 1855 he became both a councillor for the South Shields Ward and a select vestryman of St Hilda's (a role whose responsibil-ities were reducing as those of local government increased). He remained on the council for fifteen years, serving on the Town Improvement and Public Health Committee, Baths and Wash-houses Committee, Watch Committee (responsible for the police force) and Sanitary Committee. He was also appointed Mayor's auditor, no doubt influencing his son Henry's later choice of career in accountancy.

In the following year, the borough council embarked on a further major project – the construction of a mains sewerage system. It was first installed in the town centre, and in the remainder of the borough during the early 1860s. The system was improved and further extended in the 1870s to cope with a population that was still increasing rapidly, from 28,974 in 1851 to 45,336 in 1871. Although epidemics were far from over, sanitary conditions were, at last, vastly improved.

The 3rd Durham Artillery Volunteers

Not surprisingly, the attention of the council after its incorporation had focused exclusively throughout the 1850s on domestic issues – improve-ments to the town's infrastructure, public health and civic administration. With four decades of peace since the end of the Napoleonic Wars in 1815 there had been no external threats to cause concern. However, the situa-

tion changed sharply at the end of the decade, the aggressive attitude of the
Emperor Napoleon III (whose Second Empire lasted from 1852 until 1870)
sounding alarm bells in London and raising fears about the adequacy of
coastal defences if there were an invasion. In May 1859, by which time infantry volunteer units had practically ceased to exist, General Peel, Secretary of
State for War, made Public Notifications that Her Majesty's Government
would be pleased to authorise the formation of volunteer Rifle Corps,
as well as Artillery Corps and Companies, in maritime towns where forts
and batteries already existed. South Shields responded quickly. The Mayor,
Alderman John Williamson, called a public meeting on 28 November to
consider the formation of a volunteer corps. The key resolution, carried
unanimously in a packed Central Hall, was 'That, in co-operation with the
constitutional and efficient measures for national defence now so generally and prudently in course of adoption throughout the kingdom, a Corps
of Volunteers, to be called "The South Shields Volunteer Rifle Corps", be
immediately formed for this borough.' It was also agreed to set up a committee to make all the necessary arrangements, its members including the

The first drill of the 3rd Durham Artillery Volunteers, formed for coastal defence
against the perceived threat of Emperor Napoleon III, was held in March 1860.
(South Tyneside Libraries)

Mayor and Councillor Robert Chapman. Subscription lists were opened to help fund arms and equipment, £215 being raised on the night, and 140 members of the corps were enrolled within a week.

At the second meeting of what was by then called the 6th Durham (South Shields) Rifles, a 'memorial' was read out urging the formation of an artillery corps. After discussion a motion proposed by Councillor James Cochran Stevenson and seconded by Robert Chapman, 'that the memorialists be recommended to join the Rifle Corps until the artillery corps be formed', was approved. Within three weeks, just before Christmas 1859, this new unit was founded as the 3rd Durham Artillery Volunteers.[11] Four years later, in December 1863, it was agreed to amalgamate the two units, the Rifle Corps being absorbed into the Artillery Volunteers, with James Cochran Stevenson becoming the captain commandant. The following year he was promoted to major, and secured a lease for the site of a battery at the Trow Rocks, on the coast to the south of the town.

The Tyne Improvement Commission

The year 1850 was the most important one of the century for the borough of South Shields, not only because of its Charter of Incorporation but also because of the Tyne Improvement Act, which brought into being the Tyne Improvement Commission. The river had by this time become a major impediment to growth. The mouth of the Tyne, leading to Shields, was treacherous; the state of the river was deteriorating through silting; there were no docks and few quays, even though the shipping trade and coal exporting were booming. At least 95 per cent of all vessels in mid-century were still sailing ships, and for them the bar at the mouth of the Tyne and the rocks just inside the river known as the Black Middens meant that 'the Tyne was a notoriously dangerous port, to which the prudent seaman always gave a wide berth in bad weather, or if he had the temerity to essay an entrance he was often glad to save his ship by running her high and dry on the South Sands'.[12]

The problem remained compounded by Newcastle's intransigence. It had absolute authority over the whole navigable river and could levy on shipping whatever dues it saw fit. But it would not spend more than the absolute minimum on the river, instead siphoning off income for other municipal purposes. The antagonism between the two harbour boroughs of North and South Shields, and Newcastle, had been bitter and continuous for many decades. A skirmish had been successful for the Shields boroughs in 1845, when the Newcastle upon Tyne Port Act had been passed, thanks to the pressure of Shields ship owners. The Act enabled a badly needed river police to be set up, overseen by a Watch Committee with representatives of the ship owners as well as of Newcastle Corporation. And a fight had been won in 1848, when the Lords of the Treasury constituted the 'Port of Shields' as an independent customs port, even if the custom house itself was across the river at North Shields. So the time was now ripe for the major battle for control of the Tyne to be fought.

Tynemouth (the name for the recently incorporated borough, which included North Shields) took the initiative and promoted a Tyne Conservancy Bill. This sought to take control of the river from Newcastle Corporation and grant it to a Conservatory Commission, with representatives from all the boroughs on the Tyne. Equally importantly, the Bill proposed that river dues be put into a special fund for river improvements.[13] A preliminary inquiry into the merits of the Bill was held by the Lords of the Admiralty, who in 1849 sent Captain Washington to the Tyne to conduct it. He made a strong case for the Bill, reporting:

> … that the *most ordinary* duties of river engineering had been neglected by the Corporation; that sufficient quay space for the port's traffic had not been provided; that no attempt had been made to improve the bar or to prevent the deposit of sand in the harbour; that the casting of ballast in the harbour had not been stopped, and that until two years ago (in 1847) there had been neither moorings for vessels nor river police.[14]

The Lords of the Admiralty found the case for the Bill proven, and the Tyne Improvement Act was passed in July 1850. It set up the Tyne Improvement Commission as the dedicated river authority, which the harbour boroughs had sought, determining that there should be fourteen commissioners (six from Newcastle, two from Gateshead, three from Tynemouth and three from South Shields) and four life commissioners, two of whom would be appointed by the Admiralty. River dues were to be collected by Newcastle Corporation and handed over to the commission, which would have its own Tyne Improvement Fund. This major victory was celebrated enthusiastically in South Shields: 'St. Hild's Church bells were rung, tar barrels blazed in the streets all over the town, and cannons were fired on

Carpenters' Hill, one man having his jaw fractured by the explosion of a "bull-dog" or small cannon.'[15]

The commission set about its task with a sense of great urgency. Two years after its establishment it secured the 1852 Tyne Improvement Act, which gave it comprehensive enabling powers. Top priorities included piers for Shields Harbour to make it safer for shipping, and becoming a harbour of refuge. Heavy storms in January 1853 reinforced the importance of these proposals, having caused the wreck of thirty-six ships in the mouth of the Tyne and a further 110 within 20 miles of it. These figures were given by Lord Ellenborough, speaking to the House of Lords in 1854, making the case for government financial assistance for a harbour of refuge. He continued that 'during the present year I understand that not less than fifteen hundred vessels, containing two hundred thousand tons of coal, all required for the immediate use of the Metropolis, have been detained for nearly four weeks at the mouth of the Tyne, not one of them having been able to leave in consequence of the state of the Bar'.[16] In the end, despite eloquent plead-

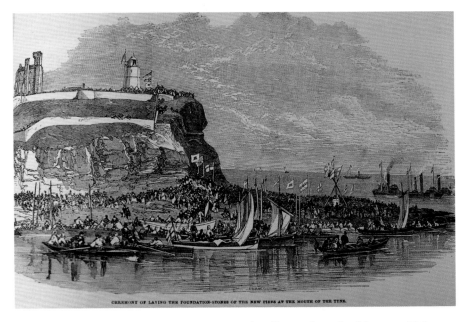

CEREMONY OF LAYING THE FOUNDATION-STONES OF THE NEW PIERS AT THE MOUTH OF THE TYNE.

A momentous day for the river recorded by the *Illustrated London News*: on 15 June 1854 Mr (later Sir) Joseph Cowen, chairman of the Tyne Commission, laid the foundation stones for the South Pier at South Shields and then for the North Pier at Tynemouth (pictured), where the Priory garrison gave an artillery salute. The huge piers would take four decades to build. (Courtesy London Library. © Joan Chapman)

ing, no government funding was ever given towards the huge cost of the North and South piers and related harbour works.

The major task of the design of the piers was given to James Walker, whose report proposed a north pier from the rocks under Tynemouth Priory to run in a south-easterly direction for 700yd, and a south pier in South Shields to run from the Herd Sand in an east-north-easterly direction for 1,400yd. Each pier would terminate in a depth of 15ft at low water, leaving an opening between their respective ends of 1,000ft, which would form the entrance to the port. Walker's report was accepted and he was instructed to prepare detailed drawings and specifications, and to supervise construction. Progress was rapid: the foundation stones for the piers were laid on 15 June 1854 by Mr (later Sir) Joseph Cowen, the first Chairman of the Commission, who would in 1865 become an influential MP for Newcastle. This event was celebrated in style:

> The Commissioners, accompanied by the Corporation of Newcastle, embarked at the Quayside, and steamed down the river in state, amid flying bunting and salutes of artillery. Landing at South Shields, they were received by the Corporation of the borough, and moved in gay procession to the Herd Sand, where the first stone was laid. Then crossing the river, they were similarly received at Tynemouth, and the second stone was laid, to the accompaniment of the National Anthem and a salute from the Priory Garrison, after which the Commissioners and the three Corporations were entertained by the Mayor of Tynemouth.[17]

In 1855, the year in which Robert Chapman became a South Shields councillor, contracts for the major section of each pier were let. Impressively enough, on this exceptionally large-scale project – which would include the building of a new railway line to bring stone from nearby Trow Quarry – the substantive works started within just three years of parliamentary approval. There would, however, be very serious setbacks before their completion some forty years later.

Harbour piers, new docks and improved navigability were the Tyne Improvement Commissioners' three priorities, and they tackled them all simultaneously. Construction of the first new dock started in 1853 at North Shields. It was a fairly straightforward project, 'an enclosure of a bight of the river by a strong wall, with the addition of the necessary basins and entrance'. This was the Northumberland Dock, formally opened in 1857 – 'the first

John Scott's iconic painting of the opening in March 1859 of Tyne Dock, which became the largest coal-shipping dock in the world. On the left is the Jarrow Chemical Works with a three-masted barque at the adjacent quay. In the middle of the procession of boats on the right is the screw steamship *Lady Berriedale*, with her funnel clearly visible. It took just fifty minutes to load her with 400 tons of coal. In the centre of the foreground is a Shields lifeboat being rowed by a full complement of pilots with their blue jackets and tall hats. (Laing Art Gallery, Newcastle upon Tyne. © Tyne & Wear Archives & Museums/Bridgeman Images. Caption, Ian Whitehead)

really effective improvement that had ever been accomplished on the river'.[18] The next dock project was immediately adjacent to the town of South Shields, and much more substantial. It was the proposal of the North Eastern Railway to cut off some 50 acres of Jarrow Slake and create a huge new dock complex. The Jarrow Dock Bill was prepared and laid before Parliament in 1854, and enacted after a supportive Royal Commission technical inquiry. Tyne Dock, as it was then called, opened four years later, in 1859. It was an enormous project, its entrance being 80ft wide, its lock 60ft wide, and the total area of the dock itself 50 acres. With its new cranes and coal-handling facilities it became the largest coal-shipping dock in the world, handling around 100,000 tons per week. Indeed, towards the end of Robert Chapman's life in 1894 Tyne Dock was loading ships with up to 140,000 tons a week, after the North Eastern Railway Company had increased the number of its staithes (coal-loading depots) and built a new dock entrance.[19]

In parallel with the new piers and dock projects, the Tyne Commission was tackling the problem of navigability. It was imperative to deepen and improve the river to facilitate access by the rapidly increasing number of ships – including the larger vessels that had started to be built – to the expanding industrial areas on both banks, up to Newcastle Quay and beyond. A comprehensive plan, drawn up by the Tyne Commission's engineer, John F. Ure, was welcomed by shipping interests and it sailed through Parliament as the Tyne Improvement Act of 1861. Within two years there were six steam dredgers in operation, assisted by a fleet of steam tugs and hopper barges. Enormous quantities of silt, sand, ballast and other material were dredged up and deposited out at sea, rising from around 750,000 tons in 1861 to over 5 million tons in 1866. By the time of Robert Chapman's death in 1894, some 90 million tons had been dredged out.

The results were spectacular. Within a decade of the 1861 Tyne Improvement Act:

> ... the silent magic of the dredger had transformed the harbour ... From the bar to the Tyne and Northumberland Docks was a waterway wide

One of the six Tyne dredgers that removed 90 million tons of silt, sand and ballast, transforming the river's navigability. (R. W. Johnson, *The Making of the Tyne* [London, 1895]. © Joan Chapman)

enough and deep enough to safely conduct the traffic of the third port in the kingdom. The Tyne was saved, and the dredger was its saviour. The port was no longer avoided by large ships; there were no longer delays in getting to sea.[20]

In carrying out all this work, and the further major projects that would follow, the Tyne Improvement Commission benefited both from much improved harbour, dock and dredging technology, and from the majority of the commissioners being 'men deeply involved in the area's industry themselves, with a keen personal interest in ensuring the most efficient and economical shipping facilities'.[21] This was certainly true of South Shields appointees to the commission, who in the 1850s included James Young, owner of the well-known West Dock shipyard and a portfolio of ships, John Clay, first Mayor of the borough and a banker and ship owner, and James Mather, wine and spirit merchant, constructor of the first ship's lifeboat, promoter of improved conditions for seamen and miners, and radical politician. It was also true of James Cochran Stevenson, a life commissioner who would later become chairman and the town's MP. Finally, it was highly advantageous that the commission was able to fund much of the very substantial improvement costs either from dues on the growing volume of port shipping or from borrowing against these increasing revenues.

Quayside Developments

Meanwhile, South Shields itself took advantage of its incorporated borough status to become steadily more independent during Robert Chapman's time as a councillor in the 1860s, though it failed to grasp two potentially significant development opportunities. At the beginning of the decade, in 1861, the council purchased – following the passage in Parliament of the South Shields Improvement Amendment Act – quays adjoining the existing landing at the Mill Dam from the North Eastern Railway Company. This became known as the Corporation Quay, but the project was only partially successful. The council decided that it wanted to erect on the site buildings suitable for a custom house and for Local Marine Board offices, as part of its decades-old ambition to become its own free-standing customs port. It had made only limited progress in 1849, when the 'Port of

Shields' (embracing both North and South Shields) was established, since the Lords of the Treasury had determined that the custom house should be in North Shields. Nevertheless, South Shields did open a register of ships, paving the way for enhanced responsibilities in due course.

In 1863 the Mayor, Alderman John Brodrick Dale (for whom Robert Chapman was the formal Mayor's auditor, signing off the borough's annual 'Statements of Monies Received and Expended'), took the bold step of laying the foundation stone on Corporation Quay of a suitable custom house and Local Marine Board offices. The buildings were opened in 1864 with much fanfare, Tyne Improvement Commissioners arriving by state barges to take part in the festivities, and benefiting from a splendid view of the impressive custom house 'of the Italian order of architecture, built of white brick with Heworth stone dressings. The façade overlooking the river is composed of eight Corinthian columns coupled, standing upon a rusticated basement of piers and arches forming an arcade.'[22] No doubt Robert Chapman would have been present at these celebrations, which were followed by his re-election as a councillor for the South Shields ward.

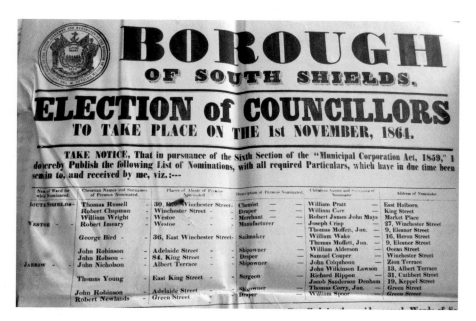

Robert Chapman was re-elected as a councillor for South Shields ward in 1864. (Tyne & Wear Archives & Museums)

Fishwives at the North Shields Fish Quay built in 1870. South Shields' plans for its own fish market never materialised. (South Tyneside Libraries)

The Mayor's courageous initiative was rewarded. With the strong support of Robert Ingham, MP, and despite the opposition of Newcastle, in 1865 the Lords of the Treasury agreed to make South Shields a separate customs port. This highly beneficial decision was a cause for great celebration, with the bells of St Hilda's in full peal, plenty of bunting on display, and a special dinner at the Mechanics' Hall. The next challenge was for the town to secure its own Local Marine Board. Fifteen years earlier a Local Marine Board for the Port of Shields had been created by the Mercantile Marine Act 1850. Located in North Shields, it was responsible for overseeing the engagement of ships' crews and for all examinations for the certificates that were required for masters and mates of foreign-going vessels. The constant dissent between North and South Shields, for example over exam locations, was finally resolved at the end of 1865, when the Board of Trade decided that there should also be a Local Marine Board in South Shields to carry out

the provisions of the Merchant Shipping Acts. It formally came into existence in January 1866, with offices in the customs building.

Unfortunately, the adjacent Corporation Quay project was not successful as a shipping facility. The borough council did not extend it as far
as the Act of Parliament would have permitted, nor did it purchase further land with development potential to the west. Its restricted area was a
major disadvantage, attempts to integrate the quay into the coasting trade
to London failing as a result. The borough surveyor also drew up plans for
the construction of a fish market at the Mill Dam, but the scheme was
abandoned, and Tynemouth stole a march by building its own fish quay
at North Shields in 1870 with ice stores and a market, thereby securing
most of the trade. The council had, in short, failed to move forward on two
important fronts, with adverse consequences for long-term growth.

Priscilla

Meanwhile, Robert Chapman's drapery business was thriving, giving him
funds for an investment to take advantage of trade from the Tyne. In 1854
he purchased a majority share in the sailing ship *Priscilla*, a three-masted
barque of 279 tons that had been built in 1841 by S. Austin and S.P. Austin
in Sunderland. In 1852–53 she was re-registered in Shields and had traded
widely – to the Mediterranean, Constantinople, the Black Sea, the Sea
of Azov, and even to Brazil. By investing in *Priscilla*, which would have
been very similar to the barque *Anne* (illustrated), Robert became what
was called a 'sixty-fourther'. Under an Act in 1854 for the Registration
of British Vessels, ship ownership had to be divided into sixty-four shares,
with owners' names and holdings being entered on Customs House
Registers. Most shareholdings were held in multiples of four, a common
holding being sixteen sixty-fourths (16/64ths). In Robert's case, he
became the majority shareholder, owning 42/64ths, with his partner, the
South Shields ship owner Thomas Young, owning the remaining 22/64ths.
Most vessels' shareholders were ship owners, shipbuilders, master mariners
and merchants like Robert himself.

His investment in a sailing ship was rather late in the day. For although
in the middle of the century there were over 1,500 merchant sailing ships
registered on the Tyne, the future was clearly with steam colliers. In fact,
'throughout the 1850s and early 1860s there was a steady decline in the
number of sailing ships acquired by Tyne owners, especially of vessels
under 300 registered tons in whose ranks most of the London sailing col-

The barque *Anne* flying the 'Blue Peter' flag from her foremast, showing she is preparing to go to sea. John Scott's 1859 painting also shows the steam paddle tug that has towed her from her berth to the mouth of the Tyne. There has been a farewell party on board, and guests of the owner Henry Milvain are being rowed back to the tug before returning to shore. In the background, just to the right of the tug, can be seen the impressive Tynemouth monument to Vice-Admiral Collingwood of Trafalgar fame. (Laing Art Gallery, Newcastle upon Tyne. ©Tyne & Wear Archives & Museums/Bridgeman Images. Caption, Ian Whitehead)

Captains of colliers from the Tyne sailed to the Baltic, the Black Sea, Africa and South America. So too did sailors from Blythe in Northumberland, the home port of Captains Dick (in top hat), Darling and John S. Clinton. (Walter Runciman, *Collier Brigs and Their Sailors* [London, 1926])

liers belonged', as indeed did *Priscilla*. While in 1850, seventy-two sailing vessels under this tonnage had been acquired, the number fell to twenty-five in 1865, and to just two in 1870.[23]

Nevertheless, trade was still booming for sailing ships. The river was, as Richard Keys so eloquently described:

> Alive with its own ships and those of other ports and other nations. They lay in tiers, sometimes seven and eight abreast. Magnificent Yankee sky-sail yarders, dainty French chasse marries, clog like Dutch jayts, rakish Greek polacres and apple bowed Yorkshire billy boys rubbed fenders with the local colliers, timber droghers, Indiamen, whalers and fruit clippers.[24]

Sometimes the huge numbers of ships in the Tyne were not there of their own free will. Two years after the investment in *Priscilla*, in the winter of 1856–57, before the Tyne Commissioners' dredging programme started, around 1,000 vessels, home to 7,000 or 8,000 seamen, were trapped between Newcastle and the sea because of a prolonged period of easterly winds and dangerous seas running on the bar at the river mouth. As soon

Main-royal

Fore-royal, with sailor

Main-top gallant sail, with sailor

Fore-top gallant-sail

Fore-top-sail

Fore-course

Preparing *Anne* for her voyage, there is a sailor up the main mast untying the gaskets (ties) from the main-topgallant sail, while another does the same for the fore–royal sail. In rough weather, 'stowing' these sails, often the job of young apprentices, was extremely hazardous. (Laing Art Gallery, Newcastle upon Tyne. © Tyne & Wear Archives & Museums/Bridgeman Images. Caption, Ian Whitehead)

as wind conditions and depth of water on the bar became favourable, there was a surge of vessels heading for the open sea – some 500 in a single afternoon in April 1857.[25]

Life at sea on sailing ships remained very harsh during the 1854–64 period of Robert Chapman's ownership of *Priscilla*. Young apprentices were often cruelly ill-treated and in a few very extreme cases – which ended up in court – were literally worked to death. Few first-hand accounts of their demanding duties and dangerous experiences survive. A notable exception were the recollections of Walter Runciman who, as a 12-year-old, ran away from school in 1859 and was taken on as a cabin boy on the brig *Harperley* at Blyth on the Northumberland coast. Two weeks later she loaded a cargo of coal for Mozambique.

Walter was keen to show willing and soon volunteered to stow the main-royal sail:

> I intimated to the officer of my watch that I would stow the royal myself next time it was ordered to be taken in by him, and when the chance came I jumped on to the topgallant rail, ran up the rigging, and was soon enveloped in the flapping sail. I put all the strength I had into mastering

it, but it very nearly mastered me. I was exhausted over and over again, but renewed the effort after a little breathing time. Meanwhile the sail was riotously covering me over and alternatively freeing itself, and I was having to hang on, as the sailors termed it, by the eyelids all the time. I wonder how a mite such as I escaped being killed or drowned, not only on this occasion, but on scores of others far more hazardous.[26]

Living conditions on board ship for sailors were uncomfortable at best and dreadful at worst. Sanitary facilities were non-existent until the end of the 1860s. Daniel Stephens, who exactly like Walter Runciman started out as a cabin boy, then became sailor, mate and master, and subsequently a successful ship owner in Newcastle, provides a striking description: 'On the *Sea Snake* we lived in a topgallant forecastle. The chain cables passed not far from our bunks, no stoves to keep the place warm, and, when at anchor, the sea would at times rush through the hawse pipes and wash the men's chests about.'[27]

During the decade 1854–64, *Priscilla* followed many of the familiar – and extensive – trading routes from the Tyne: to London for the 'coasting' trade,

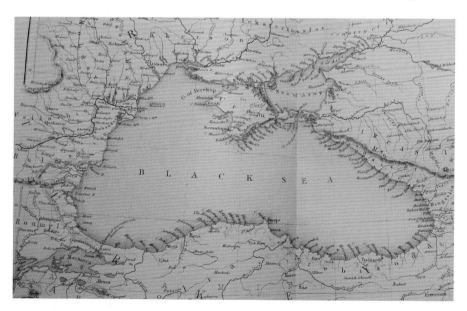

Priscilla's voyages: map showing the Sea of Marmara, the Black Sea with Sevastopol and Balaklava, the Strait of Kertch, the Sea of Azov and Taganrog. (E.H. Nolan, *The Illustrated History of the War Against Russia* [London, 1857]. Courtesy London Library. © Joan Chapman)

to the Continent, to the Baltic, to the Mediterranean, and to the Black Sea and the Sea of Azov. Her cargoes out would have been mostly or entirely coal. Her first captain (a term used interchangeably with the Victorian 'master') was George Sykes. He would have been pleased to leave the Tyne in October 1854, bound for Constantinople, since a cholera epidemic had broken out in September, when Captain Luper of the Austrian barque *Germanica*, freshly arrived in the Tyne from London, died of the disease. Several other cases were reported aboard ships moored in Shields harbour. Despite the fact that such epidemics often spread through ports, requests to the Admiralty and to Trinity House in Newcastle for a hulk to be used as a floating hospital to deal with sick sailors repeatedly fell on deaf ears.[28]

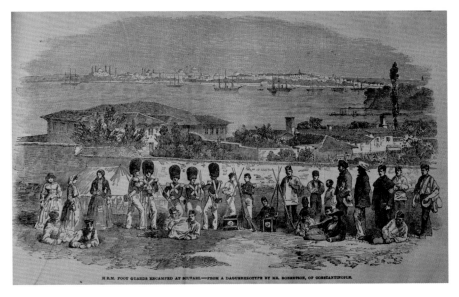

H.R.M. FOOT GUARDS ENCAMPED AT SCUTARI.—FROM A DAGUERREOTYPE BY MR. ROBERTSON, OF CONSTANTINOPLE.

'Her Britannic Majesty's Footguards encamped at Scutari' (present-day Üsküdar). This evocative daguerreotype, with views across the Bosphorus to Constantinople, appeared in the *Illustrated London News* on 15 July 1854 during the Crimean War. (Courtesy London Library. © Joan Chapman)

Captain Sykes' first voyage with *Priscilla* was to Constantinople, which she reached in June 1855. Since in March 1854 Britain had declared war on Russia and the Crimean War lasted until 1856, the voyage to Constantinople, and then to the Black Sea and the Sea of Azov, would have been 'on Admiralty account'. While most British troops went out by steamships, sailing ships were used extensively to carry horses, fodder, munitions and stores, 'bounteous profits' being made on these Government contracts.[29] Captain Sykes returned from Balaklava via Malta, arriving in South Shields in December 1855. The merchant sailing fleet often remained in port in the month of January, Captain Sykes leaving again for Constantinople in February 1856. In August he set sail for home from Taganrog, the Russian grain exporting port on the northern shore of the Sea of Azov, his last voyage on *Priscilla*.

Nicholas Smith, born in South Shields in 1817, succeeded George Sykes as captain of *Priscilla* in 1857. Seven years earlier, the Mercantile Marine Act 1850 had introduced compulsory certificates of competency, awarded after an examination (and usually referred to as 'tickets') for the posts of master and mate of foreign trade vessels. Nicholas lost no time in securing his own Certificate of Competency as master, which was awarded in December 1850 by officers of the Naval Department of the Board of Trade, and duly 'entered at the General Register and Record Office of Seamen'. Certificates of competency were not a compulsory require-ment aboard home trade vessels, which included those making voyages to near Continental ports. However, Robert and his partner Thomas Young had already shown that they also wanted to take advantage of more dis-tant trading opportunities, and indeed Captain Smith's first voyages on *Priscilla* in 1857 were to Lisbon (a five-month round trip) and then to the Mediterranean. On such voyages *Priscilla* would be trading as a 'South Spainer', the term for ships that mainly carried coal and coke to the ports of Portugal and southern Spain, returning with cargoes of sulphur ore and pyrites, lead bars, copper and iron ore for Tyneside's chemical, smelting and metal-based industries.

Over the following four years, 1858–61, with Nicholas Smith still cap-tain, *Priscilla* made half a dozen coasting trade voyages to London and the same number of Continental trade trips to Cherbourg, Le Havre and Nieuport. A further three voyages were to Hamburg, then a member state of the German Confederation, and a popular destination for British seamen. This was not surprising as the city's economy was booming, it imported much more coal from the North East than any other foreign port, it had a large English colony and harbour improvements made the city accessible at any time, sailing ships no longer having to depend on the state of the tides in the estuary of the River Elbe. And there were plenty of bars for masters and seamen.

Priscilla's voyages: map *c.* 1850 of 'The Baltic and its Coasts' showing on the eastern shore Memel in Prussia (now Klaipéda in Lithuania), and further to the north-east the Gulf of Finland leading to Cronstadt (the port for St Petersburg). (E.H. Nolan, *The Illustrated History of the War Against Russia* [London, 1857]. Courtesy London Library. © Joan Chapman)

Priscilla was also engaged in the Baltic trade, which had been big business before the war with Russia. Outward cargoes were again typically coal and coke, but also tar, grindstones, chemicals and manufactured goods. On the homeward run traders would be carrying various kinds of timber, and also barley, grain, tallow and hemp. Cronstadt (present-day Kronshtadt) on Kotlin Island, near the head of the Gulf of Finland, was the most important destination. It was traditionally the seat of the Russian Admiralty and the base of the Russian Baltic Fleet, guarding the approaches to St Petersburg, 20 miles away up the River Neva.

Cronstadt was indeed the 'water-gate of St. Petersburg', with its 'chief custom-house, and here all ships coming from the sea anchor. The smaller vessels run up to the mouths of the Neva; the larger stop here to discharge a part of their cargo before going further, or they discharge it altogether into the magazines that belong to the St. Petersburg merchants.'[30] If the magazines were impressive, 'the proper objects of imagination' were the city's

'Cronstadt from the narrow part of the Channel nearest St Petersburg', *Illustrated London News*, 15 July 1854, during the Crimean War. With its huge forts housing 600 heavy guns, it was blockaded by Vice-Admiral Sir Charles Napier. The Baltic trade recommenced after the war ended in 1856. (Courtesy London Library. © Joan Chapman)

fortifications, harbours, canals and docks. The Gulf of Finland froze over in winter, Cronstadt's permanent population being around 10,000 residents. But 'during the summer, when trade is most active, it has more than 30,000 workmen, sailors, soldiers, merchants – Russian, German and English'.[31]

Tynesiders were very much in evidence: 'Every year, as soon as the ice began to disappear from its surface, a great procession of deep-sailing vessels would set out from the coal ports of the North East coast, bound for the Baltic.'[32] There could be fifty or sixty ships, with crews of between 500 and 600 men, from the Tyne, Wear and Hartlepool lying at Cronstadt, which became the second most important foreign destination for North East coal. The importance of this trade was reflected in the nineteenth-century saying that a north countryman's idea of the four quarters of the globe were 'Roosha, Proosha, Memel and Shields' (Russia, Prussia, Memel – now Klaipéda in Lithuania – and Shields). Baltic trading was, however, severely interrupted by the war of 1854–56. At the time it was known as the Russian War, but since there was only limited naval action in the

Baltic and Gulf of Finland – where the impregnable forts of Cronstadt and
a well-organised British blockading fleet under Vice-Admiral Sir Charles
Napier produced a stalemate – it became known as the Crimean War.

The Baltic trade to Cronstadt recommenced after 1856, although
Priscilla herself did not venture there until the summer of 1858, on the first
of four such annual voyages made by Captain Smith. The port was again
bustling, not to say bursting, with its berths for at least 600 merchant ships.
Physical pleasures were well catered for and captains of Tyneside ships
would feel very much at home at a well-known watering hole whose
name, 'Jack the Blaster's', was straight out of South Shields – indicating the
town's reach as a trading partner. 'Jack the Blaster' was a real-life character
who had worked at Marsden quarries near South Shields in the late 1700s,
making a limestone cave on the beach near Marsden Grotto his marital
home. Walter Runciman recalls 'Jack the Blaster's' as a notorious Schnapps
'shop' in Cronstadt where:

> … masters of vessels were accustomed to have their nip when the sun
> was over the foreyard, and discuss with great deliberation their daily
> grievances, pleasures, and many phases of harbour news. And if they
> were hungry for conversation and in an aggressive mood, they worked
> themselves up into passion over some national reform that was needed,

The Grotto at Marsden beach near South Shields. 'Jack the Blaster' lived in one of
its caves in the late 1700s, and in Cronstadt a notorious drinking establishment was
named after him. (South Tyneside Libraries)

wherein Gladstone, Disraeli, Bright or Cowen were involved, and it depended much on the amount of vodka that had been imbibed by the debaters which fixed the dimensions of their difference of opinion.[33]

They were opinions that could equally well have been aired in similar terms back home in South Shields.

At the time of *Priscilla*'s later voyages to Cronstadt, William Gladstone was Chancellor of the Exchequer and Benjamin Disraeli was in opposition (becoming Prime Minister in 1868). John Bright was the Liberal MP for Manchester and then for Birmingham who opposed the war with Russia, and supported free trade and Irish and parliamentary reform. Joseph Cowen junior promoted revolution throughout Europe in the 1850s, supporting the Poles in revolt against the Russians. He subsequently became editor and proprietor of the *Newcastle Chronicle* and a Liberal MP for the city.

There would certainly have been plenty of topics for vodka-fuelled political arguments. But the debates also focused on local conditions and regulations for seamen in Cronstadt itself. Runciman recounted one such occasion that showed sail losing the power struggle with steam, even at anchor:

Captain Armstrong, a highly respected trader to the port of Cronstadt, was engaging the visitors to a dissertation in a deep, lordly tone of voice that indicated vodka. His theme was that a deputation should be appointed to see the Emperor [of Russia], and ask him to allow the sailing-vessels in port to have fires in their galleys and to do their cooking aboard instead of at the filthy cook-shed, where every meal had to be cooked before being brought on board by the cook in leaking lurkies, which were made of a few planks roughly nailed together in the form of a boat. He dwelt long and wearily on the number of people who had to go without their meals and the cooks who had been drowned by the lurkies capsizing, and in a jerky peroration he declared it to be a damned scandal that steamers should be allowed to have their boilers and donkey-boiler fires to drive their winches, put their cargoes out, and take them in, and galley fires to do their cooking, and the sailing-vessels couldn't have a fire to do their cooking or keep them warm when they were cold. The din of incoherent chatter grew.[34]

A violent drunken argument ensued.

These debates would not have taken place in the spring or autumn. The Baltic was just too dangerous – drifting ice when the weather became warmer, or a sudden 'freeze up', trapping vessels in their loading or discharging ports for anything up to five months. This could be commercially disastrous for owners and very unpleasant for the crews, who usually – but not always – remained on board. Just three years after *Priscilla*'s last voyage to Cronstadt, the North Shields schooner, *Arthur Fawcus*, became caught by ice at St Petersburg. Her master discharged two of the crew by mutual consent, but when they arrived home the owner, Noach S. Lotinga, refused to pay their expenses and full wages due. In the ensuing court case, which the owner won, the point was made that if they had so wished they could have remained aboard the ship on full wages.[35]

Given the risks, Captain Smith and *Priscilla*'s owners, Robert Chapman and Thomas Young, were taking no chances – all four outward voyages to Cronstadt started between May and June, and she was back in the United Kingdom between July and September. Each of these voyages lasted

The seven-man crew of *Priscilla* signed an 'Agreement for Foreign Going Ship' form before setting sail for Cronstadt in May 1861. Wages were paid monthly and the very meagre daily and monthly rations were specified in great detail. (The National Archives)

between two and four months, crews having formally signed agreements before departure. The crew agreement on the Board of Trade's 'Agreement for Foreign Going Ship' form for Captain Smith's last voyage to Cronstadt with *Priscilla*, in May 1861, still exists. His address was given as 45 Green Street, South Shields, and the 'managing owner' was Thomas Young of 98 Commercial Road. Other owners' names were not required on the form, even if, like Robert Chapman, they were majority owners. There was a crew of seven – a mate, a cook-steward, four 'able seamen' and one 18-year-old 'ordinary seaman'. Reflecting the economic migration of the times, not one had been born in South Shields itself, though the mate, Thomas Lines, was born in Newcastle. The others came from Scotland (two from Shetland), Colchester and Hamburg. Two crew members had been on *Priscilla*'s last voyage.

Monthly wages were specified in pounds, shillings and pence: £5 5s for the mate; £3 17s 6d for the cook-steward; £3 10s for the four able seamen and £1 for the ordinary seaman. Daily rations were specified, including pork, flour, peas and bread, with tea, coffee and sugar rationed on a monthly basis. 'Equivalent substitutes were permitted', but 'no spirits allowed'. The food was usually of extremely poor quality, and the rations very meagre, leading Runciman to describe them as a 'criminal disgrace'. The seamen themselves sang a song which included the lines 'Pea soup and pork amongst all hands of us; not enough for one of us.'[36]

The 'no spirits' rule reflected the fact that excessive drinking of alcohol was a major problem among crew members, but usually in port or in the early stages of a voyage, given the terms of the crew agreement. However, quite apart from infringements by crew members, 'all too many masters abused their privileged position and took to the drink when at sea'.[37] Sometimes drink led to suicide. In June 1857, while *Priscilla* was on her Lisbon voyage, the South Shields-owned sailing vessel *Catherine and Hannah* arrived in the Tyne with the body of her master on board. He had cut his own throat while suffering from what was thought to be a fit of 'delirium tremens'.

Nicholas Smith was *Priscilla*'s captain for four years, until 1861. The following year, James Henry Cook became captain. He was a South Shields man, born in the town in 1825. His Master's Certificate of Service of 1854 showed that he had been employed, as apprentice, mate and master, for nine years in the British Merchant Service in the 'Coasting and Foreign Trades'. Captain Cook was master for only two years. He was mostly engaged in the coasting trade to London, though in July 1862 he took *Priscilla* to Swinemünde, then a German industrial and naval base, with impressive Prussian fortifications, in north-west Poland (present-day Świnoujście). His last voyage was in the spring of 1864. He was bound for Bremen, situated on the River Weser in what is now north-western Germany, some 43 miles from the North Sea, then still called the German Ocean. Like Hamburg, the city had joined the German Confederation after the end of the Napoleonic Wars in 1815. Tragically, *Priscilla* did not reach Bremen. She was wrecked on the Weser on 8 April 1864, and twenty-three days later her stern was picked up off Spiekeroog, an island some 25 miles west of the river's mouth. Fortunately the crew was saved.

This was the sad end to Robert Chapman's first, and last, investment in a sailing ship. *Priscilla*'s fate was far from exceptional: 'Between 1830 and 1900, about 70 per cent of Tyne-owned sailing ships ended their days by marine peril. They were wrecked on rock bound shores, foundered in mid-ocean, caught fire, blew up, were crushed by ice, run down by other ships, or disappeared with all hands.'[38] And seamen risked their lives with each voyage: 'If disease or sickness did not get a Nineteenth Century seaman, the sea very often did. By the end of the century, actuaries had calculated that one seaman out of five, serving in the coastal trade, ended up losing his life at sea.'[39]

The Piers and the Volunteer Life Brigade

Returning once more to the mouth of the Tyne, construction of the North and South Piers had been continuing slowly but surely throughout the 1850s. The following decade saw several significant setbacks, illustrating all too clearly the concerns of the Tyne Improvement Commissioner James Cochran Stevenson: 'With an unbroken fetch to tide and wave from the North Pole to our shores, any breakwater work must be a matter of peculiar anxiety'[40] (a fetch being the distance travelled by wind or waves across open water). Several months after an inspection by Gladstone as Chancellor of the Exchequer, a great-northerly gale in December 1862 carried away a section of the completed structure of the South Pier. Exactly two years later, in December 1864, another storm wreaked similar havoc on the North Pier, destroyed one of its construction cranes, and caused further damage to the South Pier.

With the North and South Piers still under construction, the mouth of the Tyne remained ferociously dangerous in stormy weather. During the night of 24 November 1864 the Aberdeen steamer *Stanley* (pictured) and the Colchester schooner *Friendship* were both wrecked on the notorious Black Middens near the north shore at Tynemouth, with the loss of thirty-two lives. (*Illustrated London News*, 3 December 1854. Courtesy London Library. © Joan Chapman)

A month earlier, in November 1864, in another terrible gale, the schooner *Friendship* was driven on to the Black Middens, as was the *Stanley*, on her way from Aberdeen to London with thirty passengers, a crew of the same number and a deck load of cattle, sheep and pigs. Heroic rescue efforts were made by the crew of the *Constance* lifeboat from Tynemouth Haven, by the *Providence* from South Shields, and finally by the use of the Cullercoats coastguard's rocket apparatus, which managed eventually to get a line across to the *Stanley*, rescuing the remaining thirty-five passengers and crew. Nevertheless, the tragedy had ended the lives of the five-man crew of the *Friendship*, twenty-five passengers and crew from the *Stanley* and at least two lifeboat crew from Tynemouth.

As a direct result of this tragedy, a public meeting was held in Tynemouth in December 1864, leading to the formation in January 1865 of the Tynemouth Volunteer Life Brigade, the first in the country. A year later, in 1866, South Shields, with the enthusiastic support of the council (on

The South Shields Volunteer Life Brigade was formed in January 1866 as a direct response to the tragedies of the shipwrecked *Stanley* and *Friendship*. Canvas storm caps were later supplied to the volunteers. This image was taken around 1873/74. (South Tyneside Libraries)

which Robert Chapman was still sitting) and of the Tyne pilots, followed suit and established the South Shields Volunteer Life Brigade. The brigade adopted, very appropriately, the corporation's motto of 'Always Ready'. It built a wooden watch room on the South Pier, which was extended substantially a decade later to form a watch house with accommodation for shipwrecked persons, a bathroom, lookout tower, and ancillary accommodation.

The South Pier itself could still be a very dangerous place to be. In 1867, just a year after the Life Brigade was formed, 250ft of the pier – and a section of similar length on the North Pier – were carried away in a great storm. As a result, it was decided to lay the foundations some 4 to 6ft deeper, and to protect them with 36-ton concrete blocks, which were delivered to their positions on railway lines built on each pier. They were then lifted by huge 'Titan' cranes – one on each pier and reputedly the largest in existence – and finally (as the piers progressed seawards) laid by divers at depths of up to 36ft below water.[41]

Construction work would continue for another three decades, as would the perils of taking a sailing ship into the Tyne in high winds or a storm. Walter Runciman, who had progressed from cabin boy to captain, describes another rather terrifying experience in December 1874:

> A heavy gale was blowing from the east, accompanied with blinding snow squalls. I had run my distance, got a glimpse of Souter Light, and came on to the harbour mouth. I made the High and Low leading lights out [on the north bank of the Tyne], and kept them a handspike open to the south'ard, took a bearing in case they should be obscured, and let her go. Just when we were taking the harbour a heavy fall of snow came, and nothing could be seen. We had just got between the piers when a tremendous sea struck the vessel. She broached to, and was pointing for the Black Middens, at that time a most deadly danger in making for the Tyne. The bunt of the reefed square sail was let go, and the first flap sent her on her course, and in less than a minute the sail was in rags. Nothing could be made out but the glimmer of the town lights, and I was driven to quite a haphazard plan of calling out 'Port' and 'Starboard' in quick succession. Then we heard voices calling out 'Hard a port! You're running on to the [North Shields] Fish Pier!' and when I looked over the side I found it to be the life-boat going off to save the crew of some ship ashore on the South Pier or on the Herd Sands. I had resolved to run right up to Jarrow Slake, but the snow cleared

After the piers were completed in 1895 the Tyne General Ferry Company started running steamers between them in the summer months. A steamer at the South Pier's landing stage in 1906 is shown here. (South Tyneside Libraries)

off a good deal when near the Penny Ferry; one of several tugs came to our assistance, and the vessel was moored in the tier without carrying away a rope-yarn beyond the square foresail.[42]

The construction of the North and South Piers would eventually be more or less completed in 1895, although severe storms over the following two years caused further extensive damage. It was an extraordinary feat of engineering and sheer determination, helping to secure the expansion of maritime trade to the end of the century and beyond. It also facilitated recreational opportunities. Robert Chapman had, with some foresight, presented petitions to the Mayor for the erection of landing stages at both piers, which the borough council eventually approved in 1879, financial arrangements having been agreed with Tynemouth and the Tyne Improvement Commission. There was a happy outcome, since 'the Tyne General Ferry Company then began running their steamers between the piers in the summer months, a service greatly appreciated by both residents and visitors'.[43]

Family Life and the Drapery Business

By the time his landing stages petition was approved in 1879, Robert had been trading in his King Street draper's shop for forty-three years, having opened his doors for the first time in 1836. He lived above his shop for twenty-five years, having started married life there in 1841 with his wife Elizabeth. By the early 1850s the household had expanded very considerably. Their six children had been born in the house and were living with them. The two eldest, Robert and Matthew (aged 9 and 7), were schoolchildren, described in the 1851 Census as 'scholars', and the youngest, Henry, was just 1 year old. With the family lived two servants, Mary Brown and Elizabeth Ridley, and one 15-year-old draper's assistant, Matthew Grainger. The interlinked business and domestic arrangements were very typical of those in the mid-century. Retail units were 'almost invariably small, independent shops, owned and run by the shopkeeper on the spot'; 'one master, one shop was the rule'.[44] And drapers' assistants, invariably male, usually lived with the master as part of his household.

As with other occupations – whether down the mines or out at sea or in the factory – working hours were very long. In the drapery trade:

Robert Chapman, now in his seventies, continued to expand his business as a 'Linen & Woollen Draper, Silk Mercer, Hosier and Hatter'. (Chapman Family Archive)

... it was usual for the staff to rise at 6 a.m. to clean the shop and set out the stock before breakfast. The invention of gaslight – cheap, bright and exhausting to the indoor atmosphere – was no blessing to the shop assistant whose hours of work, and often his busiest hours of the day, were advanced by artificial light into the late evening. Ten o'clock at night on weekdays and midnight on Saturdays were the common closing hours.[45]

The retail environment for businessmen like Robert was favourable, with growing demand from female shoppers: 'the continued prominence of drapers and haberdashers reflected the large amount of home-sewing of dresses and shirts, underwear and night wear, to say nothing of household linen, that was still taken for granted'.[46]

Business was certainly going well for Robert Chapman in the 1850s – the decade in which he invested in *Priscilla* – but his domestic life suffered a major blow in 1855, when his wife Elizabeth died at the age of 43. At the next Census, in 1861, Robert was duly described as a 'widower (draper)'.

An 1868 view from the Market Place down King Street with its horse-drawn carriages and carts. After the premises of Humphrey & Evans, Merriman and Robson came Robert Chapman's drapery at No. 83, with a lady in a fashionable long dress and large hat looking in the window. (South Tyneside Libraries)

His eldest son, another Robert, had also died, and his 17-year-old son, Matthew, had by then become his draper's apprentice. The remaining five children at this time (William, Jane, Henry, Edward and Elizabeth, whose ages ranged from 7 to 14) were all 'scholars'. Edward had been born in 1852 and Elizabeth in 1854, just a year before her mother died. In 1863,

Robert Chapman's invoice of Christmas 1878 to his daughter-in-law Mrs Henry Chapman for some 200 purchases between July and December. (Tyne & Wear Archives & Museums)

Robert married again at St Hilda's, his second wife being Ann Alderson, aged 30 and twenty-one years his junior. Shortly afterwards they moved from King Street to Winchester Street, and by 1871 they had moved again, to 6 Challoner Terrace East in Westoe, together with at least four of Robert's children and two domestic servants. His son Matthew was now a fully fledged 27-year-old draper, and Henry was a 21-year-old bank clerk.

Robert Chapman's move from King Street to an exclusively residential area was indicative of a wider trend. In the 1870s the street was gradually taking on a purely commercial character. The Shieldsman, T. Brown, contrasted the street during this period with his childhood memories: 'The street has vastly improved since then, the many handsome fronts indicating the prosperity of the town. No longer do the shopkeepers and their families occupy the rooms above. The entire aspect of the street has changed.'[47]

He first describes the north side of King Street, and then, 'Beginning again at the Market end, on the opposite side, were Humphrey and Evans, grocers; Merriman and Robson, hatters; Chapman, draper; 'Gazette' Office; a deaf and dumb gentleman as engraver; Hodgkin, Barnett, Pease and Spence, bankers; H.T. Duncan, solicitor; and Learmount, stationer.'[48]

Robert was related by marriage to the proprietors of both Merriman's and Robson's, who trading next door to Robert's shop were also drapers, and not solely hatters. The concentration of drapers' shops in King Street and the Market Place was commercially advantageous: 'Plenty of trade in the road if the shops were all drapers,' as the highly successful Liverpool draper Owen Owen observed.[49] Away from his shop, Robert remained active as a select vestryman of St Hilda's, supporting the vicar, T.H. Chester, MA, and his two curates. A plaque on the west wall of the entrance vestibule records their names in August 1871, when 'This Church was fitted with open settings and with new warming and lighting apparatus at a

Designed by the well-known local architect J.H. Morton, No. 83 King Street was rebuilt to provide additional floor space.
(Ian Whitehead)

A roundel in the gable of No. 83 King Street records the date of Robert Chapman's extension: 'Rebuilt R C 1883'. (Ian Whitehead)

cost of £1,200, raised by voluntary subscriptions.'

Robert was now describing himself as a 'Linen & Woollen Draper, Silk Mercer, Hosier & Hatter'. He gave generous credit terms, at least to family. At 'Xmas 1878' he sent an invoice to his daughter-in-law, Mrs Henry Chapman, for all her purchases from July to December, some 200 in all, including for chintz, sarsenet, Alhambra quilt, black alpaca, servants' caps, gloves (white taffeta, 'colored kids' and Spring Top), twilled sheeting and ribbon (scarlet, bronze, brown, pink, blue and 'Cardinal') – a veritable cornucopia of drapery and haberdashery.

Three years later, in 1881, Robert celebrated his seventieth birthday. He was still very actively engaged in his business. His son Matthew, now 37, was working with him in the shop, and his son William was a 'draper traveller'. His daughters Jane and Elizabeth, 32 and 27, respectively, were unmarried and still living at home, and Henry was a busy chartered accountant in private practice. Business continued to thrive, and Robert decided that the time was right to expand his premises. In 1883 he rebuilt the shop, adding additional storeys in a rather attractive Dutch style designed by the well-known and talented local architect J.H. Morton. In a roundel on the gable he added the inscription 'Rebuilt RC 1883'. Some two years later, in 1885–86, he ceased being a sole trader and incorporated the business as Chapman & Co., formally bringing in his son Matthew. This coincided with a further domestic tragedy: Robert's second wife, Ann, died in 1886, at the age of 53. So Robert became a widower for the second time. Matthew subsequently decided to plough his own furrow, and moved to London, where he died in 1891 at the age of 48. By then, Robert had himself retired from the drapery trade, and could look back on more than half a century of commercial success on King Street.

Meanwhile, he had new external responsibilities to fulfil. He became a JP (Justice of the Peace) in 1887, or in the language of the time 'he received the commission of the peace for the borough'. He was an active magistrate, continuing his duties after the new Central Police Buildings, with their principal entrance in Keppel Street, were opened in 1893. They included two courtrooms, in which the borough and county petty sessions (a court held by two or more justices, exercising summary jurisdiction in minor offences) were held, and in which the county court judge held his sittings, together with magistrates', solicitors' and witnesses' rooms.

Opening in 1893 of the Central Police Buildings with two new courtrooms in Keppel Street by the Mayor, Councillor Robert Readhead (at the top of the steps). Robert Chapman, JP (in black top hat and holding a cane), is second from the front on the right. (South Tyneside Libraries)

A year later, in 1894, Robert Chapman sat for the last time as a Justice of the Peace, less than two months before he died, on what became a notorious and protracted case. On 3 November the notice of the trial date stated that 'Thomas Sinclair Leinster, of 41 Linskill Terrace, North Shields, ship owner, stands charged on a warrant with having set fire to his vessel, S.S. *Richmond*, while on a voyage from London to the Tyne'. It was a long and complicated case in which Captain Leinster was accused of boarding his own vessel in Algiers, leaving it in London and then re-embarking disguised as a bearded deaf and dumb passenger, setting fire to its cargo of North African esparto grass (used in paper-making) with paraffin shortly before the vessel reached the Tyne, and successfully making an insurance claim. Captain Leinster absconded, but was caught several years later, tried at the Durham Assizes, found guilty and sentenced to five years' penal servitude, dying at Parkhurst prison on the Isle of Wight.

The case was long and exhausting, and Robert's last as a Justice of the Peace. He died a few weeks after the initial hearings, on 31 December 1894. Tribute was paid to him by the Mayor of South Shields, Alderman Robert Readhead, at the police court, which sat on New Year's Day. The Mayor, as reported by the *Shields Gazette*, said:

> I have to regret the death of one of our colleagues, Mr Chapman, who was appointed a magistrate in 1887. From that day until the last time he presided at the court he has been very industrious indeed in attention to the duties of the position. I regret to say that one of his last acts was to sit here for two consecutive days over long periods in the trial of the Leinster case. That was no doubt one of the causes of shortening his life, and the best we can do is to offer our condolences to the family.

Robert Chapman was 83 years old when he died. In his long life he had seen, and contributed to, the extraordinary growth of South Shields. And his son Henry was, at the age of 33, already well established in his chartered accountancy profession, at Waterloo Chambers in King Street.

The future for the town in the final years of the century continued to look promising. The well-known Victorian novelist and *Newcastle Daily Chronicle* journalist William Clark Russell described in upbeat terms the scene from a trip down Tyneside's 'broadest street':[50]

> As the little steamer's head swept round up stream I stood looking at the wintry picture of old South Shields. Who says there is no beauty nor poetry in coal and grime and smoke, in huddled tenements, high chimneys, and such things? I never remember a finer sight in its way than this old black town viewed from the rushing, broken, tossing river, its foreground of colliers crowded in tiers lifting their ill-stayed spars into the whirling gloom of the tempestuous December day, its roofs whitened with snow which made every wall look to be built of coal, upon which here and there the red and black funnel of a steamer planted a spot of colour ... Assuredly the Tynesider has a right to be proud of his noble stream, and to resent our southern ignorance of the magnitude of its

interests, the wealth of its industries, the amazing spirit of progress that characterises its history and that is shaping its colossal future. Even as I write I hear of projects which in a few months will be completed – new shipbuilding yards, new graving and dry docks, extensions of established works. If this present rate of movement is persevered in, what must be the sight the river Tyne will offer twenty years hence?[51]

PART 2

WESTOE

3

FULL STEAM AHEAD

The 1850s significantly improved the fortunes of South Shields through its new status as an incorporated borough and the setting up of the Tyne Improvement Commission. And it was at the very beginning of that decade, in March 1850, that Henry Chapman, the fifth child of Robert and Elizabeth, was born at 83 King Street. The family was still living above the shop, his father's drapery business was flourishing, and South Shields was booming. If he did look back on his youth when he married at the age of 26, he would no doubt have agreed with the judgement of G.M. Young, the famous twentieth-century historian of Victorian Britain, that 'Of all the decades in history, a wise man would choose the eighteen-fifties to be young in.'[1]

Henry received a decent education. He was sent first to William Brockie's private school in nearby Russell Street, at a time when around 4,000 children were studying at private schools in the town. It was a good choice because William Brockie was a well-known man of letters and an exceptional linguist who had been the first editor of the *North & South Shields Gazette and Northumberland and Durham Advertiser*. His editorship lasted only three years, until 1852, but during that period he published, through its columns, his acclaimed *History of Shields* and *The Folk of Shields*.[2] Ill-health forced him to give up his post, after which he started his school in Russell Street and became a borough councillor, and therefore a colleague of Henry Chapman's father, Robert, in the Town Hall.

From Russell Street, where Henry would have been instructed in 'English Reading, Writing, Arithmetic, Grammar and Geography',[3] he moved to what would become the Royal Grammar School in Newcastle. The school,

William Brockie, painted here by John Scott, was a well-known man of letters. After stepping down from the editorship of the *Shields Gazette* he founded a private school in Russell Street, where Henry Chapman was a pupil. (Sunderland Museum & Winter Gardens, Tyne & Wear. © Tyne & Wear Archives & Museums/Bridgeman Images)

although founded by a charter of Queen Elizabeth I in 1600, was not generally known as 'Royal' until 1900. Throughout the nineteenth century it was known as the 'Newcastle Free School' or simply as the 'Grammar School'. The timing of Henry's entry in the 1850s was fortunate, or well judged by his parents. The period from 1820 to 1847 had seen the school in the doldrums, and far from being the most significant in the city. In fact, total numbers were down to a mere two dozen pupils by 1847 when the 30-year-old James Snape D.D. took over the running of the school. The Grammar School had been under-funded during this period, and many of the leading city mercantile and professional families sent their sons to boarding schools in the country.

Although only taking day boys, James Snape became a highly successful headmaster, who transformed the fortunes of the school. He moved it to new premises in 6 Charlotte Square in 1848, and managed to increase the number of pupils substantially. During Henry Chapman's attendance there were between 150 and 230 boys in total, half of whom lived outside Newcastle. This increase in numbers was facilitated by the spread of the north-eastern railways, links through Northumberland as far as Carlisle in the west, and to South Shields and other County Durham towns having been completed by 1840. Henry himself would have had the choice of travelling by train to Newcastle (the High Level Bridge from Gateshead having been opened in 1849), changing at Brockley

The School at Charlotte Square, 1867.

Newcastle Grammar School boys at Charlotte Square, 1867. Henry Chapman benefited from the outstanding teaching of the headmaster, Dr James Snape. (Royal Grammar School, Newcastle upon Tyne)

Whins, or by steam ferry from the Mill Dam to the city. The social composition of the Grammar School was mixed. In the mid-1860s, around three-quarters of pupils came from shop-keeping, artisan and working-class families. Fortunately for them, the Grammar School's endowments enabled the fees charged to be very substantially below the actual cost of providing the boys' education.

James Snape was an outstanding teacher at the Grammar School:

In the mid-century, when parents put their sons into the Grammar School they did so in order to have them made proficient in literacy and numeracy so that they could find work in non-labouring jobs. Skill in the lower levels of mathematics and accuracy in English was what Snape was expected to impart. It was these very subjects that he taught brilliantly. 'Few undergraduates in a college lecture room could have surpassed these lads in the repetition of propositions or in the explanation of the successive steps required for the constructions and proofs.[4]

A. Reid and Co., Ltd., Newcastle.   VIEW ON TYNE.

"The Tyne is not the longest river in the United Kingdom, nor the broadest nor the deepest; but historically it is one of the most interesting; naturally, one of the most diversified; commercially, one of the most important."—*Rivers of the United Kingdom.*

TYNE GENERAL FERRY COMPANY.

HALF-HOUR SAILINGS
FROM
QUAYSIDE, NEWCASTLE
} TYNEMOUTH FARES: 6D. SINGLE.   SHIELDS FARES: 4D. SINGLE.
          "   "   9D. RETURN.   "   "   6D. RETURN.

The Tyne General Ferry Company's landing stage at the Mill Dam. Henry Chapman would probably have taken a ferry to school in Newcastle. (South Tyneside Libraries)

Henry's Grammar School education laid the academic foundations on which he would build, in due course, a very successful professional and business career. His first job, however, as a 15-year-old school leaver in 1865, took him briefly in a different direction: he became an apprentice in Charles Palmer's hugely successful Iron and Shipbuilding Company Ltd. However, having decided that shipbuilding was not for him, he left Palmer's after two years. In 1867 he joined the National Provincial Bank, where he became an accountant and remained for eight years.

The year 1867 was a good one in which to join an expanding, national, well-capitalised joint-stock bank (where capital is held jointly by many different shareholders). Just a decade earlier, in 1857, the largest regional joint-stock bank based in Newcastle, the Northumberland and Durham District Bank, 'failed for an enormous amount, and by the misery and distress it caused, eclipsed all previous bank failures in the North of England'.[5] Unlimited liability existed for partners (and for a time also for shareholders in joint-stock banks) until the law was changed in 1862, when limited liability was introduced. Fortunately, in the case of the District Bank, the Newcastle branch of the Bank of England, which had been set up in 1828, had seen the writing on the wall and had made careful preparations. It was able to provide immediate and substantial funds to the commercial customers of the failed bank, including local colliery companies, enabling them to pay their workers.[6]

The National Provincial Bank of England, to give its full name, was the brainchild of Thomas Joplin, who was born in Newcastle upon Tyne. It was founded in 1833 in London with capital of £1 million, to be subscribed in shares of £100 each. Joplin was one of the original directors. It was, as its name suggests, specifically set up to have 'branches in the provincial towns' – the South Shields branch opened in 1848 – with business conducted by 'Boards of Local Directors'. Indeed, for the first thirty years of its existence the National Provincial was a country bank, with its headquarters in London but no banking facility open to the public. It expanded remarkably quickly, and by 1866 – a year before Henry Chapman joined and the year in which it did finally open for banking business in London – it had 2,000 shareholders and a nationwide network of 122 branches, including in Newcastle and North Shields.[7] Many of these branches came from the acquisition of local private banks, such as the Stockton and Durham County Bank in 1846.

Henry Chapman gained valuable commercial experience at the National Provincial. However, he was a budding entrepreneur who had been planning very carefully to start two new ventures simultaneously. In 1875 he celebrated his twenty-fifth birthday, left the bank, walked a few yards down King Street, and set up his own accountancy practice. This would become Henry Chapman Son & Co., where he would be senior partner until his death sixty years later. In July of the same year he founded the South Shields Commercial Permanent Building Society, and became its first secretary. He would remain in that post for fifty years, and both businesses would be going strong a century after he founded them. Meanwhile, Henry rather cleverly complemented them by becoming an insurance agent for three companies – Atlas Steam Ship Insurance Association, Norwich and London Accident, and Commercial Union.

Not content with these challenges, just a year later, on 8 August 1876, he also transformed his domestic life: he married Dora Gibson at St Peter's Church in Harton, moving from his parents' house in Challoner Terrace, Westoe, to nearby 34 Winchester Street. Dora came from a Harton ship-owning family. Her father, George Gibson, had started out as a sail-maker and ships' chandler and diversified into ship owning, as was quite usual

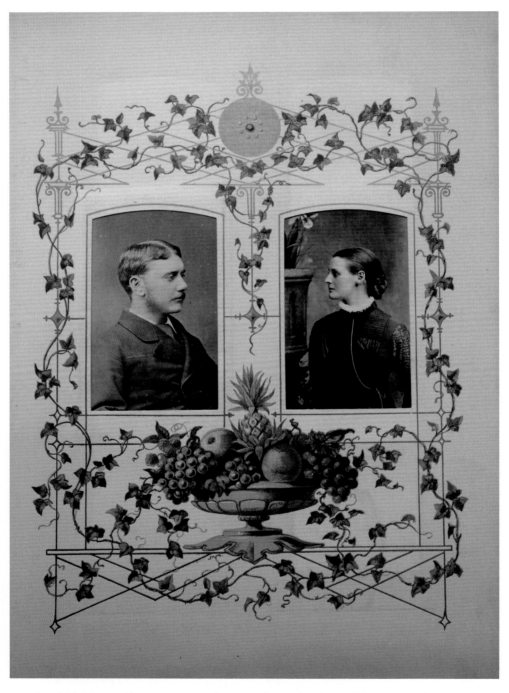

Aged 26, Henry Chapman married Dora Gibson, daughter of the Harton ship owner George Gibson, in 1876. (Chapman Family Archive)

among businessmen in nineteenth-century South Shields. By the time of the 1861 Census, he was part-owner of at least five sailing ships. Tragically, George died in 1865 aged 40, leaving his widow Elizabeth and four children, Dora being the eldest.

Happily married, Henry and Dora lost no time in starting a family. Their daughter, Ethel, was born in May 1877, a year after their marriage, Henry confirming his profession of 'Accountant' on her birth certificate. The second child was a son also called Henry, born a year later in 1878, followed by Robert (later Sir Robert), born in 1880 at 6 Wood Terrace, Henry and Dora having moved from Winchester Street. They would have a large family even by Victorian standards: Dora gave birth in quick succession to seven boys and four girls between 1877 and 1892.

The year 1880 was an important milestone in Henry's professional life: he became a Fellow of the newly established Institute of Chartered Accountants in England and Wales in September. And two months later he founded a new professional practice, taking advantage of the growing demand for accountancy services. The Winding-Up Acts of 1848 and 1849 (used extensively with the many railway companies that became insolvent), and the succession of Companies Acts and corporate start-ups following the Limited Liability Act of 1855 were key drivers of this rising demand.

Professionalisation of accountancy activities had been a slow process, and it was not until 1870 that the Incorporated Society of Liverpool Accountants and the Institute of Accountants in London were formed. It would take a decade of protracted discussions and negotiations before a Royal Charter was granted in May 1880 to the Institute of Chartered Accountants in England and Wales, which incorporated nearly all the members of the five separate pre-existing institutes and societies of accountants.[8]

Henry Chapman had moved very quickly indeed, as an existing practitioner first at the National Provincial Bank and then in private practice, to become a Fellow of the Institute in September 1880, just four months after its formation. He was, by then, already practising on his own account in Newcastle as well as in South Shields, and in November 1880 he made the decision to expand the Newcastle office by taking William Castle Fletcher into partnership with him, at 24 Grainger Street West.

'The Agreement of Partnership' of Chapman Fletcher & Co. ran to twenty-five clauses. William Fletcher was entitled to a sum of £100 a year, payable monthly, before net profits were distributed equally between the two partners on the basis of half yearly accounts. If net profits were less than

£100 in a year, Henry Chapman would make up the difference out of his own resources. William was very much the junior partner: 'he shall at all times devote the whole of his time and attention to the said partnership business and diligently and faithfully employ himself therein and carry on the same for the greatest advantage of the partnership'. On the other hand, 'it shall not be necessary for the said Henry Chapman to take any part in the said joint business otherwise than as the said Henry Chapman shall think fit but so that he shall not neglect the interests of the said partnership business'.[9]

The reason for this clause was to ring-fence Henry's existing South Shields business:

> Henry Chapman shall be at full liberty to continue to carry on the busi-
> ness of an accountant as at present carried on by him at South Shields
> on his own separate account and all profits made by him from business
> located within the Borough of South Shields and also anything arising
> out of or in the nature of Bankruptcy or Liquidation or composition
> [agreements with creditors] introduced by the said Henry Chapman at
> South Shields or elsewhere by Solicitors practising at South Shields or
> in the auditing of accounts as at present made or held by the said Henry
> Chapman at North Shields shall belong to the said Henry Chapman
> absolutely and shall in no way form part of or be dealt with or treated by
> the said partnership business.

This was despite the fact that the 'style' Chapman Fletcher & Co. would also be used for the South Shields office.

Henry also protected his other existing business interests, notably as Secretary of the South Shields Commercial Permanent Building Society: 'Neither of the said partners (except the said Henry Chapman and then so far only as regards the business at present carried on by him at South Shields) shall engage in or undertake any trade or business save as afore-said without the consent in writing of the other partner.' Henry displayed loyalty to his previous employer, the agreement stipulating that the part-nership's bankers should be 'The National Provincial Bank of England', unless the partners agreed otherwise. And the partners should themselves display mutual loyalty: 'Each partner shall be just and faithful to the other partner in all transactions relating to the business of the partnership and shall give a true account of the same to him when and so often as the same shall reasonably be required.'

The agreement was for a term of three years. Although seemingly very one-sided, it clearly worked well for both partners, and was renewed for a further three years in November 1883, when the Chapman Fletcher office in Newcastle moved to Bank Chambers in Mosley Street. It was renewed again in 1886, but the partnership was dissolved 'by mutual consent' at the end of January 1889. The next month William Castle Fletcher secured long-term career advancement by becoming the Newcastle 'Resident Partner' of R.F. Miller & Co., whose main office was in Manchester. In South Shields, Henry Chapman moved a few yards from 70 King Street to Waterloo Chambers at No. 67. He practised there with his professional team for the next seventeen years.

Family Life in Westoe

If Henry had plenty on his plate in the 1880s with his expanding business interests in South Shields, his wife Dora had even more on hers. After

Henry Chapman spent his whole life in or very close to Westoe village, which became increasingly popular among business families. This image was taken in 1868. (South Tyneside Libraries)

Henry Chapman built *Seacroft* on the eastern
edge of Westoe Village in 1887. With its twenty
rooms, the house accommodated comfortably
his and Dora's eleven children and four servants.
(Historic Environment Scotland)

the birth of their third child,
Robert, in 1880 came Hilda
in 1881, George in 1882,
Alan in 1883, Dora Elizabeth
in 1884, Laurence in 1886,
Frederick in 1887, and
Marion Dorothy in 1890.

Henry and Dora con-
sidered the move to Wood
Terrace as temporary, since
in 1878 Henry and several
fellow businessmen had
bought the fields adjacent to
Westoe House (until then the
home of the Ingham family,
prominent local landowners
and benefactors), just to the
east of Westoe Village. This
parcel of land, known as the
Westoe Park Estate and formerly also part of the Ingham estates, was developed with four very large houses, each standing in extensive grounds.[10] In
1887, Henry built *Seacroft* on his plot. It was a magnificent mansion with
over twenty rooms – whose layout would have been along similar lines to
nearby *Rockcliffe*, built in 1885. On the ground floor there was a spacious
entrance hall, breakfast room, drawing room, dining room and kitchen, with
a principal staircase, and separate servants' stairs next to the kitchen, leading
to the first floor. There was a principal bedroom with adjoining, though
not interconnecting, dressing room, and four other bedrooms, but only one
bathroom and WC. There was also a housemaid's room and large linen cupboard. The attic floor, where the rest of the servants would have lived, had
even more useable space than the first floor.[11]

Henry and Dora certainly needed a large house. At the time of the 1891
Census there were fifteen household members living with them: ten children, Dora's sister Marion Gibson and four servants. One of the servants
had been born in South Shields, one in North Shields, one in Plymouth
and one in Portsmouth, demonstrating the perennial 'pull' of a town with
an expanding economy. The household was completed a year later, with
the birth of the eleventh child, Charles Lancelot.

What was the village of Westoe like when Charles was born? Aaron Watson, editor of the *Shields Gazette* from 1885 to 1892, describes it in glowing terms:

> Westoe is one of the prettiest villages in England. It has given its name to the largest of the townships of which South Shields is composed, and it is no longer what it was in times past, a quaint congregation of houses detached from any larger centre of population, but it remains a village still, with an air of separateness and aloofness, though several roads and streets converge upon it. At Westoe reside the wealthier inhabitants of South Shields. On one side of the single street of the village several large mansions have been erected; other mansions straggle away into the fields and the neighbourhood of the sea. Westoe Village has a prosperous and orderly look, but it also has a retired appearance, as if it were still remote from towns. It is pleasantly shaded by trees; a family of rooks inhabits the elms; in spite even of quite modern innovations the place retains a flavour of antiquity.[12]

The Children's Education

Henry and Dora's children were lucky enough to grow up in a very large house in a splendid location. The eldest was Ethel, and decisions were soon taken about her education. She and her sisters would be sent away to boarding school, and the boys would stay at home and go to the new day school in Westoe itself.

By the time the older girls went to boarding school in the 1890s there had been a transformation in the choices available:

> The real breakthrough came with the Schools Inquiry Commission of 1864–67. Appointed to survey middle-class education, it was persuaded to include girls' schools within its remit and became the first royal commission to take evidence in person from women witnesses. Its survey of the inadequacies of provision for girls' education made the case for mobilizing resources for reform. The state did not yet fund secondary education in Britain, but the Endowed Schools Act of 1869 provided for the redeployment of educational endowments to found grammar schools for girls as well as boys.[13]

By the end of the century more than ninety girls' grammar schools or 'high' schools had been founded under this Act in towns throughout Britain, though South Shields was not one of them. Some thirty were formed by the Girls' Public Day School Company, for whom Cheltenham Ladies' College was an important model. The college had been founded in 1853 'to provide a sound academic education for girls', and its excellent reputation was entirely due to the successful efforts of the formidable Dorothea Beale, who became its Principal in 1858 at the age of 27. She personally gave evidence before the Schools Inquiry Commission and arranged, at her own expense, for the sections on girls' education in the commission's report to be published separately, with a preface that she wrote.

Several of the girls' schools founded in the last quarter of the nineteenth century would also become very well known. 'St. Leonards, St. Andrews (1874), Roedean School (1885), and Wycombe Abbey (1896) offered, like Cheltenham Ladies' College, a female equivalent to the boys' public boarding school, with an emphasis on the character building value of sport.'[14]

In the event, Henry and Dora chose Cheltenham Ladies' College for their eldest daughters, Ethel and Hilda. In September 1891, aged 14, Ethel was admitted to the college and placed in Miss Bere's house, situated in Fauconberg Terrace. By the time Ethel went to Cheltenham, Dorothea Beale, who was still principal, had created an exceptional educational establishment on the site of the original Cheltenham Spa, where, also demonstrating skilful financial management, she oversaw the building of 'a large Gothic pile architecturally much influenced by Ruskin, whom she admired and who approved her aspirations'.[15] In addition to classrooms, the college had music rooms, a library and laboratories. A wide syllabus, including mathematics and classics, had been taught since 1880.

Ethel was strong academically, and girls were encouraged to take public examinations, notably the University of Oxford Senior Local Examination and the University of Cambridge Higher Local Examination (which were broadly equivalent to today's GCSE and A Level qualifications, respectively). In 1894 she was awarded a 'Distinguished in English' grade in the Oxford Senior exam, and subsequently passed the Cambridge Higher exams in English Language and Literature, History of English Literature, Early English, Arithmetic, English History, Constitutional History, French History and French.

"Dante" by the C.L.C. Guild.
July - 1900.

The first meeting of Dante and Beatrice

DB/370/12 R

Henry and Dora's eldest daughters Ethel and Hilda were educated at Cheltenham Ladies' College, whose principal was the formidable Dorothea Beale. As alumnae, they both performed in the Guild's 1900 production of *Dante*. (Cheltenham Ladies' College)

Ethel was the prize winner among the 'Honour candidates' in an exam following a Course of Extension Lectures given in the college on the Stuarts and the Puritan Revolution. The examiner, Mr J. Hassell, MA of Christ Church, Oxford University, commented that 'the questions were by no means easy, and some of them required considerable knowledge and no little thought'. She took piano and singing lessons as extras, and participated in various Handiwork Exhibitions, where her 'nicely embroidered handkerchief sachet' and table cloths were commended. So what were traditionally called 'Accomplishments' were still taught, alongside a rigorous academic education.

Ethel left in 1894 and Hilda (who had started as a 14-year-old in 1895) left in 1898, both becoming members of the Guild, as the alumnae association was called. They returned to Cheltenham in 1900 – the year in which the Ladies' College won a gold medal at the Paris Exhibition for its educational exhibits[16] – to perform in the Guild's production of *Dante*. He was a particular favourite of Dorothea Beale. In her lectures on him, she would focus on the moral and spiritual virtues of Beatrice, who was held up as an important example for the girls since 'Dante tells us with what reverent worship he cherished the ideal of Beauty and Goodness revealed to him in Beatrice.'[17]

On the 1900 production, the college magazine reported that 'In the Second Act, Casela's song "Love, reasoning of my lady in my mind" was sweetly sung by Miss E. Chapman' (Casela being a Florentine musician). Hilda also appeared in Act II, possibly as one of the three Christian Graces (in red, white and green respectively) or as one of the Cardinal Virtues (in purple).[18] The play certainly seemed fully to reflect the college's motto of *Cœlesti Luce Crescat* (May she grow in heavenly light). Ethel and Hilda were indeed fortunate to have attended Cheltenham Ladies' College, whose reputation had spread throughout Britain and the British Empire. 'By 1900 the small and initially struggling day school had become a thriving community of over 1,000 pupils, with boarders, day girls and part-time students, studying from Kindergarten to Degree level.'[19]

Dorothea Beale also established St Hilda's College, Oxford, and a teacher training school. Boundlessly energetic, she also found time to be President of the Association of Headmistresses, succeeding the equally indomitable Frances Buss. They had been contemporaries at Queen's College, Harley Street, in London, and Buss became the first Headmistress of the North London Collegiate School for Ladies, and a Life Member of the Council of Cheltenham Ladies' College.

The two women were the butt of a contemporary satirical rhyme in *Punch* magazine:

Miss Buss and Miss Beale,
Cupid's darts do not feel,
How different from us,
Miss Beale and Miss Buss[20]

The two youngest daughters – Dora Elizabeth and (Marion) Dorothy – did not follow their older sisters to Cheltenham Ladies' College. They were sent to St Leonards, in St Andrews, Scotland, one of the new wave of the Girls' Public Day School Company schools founded in the 1870s.

There were, however, important links between the two schools. The first headmistress, (Dame) Louisa Innes Lumsden, one of the first graduates of Girton College, Cambridge, was recruited to the new school in St Andrews (St Andrews School for Girls, which later took the name St Leonards) in 1877, having been teaching classics for a short period at Cheltenham Ladies' College. She, like Dorothea Beale, was also a well-known 'suffragette' (as she described herself).

St Leonards 'was the first (Scottish) girls' school to be modelled on the English public schools, incorporating a house system and a sixth form collectively responsible for the duties of prefect', with a strong emphasis on games and exercise.[21] When Louisa Lumsden resigned in 1882, her successor as headmistress was her colleague (Dame) Frances Dove, who had also been not only at Girton College, Cambridge, but also at Cheltenham Ladies' College, where she taught mathematics and physiology. She had thirteen successful years at St Leonards, achieving a reputation for excellence and doubling the numbers of pupils ('scholars' as they were described in nineteenth-century Census returns). In 1896 Dove moved south, becoming the first Headmistress of Wycombe Abbey School in Buckinghamshire.

Two years later, in 1898, Frances Dove edited, with Dorothea Beale and Lucy Soulsby (who had been headmistress of Oxford High School for Girls), *Work and Play in Girls' Schools*:

> She argued that women should be taught corporate virtues, and that to be good citizens it was essential to have wide interests, a sense of discipline and *esprit de corps*. She applied these principles at Wycombe, believing that the best place to instil ideals of citizenship was the school. Like headmasters of boys' public schools, she regarded team games as the best medium for developing character, and introduced cricket, hockey and lacrosse as compulsory activities.[22]

These games were already very important activities at St Leonards when Dora Elizabeth Chapman went to Bishopshall East House in 1899, at the age of 15. Her good friend from Westoe, Bessie Gowans, daughter of the well-known South Shields doctor, Dr W. Gowans, who was Scottish, went with her to the same house in the same year. Their parents' friendship might well explain Henry and Dora Chapman's decision to send their youngest daughters to St Leonards, rather than to Cheltenham Ladies' College.

Dora Elizabeth and Bessie would make a new friend in the following year, 1900. This was the 14-year-old Hélène Paris Macgowan, who had indeed been born in the French capital. Hélène won cups for her swimming prowess, played hockey and cricket for her house (Bishopshall West, whose boarders were known as Abernethys after its house mistress Miss Abernethy) and was taken to Westoe to stay with the Gowans family. There she met her future husband, Robert, Henry and Dora's second son. Hélène's sister, Isabelle Stuart Macgowan, spent two years at Bishopshall West, where she also played hockey and cricket for the house. She left at the same time as Hélène, in 1904, and subsequently went to Girton College, Cambridge.

Marion Dorothy Chapman (known as Dorothy) followed in her sister's footsteps to Bishopshall East house in 1903, aged 13, and left five years later. She must have displayed outstanding *esprit de corps* as she became captain of house, and she was certainly very sporty, becoming captain also of the hockey team and playing on the lacrosse team.[23] St Leonards was par-

Dorothy Chapman captained the Bishopshall East hockey team in 1908. Back row, left to right: M. Jackson, M. Moir, J. Ross and M. Baron; middle row, left to right: K. Robertson, H. Taylor, D. Chapman (Captain), G. Bacon and K. Haggie; bottom row, left to right: F. Ritson, D. Potts and N. Young. (St Leonards School, St Andrews)

Dora Elizabeth and Dorothy Chapman, the youngest daughters of Henry and Dora, went as boarders to St Leonards School, St Andrews. There they met Hélène Paris Macgowan (pictured in the back row, extreme right, in an Abernethys house photo), who would become their sister-in-law. Hélène's sister Isabelle is also in the picture (on the right-hand side of the group, blonde hair, hands in front of her, seated just above the two girls on the bottom row). (St Leonards School, St Andrews)

Before motor bus services reached St Leonards St Andrews: girls in a horse-drawn coach, 1904. (St Leonards School, St Andrews)

ticularly proud of its lacrosse record. The game was brought to the school by Louisa Lumsden and Frances Dove, who had first seen it played on a visit to Canada in 1884. As Louise Lumsden later recalled:

> … we went to see a great Lacrosse match between the Canghuawaya Indians and the Montreal Club. These Indians live not far from Montreal, above the Lachine Rapids, and are, of course, civilised, and many of them very wealthy. They were in ordinary costume – dark-blue jerseys, velvet breeches, hats and all dark blue, and their dark faces and legs, bare from the knee, gave them a most picturesque appearance. Their chief was called White Eagle. But the whites were a stronger team, and won the game. It is a wonderful game, beautiful and graceful. (I was so charmed with it that I introduced it at St. Leonards.)[24]

Henry and Dora's four girls went to two leading boarding schools. All seven of their sons went to a new boys' day school very close to home – the South Shields High School. Following the Girls' Public Day School Company's successful launch of some two dozen schools, the Boys' Public Day School Company was formed in London in 1882 for the provision of higher intermediate education throughout the country. Its president was the well-known educational reformer, Lord Aberdare. Before being elevated to the peerage, he had been, as Henry Austin Bruce, MP, a leading supporter of the Bill introduced during Gladstone's first government, which became the famous Elementary Education Act of 1870. Under this legislation, school boards were created by local authorities, South Shields being quick off the mark to set one up and embark on an ambitious school building programme (including a school for 1,500 children in Ocean Road).

The formation of the Boys' Public Day School Company was welcomed by a group of South Shields residents led by Samuel Malcolm, and in January 1883 James Cochran Stevenson, South Shields' MP, presided over a public meeting in the Marine School that resolved to enter into discussions with the company.[25] Leading supporters of the proposal, who included Henry Chapman and his friend and business partner, the solicitor James Henry Rennoldson, 'signified their willingness' to serve on a 'Provisional Committee' to persuade the company to select South Shields for the establishment of one of its new schools and, importantly, undertook to buy shares to ensure that adequate finance would be available. Negotiations took place in the spring with Samuel Malcolm, Joseph Mason Moore (the town clerk) and Alexander

The new South Shields High School for Boys opened in 1885. By the time of this advertisement in 1892, five of Henry and Dora Chapman's seven sons were pupils. The youngest two, Laurence and Frederick, started in 1894 and 1895. (Aaron Watson, *South Shields: A Gossiping Guide* [South Shields, 1892])

Scott (the Head of Ocean Road Schools) pressing the company to agree to provide a school whose pupils could go straight on to university. Agreement was soon reached to establish the South Shields High School on the basis that at least 1,000 newly issued shares (at £2 each) would be taken up.

A 4-acre site adjoining Mowbray Road in Westoe was identified, and a sale price of £1,870 was agreed with the Ecclesiastical Commissioners (very large landowners in South Shields). To speed up the process the local committee members undertook to be financial guarantors, and plans were quickly drawn up for a building intended initially for 200 boys. The architects were Oliver and Leeson of Newcastle upon Tyne, well known for the design of school buildings. Construction soon started and Lord Aberdare laid the foundation stone in May 1884. A Headmaster, Walter Hibbert Phillips, MA (formerly Second Master and Head of Science at Bedford County School) was appointed, and in May 1885 the first thirty-seven pupils enrolled.

The May 1885 intake included boys whose fathers were well known to Henry Chapman in the business and social community of South Shields.

Most of them would become close friends of Henry's son Robert. The new boys (whose ages ranged from 9 to 15) included: Robert Readhead and his cousin John of the shipbuilding family; William Grant, son of James Grant the jeweller; Walter Runciman (who would later become a well-known MP and President of the Board of Trade); Forster Moore Armstrong, son of Joseph Forster Armstrong MD, who would become a solicitor before being killed in the First World War; Victor Grünhut, son of Jacques Grünhut the industrial chemist, who would practise as a solicitor in the town for fifty years; and Harry Eltringham, son of the shipbuilder Joseph T. Eltringham. Later entrants included the five sons of John Barbour, the draper. The eldest, Malcolm M. Barbour, would become Mayor immediately after the Second World War.

Henry and Dora Chapman's eldest son, also called Henry (and known as Hal), entered the school in 1887, aged 9, by which time there were around sixty boys. He took the Cambridge Junior Locals exam, distinguished himself in Religious Knowledge and left as a 17-year-old. 'To be an architect. Articled to D. H. Grieves' was the 'cause of withdrawal' noted in the school record. Robert Chapman, Hal's younger brother, also started at the school in 1887, at the age of 7. Other boys who started at the same time included Ralph Henry Morton and Albert Hale Morton, sons of the well-known South Shields architect, Joseph Hale Morton.

Robert made a strong start, being awarded the IVth Form prize in 1891. This was *Heroes and Kings: Stories from the Greek*, written by the Rev. Alfred J. Church, MA, Professor of Latin in University College London, and published the year before with a gilt-edged Morocco leather cover. The stories, from Homer, Herodotus and Appollonius Rhodius, are full of the ruthless and perfidious deeds of gods and mortals. *The Story of Polycrates of Samos*, from Herodotus, exemplified the utility of succinct and plain speaking, which would stand diligent readers such as Robert in good stead in adult public life. A delegation from Samos went to Sparta, seeking help against King Polycrates. 'And when the rulers of Sparta gave them audience they made their request, using many words, as men are wont to do when they desire a thing exceedingly. The rulers answered, "What ye said at the first we have forgotten, and what ye said afterwards we do not understand."'[26]

Robert took the Cambridge Junior Local Examination in 1892, achieved a first-class result in the 1897 Matriculation exam and second class in the Intermediate exam the following year. He was the only one of his family to obtain a Bachelor of Arts external degree from London

University at the school as a 19-year-old. He became school captain, and left in 1899 to go full-time into his father's chartered accountancy office.

Henry and Dora's third son, George Gibson Chapman, was admitted in 1890. He had the most distinguished academic record of all the brothers. After the Cambridge Local exams he achieved a first-class result in the Matriculation exam, and in 1899 won an open scholarship (worth £40) to Peterhouse at Cambridge University at the age of 17. Tragedy struck Alan Edward Chapman, Henry and Dora's fourth son, who had also started at the High School in 1890. While still a pupil he contracted pernicious anaemia and died in 1898, at the age of 15.

George and Alan's enrolment at the school coincided with the appointment of a new headmaster, George Doherty Dakyns, formerly assistant master at Newcastle High School in Staffordshire. He came at a challenging time, since in 1891 the school was in financial difficulties, having failed to attract suffi-

South Shields Boys' High School Old Boys' rugby team in 1897/98 included Hal and George Chapman. Front row, left to right: Holmes Glover – Briton Robson – Thomas Cowan – James Readhead – Stanley Readhead. Second row, left to right: Thomas Bone – John Readhead – Frank Hudson – Matthew Henderson – George Chapman. Back row, left to right: Thomas Vasey – Arthur Fitzgerald – Henry (Hal) Chapman – Matthew Hall – Rev (Tardy) Clarke. (www.boyshighschool.co.uk/ photos/schoolphotos/1897-rugby.htm and Chapman Family Archive)

cient pupils. The failure was attributed to the fact that the London-based Boys' Public Day School Company had not appointed a local board of governors to oversee the school and take an active role in its development. Fortunately the potential crisis was quickly averted when the company agreed to sell it, together with its buildings, grounds and debts, to the specially formed South Shields High School Company Limited, for the sum of £4,500.

Three years later, in 1894, Henry and Dora's fifth son, Laurence Alfred, entered the school at the age of 8. He took the Cambridge Local Preliminary and Junior exams, received several distinctions, and left in 1902 to go into his father's business alongside his elder brother Robert. However, he was not cut out to be an accountant, and left to become an agricultural chemist, working on tea plantations in Assam. Henry and Dora's sixth son, Frederick Ernest Chapman (known as 'Fred' or 'Freddie'), started at the High School in 1895, also at the age of eight. After passing the Cambridge Local Preliminary and Junior examinations, he took both the Durham Preliminary Arts and the Edinburgh Medical Preliminary exams, leaving the school in 1905 to go to Durham University's College of Medicine. He later combined a medical career with international rugby.

A year after Frederick enrolled, in 1896, Wallace Moir Annand joined the school as a 9-year-old. He was the son of Robert Cumming Annand, described in the register as 'Engineer and Newspaper Proprietor', and who would become Managing Director of the *Shields Gazette*. Wallace, who went on to study at Durham College of Science, would marry Henry and Dora's daughter Dora Elizabeth (always known as Bessie) in 1914, thereby becoming a brother-in-law to the Chapman boys. Tragically he was killed at Gallipoli the following year. Charles Lancelot Chapman, Henry and Dora's seventh son, entered the school in 1901, at the age of 9, two years after a brand new science and art wing had been opened by old boy Walter Runciman, who had become the MP for Oldham.

Unfortunately, with pupil numbers never exceeding seventy, the governors – who included Henry Chapman – were not able to put the High School's finances on to an even keel, and in 1908 (the year before Charles Chapman left to become an articled clerk in a chartered accountancy office) the school was sold to the South Shields Corporation for the sum of £8,562. Governance issues were soon addressed by the South Shields Board of Education, which approved a new Scheme of Management in 1910. Thirteen new governors were appointed, under the chairmanship of the engineer and shipbuilder Alderman Joseph Middleton Rennoldson, who lived in *Fairfield*,

Westoe. Several previous governors were reappointed under the new scheme of management, including Henry Chapman and Dr William Gowans. The future of the school was, finally, assured, with admissions rising considerably. Twenty years later new challenges would arise, and again be overcome.

Developing the Accountancy Business

While his sons were at the South Shields High School, and his daughters boarded at Cheltenham Ladies' College and St Leonards, Henry expanded his business interests substantially, and continued to do so until the outbreak of the First World War. After the amicable termination of the Chapman Fletcher & Co. partnership in 1889, he remained in Waterloo Chambers, 67 King Street, as a sole chartered accountant practitioner. He also continued to manage the

Robert Chapman did rather well in the final examination set by the Institute of Chartered Accountants in England and Wales. In 1902 he received a Certificate of Merit for achieving fifth place nationally, having been in first place in the intermediate exam. (Chapman Family Archive)

South Shields Commercial Permanent Building Society and the North-
Eastern Investment Trust Ltd, both of which he had founded. A man of
considerable energy, he steadily built up these businesses as well as his accountancy base of audit clients, which would in due course comprise many of the
leading companies in the town. Fortunately for him, his son Robert wanted to
become a chartered accountant and join him in practice.

The first step was taken in December 1896, when 16-year-old Robert,
still studying at the Boys' High School, became an 'Articled Clerk'. Under
the Articles of Agreement, formally signed by father and son, Robert agreed
to 'place and bind himself Clerk to the said Accountant' for a term of five
years. He also agreed that he should not 'at any time during such term cancel
obliterate spoil destroy waste embezzle spend or make away with any of the
Books papers moneys or other property of the said Accountant ... or any
of his Clients or Employers'. Equally importantly, 'he shall not divulge the
names or affairs of such cli-
ents and Employers, and shall
readily and cheerfully obey
and execute ... their lawful
and reasonable demands'. The
remuneration to Robert under
the agreement was just 10*s* in
total for the full five-year term,
with Henry also agreeing to
'afford him ... such reasonable opportunities and work as
may be required to enable him
to acquire the art science and
knowledge of a Professional
Accountant'.[27]

To succeed, Robert needed
to study – hopefully also

Henry's architect son Hal Chapman drew up
plans for his father's new office in Barrington
Street, and had them published in *The Builders
Journal and Architectural Record*, 25 April, 1906.
(RIBA Collections)

'readily and cheerfully' – for his national accountancy exams. He would do
exceptionally well in them. In January 1901 he received a letter from the
Institute of Chartered Accountants in England and Wales (whose succinct,
problem-resolving telegram address was '"Unravel", London') informing him that he had passed the Intermediate Examination, 'placed 1st in
Order of Merit'. Henry Chapman, who became a Justice of the Peace in
the same year, must have been a very proud father. Eighteen months later

Robert took the Institute's Final Examination, this time being placed fifth in the Order of Merit of all candidates in England and Wales.

Robert immediately became an 'Associate in Practice' with his father, who felt that he had now outgrown his King Street office. Henry found a suitable plot of land in Barrington Street, and asked his eldest son Henry (Hal), an architect, to draw up plans. Hal was now 28, and as an ambitious young professional he had his drawings and plans published in the well-known weekly, *The Builders Journal and Architectural Record* of April 1906, the year after his father and brother Robert moved into the new offices. Hal's drawings show that the elevations for the new office were fully sympathetic with its distinguished neighbour, the 1881/82 Poor Law Union offices designed in 'Domestic Revival' style by the well-known South Shields architect, J.H. Morton. Henry and Hal took no risks with the construction contract. They had appointed the tried and trusted Messrs Summerbell & Son as contractors. The firm had carried out extensive works to *Seacroft*, Henry's house adjoining Westoe Village. Its principal, Mr R. Summerbell, had also been appointed by Henry in 1890/91 as one of the surveyors to the South Shields Commercial Permanent Building Society, a position he still held fifteen years later.

A Marital Interlude

Four years after the office move, on 10 November 1909, Robert married Hélène Paris Macgowan. He had first met her in Westoe, where she was staying with his sister Dora's friend Bessie Gowans, all three girls being boarders together at St Leonards in St Andrews. After leaving St Leonards in 1904, Hélène went to a 'finishing school' in Heidelberg. She had won swimming prizes in Scotland, and while in Germany she swam down the Rhine from Heidelberg to Mannheim, a distance of 11 miles and a record for her. Keeping closely in touch with Robert, Hélène returned to Paris, where her father James George Macgowan managed the business interests of John D. Rockefeller's Standard Oil Company from offices at 25 Boulevard Haussmann. It would have come as no surprise to him when Robert broached the subject of marrying Hélène, and he was delighted to give his consent.

The wedding took place at East Church, Stirling, the Macgowan ancestors having settled down as farmers nearby 300 years earlier. The East

The wedding of Robert Chapman and Hélène Macgowan in Stirling, November 1909. Front row, seated, left to right: Henry Chapman, Mrs James Macgowan (Hélène's mother), Dora Chapman (Robert's mother), James George Macgowan (Hélène's father). Standing: the Rev. J.P. Lang, Laurence and Bessie Chapman (Robert's brother and sister), Hélène and Robert, Isabelle Macgowan (Hélène's sister), Hal Chapman (Robert's brother), Miss Macgowan (Hélène's aunt). (Chapman Family Archive)

Church was part of the old parish church of Stirling, the Holy Rude.[28] In the seventeenth century a dispute among parishioners led to the church being partitioned and the formation of two separate congregations. Hence the 'East Church' and 'West Church'. As James Macgowan, the bride's father, reminded guests, it was in 1567 at the original Holy Rude Church that the infant King James VI (who later also became King James I of England and Ireland), son of the Catholic Mary, queen of Scots, was crowned as a Protestant, following her abdication. John Knox, the virulently anti-Catholic leader of the Scottish Reformation, had preached the sermon. So the church had a well-known history.

Robert and Hélène's marriage service was taken by the Rev. J.P. Lang, uncle of the then Archbishop of York. The wedding was given full coverage in the *Stirling Journal* on 12 November 1909:[29]

Wedding in East Church

Miss Macgowan, Paris, And
Mr Robert Chapman, Westoe
The wedding of Miss Hélène Macgowan, daughter of Mr Macgowan, Paris, and niece of the Misses Macgowan, Snowdon Place, with Mr Robert Chapman, Westoe, which took place on Wednesday in the East Church, was a very pretty sight. The stately old church forms a very effective setting to any such ceremony, while the artistic massing of the plants and flowers, and the handsome dresses worn by the guests heightened the general effect. The bride, who was given away by her father, was simply dressed in a charming robe of soft white satin, with court train, draped with pointe d'aiguille. She had a wreath of orange blossoms, over which fell her tulle veil. A pearl and diamond pendant was her sole ornament. She was accompanied by her sister, Miss Isabelle Macgowan, and the bridegroom's sister, Miss Bessie Chapman, as bridesmaids. These ladies were attired in pale blue and pale pink moiré frocks respectively, with antique silver trimmings. They wore large black picture hats with white aigrettes, and gold watch bracelets, the gift of the bridegroom.

The *Stirling Observer* noted that the reception in the Golden Lion Hotel was 'numerously attended', and described in great detail the dresses of the bridal party. 'The bride's mother was dressed in black charmeuse trimmed with old lace and peacock blue embroidery, black velvet hat with sable and blue aigrettes, sable stole and muff.' Following the strict reporting conventions of the time, presents to the lucky couple were also listed: 'To the bride, the bridegroom gave a grand pianoforte. The bride's present to the bridegroom was a gold hunting watch and curb chain.' Soon it was time to leave: 'After the reception the bride went away in a royal blue travelling dress with braided cuirass, a large beaver hat with cock's feathers, ermine stole and large ermine muff.'

Henry and Dora returned to Westoe in high spirits. They now had a son who was a highly qualified accountant, and a vivacious and energetic daughter-in-law. Looking to the future, Henry decided the time was right to change the legal structure of his practice, which in 1910 became Henry Chapman Son & Co., with Robert as his partner. The following year Henry and Dora became proud grandparents, with the birth of Robert and Hélène's son, Robert (Robin) Macgowan, followed in early 1914 by the birth of a second son, Henry James Nicholas.

Henry Chapman Son & Co. and the South Shields Commercial Permanent Building Society

Henry Chapman Son & Co. was a thriving practice and had become the largest in South Shields. Its corporate clients included the South Shields Gas Company, the South Shields Savings Bank, the *Shields Gazette*, the Jarrow Chemical Company and J.T. Eltringham & Co., shipbuilders. With some clients there were multiple and long-standing links. The Gas Company was a good example: Henry's father Robert had been external auditor; Henry's firm became auditor, and Henry himself became a director and then vice-chairman. Later, when his son Robert and then his grandson Robin became senior partners, Henry Chapman Son & Co. would remain auditors of the Gas Company for a further thirty years.

Henry's successful accountancy practice did not prevent him from growing the South Shields Commercial Permanent Building Society, which he had founded in 1875. Building societies had started a century earlier as small self-help organisations ('friendly societies') for working people. They did not in fact build houses, but rather enabled subscribing

Henry Chapman, JP, founder of the chartered accountancy firm Henry Chapman Son & Co., the South Shields Commercial Permanent Building Society, and the North-Eastern Investment Trust. (Chapman Family Archive)

members over a period of time to realise the value of their shareholding and then to borrow funds for house purchase. When all members had bought their properties, having been allocated their share, the societies' objectives were fulfilled, and they wound themselves up. Hence they were known as 'terminating societies'.

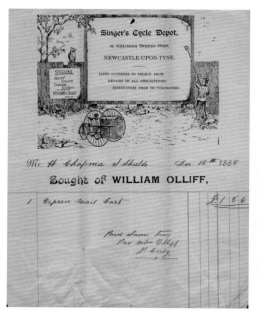

Henry Chapman purchased an 'Express Mail Cart' to expedite business correspondence. Singer's Cycles promoted the virtues of 'Health, Utility, Pleasure and Economy'. (Tyne & Wear Archives & Museums)

However, from the middle of the nineteenth century, so-called 'permanent' societies developed. They took 'deposits from investors seeking interest rather than loans or houses, to increase the funds available for members wishing to borrow. Later subscriptions from bor-rowers repaid investors with interest.'[30] Investors could become members of societies at any time, and withdraw their money whenever they wanted; borrowers received loans (mostly, but not exclusively, for house purchase), which they repaid over a fixed number of years. A Royal Commission report of 1872 observed that 'a building society, with its money secured on freehold land and leasehold property, and a constant incoming of repayments by monthly instalments may fairly be preferred … to a bank'.[31] Many permanent societies rapidly became substantial financial institutions, needing skilled management rather than administration on an amateur basis by officers elected from the members (typically working class in the case of terminating societies). 'The new type of members wanted little involvement in running the societies, and the changing requirements of management were met by the influx of the educated bourgeoisie, whether socially, religiously or com-mercially minded.'[32]

In 1874, there was a new Building Societies Act, which drew on the recommendations of a Royal Commission, and which was very helpful to those, like Henry Chapman, who were actively considering setting up a new building society. The Act permitted 'any three or more persons' to set one up and introduced corporate status for societies:

… members gained limited liability while the society itself, rather than trustees, could now hold mortgage deeds and stand security for loans. Permanent societies were permitted to issue small denomination 'paid up' shares akin to modern ordinary shares rather than only subscription shares involving long-term saving, and could borrow from depositors up to two-thirds of the sum secured by mortgages. Investment of surplus funds was restricted to mortgages or securities carrying a government guarantee, thus prohibiting direct investment in land or other property, companies, etc.[33]

In short, 1875 was a very good year in which to set up a new building society taking full advantage of the favourable provisions of the new Act. There were seventy 'new formations' in that year alone in England and Wales, and a further 627 over the following four years.[34] Henry's timing had been typically shrewd, and the South Shields Commercial Permanent Building Society turned out to be a success. In sending out the notice for its second annual meeting on 20 September 1877 at 70 King Street, Henry Chapman, as secretary, reported 'that the business transacted has been of a most satisfactory character'. There were by then 135 members, whose names were all listed. The number of shares stood at 429, an increase of fifty-nine from the previous year; £9,150 had been 'advanced' (as mortgages) to sixteen members; assets were £15,000 and 'the Balance of Profit now standing to the credit of the Society' was slightly over £92 (it had been £24 at the end of the first year). Henry himself received a salary of £62 as secretary.

The society's 'Officers for 1876–77' were all leading figures in the town. There were close links with the borough council

THE SHIELDS DAILY NEWS, FRIDAY, MAY 8, 1891.

IMPORTANT TO BORROWERS AND INVESTORS.

COMMERCIAL PERMANENT BUILDING SOCIETY, 67 KING STREET, SOUTH SHIELDS.

ALDERMAN WARDLE, J.P., CHAIRMAN.

ASSETS...£74,783.
SURPLUS FUNDS.............................£2,002.
NO PROPERTIES ON HAND.

Advances promptly made under reduced scale of monthly repayments or on DORMANT LOAN. PREFERENCE or INVESTING SHARES issued. Bonus to Members No Entrance or Loan Fees.

J. H. RENNOLDSON, Solicitor.
HENRY CHAPMAN, F.C.A., Secretary.

THE NORTH-EASTERN INVESTMENT TRUST, LIMITED, 67 KING STREET, SOUTH SHIELDS.

ALD. ELTRINGHAM, J.P., CHAIRMAN.

Debentures issued bearing Interest at the rate of 4½ per cent. per annum, payable half-yearly. The Debentures are secured by having a first claim upon all the Assets, Securities, and uncalled Capital of the Company. Deposits received. Full particulars on application to
HENRY CHAPMAN, F.C.A., Manager.

Shields Daily News advertisement for the South Shields Commercial Permanent Building Society and the North-Eastern Investment Trust, 8 May 1891. (South Tyneside Libraries)

Reg. No. 36
County Durham.

THE SOUTH SHIELDS
COMMERCIAL PERMANENT BUILDING SOCIETY,
INCORPORATED.

OFFICES :—67, KING STREET, SOUTH SHIELDS.

NOTICE IS HEREBY GIVEN, that the Twenty-first Annual Meeting of the above Society, will be held at the Offices of the Society, No. 67, King Street, South Shields, on Friday, the 28th day of August, 1896, at Eight o'clock in the Evening, for the purpose of receiving the Directors' Report and Financial Statement, appointing Officers for the ensuing year, and transacting other business.

By order,

HENRY CHAPMAN, Secretary.

OFFICERS OF THE SOCIETY.

Directors :

Mr. JOHN P. WARDLE, J.P., Chairman.
Mr. J. T. ELTRINGHAM, J.P., Deputy-Chairman.

Mr. M. CAY, J.P.	Mr. JAMES HOGG.	Mr. J. M. RENNOLDSON, J.P.
Mr. WILLIAM CAY.	Mr. J. R. LACKLAND.	Mr. W. R. SMITH, J.P.
Mr. D. W. FITZGERALD.	Mr. JAMES READHEAD.	Mr. J. J. SNAITH.

Treasurer.
Mr. WM. J. HUMPHREY.

Bankers :
Messrs. WOODS and COMPANY.

Auditors :
Mr. W. M. BIRD.   Mr. J. STABLEFORD, F.S.A.A.

Stewards :
Mr. W. J. HUMPHREY.   Mr. J. GRIMES.   Mr. R. O. MIDDLETON.

Surveyors :
Mr. J. P. WARDLE, J.P.   Mr. W. R. SMITH, J.P.   Mr. R. SUMMERBELL.   Mr. JAMES YOUNG.

Solicitor :
Mr. J. H. RENNOLDSON.

Secretary :
Mr. HENRY CHAPMAN, Chartered Accountant.

Notice of the twenty-first Annual General Meeting of the South Shields Commercial Building Society, held on 28 August 1896. (Tyne & Wear Archives & Museums)

itself: the president was Councillor John P. Wardle, a prominent timber merchant and a future Mayor; the four vice-presidents included the then Mayor, Alderman Matthew Stainton, whose family firm was T. Stainton & Co., ironfounders; and of the nine directors, three were councillors (a brewer, a contractor and a commission agent). The other vice-presidents included James Purdy Rennoldson, shipbuilder, and Bamford Williamson, chemist and druggist.

Among the other directors were Robert Chapman (Henry's father, who would later become a vice-president) and Joseph T. Eltringham, shipbuilder, a close business associate of Henry, and another future Mayor. He was chairman of the North-Eastern Investment Trust, which Henry had founded and managed. The society's solicitor was another close friend and colleague, James Henry Rennoldson, whose legal practice was also based at 70 King Street. The society employed three 'stewards' (managers) and four surveyors (one of whom was the builder Mr R. Summerbell) and banked with Woods & Company, the well-known private bankers who would eventually be taken over by Barclays.

Henry achieved steady expansion over the next two decades, which was remarkable given the national economic situation:

> The 20 years after 1874 were a period of economic depression generally, an era of falling prices and interest rates and also falling property values. Building societies, by maintaining their mortgage rates were able to attract an increasing volume of savings, but falling property values and the rising volume of surplus funds meant that demand for loans backed by adequate mortgage security was inadequate to absorb the societies' funds. Societies with surplus funds extended their business into increasingly risky areas, and many got into difficulties.[35]

Indeed, the country's largest society, the Liberator, had crashed spectacularly in 1892 with liabilities to shareholders and depositors standing at a total of £3,300,000. Its assets consisted almost entirely of second and third mortgages.[36] Shockwaves reverberated throughout the building society movement.

Henry Chapman had not made these commercial mistakes. The South Shields Commercial Permanent Building Society's assets as at June 1892, a few months before a compulsory winding-up order was served on the Liberator, stood at just over £100,000, and they rose to £108,000 by June

1895. A prudently managed local society could, and in South Shields did, weather the storm. The principal officers of the society were still in place in 1895, twenty years after its formation. John P. Wardle, JP, remained as chairman (the term 'president' having just been dropped); J.T. Eltringham, JP, who had been Mayor in 1885 and 1886, became deputy chairman in 1894/95; J.H. Rennoldson continued as solicitor. However, new blood was also brought in after the 80-year-old Robert Chapman resigned. J.M. Rennoldson became a director in 1891/92, the year in which he was Mayor, and James Readhead, the chairman and managing director of the very well-known South Shields shipbuilding company, joined the board four years later.

In 1899 the society issued a prospectus, outlining the benefits it offered both to investors and borrowers. The advantages to tenants of buying the properties they rented were highlighted, at a time when well over 90 per cent of all households − both middle class and working class − rented. 'Open to all' was the attractive message for investors:

> To persons desirous of investing large or small sums this Society offers important advantages. It is adapted to the wants of all classes. For investment of small sums periodically it affords a first-class security which usually can only be obtained by capitalists, while at the same time investors are saved the trouble involved by personal management, and protected against any adverse contingencies to which their security might be subject.

The prospectus added that 'Females, whether married or unmarried, and minors may become Members.'

The prospectus emphasised that the society was managed by a board of directors, chosen by the members, and that 'Many of the Directors and Officers have had great experience in the Management of Building Societies, and being all interested pecuniarily, they have a direct personal interest in working the Society to best advantage.' Indeed they did, and there were other financial interests as well. The chairman, John P. Wardle, had been one of the society's valuation surveyors for a decade or more, as had another director, W.R. Smith. Directors' fees were paid to all board members and had become a separate line entry in the annual accounts. Henry Chapman and J.H. Rennoldson also received remuneration as secretary and solicitor, respectively.

The secretary had for many years described himself as 'Mr. Henry Chapman, Chartered Accountant', no doubt to highlight the professionalism and prudence of the society's management. This remained an important message to be conveyed to prospective borrowers and investors (to whom the prospectus offered an annual interest rate on shares of '4½ per cent per annum'), since there had been a number of cases of building society fraud and financial mismanagement in the years following the crash of the Liberator. This episode had prompted the new provision in the 1894 Building Societies Act that one of a society's auditors must be a person 'who publicly carries on the business of an accountant'. In the case of the South Shields Commercial Permanent Building Society, this requirement was met by its joint auditor, Mr J. Stableford, FSAA (Fellow of the Society of Accountants and Auditors).

The prospectus had been issued in 1899. As it turned out, 'The first decade of the twentieth century ... witnessed one of the most pronounced declines in housing activity and house prices in British housing history.' Levels of activity in 1912 and 1913 were lower than those of any time since 1895, and house prices were estimated to have fallen by as much as 40 per cent.[37]

Rents, however, remained fairly constant, so house purchase became more attractive and more accessible to those on regular incomes. In principle this should have been advantageous to the building society movement, whose mortgage assets did indeed increase by around 30 per cent between 1903 and 1914. However, there was considerable variability. The country's largest building society, the Leeds Permanent, saw its annual advances decline by a third during this period. Others, notably the Cooperative Permanent Building Society, whose strong marketing through a network of retail stores enabled it to provide mortgages to a predominantly working-class clientele, grew very rapidly, doubling its lending in the same period.[38]

The South Shields Commercial Permanent Building Society followed a middle, fairly static, course. At the last annual meeting before the First World War, held on 29 September 1913, still under the chairmanship of John P. Wardle, JP, assets stood at £119,000, a very modest increase from £108,000 in 1895. Membership, too, seemed to have plateaued: indeed it was very slightly down, from 307 members in 1895/96 to 303 in 1912/13. Maybe the secretary and solicitor, having weathered successfully an exceptionally difficult period, were starting to pin their expansionary ambitions on the next generation. Certainly J.H. Rennoldson had now brought in his son H.F. Rennoldson as joint solicitor, and Henry Chapman, now in his early sixties, had done the same: Robert Chapman was now joint secretary. As it turned out, Robert would not have any time to devote to that role once war was declared the following year. Fortunately, the society's prudent policies and financial management would stand it in good stead, not only during the war itself, but for the following half century and beyond.

4

BUSINESS AND COMMUNITY LEADERS

Westoe Village, just a mile from the centre of South Shields, was a tightly knit community. Residents, many of them prominent in the town's affairs, were linked by ties not only of propinquity, but also of business and by a shared involvement in philanthropic and leisure activities.

Henry Chapman's closest neighbours included the Stevensons, Readheads, Rennoldsons, Eltringhams, Wardles, Mortons and Armstrongs – all leading families from 'the mercantile classes' and the professions.[1] Other prominent families lived nearby, including the Runcimans and Annands. All these families sent their sons to the South Shields Boys' High School (except for the Stevensons, whose three eldest sons were in their twenties when the High School opened in 1885).

James Cochran Stevenson

James Cochran Stevenson of *Westoe Mansion* was a towering figure in the town and on Tyneside. Born in Scotland, his father James Stevenson moved his family to South Shields in 1843 when he bought Cookson and Cuthbert's chemical works in Templetown just to the west of the town, and founded the Jarrow Chemical Company, alkali manufacturers producing soda ash, acids and bleach. James Cochran Stevenson and one of his father's partners, John Williamson, took over the company in 1854, by which time it was trading very successfully. Before long it became the

Map of Westoe Village in 1897, identifying the houses occupied by the leading businessmen of South Shields. Henry Chapman lived in *Seacroft*, to the east of *Westoe House*. (South Tyneside Libraries)

James Cochran Stevenson of *Westoe Mansion* was a towering figure in South Shields and on Tyneside. Founder of the Jarrow Chemical Company, he became Liberal MP for the town, proprietor of *The North and South Shields Gazette* and chairman of the Tyne Improvement Commission. This portrait was painted by Sir William Quiller Orchardson, RA in 1889. (Courtesy Hew Stevenson)

largest chemical works in England, employing around 1,400 men and generating annual profits of around £90,000, of which Stevenson's share was more than £20,000.[2] This income enabled him to purchase three large plots of land in Westoe Village, and to build *Westoe Mansion*, into which he and his wife and six children (there would eventually be twelve) moved in 1866. It was designed by his well-known architect brother, John James ('Jaughty') Stevenson and became, not surprisingly, 'his beloved Gothic family home'.[3]

James Cochran Stevenson was deeply involved in public affairs. He was elected to the borough council in 1862 (joining Henry Chapman's father, Robert), becoming an alderman in 1865 and Mayor in 1867. He was the energetic leader of the 'Progressives', persuading the council to undertake major sanitation and road-widening schemes financed by municipal borrowing, thereby overturning 'the curious economic heresy that all works undertaken, no matter how permanent in character, should be paid for out of the current rates'.[4] He resigned in October 1868 to stand as a Liberal for Parliament (the Parliament of the United Kingdom of Great Britain and Ireland, as it was then) on the retirement of South Shields' first MP, Robert Ingham. His opponent was the fellow Liberal and equally well-known South Shields businessman, Charles (later Sir Charles) Mark Palmer, founder of the hugely successful Iron & Shipbuilding Co. Ltd in Jarrow. The contenders were evenly matched, and following the 1867 Reform Act, eligible male voters in South Shields increased fourfold, from just under 1,300 to over 7,000. The election result was anything but a foregone conclusion.

Perhaps not surprisingly, the November hustings developed into a bruis-
ing battle between the candidates, with taunts freely traded. A pro-Palmer
poster declared that 'Mr. Stevenson's whole life, from beginning to end,
shows him in temperament to be largely despotic and unloveable – one
of the class of men who should never be entrusted with political power
to wield over his fellows, seeing that he would be sure to abuse it.'[5] The
Stevenson camp gave as good as it got. One of its cartoons 'showed Palmer
as a swaggering colossus, juggling many balls in the air':

'My Railways, My Estates, My 10,000 men, My collieries, My glassworks,
My coke-ovens'… the biggest shipbuilder and ship owner in the North,
who would 'make a railway to the moon, extract the spots from the sun,
and build a ship to float in the regions of space'. Even better, he would
send hares and pheasants from his Yorkshire estate to all his supporters.

The final result was nail-bitingly close. Stevenson scraped home by
300 votes, and remained MP for the town until 1895, by which time
Palmer had become Liberal MP for Jarrow.

Stevenson managed to combine Westminster with numerous important roles on the Tyne and in South Shields itself. Already influential as a
Life Commissioner of the Tyne Improvement Commission, he became its
chairman in 1880, holding this office for the next twenty years. He was also
chairman of the Tyne Pilotage Board, a magistrate and the first president
of the South Shields Chamber of Commerce. He was also a newspaper
proprietor, having purchased *The North and South Shields Gazette and
Northumberland and Durham Advertiser* in 1865 from his father. The business
expanded rapidly under its managing director, Robert Cumming Annand,
brother of the then editor, James Annand. The newspaper's auditor became
Henry Chapman.

There was a further link with Henry. Stevenson was appointed commanding officer of the 3rd Durham Volunteer Artillery Corps, receiving
his commission as major in 1864. In this role he was well known to Henry,
who had become a cadet as an 11-year-old in 1861, and who himself
received his commission as 'Lieutenant, Volunteer Forces' in 1884 (by
which time he was a married man with seven children), three years before
Stevenson retired and became honorary colonel.

Unfortunately, the story of the Jarrow Chemical Company did not
have a happy ending. A new and very efficient process of making alkali,

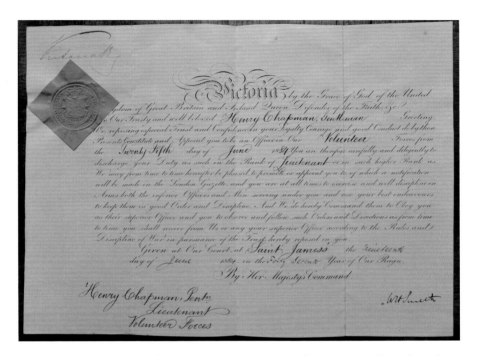

Henry Chapman received his commission in 1884 as a lieutenant in the 3rd Durham Volunteer Artillery Corps, where James Cochran Stevenson had been appointed commanding officer twenty years earlier. (Chapman Family Archive)

without the need for sulphur (which the Jarrow plant's noxious and polluting Leblanc process required), had been developed in the 1870s. This Solvay ammonia-soda process became adopted widely, eroding irrevocably the competitive position of Jarrow and other Tyneside plants. Stevenson did try hard to stem the tide. He was the prime mover in effecting a large-scale merger of Leblanc producers, by forming the United Alkali Company in 1890. However, the new company, in which he did not have a controlling stake, decided to close the Jarrow chemical works in 1891, with the result that Stevenson's income was decimated. He shut up his house in Westoe in the same year, and moved permanently to London.

The Readheads

The Readheads became the pre-eminent shipbuilding family in South Shields, and the owners of more houses in Westoe Village than any other.

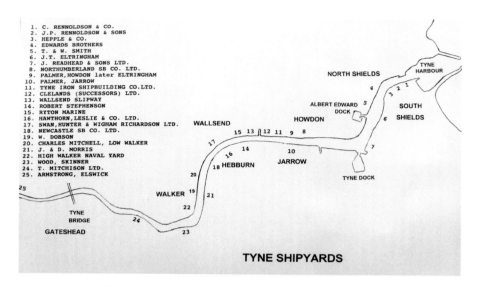

1. C. RENNOLDSON & CO.
2. J.P. RENNOLDSON & SONS
3. HEPPLE & CO.
4. EDWARDS BROTHERS
5. T. & W. SMITH
6. J.T. ELTRINGHAM
7. J. READHEAD & SONS LTD.
8. NORTHUMBERLAND SB CO. LTD.
9. PALMER, HOWDON later ELTRINGHAM
10. PALMER, JARROW
11. TYNE IRON SHIPBUILDING CO.LTD.
12. CLELANDS (SUCCESSORS) LTD.
13. WALLSEND SLIPWAY
14. ROBERT STEPHENSON
15. RYTON MARINE
16. HAWTHORN, LESLIE & CO. LTD.
17. SWAN, HUNTER & WIGHAM RICHARDSON LTD.
18. NEWCASTLE SB CO. LTD.
19. W. DOBSON
20. CHARLES MITCHELL, LOW WALKER
21. J. & D. MORRIS
22. HIGH WALKER NAVAL YARD
23. WOOD, SKINNER
24. T. MITCHISON LTD.
25. ARMSTRONG, ELSWICK

TYNE SHIPYARDS

Norman L. Middlemiss' sketch plan of Tyne shipyards highlights those of the Readheads, Rennoldsons and Eltringhams. (Norman L. Middlemiss, *British Shipbuilding Yards, Volume I: North-East Coast* [North Shields, 1993])

View in the 1870s from North Shields across the river to Readhead's shipyard at the Lawe. In the foreground is a paddle sailing ship. (South Tyneside Libraries)

The founder of the family firm was John Readhead, a millwright turned shipwright who in 1865 set up the partnership of Readhead & Softley in a small shipyard in Pilot Street at the Lawe, near South Shields harbour. They built eighty-seven ships in seven years, the first three being the collier brigs *Unus*, *Duo* and *Honor* for the Baltic trade. Iron screw steamers and steam tugs followed, but the partnership was dissolved in 1872 during a period of economic depression and uncertainty.

John Readhead was a determined man. He continued trading on his own account, overcoming strikes, cash flow problems and accidents. His business, incorporated as John Readhead and Company, started to flourish, and after seven or eight years outgrew its yard in the Lawe. In order to expand, he purchased a 10-acre site to the east of Tyne Dock that included the well-known West Dock shipyard, formerly belonging to James Young. In 1881 the new West Dock Shipbuilding Yard was opened, by which time Readhead's was a very substantial enterprise:

> The yard is fitted with plant of the newest and most approved construction, a large number of hydraulic machines being employed, and the workshops and sheds, etc., lighted with electricity throughout. The works also include a large marine engineering establishment, the firm engining all the steamers they build. They employ a working staff of about 2000 hands in the various departments.[6]

A large graving dock nearby was later bought for the ship-repairing side of the business.

When he moved to West Dock, John Readhead took his clients with him. The most important was Edward Hain, heir to the Hain Steamship Company in Cornwall, which had already placed an order for a screw streamer, *Trewidden*. This turned out to be the beginning of an extraordinarily long and mutually beneficial commercial relationship. Over the next decade to 1888, John Readhead built fifteen ships for Hain, all with alliterative Cornish names, from *Trewidden* through *Trekieve* and *Treloske* to *Trewavas*. By then the firm had, very appropriately, been rechristened John Readhead & Sons. All four sons had joined the company, each with clearly defined roles: Robert and John ran the engineering side of the business; James ran the shipbuilding; and William managed the drawing office.

John Readhead was also active in civic affairs. He was a contemporary of Robert Chapman on the borough council, becoming an alderman, and was twice Mayor, in 1878 and 1879. He was a magistrate, president of the Conservative Association and a director of the South Shields Gas Company, where Robert was external auditor. Like Henry Chapman, and many other successful contemporaries, he was attracted to Westoe Village, moving into *Southgarth* in 1888.

The house had been built in 1874/75, another architectural project of J.J. Stevenson, this time for his brother Archibald, who worked with his older brother James Cochran Stevenson at the Jarrow Chemical Company, becoming managing director of their Willington Quay Copper Works. The house was a splendid creation, much admired by Nikolaus Pevsner during his 'perambulations' from South Shields to Westoe Village: 'The style is the freest "Queen Anne" of the Norman Shaw type with irregular fenestration pulled together under one big gable, a boldly projecting oriel, and tall plain chimney-stacks: crisp and studied.'[7]

Tragically, Archibald Stevenson was drowned in 1877 while on a ship bound for Australia, and in 1878 *Southgarth* was bought by James Cochran Stevenson's business partner and electoral campaign manager, Alderman John Williamson. It was on his death in 1888 that the house was sold to John Readhead, who had the pleasure of seeing his son Robert become Mayor shortly before he died in 1894. The house stayed in the Readhead family, and indeed it was Robert Readhead himself who inherited *Southgarth* from his father.

The family shipbuilding business continued to go from strength to strength. James (later Sir James) Readhead became chairman and managing director, and the firm became a private limited company in 1909, with a nominal capital of £300,000, mostly held by the four

Sir James Readhead was chairman and managing director of John Readhead & Sons. He purchased *Westoe Mansion* from James Cochran Stevenson, and became president of the Ingham Infirmary. He was created a baronet in 1922. (South Tyneside Libraries)

brothers. Their main customer remained the Hain Steamship Company, for whom seventeen tramps (cargo ships) were built between 1909 and the outbreak of the First World War. Other important domestic customers included Walter Runciman's Moor Line, and export orders were won from ship owners in Norway, France and Greece.[8]

The firm had two further strengths in addition to its loyal shipbuilding client base. Its engine building works had an excellent reputation, continuing to build most of the engines for Readhead's own ships, as well as selling them as standalone components to other shipbuilders. And the ship-repairing operation was extensive and very profitable. This commercial success enabled James Readhead to purchase *Westoe Mansion* from James Cochran Stevenson in 1894, three years after the latter's move to London in 1891. He rechristened the house *Westoe Hall*, and his wife and three children lived there in considerable style. His elder brother, John, meanwhile was already well established in nearby *Rockcliffe*, a substantial house by any standards except those of palatial *Westoe Hall* itself.

James Readhead had close links with Henry Chapman, having joined the Board of the South Shields Commercial Permanent Building Society in 1896. He also became Chairman of the South Shields Gas Company, where Henry had been auditor (succeeding his father, Robert), and then a director, for many years. James was not as active in civic affairs as his father had been, although he was a magistrate. However, on the philanthropic front, he strengthened the family's already close links with the Ingham Infirmary, and became its president in 1911.

The Rennoldsons

The Rennoldsons were well known as shipbuilders and solicitors, tracing their descent from George Rennoldson who had established in 1826 the earliest marine engineering works in the town. He had two sons, James Purdy and James Henry. James Purdy continued the marine engineering business, added ship repairing, and moved into iron shipbuilding in the 1870s. Through Henry Chapman, he was also one of the first vice-presidents of the South Shields Commercial Permanent Building Society.

On his death in 1878, the firm became Messrs J.P. Rennoldson & Sons, the partners being his sons Joseph Middleton Rennoldson and Charles Rennoldson. Under their management the business doubled in size by the mid–1880s. The works were again expanded very considerably in 1898, when the shipyard at the Lawe, formerly occupied by Readhead's, was acquired. Hodgson noted in 1903 that, 'The firm has made a speciality of building paddle and screw tugboats and trawlers, passenger boats, ferries etc., their output including the most powerful tug afloat, the S.S. *Titan*, built [in 1899] for the Suez Canal Company for special service in the Canal. The firm's output in 1900 was six vessels of 2,206 tons, in 1901 seven vessels of 2,609 tons, and in 1902 eight vessels of 1,632 tons.'[9] Five years later, the screw tug *Hercules* was built specifically for service on the Tyne.

Titan II, a large, powerful, twin screw tug, was purpose-built by J.P. Rennoldson & Sons in 1899 for the Compagnie Universelle du Canal Maritime de Suez to haul off large ships that had run aground on the banks of the canal. Across the river in North Shields can be seen the Low Light of 1810, with its seaward-facing wall painted white. (South Tyneside Libraries. Caption, Ian Whitehead)

The Rennoldsons' reputation for their screw tugboats was international. In 1909 alone they launched the *Derwen*, for delivery to the Peninsular and Oriental Steamship Company in Bombay, and the *Nyora* for clients in Melbourne. Their tugs were known to have staying power, the *Shields Gazette* noting in September 'an excellent piece of towing performed by the Screw Tug *Champion*', built in 1895 for Messrs J. & A. Brown, also in Melbourne. As the *Gazette* reported on 30 September 1909:

The *Champion* accomplished a 1,281 miles run against continuous gales with the big sailing ship *Leicester Castle* in tow. The voyage was from New Zealand to Port Jackson, Sydney, and the tow provided one long dreary battle against head winds and seas. During one twenty-four hour gale, it is stated, the crew of the *Leicester Castle* were unable to catch a glimpse of the *Champion*.[10]

Joseph Middleton Rennoldson, the elder brother, was very active on the borough council. He was an alderman, and Mayor in two successive years, 1891 and 1892. He was a close business colleague of Henry Chapman, joining the board both of the South Shields Commercial Permanent Building Society (during his mayoralty) and of the North-Eastern Investment Trust, where he became chairman in 1898. He also became chairman of the town's Electric Lighting Company, this novel source of power being first used for street lighting in 1896. King Street, Market Place and Dean Street were the first streets to be 'illuminated'. The novel nocturnal brightness caused alarm in the shipyards. As the *Shields Gazette* reported in January 1879:

The shipbuilder Joseph Middleton Rennoldson was Mayor of South Shields in 1891 and 1892. A close business colleague of Henry Chapman, he built *Fairfield* next door to Henry at *Seacroft*. (South Tyneside Libraries)

Last night the electric light was in operation for the first time in South Shields, at Messrs Edwards' High Dock, and attracted much attention. A bright light was thrown over the whole of the dock and a pin might have been discerned upon the ground with the same ease as if it had been daylight. Many persons unaware of the experiment, rushed to the place, believing a fire had broken out.[11]

Joseph Middleton Rennoldson and Henry Chapman became next-door neighbours, Rennoldson building *Fairfield* in the early 1880s on the large plot purchased from the Ingham Estate at the eastern end of Westoe Village. He lived there with his wife and daughters Marion, Alice and Dorothy. His brother Charles, having been his partner in their successful shipbuilding business for some thirty-five years, took the bold step of setting himself up independently in his own shipyard in 1913. He did well enough, quickly securing orders for two coasters and a cargo ship, but he had left it rather late in life to go it alone.

James Henry Rennoldson was a leading solicitor and notary in the town, practising from offices at 70 King Street. He was Henry Chapman's closest business partner, for some forty years acting as solicitor to the South Shields Commercial Permanent Building Society, and no doubt also acting for Henry's North-Eastern Investment Trust, where he was a shareholder. Another Westoe Village resident, he was Henry's neighbour to the east of *Seacroft*, having also purchased a large plot from the Ingham Estates, on which he built *Ingleside* in the 1880s. He lived there with his wife, Gertrude Louise, daughter Gertrude and son Henry Francis, who in due course joined his father's solicitor's office, which became J.H. and H.F. Rennoldson. Like so many of his prominent contemporaries, he played an active role at the Ingham Infirmary. He was a vice-president and chairman of the special committee set up to oversee the construction of a new wing. At the same time he was chairman of the South Shields Poor Law Union.

The Eltringhams

Joseph Eltringham founded J.T. Eltringham & Co. as shipbuilders, engineers and boilermakers in 1864, at the Stone Quay, High Holborn, an area between the Mill Dam and Middle Docks. Although the yard was rather cramped, he increased its output steadily, until he was building six to ten tugs and trawlers annually. Ship repairing and boiler making were also integral parts of the business. He reputedly built the first steam trawler in the world, *Normandie*, and an important client was the highly successful Prince Fishing Company in North Shields.

Joseph Toward Eltringham had very close business links with Henry Chapman, who was auditor to J.T. Eltringham & Co. Henry brought him in as a founding director of the South Shields Commercial Building Society, and he became deputy chairman eighteen years later, in 1894. Eltringham also became the first chairman of the North-Eastern

Investment Trust, which Henry had founded in 1890. The Trust, where Henry was both a director and manager, duly launched its 'First Issue of Debentures for £25,000 carrying interest at the rate of £4 10s per cent per annum, payable half yearly'. It was soon fully subscribed. The Trust made investments in a very wide range of stocks and shares, including local companies (George Angus & Co., Newcastle Breweries, United Alkali Co. Ltd), and national companies (Bryant & May, Swan United Electric Light Co. Ltd). Overseas companies were strongly represented in the portfolio: United States Breweries, Gold Fields of South Africa, Cuba Submarine Telephone Co., Bank of Victoria and New Zealand Trust & Loan Co.

The 'Wouldhave and Greathead Memorial of the Lifeboat' on Pier Parade by the architect J.H. Morton was unveiled by Alderman Joseph Eltringham in 1890. The building to the right housed the lifeboat *Tyne*, built in 1833, under a cast-iron canopy. (South Tyneside Libraries)

Joseph Toward Eltringham was also very well known in civic affairs, as a magistrate, councillor and alderman. He was twice Mayor, in 1885 and 1886, supporting the proposal to erect a joint 'Wouldhave and Greathead Memorial of the Lifeboat', a tribute to the lifeboat designed and built in South Shields towards the end of the eighteenth century. The finally

The splendidly situated North and South Marine Parks with their extensive recreational facilities were opened on 25 June 1890 to scenes of 'great public rejoicing'. (South Tyneside Libraries)

approved design, by the South Shields architect J.H. Morton, was for a baroque clock tower, happily positioned between the newly completed North and South Marine Parks. It was Alderman Eltringham who unveiled the monument built to commemorate Queen Victoria's Jubilee of 1887, at the official opening of the Marine Parks in 1890 by the Ecclesiastical Commissioner Sir John Mowbray. 'There was great public rejoicing,' as George Hodgson recalled. 'The ugly, unsightly ballast hills became handsome parks, with well-wooded borders, grassy slopes and blossoming flower-beds', not to mention promenades, bowling greens, tennis courts and a large lake.[12]

Joseph Eltringham also joined the Westoe Village 'club', purchasing a large part of the garden of *Westoe House* from ship owner Matthew Cay, who had purchased the property on the death of Robert Ingham, MP, in 1875. Eltringham built *Eastgarth* on his new plot, and lived there with his wife and their son, Harry. He took an active interest in the Ingham Infirmary, becoming a vice-president from 1893 to his death in 1897, years in which he also served as a Tyne commissioner.

Dr Harry Eltringham remained a director of the family shipbuilding company after his father's death, but his passion was breeding butterflies, and he became a distinguished entomologist at Oxford University. The driving force in the shipyard, which continued to prosper, became Durham Walker Fitzgerald of Wood Terrace, Westoe. He was successful in maintaining close links with the Prince Fishing Company, and in 1907 the twenty-sixth trawler was launched for them by Eltringhams. Five years later, in 1912, Fitzgerald formed a public company, Jos. T. Eltringham & Co. Ltd, with an authorised share capital of £50,000, to enable further expansion. He became chairman, his co-promotor being George Renwick, Newcastle upon Tyne MP. They moved quickly to acquire Charles Palmer's Shipbuilding and Iron Company's yard at Willington Quay, Howdon, on the north bank of the Tyne, following its closure in the summer of 1912. This 4-acre site, with 460ft of river frontage, was ideal for a 'thoroughly up to date' multi-berth shipyard and marine engineering works.[13] The last ship to be launched at the old stone quay yard in South Shields, in October 1913, was the *Northern Prince* for James (later Sir James) Knott's Prince Line, by then the third largest shipping line in the world.

The Wardles

John Potts Wardle, a prominent timber merchant, built *Stanhope House* on the plot he had purchased from the Ingham Estates at the same time as his friends and business associates, Henry Chapman and the Rennoldson brothers had purchased theirs. He lived in his impressive property with his wife Mary and their large family. He, too, was a magistrate, an active borough councillor and future Mayor, whom Henry had chosen to be the first president of the South Shields Commercial Permanent Building Society in 1876. His title was subsequently changed to chairman, a post he still held in 1913, thirty-seven years after his original appointment, a notable example of the long-term business partnerships Henry developed.

The Runcimans

Walter Runciman (later Sir Walter, and finally Baron Runciman) was born at Dunbar in Scotland in 1847. The family moved to Cresswell in

The Rt Hon. Lord (Walter) Runciman started life as a cabin boy and became a captain, a Westoe resident and borough councillor, an extremely successful ship owner, MP for Hartlepool, and a baronet who was subsequently elevated to the peerage. (South Tyneside Libraries)

Northumberland on his father's appointment to the coastguard service. Young Walter ran away to sea at the age of 12, some of his adventures during a merchant marine voyage from cabin boy to ship's master having been recounted in Chapter 2.[14] In 1884, after twenty-six years at sea, his 'medical men' urged him to live ashore, and he settled in South Shields, determined to become a ship owner. By this time he had built up a 'small well-invested nest-egg' and the following year he purchased his first vessel. Shipping in the mid–1880s was in a 'seriously depressed condition'. With prices low he was able to buy a dozen more vessels over the next few years, all of them financed on the old 'sixty-fourth' shareholding system. He ordered his first new ship, the *Blakemoor*, from John Readhead & Sons, making 'the beginning of a close business and personal friendship which has never at any time been shaken'. Runciman was now well on the way to becoming a successful ship owner, and in 1889 he formed the South Shields Shipping Company with a capital of £150,000.

Meanwhile, living in Westoe's Wood Terrace, with his son at the Boys' High School, he described South Shields as being 'ablaze with sharply divided party and indeed social antagonisms' and decided to enter local politics. He first campaigned, unsuccessfully, on a 'Fish Dock and Temperance' ticket, being a keen supporter of both. However, moving on to advocacy of sanitary reform and housing improvement, he was elected in 1891 when the Mayor was Councillor Joseph Middleton Rennoldson, the Deputy Mayor was Alderman Joseph Toward Eltringham and the former Mayor, Alderman John Potts Wardle, was still a borough councillor – all of them living just a short walk away from Wood Terrace.

As Runciman recalled in *Municipal Life – A Merry Interlude*, at first, 'Everybody, especially the aldermen and councillors who had a bit of property, thought I was attacking them personally, and I met with bitter opposition on the Council.'[15] However, his campaign received the vigorous support of Aaron Watson, the influential editor of the *Shields Gazette*, their having visited the awful slums together, and 'before very long the whole Council were sanitary reformers'. This was an impressive achievement in just three years, because in 1895 Runciman decided to step down from the council. The reason was simple enough: 'Each vein of me was throbbing with the desire to build up a large ship-owning firm, and my instinct told me to cease flirting with politics or other fascinating public work until the fabric was firmly established.'[16] His single-mindedness certainly paid off. He increased the nominal capital of the South Shields Shipping Co. to £500,000, changed its name to the Moor Line Ltd (after the Blakemoor estate owned by his wife's relatives), and moved the head office to Newcastle. He was created a baronet in 1906, and by 1908 he was the largest ship owner on the north-east coast after Sir James Knott's North Shields Prince Line. With the commercial 'fabric' of the Moor Line so firmly established, he could afford to devote some of his time to public affairs, and in 1910 he was elected President of the Chamber of Shipping of the United Kingdom. By 1914 the Moor Line owned forty steamers and managed a total of 120 vessels. Its growth seemed unstoppable.

The Mortons

Joseph Hall Morton was born in 1850, the same year as Henry Chapman. He started an architectural practice in South Shields in 1871, becoming a Fellow of the Royal Institute of British Architects in 1882. His son, Ralph Henry, became his partner in 1900, and the family moved to *Dinsdale House* in Westoe Village four years later. Joseph was a very talented architect who turned his hand to many different types of building: shops, houses (new and refurbished), workhouses, offices, churches, banks and memorials. He had produced the plans for Robert Chapman's rebuilt drapery shop in 1883 with its engaging Dutch gable, and, even nearer to home, designed numerous residential projects in and around

Dinsdale House and *Westoe Tower* on the north side of Westoe Village. Bunting on the houses celebrated the Relief of Mafeking in May 1900, during the Boer War. The well-known architect Joseph Hall Morton moved into *Dinsdale House* in 1904. (South Tyneside Libraries)

Westoe Village, including in 1896 the new *Manor House* on the plot next to James Readhead's *Westoe Hall*.

His biggest project was the new South Shields Poor Law Union work-house, school and infirmary on Harton Lane, completed in 1880. He later designed the Union's new premises in Barrington Street, immediately next door to Henry Chapman's accountancy office. His South Shields Poor Law institution scheme led to many other similar projects, and indeed he developed an international reputation for them: 'Mr. Morton had the honour of sending designs for workhouses

The South Shields Poor Law Union Workhouse, designed by Joseph Hall Morton, also contained an infirmary and a school. Able Seaman Charles Amey (pictured), a veteran of voyages to the Baltic, Crimea and Burma, was discharged into 'comfortable lodgings' in 1908. (South Tyneside Libraries)

and infirmaries to the Russian Government in the time of the late Czarina, who was interested in this class of building. He was also asked by the Government to send similar designs for the Government of Venezuela.'[17]

His ecclesiastical commissions in South Shields included the new churches of St Aidan and St Jude and restoration work at St Hilda's and St Stephen's. His portfolio of commercial buildings included Martins Bank on King Street in 1909, which rather elegantly turned the corner into Fowler Street. Rather unusually among prominent Westoe Village residents, Morton was a Freemason, being a member of St Hilda Lodge, a Provincial Grand Superintendent of Works (Durham), and 'the designer of many notable buildings of the craft'.[18]

The Annands

The Annand brothers, James and Robert Cumming, played a leading role in the expansion and commercial success of the *Shields Gazette* over a period of almost four decades. James Cochran Stevenson appointed the fellow Scotsman, James Annand, editor in 1879. It was a good choice. Annand was 'the foremost Liberal journalist on Tyneside', who had previously been the successful editor and chief leader writer of the *Newcastle Daily Chronicle*. However, he had fallen out with the proprietor, Joseph Cowen, MP, for expressing radically different views on foreign policy (the 'Eastern Question') to

James Annand, editor of the *Shields Gazette* from 1879 to 1885, 'made the paper the recognised Liberal organ of the North'. (South Tyneside Libraries)

those being put forward by Cowen in Parliament. So eventually Annand resigned.[19]

The North and South Shields Gazette – to give the paper its full title – had been going through a long period of editorial stagnation. James Annand immediately raised its profile: 'His leading articles were a political education, not only to the borough, but to Tyneside generally', and they 'soon made the paper the recognised Liberal organ of the North'.[20] In 1882 James Annand's brother, Robert Cumming Annand, was appointed as manager, and would prove to be 'as notable a manager as his brother was editor'.[21] Their contribution to the newspaper's success was recognised by James Cochran Stevenson a year later, when he reconstructed the business as the Northern Press Company Ltd, with the Annand brothers each acquiring a 10 per cent shareholding. By this time the *Shields Gazette* had outgrown its King Street premises. Stevenson commissioned his architect brother, J.J. ('Jaughty') Stevenson, to design new offices, large enough to house a state-of-the-art rotary printing press, on land he owned in Barrington Street. The result was an elegant new building, demonstrably 'Queen Anne' in character.

After six years as editor, James Annand received an offer he could not refuse:

> A group of Newcastle Liberals (who had also disliked Cowens' policy in the *Newcastle Daily Chronicle*) invited Annand to launch a rival paper for the city. The first number of the *Northern Weekly Leader* was issued from the *Gazette* office in South Shields on 9 February 1884 and was so successful that the group of Liberals, headed by the coal owner Sir James (later Lord) Joicey, took it over and converted it into a morning newspaper – the *Newcastle Daily Leader*.[22]

It now needed a full-time editor, and Annand resigned from the *Gazette* in 1885 to take on this new challenge. He remained on good terms with his previous colleagues, retaining his shareholding in the company.

While at the *Newcastle Daily Leader*, Annand developed parliamentary ambitions, and secured the Liberal candidacy at Tynemouth in 1892. However, Joicey did not support Annand's attempt to win a seat in the House of Commons, putting it to him that he could not be a parliamentary candidate and a newspaper editor at the same time – at least if Joicey were the proprietor. Annand decided to withdraw his candidacy, resigning as editor three years later, the underlying reason probably again being the 'conflict between the proprietor's wishes and Annand's inflexible adherence to the principle of editorial independence'.[23] However, he was now free to seek a parliamentary seat elsewhere, eventually returning to Scotland, where his political ambitions were realised, but all too briefly.

In January 1906 he was elected Member of Parliament for East Aberdeenshire, but died, tragically enough, in London just sixteen days later, before he had an opportunity to take his seat in the House of Commons.

By the time his elder brother stood down from the *Newcastle Daily Leader*, Robert Cumming Annand had been at the *Shields Gazette* for twenty-three years and was thoroughly entrenched as its outstandingly successful managing director. As it had turned out, he was a 'brilliant inventor of printing machines', creating new and very lucrative lines of business for the Northern Press Company. Starting with a workshop to maintain and repair the *Shields Gazette*'s own machinery, 'He began to invent and patent improvements

Robert Cumming Annand, James' brother, joined the *Shields Gazette* in 1882 and became an outstandingly successful managing director and 'brilliant inventor of printing machines'. In 1901 he moved with his family to Harton Lea near Westoe. (*Shields Gazette*)

in printing equipment and before long was manufacturing whole printing presses in the South Shields office.'[24] The success of this fast web printing operation made the engineering division more profitable than the newspaper, leading the company to rebrand itself in 1889 as the Northern Press and Engineering Co. Ltd.

On the domestic front, Robert Cumming Annand had been living in Challoner Terrace in Westoe, almost next door to Robert Chapman. However, his commercial success enabled him to buy a larger plot in Harton Village – just up the road – and by 1901 he was comfortably installed with his wife Margaret and their six children (William, Robert, James, Wallace, Margaret and Alan) in his spacious new house, *Harton Lea*. He probably needed all the space he could get, since at the time of the Census there were fifteen people living in the house: seven 'nuclear' family members, four relations, three servants and a cook.

At work, everything looked rosy. The Northern Press was expanding, and in 1909 the company bought its rival newspaper north of the river, the *Shields Evening News*. The engineering side of the business continued its 'meteoric growth': 'streams of printing presses were leaving the factory for national and local newspaper offices across the country and soon were being sent all over the world – including Egypt, South Africa, China, Australia and Newfoundland'. Annual profits were running at around £20,000, and Annand's salary had been increased to £1,000 a year (more than twice the salary of the *Shields Gazette*'s well-known editor, George Bryan Hodgson).[25]

Owning with his brother James 36 per cent of the share capital of a successful company, and no doubt confident about its future prospects, Robert Cumming had brought his son Wallace Moir Annand into the business. In 1913 Wallace was elected a director, and in January 1914 he married Henry and Dora Chapman's daughter Dora Elizabeth (always known as Bessie) at St Michael's Church, South Westoe. But tragedy and dissension lay ahead, and by the end of the First World War there would be no Annands left at the Northern Press. However, the Annand name would again become famous in South Shields during the Second World War.

The Armstrongs

The solicitor Joseph Mason Moore became Mayor in 1870, resigning to become town clerk, an office he held with great distinction for twenty-one years. He lived in *Harton Hall* near Westoe. (South Tyneside Libraries)

Joseph F. Armstrong moved from Tynedale to South Shields in the 1860s.[26] He became a doctor and then a surgeon (at the Ingham Infirmary) whose first marriage, in 1867, was to Elizabeth Jane Anderson. Her father, who lived in *Bents House*, Westoe, was James Anderson, a timber merchant and councillor in the town, where he was Mayor the year before his daughter's marriage. Elizabeth Jane had two children, William Anderson and her namesake, Elizabeth Jane, but sadly she died of scarlet fever in 1870, shortly after her daughter's birth.

Five years later, Dr Joseph Armstrong remarried into a

prominent South Shields family. His second wife was Sarah Jane ('Poppy') Moore, daughter of Joseph Mason Moore, a man of many talents. He was a practising solicitor, partner in the law firm Maxwell and Moore, and a magistrate. He became a borough councillor alongside Robert Chapman in 1865, and Mayor in 1870. During his mayoralty he made a most unusual career change. The previous town clerk, Thomas Salmon, died suddenly, and Moore resigned 'the civic chair to accept the town clerkship. Mr. Moore proved himself equally devoted to the town's interests, many of the most important improvements effected during the (twenty-one) years he held the post being due to his initiative.'[27] He retired from the council in 1892, but continued his legal practice. He lived near Westoe in *Harton Hall*, whose beautiful gardens, with their fountains and hot houses, he opened to the public, laying on musical entertainment. He was closely involved with the Ingham Infirmary, becoming president in 1905.

Joseph and Sarah Jane Armstrong moved into Charlotte Street in Westoe, where they had seven children together. The eldest was Forster Moore Armstrong, who, like the vast majority of the sons of leading Westoe families, was educated at the South Shields Boys' High School, becoming a close friend of Henry Chapman's sons Robert and Charles. Dr Joseph's medical practice flourished, enabling his son (by his first wife) William Anderson Armstrong to study law at Trinity College, Cambridge, before becoming a solicitor in 1893. Joseph Mason Moore, his step-grandfather, then made him, and William's half-brother Forster Moore Armstrong, partners in his law firm, which he renamed J.M. Moore and Armstrong. They had numerous clients in South Shields, including Henry Chapman and his family.

Dr Joseph Armstrong and his wife Sarah Jane, daughter of Joseph Mason Moore, moved into elegant *Westoe House* in the early 1900s. It had formerly been the home of Robert Ingham, MP. (South Tyneside Libraries)

Joseph and Sarah must have been delighted when an opportunity came up to move into *Westoe House*. Mostly built in the eighteenth century, with later additions, it was described in glowing terms by the well-known local historian Amy Flagg: 'Of all the older homes in the Village, the gem is *Westoe House*.'[28] The ship owner Matthew Cay had bought the house in 1878/79 from the estate of Robert Ingham, MP, who had lived there himself until his death in 1875. Cay died in 1896 and his widow continued to live in the house until her death in 1902, when the property was purchased by Mrs Joseph Toward Eltringham of neighbouring *Eastgarth*, widow of the shipbuilder. She let out the property to Dr Joseph Armstrong, who died in 1911, and she subsequently sold it to his son by his first marriage, William Anderson Armstrong.

William and his wife Helen Marianne had five children – Margaretta Elizabeth, John Anderson, Josephine, Kathleen Marianne and Ruth Pauline – all of whom grew up in the splendid family home of *Westoe House*, becoming close friends with Henry and Dora Chapman's family. As with so many Westoe Village families, there were close links with the Ingham Infirmary, William Anderson Armstrong in due course becoming a trustee, chairman of the general committee and, finally, president.

The Ingham Infirmary and its 'Annual Full and Fancy Dress Ball'

'All work and no play makes Jack a dull boy' was a common adage in Victorian times, at least among the mercantile and professional classes who had enough time and money for leisure activities. Prominent among those activities for leading Westoe and South Shields residents was the Ingham Infirmary's Annual Ball.

The Ingham Infirmary, which incorporated the old South Shields and Westoe Dispensary, was built on land donated by the Dean and Chapter of Durham on the east side of Westoe Lane, just a stone's throw from Westoe Village. The hospital was completed in 1873, a shield on the façade recording that 'this building was erected by public subscription for the benefit of the sick and suffering, and called the "Ingham Infirmary" to commemorate the public service and private worth of Robert Ingham, Esquire, QC, of Westoe, the first member of Parliament for the Borough, and its representative for twenty-five years'.[29] James Cochran Stevenson's Jarrow

The Ingham Infirmary, just a stone's throw from Westoe Village, was opened in 1873, and the John Readhead Wing was added in 1899. Its annual Full and Fancy Dress Ball was a highlight of the town's social calendar. (South Tyneside Libraries)

Chemical Company partner, Alderman John Williamson, performed the opening ceremony, the company having donated £4,000 to the building. Williamson became the first president of the infirmary, and he was succeeded in 1888 by Stevenson.

The infirmary's original trust deed had specified that it should benefit 'the sick and lame poor residing or being in the Borough of South Shields and in the surrounding district'.[30] It rapidly gained the support of all sections of the population, with small, regular weekly subscriptions from workers in the local shipyards, chemical works, factories and other industries adding up to a significant proportion of annual running costs. These subscribers were entitled to 'elect a number of working men Governors of the Institution'[31] – a rather enlightened arrangement at the time.

The scale of the facilities at the infirmary soon became inadequate, with the population of booming South Shields continuing to rise rapidly, from 45,500 in 1873 to 78,500 in 1895. This was the demographic background to the decision to expand the infirmary, the result being the opening of a new wing in October 1899. James Readhead and other family members contributed nearly half of its costs, and hence it was called the John Readhead Wing in memory of the shipbuilding company's founder. In addition to the Readhead family's £4,000 donation to the total costs of around £9,000, the town's workmen made, collectively, an additional contribution of £1,200. Their regular subscriptions continued to fund nearly half of the infirmary's annual running costs. The new wing increased facilities considerably, accommodating forty-eight patients in six wards (the original building had only twenty-one beds) together with a convalescent day room, nurses' kitchens and sitting rooms.

Regular fundraising events were held in the town to meet running costs and capital expenditure. The most significant, and the most enjoyable for participants, was the Annual 'Full and Fancy Dress Ball' held at the Royal Assembly Hall each December. It had started life in 1874, eighteen months after the infirmary opened, and had spawned an Annual Children's Ball in 1893. Both balls were as popular as ever at the turn of the century and well beyond.

Around a hundred couples and their children celebrated at the Seventh Children's Ball on 10 January 1900, and 'choice music was rendered by Mr. J.H. Amer's Band' to accompany dancing from 7.30 p.m. to 1.30 a.m. All the leading Westoe families were there in strength: a dozen Readheads, nine Rennoldsons, half a dozen Armstrongs, Eltringhams, Fitzgeralds and Wheldons, with a sprinkling of Annands, Brighams, Gowanses, Grants, Grieveses, Mortons, and Wardles. Mrs (Dora) Chapman was there, with her son Mr Robert Chapman, the Misses Hilda, Bessie and Dorothy Chapman and Master Fred Chapman. The *Shields Gazette*'s reporters were indefatigable in listing each and every adult and child who attended. Where readily identifiable, the *Gazette* also listed the children's fancy dress, whose characters ranged far and wide, from *Blyth* (just up the Northumberland coast) to *Greek Brigand*, *Russian Skater* and *Geisha*. Also visible were *Page*, *Jester* and *Jack Tar*. In a brave if unsuccessful effort to master the French language, Miss Dorothy Chapman was reported as representing *Madam Sans Gene*. No doubt her mother had in mind something witty like 'Madam doesn't feel embarrassed'. There were allusions to the Boer War which had started just three months before the ball. One child represented *Kruger, junior* (Paul Kruger being President of the Transvaal), and another *Cape Colony* (into which Boer forces had already made incursions).

The Boer War had not finally run its course by the time the Twenty-seventh Full and Fancy Dress Ball was held on 13 December 1901. The committee for the ball was again drawn from the good and the great of Westoe, together with strong representation from organisations providing financial services to them, including Barclays Bank, the National Provincial Bank and the North-Eastern Bank. This time it was Henry Chapman's turn to act as Master of Ceremonies, jointly with James Readhead. The ballgoers' energy was undiminished: dancing started at 8.30 p.m. and continued until 2 a.m., to the music of Mr Amers, who had upgraded his colleagues from a 'band' to an 'orchestra'.

After the Children's Ball in January 1902, the Ingham Infirmary celebrations were over for another year. The more sporty Westoe residents were now looking forward to energetic activities outdoors, including rowing, swimming, rugby football, cricket and lawn tennis.

5

SPORTING LIVES

Henry Chapman was a lucky man. He was a gifted sportsman, and had the time and money to take advantage of the unprecedented growth of sporting activities on Tyneside in the second half of the nineteenth century. He was an active participant in the South Shields Amateur Rowing Club, the South Shields Amateur Swimming Club, the South Shields Cricket Club and the Westoe Rugby Football Club.

South Shields Amateur Rowing Club

It comes as a surprise to discover just how popular Tyne rowing was in the nineteenth century. The South Shields Amateur Rowing Club was formed in 1868, and the 18-year-old Henry Chapman was a founding member. By the late 1860s there were five amateur rowing clubs on the Tyne, and their members had drawn inspiration from the extraordinary success of professional rowers on the river. The first official boat race had taken place in Newcastle forty years earlier on 1 August 1821, the anniversary of the 1798 Battle of the Nile where Rear Admiral Sir Horatio Nelson annihilated a French fleet, during the Napoleonic Wars. The next half century would become the 'golden age of Tyne rowing'.[1]

Competitive, professional, rowing became by far the most important spectator sport, and leading Tyne oarsmen had a national – and indeed international – reputation. These highly respected north-east rowers:

… developed over the years a special relationship with the crowds that came to watch them. The many thousands who were reported as supporting the races behaved much like sporting crowds anywhere, indulging themselves heavily in gambling and drinking in the fashion of the day, encouraged by the owners of the many taverns and ale-houses along the banks of the river. But over and above all this, there emerged a rapport between the oarsmen and their public that was distinctive and special. It was to make the Tyne the most important river in the history of rowing.[2]

There were three outstanding professional oarsmen during this period: Harry Clasper, Robert Chambers and James Renforth.[3] Clasper, who began work as a 15-year-old at the Jarrow Pit, was apprenticed as a carpenter and became a wherryman, led the way.[4] He developed lighter and technically more advanced boats than his competitors, and with his uncle and three brothers (one as coxswain) won the final of the fours race at the Thames Regatta in 1844. This victory over the cockneys was particularly sweet, being the first time the Londoners had lost the championship of their home river. There were huge celebrations, bell ringing and gun salutes in Newcastle. Clasper did not disappoint his fans, going on to win six further Champion Fours races at the Thames Regatta, achieving his last championship victory at the age of 47 in 1859. He died in 1870, with around 100,000 supporters witnessing the funeral procession and burial.

Robert Chambers spent several years working in an ironworks as a 'puddler', whose exhausting job it was to stir molten pig iron with a long heavy ladle to release impurities from the metal. He was trained by Harry Clasper, joining his crew in 1856. He then proceeded to demolish the best of the Thames scullers one by one, including Tom White of Bermondsey, who had been chosen in 1859 'to do battle in the interests of Cockneydom', the stake for the race being £200, an enormous sum in today's money. Chambers became the Tyne, Thames, England and – in 1863 – the World Champion Sculler, dying of tuberculosis in 1868, at the age of 37. The last of the famous professional rowing trio was James Renforth, who started out as a smith's 'striker' or hammerer in an iron foundry. He, too, built an exceptional career as a professional oarsman, becoming World Champion Sculler and stroke of the famous Tyne Champion Four which defeated the St John, New Brunswick Four in Canada in 1870. Tragically, he died during the return match in Canada a year later. He was just 29 years old.[5]

Bob Cooper v. Bob Chambers. Oil painting by John Warkup Swift, 1865. This race took place on 5 September 1864, in the roughest conditions anyone could remember. Chambers' boat was soon holed, and, as it began to sink, the race was stopped. A rerow took place the next day, which Chambers (on the right) won. (Shipley Gallery, Gateshead, Tyne & Wear © Tyne & Wear Archives & Museums/Bridgeman Images. Caption, Ian Whitehead)

The national and international success of professional Tyne oarsmen had given a tremendous stimulus to the growth of amateur rowing. Henry Chapman became keenly interested in the sport, and would have been able to watch professional races on the Tyne, both when he was at the Grammar School in Newcastle and subsequently. Boat races and club regattas were reported at great length in the *Newcastle Daily Chronicle*, whose sports correspondents' vividly descriptive writing enabled readers to follow the fortunes of oarsmen and crews almost, it seemed, stroke by stroke. This was in fact carefully crafted editorial policy. The proprietor of the *Newcastle Daily Chronicle* was Joseph Cowen, who later (in 1873) became a Member of Parliament. He was:

> A most eager, almost a fanatical, politician, (but) nevertheless perceived with incisive clearness that a newspaper is not made by its politics. The public must be attracted to it by other means, and, as the public of Tyneside was a sporting public, Mr. Cowen organised his sporting department on a scale and with a completeness up to that time unattempted by any other provincial journal. In that particular he was one of the first of those who determined to 'give the people what the people want'.[6]

South Shields Amateur Rowing Club members and readers would soon benefit from the depth of the *Chronicle*'s reporting. Henry Chapman was quickly establishing a reputation as an able 'stroke oar' of coxed four boats, and the club was actively preparing for its first regatta, in July 1870. It purchased a splendid four-oared boat built in what the *Chronicle* called the 'world-famed establishment' of the Tyne boatbuilder, Robert Jewitt. It was named *The Williamson* after their president, Alderman John Williamson.

Henry and his crew proceeded to win triple victories in the fours races at the regatta, a full report duly appearing in the *Newcastle Daily Chronicle* on 30 July:

> The annual regatta of this prosperous club was held yesterday, and in spite of serious drawbacks against which it had to contend, was highly successful. It was at first arranged that the rowing should take place alongside the South Pier, over a course of half a mile in length, but a strong easterly breeze driving in the sea in heavy rollers at the place indicated, a change had at the last moment to be made. The fine piece of water in front of Jarrow Slake was then pitched upon to bring off the

racing, and clear of traffic as it was, no better course could have been selected. The steamer *Harry Clasper* was chartered to carry the members of the club and their friends, and it was heavily freighted with visitors, including a large number of the fair sex. The *Wansbeck* and *Margaret* also attended the regatta, and amongst the company on board the various steamers we noticed the Mayor of South Shields, Mr. Ald. Williamson, Mr. Ald. Dale and Mrs. Dale.[7]

Councillor Robert Chapman (Henry's proud father) was present, as were officers of the 98th Regiment, whose band, 'under the direction of Herr Carl Fricke, performed a choice selection of music on board the *Harry Clasper*', a fitting name for the club's vessel at its regatta. Henry's final victory as stroke, with crew members R. Oliver, J.C. Holmes, F.E. Buckland and Reed as cox, rowed over a distance of half a mile off the South Pier, won them the Ladies Prize – all regattas had a 'Ladies Prize' – presented afterwards at the Golden Lion Hotel on King Street.

A fortnight later, Henry took the plunge at the Annual Gala of the South Shields Amateur Swimming Club, which was founded in 1862 and claimed to be the oldest in the country. In 1870 it was still true to its origins as a club for sea water bathers, and the gala was held alongside the South Pier. Spectators lined the pier and filled steamboats and cobles alongside the course, and the *Harry Clasper* was again in evidence as a club boat, this time hosting the band of the 3rd Durham Volunteer Artillery. Henry, having previously won at least one cup as a junior, entered the most challenging ('1st class') race, for seniors over 440yd. As described by the *Newcastle Daily Chronicle* it was 'a very severe contest'. Henry finished second to T. Edwin White, with Joseph Eltringham in third place – both of them friends and Amateur Rowing Club colleagues.

In the following year Henry took up his oar again and competed in the Tyne Regatta, which included races both for professionals and for 'gentlemen amateurs'. The South Shields ARC generously lent their boat ('one of the finest that has ever been turned out of Mr. Robert Jewitt's establishment') to James Renforth, who proceeded to win the professionals' four-oared race. Shortly afterwards, Henry also competed in the senior skiff and fours races in the South Shields regatta, narrowly missing further prizes. Undaunted, he went into the 1872 season – his last – determined to achieve further victories. He was not disappointed. Again he stroked his crew to victory, winning the Steward's Plate (a four-oared race for junior

crews) at the Durham Regatta in June. Then came the big challenge of the
Tyne Regatta in July.

The regatta, one of the highlights of the sporting year, received detailed
coverage over several days in the *Newcastle Daily Chronicle*. The fifty patrons
included the great and the good of Tyneside and adjoining counties: the
Duke of Northumberland, Earl Grey, the Earl of Durham, eleven Members
of Parliament (including Sir Joseph Cowen, James C. Stevenson and Sir
Hedworth Williamson), the Mayors of Newcastle, Gateshead, Tynemouth
and South Shields, officers of the 14th Brigade of Royal Artillery, the
Master and Brethren of the Trinity House, Newcastle, and the chairman and
directors of the Tyne General Ferry Company. The names of the General
Committee and Executive Committee members were all listed, as were
those of the two honorary treasurers (Archibald Stevenson of South Shields
being one of them). In short, the regatta was a major event by any standards.

Henry Chapman and his South Shields ARC crew rose splendidly to
the occasion. They competed for the Tyne General Ferry Challenge Cup,

BOAT-RACE ON THE TYNE.

Boat race on the Tyne, *Illustrated London News*, 9 August 1873. Above the rowers is
the famous High Level Bridge, linking Newcastle and Gateshead. Completed in
1849, its roadway is suspended below the railway line. (Courtesy London Library.
© Joan Chapman)

valued at £60 and presented by that company's chairman and directors for junior 'gentlemen amateurs' in coxed fours, racing over a distance of about ¾ mile. Henry was again 'stroke oar' and his crew mates were George Coward, Thomas Henry White, Thomas Edwin White and J. Brown (cox). There were strong competing crews from Newcastle, Middlesbrough, York, Berwick and Blyth. In the first heat, South Shields was up against Newcastle and Middlesbrough. The race was tight, and the umpire decided, somewhat controversially, that both Newcastle and South Shields should go through to the final, where they were up against York. Further controversy followed in the final race, which Newcastle thought it had won by half a dozen lengths. However, its crew was disqualified, the *Newcastle Daily Chronicle* reporting that the umpire:

> … ordered the York and South Shields men to row over again. This order was at once complied with, and the two boats came away to an excellent start, and rowed nearly level until approaching the Suspension Bridge. South Shields crew then forged ahead, and passing underneath the structure half a length in advance, increased their lead to a length as they passed the Stand. The York crew then came up with a brilliant spurt, and reaping the benefit of the bend, placed their boat fairly alongside of the South Shields crew. As they passed the Derwent Gut, the South Shields crew, however, then got the best of it, and slowly but surely improving their advantage throughout the remainder of the distance, won cleverly by a length and a half.[8]

South Shields ARC had won the coveted Tyne General Ferry Challenge Cup, for the first and last time in its history.

Henry had decided that 1872 would be his last season of competitive amateur rowing. Could he end it on a high note at the South Shields ARC's own Annual Regatta in August, which, the *Newcastle Daily Chronicle* informed its readers, was 'favoured with most magnificent weather and came off with the most triumphant success'?[9]

The judge was Henry's friend Joseph Eltringham and the umpire was William Fawcus from the Tynemouth ARC, a very well-respected rower who had won the Diamond Sculls at the Henley Regatta the year before – the first Northerner to do so.

Henry entered the four-oared race competition for the President's Prize, which comprised four silver cups and a silver pencil case for the coxswain. He was again 'stroke oar', but there was no continuity with his winning Tyne Regatta crew. This time Henry's crew mates were John T. White, B. Dale, Christison and Bell (cox). They won their heat comfortably, 'having the advantage of smooth water close to the pier', and they were now in the final. The *Newcastle Daily Chronicle*, as ever, reported on the outcome:

> This was looked upon as the contest of the day, and the magnificent race that ensued between the two crews justified the anticipations of the spectators. The crews were very fairly balanced, and both went away to a good start. Pulling well in time and with great speed, the two crews kept in close company for fully one-half the distance, when, however, Chapman's crew began to draw in front, and continued to advance before Coward's crew – who never failed to keep their boat going at a splendid speed – until the finish, when [Chapman's] inside boat was hailed the victor by between two and three lengths.[10]

Henry certainly completed his final regatta on a high note. By good fortune, he was rowing when the Tyne's reputation was pre-eminent. The Americans regarded the Tynesiders as 'the best oarsmen in the world', and the rowing community regarded the river as a 'beacon of athleticism, innovation and professional excellence'.[11] However, seismic change was under way. The three famous professionals – Harry Clasper, Robert Chambers and James Renforth – had all died in just three years, between 1868 and 1871. The Tyne never produced another sculling champion. Moreover, the separation of professional and amateur rowing was rapidly becoming deeper. Amateur clubs wanted to stage amateur-only regattas: the last mixed professional and amateur (pro-am) pair-oar race was probably held in 1869. And wealthy amateurs seemed much less inclined to provide stake money for local professionals. The result was that 'professional rowing began to be banished to the margins'.[12]

However, it was football that provided the knock-out blow to professional rowing as the Tyne had known it. The Football Association, the game's ruling body, had been founded in 1863 and the game was flourishing in the 1870s, and spread very rapidly in the 1880s. The Football League was formed in 1888, and the following year an attendance of 10,000 was recorded at a local match in Sunderland.[13] Spectators on the Tyne were now watching a minority sport.

Nevertheless, amateur rowing continued to be popular, with South Shields ARC scullers and fours winning prizes at the Durham Regatta throughout the early 1870s and its crew triumphing over a rival boat with several Oxbridge oarsmen to win the Londesborough Grand Challenge Cup at York in 1877. Further Grand Challenge Cups were won at Durham Regattas in the 1880s. Marking the end of the decade, Henry Chapman and Joseph Eltringham, as vice-presidents, attended the Club's AGM in May 1890, where the captain, Fred Rennoldson, presided. He reported that the club had been represented at 'all the regattas', namely Durham, Talkin Tarn near Carlisle, and Tynemouth, the 'stock of boats was undoubtedly the best on the Tyne' and the financial position was 'fairly good'. However, the number of members had declined from forty-nine to forty-two, and the club itself had not held a regatta since 1883. The next one would not be held until 1899. Henry Chapman remained a vice-president all his life, and the club had boats named after him and his son Robert Chapman. But the glory days were over.

Westoe Rugby Football Club

If amateur rowing was in decline, rugby football was in the ascendant. The Rugby Football Union was founded in January 1871, with twenty-one clubs at the initial meeting. A code of rules, the 'Laws of the Game', was quickly drawn up and the first international match, between England and Scotland, was played just two months later. The game's popularity spread very quickly and by the time Westoe Rugby Football Club was formed in 1875 there were around ninety clubs affiliated to the RFU. The club's home pitch was the initially unlevelled west side of the South Shields Cricket Club's ground of 4 acres at Wood Terrace in Westoe, former farmland that the cricketers had leased from the Ecclesiastical Commissioners in 1868. The cricket club itself had been founded in 1850, and its first honorary secretary was George Gibson, father of Henry Chapman's wife, Dora. Henry became vice-president of the Rugby Football Club in 1878, the notable year in which the Westoe player J.L. Bell was capped for England in its match against Ireland. J.J. Gowans, one of the six sons of Dr W. Gowans, was another well-known Westoe player, who won eight caps for Scotland between 1894 and 1896.

Five of Henry's own sons – Robert, George, Laurence, Charles and Fred – played for Westoe in the years leading up to the First World War.[14]

Robert (later Col Sir Robert) was a talented player, appearing ninety-three times for the First XV between 1900/01 and 1907/08 and once, alongside his brother Fred, for Durham County. Robert was team captain in 1901/02. George played four times for the Westoe First XV in the 1901/02 season. He also played for the South Shields High School Old Boys Club, as did his elder brother Hal, and later for his Cambridge University college, Peterhouse. Laurence Chapman played twenty games for the club (two for the First XV) between 1902/03 and 1907/08 before moving to Assam as an agricultural chemist advising tea plantations. Charles Chapman, like Robert, was a talented player, making ninety-one appearances (fifty for the First XV and forty-one for the Second XV) between 1907/08 and 1912/13.

However, the star of the family was Frederick Ernest ('Fred' or 'Freddie') Chapman, widely recognised as one of rugby's great players.[15] His appetite for the game would prove to be prodigious. He first played for Westoe as a 15-year-old in 1902/03, and his final season for the club was in 1911/12. During that time he played six games for the Second XV and sixty-one for the First XV. This participation showed his intense loyalty to the club, because while a playing member of Westoe RFC he also played for Durham County, Durham University and England. Over his long eighteen-year career (1902–20) he played for Durham County on thirty-one occasions, frequently as captain, scoring fourteen tries, twelve goals and three penalty goals in the process.[16]

Fred first came to national – and indeed international – attention when he was selected for the Anglo-Welsh team, captained by A.F. Harding (Wales), that toured Australia and New Zealand in the summer of 1908. The party included fifteen caps – nine English and six Welsh – and had a convincing overall result against provincial sides, winning twenty-five of their thirty-one matches and scoring 323 points against 202.[17] However, the three international matches ('Tests') against the strong New Zealand side were far from successful. The first and third Tests were crushing defeats (3-32 at Dunedin and 0-29 at Auckland), although the visitors managed a 3-3 draw in the second Test, at Wellington.[18]

Fred Chapman's performance on the tour must have been creditable, because he was also selected to play for the Anglo-Welsh squad that hosted the first visiting team from Australia (the 'First Wallabies') at the end of 1908. The visitors won twenty-five of their thirty-one matches. Fred's career was now about to take off spectacularly. 'In 1910 he upset the apple cart

The Anglo-Welsh team on tour to New Zealand and Australia in 1908. Fred Chapman, in a pale suit, is arrowed. (Chapman Family Archive. © Joan Chapman)

Fred Chapman, captain of the Durham County team against Midlands Counties, March 1914. Seven of his team mates would be killed in the First World War. (C. Berkeley Cowell and E. Watts Moses, *Durham County Rugby Union, 1876–1936* (Newcastle upon Tyne, 1936). © Joan Chapman)

by helping a "Rest of England" side to defeat England comfortably on the eve of the opening fixture of that year's 5-Nations Championship. As a result he was one of a number of players parachuted into the England team to face Wales in the very first international fixture to be played at Twickenham',[19] on Saturday, 15 January. The importance of the occasion was marked by the prominent presence, among the 20,000 spectators, of the Prince of Wales, a noted rugby fan who would a few months later ascend the throne as King George V.

Adrian Stoop was England's captain and fly-half; Fred Chapman was right wing. *The Times* reported the match in full:

England beat Wales on the new Rugby Union ground at Twickenham on Saturday for the first time since 1893 by one goal, one penalty goal, and one try (11 points) to two tries (6 points). England deserved to win; but there was not much to choose between the two teams, and until the final whistle was blown no one could feel quite sure that Wales might not at least draw level. The weather was unfavourable. A drizzling rain fell throughout the game, and the ground, which was already soft, became in parts a sea of mud, and in these circumstances the game was chiefly confined to the forwards.[20]

English fifteens have often been accused of taking a long time to settle down to their game, but this was not the case on Saturday. Indeed, the beginning of the match was sensational. B. Gronow kicked off for Wales, and the ball went to A.D. Stoop, who ran through to the centre and then punted over the Welsh backs. The Englishmen followed up and tackled their man; there was a scrummage, and then Stoop, getting the ball again, passed to J.G.G. Birkett, who passed again to F E. Chapman at the right moment and a try was scored. Chapman took the place-kick and only just failed at an awkward angle … England were hard pressed at one point, and from a penalty J. Bancroft [Wales] nearly kicked a goal. Subsequently England attacked strongly, the forwards playing splendidly and making more than one magnificent rush. Chapman nearly got in again, and soon afterwards he kicked a goal from a penalty awarded for a foul tackle, and England were thus six points up at the end of a quarter of an hour's play. Wales, however, soon reduced this lead [with T. Evans scoring a try]. Soon afterwards a very fine piece of play by B. Solomon gave England another try, and this was converted [by Chapman]. After a rush the ball came through two or three hands to Solomon, who deceived the Welsh backs by feinting to pass, and went over himself. Soon after this the teams changed ends, and at half-time, therefore, England were leading by 11 points to 3.[21]

In the second half Wales scored, and although England were on the defensive most of the time they held on to their lead, eventually winning by 11 points to 6. No wonder *The Times* reported that 'Chapman confirmed all the good things that had been said about him.' In his first game for England and the first international at Twickenham, Fred Chapman had scored the first try in the first minute of the match, the first penalty goal and the first conversion – eight points out of England's total of eleven. Just as impressively, it was the first time England had beaten Wales in seventeen seasons. The newspaper concluded that:

> The Selection Committee must be well pleased, as they ought to be, with their choice of the fifteen; and after so brilliant a victory over such formidable antagonists they are not likely to make many alterations in the English team for the International matches against Scotland and Ireland.[22]

The Times' predictions were correct. Fred Chapman (still representing Westoe) was indeed selected to play for England against Ireland a month later, in February 1910. The result was a draw. For Westoe RFC 'this was the famous game, when, the week before, the Irish prop O.J.S. Piper informed an unsuspecting Committee that he was not able to play for the club the following week, as he was playing for Ireland'.[23] Never again was Westoe in the very unusual situation of providing a player for each side in an international match. In March, Fred Chapman played for England against France (England won 11-3) and Scotland (England won 14-5). He played very little rugby in 1911 as he suffered injuries and was also in his final year of medical studies at Durham University's College of Medicine.

In January 1912 he continued his career for England, playing again against Wales (England won 8-0). This was the year in which he moved, as Dr Chapman, to Hartlepool, having been appointed house surgeon at Hartlepools Hospital. He then joined Hartlepool Rovers and played two more games for England before the First World War – against Wales in January 1914 (England won 10-9), and against Ireland in February 1914 (England won 17-12) – thereby making a significant contribution to England's 'grand slam' victory in that year.

Fred's career as an England player became legendary. He won seven caps, he scored in each game and England won every match in which he played (except in the no-score draw with Ireland). His versatility was exceptional, and he played with assurance on either wing or in the centre or as a back. And in addition to his reputation as a kicker 'he was regarded as the greatest exponent of side-stepping during his long career'.[24]

Westoe Lawn Tennis Club

Fred Chapman's sporting prowess was not limited to rugby football. He was also a talented tennis player, and an active member of the Westoe Lawn Tennis Club. The game became very popular in the 1870s, and in 1880 the South Shields Cricket Club had members playing tennis on its field at Westoe. Not everyone was happy about this expansion of sporting activities. In the following year a local butcher, Thomas Raffle Lawson, wrote a letter of complaint to the cricket club:

> I beg to request a reduction of rent for the eatage of grass on your field by one half as when I took it, it was used for cricketing and your sports alone, and was then worth the rent which I paid, now it is used for all kinds which destroys the grass very considerably.

The rent was duly reduced, but only from £15 to £12.[25]

There was no stopping the growing popularity of the game among both men and women. By 1884 the cricket club had forty-six lady members playing tennis and two years later it appointed a sub-committee, which included Henry Chapman, 'to carry out all the business in connection with the Tennis Club'.[26] He would have a close involvement with the club for the next half century. Two years later, in August 1886, the first Westoe Lawn Tennis Tournament was held:

> Most of the early tennis was played in a Garden Party atmosphere, and perhaps it is not difficult to visualise August Bank Holiday, a lazy Summer's day, the band [of the 3rd Durham Artillery Volunteers] playing, ladies in their long Victorian dresses and gentlemen in their brightly coloured blazers and straw hats strolling leisurely over the green with only the rhythmic sound of racquet on ball and the calling of the umpires to disturb the harmony of those far-off peaceful days.

There was certainly a party atmosphere, since 'after the conclusion of the tournament there was an open concert with dancing on the green'.[27]

The Westoe tournament steadily expanded in scope and duration. In 1890 the first open events – the ladies' and gentlemen's doubles and the gentlemen's doubles – were held, and in the following year the tournament became a two-day event. In August 1892 a new ladies singles handicap event was introduced, which was won by Henry's daughter Ethel ('Miss E. Chapman'), who no doubt had honed her tennis skills at Cheltenham Ladies' College. This was also a good year on the sporting front for Henry, who, with two other cricket club colleagues, had played a leading role in the establishment of Durham County Cricket Club just three months before the Westoe tournament.

County tennis links were also being forged. In 1896 the Durham County Lawn Tennis Association was founded, and Westoe joined shortly afterwards, its formal club title now being the 'South Shields Cricket and Westoe Lawn Tennis Club'. Henry Chapman became chairman, and in 1899 the club became a founding member of the Northumberland and Durham Inter-Club Lawn Tennis League, which grew to be one of the largest in the country. The Chapman family — Henry and five of his adult children — became even more active in the club between the death of Queen Victoria in 1901 and the outbreak of the First World War:

The 1907 Westoe Lawn Tennis Club team, winners of the Durham County Challenge Cup. Left to right: M.H. Duncan, T. Dilks Page (captain), T.A. Binks, R. Wheldon, G. Scott (jnr), Hal Chapman. (South Tyneside Libraries)

The 1905 season commenced with Henry Chapman, long a loyal and wise counsel in club matters, being elected president to succeed James (Cochran) Stevenson, who had died after holding the office for almost 28 years. Unlike his predecessor, Chapman rejected the figure-head role and club rules were amended to make him an active ex-officio committee member.[28]

Henry's eldest son, Hal Chapman, became a prominent Westoe LTC player. He was on the team that won the Durham County Challenge Cup in 1907. He became honorary secretary of the club in 1908, and men's captain for three seasons from 1909. That was a good year for tennis and the Chapmans: Fred showed that his ball-playing talents extended well beyond rugby football by pairing with W.L. Clements and winning for Westoe the Northumberland and Durham League Doubles Championship, a feat not repeated during the Lawn Tennis Club's first hundred years.

Ethel Chapman – sister of Hal and Fred – continued to be a very active club player. At a meeting of the club early in 1914 at St Paul's Hall in Westoe Road she was elected to the ladies committee, and became captain, a position she was to hold for five years. By the time she stood down she had been playing competitive tennis for twenty-seven years.

Charles Lancelot Chapman, the youngest brother of Hal, Ethel and Fred, was also a tennis player. He was elected to the all-male main club committee as honorary secretary early in 1914. Other members included Wallace Moir Annand (Henry Chapman's son-in-law) as honorary treasurer, and J.H. and S. Readhead. Those members would never all meet again as a committee. The annual tournament was in full swing when war was declared against Germany on 4 August 1914. 'The Hon. Secretary, Mr. C.L. Chapman, was unable to see the tournament through, "being called to the higher duty of serving his King and Country, and unfortunately was later to make the supreme sacrifice"'[29] – as indeed would Wallace Moir Annand.

Finally, Henry Chapman's daughter Dorothy, who had been so successful at school hockey and lacrosse at St Leonards St Andrews, was also a keen tennis player. She entered the 1914 tournament, which, 'Despite many unavoidable withdrawals … was brought to a finish. C.J. Tindel-Green of Sunderland won the Men's Singles, and the Ladies' final was won by Westoe member, Miss Dorothy Chapman who was later to die in Egypt on active service.'[30]

Those young men and women who went off to war with their heads held high had no idea what horrors awaited them.

PART 3

THE FIRST WORLD WAR

6

WAR ON ALL FRONTS, 1914–18

When Britain's ultimatum was given to Germany on 4 August 1914 demanding the evacuation of Belgium it was ignored, leading immediately to the First World War. Henry and Dora's family were actively engaged in the fighting, and in medical and nursing care. Like so many other parents, they would have to cope with four anxious years, and grieve the deaths of loved ones.

Five family members served in three different war zones: Wallace Annand, husband of their daughter Dora Elizabeth (known as Bessie), fought with the Royal Naval Division at Gallipoli; Charles Chapman served with the 50th (Northumbrian) Division and 36th (Ulster) Division at Ypres; Dorothy Chapman became a nurse with a Voluntary Aid Detachment in Egypt; Fred Chapman joined the Royal Navy as a temporary surgeon and later moved to the Royal Army Medical Corps; and Robert Chapman served with the 50th (Northumbrian) Division at Ypres and on the Somme.

Lt Cdr Wallace Moir Annand, RNVR

In 1907 Wallace Annand joined the Tyneside Division of the Royal Naval Volunteer Reserve (RNVR), which had been formed four years earlier to attract civilians. As with all volunteer units, service was a part-time activity, fully compatible with Wallace's day job as a director of the

Lt Cdr Wallace Moir Annand, RNVR, in Royal Naval Division uniform. (© Imperial War Museum [HU 112900])

Shields Gazette, although reservists were required to attend an annual two-week course at sea. He started out as a midshipman, and was promoted first to sub-lieutenant, then to lieutenant in June 1914.

After the declaration of war, Wallace volunteered for full-time service and was attached to the Collingwood Battalion of the Royal Naval Division at the Crystal Palace Depot in London. The division had only just been formed – in September 1914 – to fight on land alongside the Army, making productive use of the huge surplus of Royal Navy reservists. It consisted of personnel brought together from the Royal Naval Reserve, Royal Fleet Reserve, Royal Naval Volunteer Reserve and a brigade of Royal Marines, together with Royal Navy and Army personnel. Of the latter, some 2,000 were miners from Durham and Northumberland who were transferred from northern regiments.

Wallace had joined the RNVR because he wanted to serve at sea, not on land. So in November 2014 he applied for a transfer to the Royal Naval Motor Boat Reserve, which carried out coastal work including minesweeping, but was told that there was no vacancy. He had become too valuable to be allowed to transfer, and in December he was promoted to adjutant in what by then was called the 4th (Collingwood) Battalion of the 2nd Royal Naval Brigade.

In February and March 1915 the battalion moved from the Crystal Palace to Blandford Camp in Dorset for a period of intense training in field operations – including rifle range instruction (still called 'musketry'), machine gun courses, trench digging and deploying into shallow col-umns in firing lines. Discipline had to be maintained. Wallace Annand's adjutant's diary noted that one soldier broke out of camp, and was absent for precisely 159 hours. When he eventually returned, his sentence was twenty-one days' detention and twenty-five days' pay forfeited. Closer to base, problems at the White Hart Inn in Blandford led to its being placed 'out of bounds' for three weeks. In April 1915, Wallace wrote in his adjutant's diary that 'serious complaints have been received of men going to & returning from the rifle ranges firing ball ammunition at rabbits & hares in the fields … Any cases of men being found in possession of live ammunition (except on the Ranges) are to be severely dealt with.'[1]

There was some light relief from the hard grind of training. On 14 April all officers and men were invited to a Grand Evening Concert in the YMCA hut. The battalion's commandant was Cdr Alexander Spearman, the second in command was Lt Cdr Charles West, and Wallace Annand remained adjutant. An amusing piece of doggerel, *Collingwood personalities*, was doing the rounds at the camp:

Our blue water Collingwood skipper,
To defaulters as grim as Agrippa;
But he shoulders his pack,
And he heads the attack;
And we vote him a regular ripper.

I'm sure you would never have guessed
What a subtle Commander is West;
He looks half asleep;
But he shepherds his sheep,
And men run at his lightest behest.

Our adjutant, (Wallace) Annand,
Not a ha'p'orth of nonsense he'll stand;
Six feet in his socks,
With a voice like an ox,
You can see he was born to Command.[2]

(Note: A 'ripper' was an excellent fellow, and a 'ha'p'orth' was a half-pennyworth.)

When he was promoted to the rank of lieutenant commander in May 1915, Wallace would have been well aware that the Royal Naval Division had been in action at Gallipoli since 25 April. The British, and the French, were there to help their Russian allies. The Ottoman Empire had entered the war on the German side in October 1914, and a Turkish offensive was soon causing major problems for the Russian army in the Caucasus. Even

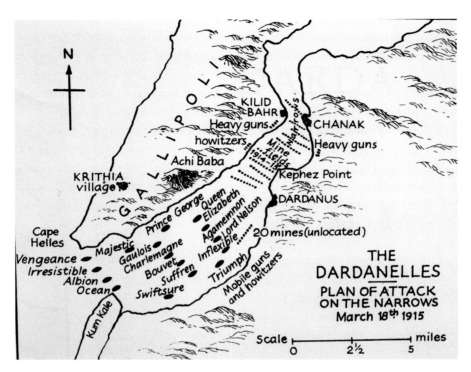

Map of the Dardanelles and 'Plan of Attack on the Narrows', 18 March 1915. (H.M. Denham, *A Midshipman's Diary* [John Murray Publishers, an imprint of Hodder & Stoughton, London, 1981])

worse, the Dardanelles were blockaded by the Turks and their German allies, which meant that essential imports to Russia through the Black Sea were blocked, and its export trade (largely grain from the south) declined dramatically. At the beginning of January 1915 Grand Duke Nicholas appealed to Britain for help.

In mid-January the War Council, whose members included Winston Churchill as First Lord of the Admiralty and Admiral Lord (Jacky) Fisher as First Sea Lord, decided on a bold scheme. This was, as they described it, to 'force' the Dardanelles Straits, making use of a surplus of pre-Dreadnought battleships, take Constantinople, which would be handed over to the Russians, and topple the Ottoman government. It was not initially intended that there would be any military action on the Gallipoli peninsula, but naval efforts to sail up the Straits were halted in March 1915 by mines laid in the waterway and by Turkish mobile howitzers on both shores. So it was decided to land a military force to eliminate those batteries on the peninsula itself.

The British and French fleets were in place by 24 April. Midshipman Henry Denham, on HMS *Agamemnon*, in the entrance to the Straits, noted in his diary that day:

> The eve of great events. We took in 120 tons of coal early in the forenoon from *Cairngowan*. In the *Dog Watches* [two-hour watches between 4.00 p.m. and 8.00 p.m.] *Swanly* came alongside and we started taking in various stores; three destroyers then came alongside us for stores. Several transports came round during the night. Landing conditions … seem very favourable for a landing tomorrow.[3]

He judged correctly and the next day he wrote:

> Landing of the Allied Army in Gallipoli. At 5.15 it was quite light and many ships were following a long way astern of us: transports, trawlers full of troops, and lighters all ready for landing. The whole setting was most dramatic. We were conscious of a mighty armada – setting forth to conquer the Dardanelles, to open the way to Constantinople, and perhaps end the War.[4]

The campaign's aims were spectacularly unfulfilled. Detailed intelligence, planning and preparation were all lacking 'for what would be the first amphibious assault in history mounted against on-shore opponents armed with machine guns'.[5] The Turks, capably advised by the head of the German military mission to Constantinople, were ready and recently reinforced. As they well knew, landing places were limited, at Cape Helles itself to a few small sandy beaches. The Allied troops, including not only the Royal Naval Division but also the all-regular 29th Division, were inexperienced. There were no towns, just a few settlements, Krithia in the south being the most important; and the roads were unmade tracks.

The 29th Division was assigned to the main landings at Cape Helles to capture the forts at Kilid Bahr. The landings were spread over five beaches around the point of the peninsula, but, due to witheringly effective fire from the well-prepared Turks, only limited beachheads could be gained. Despite valiant efforts, the troops could not attain their first objective of taking Krithia, and the Turks remained in possession not only of the hill of Achi Baba behind the village, but also of the high ground generally. By 5 May the 29th Division had lost half of its initial strength, including two-thirds of its officers. The Royal Naval Division was faring no better, and badly needed reinforcements.

This was the situation on the ground when Wallace Annand and the Collingwood Battalion left Blandford by train on 10 May and sailed from Devonport aboard HM Transport *Ivernia*, a former Cunard liner, under orders for 'service in the Mediterranean'. The battalion knew precisely where it was going, since officers had been informed that letters from home should be sent to the British Expeditionary Force, Dardanelles. Six days later *Ivernia* arrived at Gibraltar and dropped anchor fairly close to the harbour wall. The commanding officer went ashore to receive orders from the admiral, which:

> ... came promptly enough, viz., to proceed to sea immediately as, owing to the presence of submarines in the vicinity, our ship was likely to be an object of interest if she remained in harbour. We, therefore got under weigh [sic] again at 5pm. Glorious weather prevailed all this time, and the sea was a perfect blue.[6]

Next stop, on 19 May, was Valletta, Malta, also being used by the French as a base. Leave was given in the evening and the following morning, a much-appreciated opportunity to 'indulge in the novelties and joys of an Eastern city' which included buying lace and silk to be sent home as presents, and watching roaming goats being milked on the locals' doorsteps.[7] After 'coaling ship' (refuelling), *Ivernia* reached Lemnos twenty-four hours later, and when she entered the harbour of Mudros, being used as the forward base for Gallipoli operations, 'there was disclosed before our eyes one of the finest naval harbours in the world, capable of sheltering several fleets'.[8] There were 120 ships already at anchor, with room for plenty more. The sea journey from Devonport to Mudros was the last enjoyable experience the battalion would have. Its task was to reinforce the Royal Naval Division, and it was joined by the Hawke and Benbow Battalions, together with a draft of 500 men from other units. They would discover all too soon that the task was impossible.

On 29 May the Collingwood Battalion, having transferred to four lighters, arrived at Cape Helles in the early hours of the following day. During the evening of 1 June its troops, having received the necessary equipment and stores, left the beach area for the front-line trenches facing Krithia, which they reached without any casualties. They were about to join the third battle for this small, but strategically important, village. The

Manchesters of the 127th Brigade, 42nd Division, had managed to take the last organised Turkish trenches before the outskirts of Krithia:

> Next in line were the RND, who launched the 2nd Naval Brigade into the attack. This previously ramshackle formation had gained an impressive variety of military skills over the past month, but the blast of fire after the temporary suspension of the bombardment had let them know that the Turks were well and truly ready for them.[9]

Still, over the top on 4 June went the Anson, Howe and Hood Battalions.

The 'White House', a position captured by the Hood Battalion, Royal Naval Division, at Gallipoli. (© Imperial War Museum [Q 61127])

As Ordinary Seaman Joe Murray of the Hood Battalion recalled:

> Off we go and up we went over the ladder. The moment we started to leave the trench at this traverse, 10–12 feet long, there were men falling back into the trench or on the parapet. There was dead all over the place. My Platoon Commander got through. I followed him up there. Parsons had already been killed. We got into dead ground. The Petty Officer said, 'Well, come on lad! C'mon!' We moved again and … I got

to the (Turkish) trench and in I go – it was 10 feet deep. There was one or two dead, nobody alive.[10]

The Hood Battalion had succeeded in taking three trenches, but had suffered severe casualties, and withdrew.

The Collingwood Battalion started their attack at noon, by companies, ten to fifteen minutes after the other battalions. The Turkish trenches they were attempting to reach were some 400yd away, and the battalion was exposed to deadly enfilading fire from their right flank. They lost hundreds of men before they even reached the original British front line. Wallace Annand, aged 29, was among the first of the battalion to be killed (as was Cdr Spearman) in the initial moments of the attack. As General Sir Ian Hamilton, Commander-in-Chief of the Mediterranean Expeditionary Force, wrote in his war diary, 'As to the Collingwoods, they were simply cut to pieces, losing 25 officers out of 28 in a few minutes.'[11] Casualties among the men reached 500. The battalion was annihilated, and the 2nd Naval Brigade as a whole lost sixty out of seventy officers in just forty-five minutes. Four days later, on 8 June, came the decision to break up the Collingwood, with the survivors transferred to the Anson, Hood and Howe Battalions.

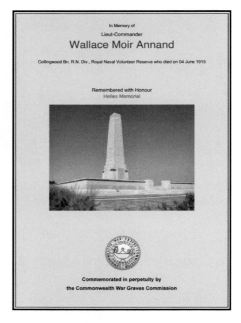

The offensive by the British and French had now completely ground to a halt. 'Their aspirations were no longer Kilid Bahr or Achi Baba or even Krithia, but merely the unprepossessing vista of the next in an endless sequence of trenches. The British had suffered 4,500 casualties and the French 2,000 at the Third Battle of Krithia; the Turks had lost about 9,000 men.'[12] A final effort to break the stalemate on the peninsula by a major offensive through Suvla Bay, where 20,000 men were put ashore later in the summer, might

The Helles Memorial, Gallipoli, where Wallace Annand's name is inscribed on the Royal Naval Volunteer Reserve panels. (Commonwealth War Graves Commission)

well have succeeded if divisional leadership had been more decisive. But it was not, and that offensive also ground to a halt. The only exceptionally well-planned and executed operation was, ironically, the withdrawal from the peninsula (from Suvla Bay and Anzac Cove on 18 December, and from Cape Helles on 8 January 1916) with practically no loss of life.

This was cold comfort to Wallace's wife Bessie. She was pregnant when her husband went off to the war, and their child was born three months later on 5 November 1914. Richard Wallace Annand would win the Victoria Cross in the Second World War, but would never know his father. And Bessie remained a widow for the rest of her life.

Major Charles Chapman, MC

Charles, the youngest son of Henry and Dora, had been born in August 1892 and looked all set to become an accountant. Having passed the preliminary exams of the Institute of Chartered Accountants in England and Wales in 1909, as an articled clerk in his father's office, his career aspirations seemed to point in one direction only.

Maj. Charles Chapman, MC, on horseback. (Chapman Family Archive)

Two years later, in 1911, the 29-year-old Charles was commissioned, after War Office approval, as a second lieutenant in the 4th Northumbrian (County of Durham) Howitzer Brigade of the Royal Field Artillery. This was a unit of the Territorial Force, formed in 1908 following the Territorial and Reserve Forces Act of 1907, which was one of the successful initiatives of Richard Haldane, Secretary of State for War, who carried out major reforms of the British Army.[13] The purpose was to provide a Home Defence Army organised in field divisions and with coastal artillery units close to naval bases and defended ports, as on Tyneside. During peacetime the units, all manned by part-time volunteers, would train with the armaments they would use in war, and they would be ready for rapid mobilisation should hostilities break out.

A Territorial Force gunner (a 'Terrier') like Charles would enlist initially for four years, and be obliged to perform twenty drills a year and attend fifteen days' annual training in camp (during which time he would be paid). The priority was home defence, though Terriers could volunteer to serve overseas in times of war. Charles' brigade consisted of a small headquarters, at the drill hall in Bolingbroke Street, South Shields, and two batteries. The 4th Durham Battery (which absorbed what had originally been the 3rd Durham Volunteer Artillery) was also quartered at South Shields, together with the brigade's ammunition column, while the 5th Durham Battery was based up river at Hebburn. As for armaments, the brigade had to make do with the 5in BL howitzer, which being 'a weapon of a certain age and dignity' was already outdated.[14]

Charles was very enthusiastic about his involvement and was soon devoting practically all his spare time to the unit. Training included horsemanship, and a riding school was opened in Bolingbroke Street in 1912 by no less a personage than Lord Haldane (ennobled the previous year). In the following year Charles was promoted to lieutenant shortly after a visit to the brigade's drill hall by Lt Gen. Sir Herbert Plumer, head of Northern Command. The summer camp was held at Redcar on Teesside and at Buddan, near Dundee in Scotland. Charles sent a postcard to his mother, in which he referred to an artillery competition: 'Glorious weather. We have had a very successful Camp, but have lost the Cup. Charlie.'

The summer camp in June 1914 was closer to home – at Bellingham and Redesdale in Northumberland, appropriately enough since the brigade was under the command of the Northumbrian Division (later known as the 50th Division), part of the Territorial Army. It had three

infantry brigades (the local one being the Durham Light Infantry), three
field artillery brigades and one howitzer brigade (in which Charles
served), one battery of Royal Garrison artillery (so-called 'Heavies'),
two field companies and one signal company of Royal Engineers, three
field ambulances, and four companies of horsed transport of the Army
Service Corps (Transport and Supply). There were around 20,000 men
in total and as a typical Army division, 'it was in effect a complete and
self-contained fighting force'.[15]

The summer camp had no sooner finished when, on 28 June 1914,
Archduke Franz Ferdinand of Austria-Hungary was murdered in Sarajevo,
and the countdown to the First World War began. On 3 August, Charles
left the annual Westoe Lawn Tennis Club tournament in a hurry, all
Northumbrian Division units having received orders to report to their
respective headquarters – in Charles' case just a mile down the road in
Bolingbroke Street. At about 5 p.m. on 4 August, the expected telegram,
'mobilise', was received. Charles was now 'embodied', meaning that he was
on full-time active service. By 5 August, most of the officers and men of
the 4th Northumbrian Howitzer Brigade had reported to their drill halls
in Hebburn and South Shields, and, in accordance with Army procedures,
mobilisation was proclaimed. This was no mean feat, since, for Artillery
Brigades, previously catalogued and requisitioned horses had to be brought
in, ammunition had to be collected, sorted and packed into limbers[16] and
wagons, and new harnesses had to be fitted to horses and mules.

Before dark on 5 August, Charles and the 4th Durham Battery (commanded by his elder brother, Maj. Robert Chapman), the ammunition
column (under Capt. C.W. Brims) and headquarters staff had marched off
from South Shields to a camping ground at Hebburn. As expected, all members of the brigade agreed to serve overseas. By the middle of September
the whole brigade, under Lt Col Stockley, had moved to Newcastle, where
it was encamped on the edge of the Town Moor. Officers and men lived in
tents until November – when Charles Chapman was promoted to temporary captain – and then in billets in nearby West Jesmond.

In December 1914, it became clear that there would be direct attacks
on Britain itself, in addition to campaigns abroad. Imperial German Navy
warships shelled Scarborough and Whitby in Yorkshire and, closer to home,
Hartlepool on the County Durham coast, where Charles' brother Dr Fred
Chapman had moved several years earlier. The naval bombardment of the
town killed 130 civilians and military personnel, wounding a further 500.

These attacks reinforced the importance of the training, including 'sham fights' and route marches, which Charles' brigade and other units of the Northumbrian (50th) Division were undertaking from their Newcastle base. This heightened military activity and awareness did not preclude taking advantage of 'ample opportunities for small dinner parties in nearby restaurants and visits to the local music hall',[17] and no doubt also to the many variety theatres in the city.

Those social diversions could not, however, hide the fact that the brigade's training in actual gun practice was as limited as its ordnance was outdated. Certainly, officers such as Charles and many of the longer-serving men had experience of shooting practice at annual camps, 'but there were quite a number whose only familiarity with gun-fire before leaving for the Front was a two-day brigade visit to Salisbury Plain where each battery fired a few rounds at easy targets to accustom the gun detachments to artillery fire'.[18] As for the guns themselves, the brigade had hoped to be equipped with the modern 4.5in QF howitzer. However, hopes were dashed and the gunners were stuck with their obsolete 5in BL howitzers.

Those were the guns they took with them when – to use the military description – they entrained at Newcastle on 19 April 1915, bound first for Southampton, where they embarked on the *Anglo-Canadian* for Havre, arriving the next day. Having collected their stores from its vast ordnance depot, they travelled again by troop train ('with its exhilarating rush through the air at the rate of at least eight miles an hour!'),[19] reaching the French town of Hazebrouck, south-west of the Belgian towns of Poperinghe and Ypres, on 22 April. These towns would become all too well known to the troops as 'Pop' and 'Wipers', respectively.

A few days earlier, the Second Battle of Ypres had begun, with a German push to try to break what was already a stalemate on the Western Front. On the evening of the 22nd itself, after a violent bombardment by German heavy howitzers, 'British officers … observed two curious clouds of a greenish-yellow tint creeping slowly along the ground on either side of Langemarck from the German lines … [and which] took on the appearance of a light mist enveloping the French positions.'[20] This was chlorine gas, 168 tons of it, released across a 3½-mile front.

The positions had to be abandoned:

…along the roads leading to Ypres, and to the western bank of the Yser Canal, came crowds of coughing, gasping and suffocating French

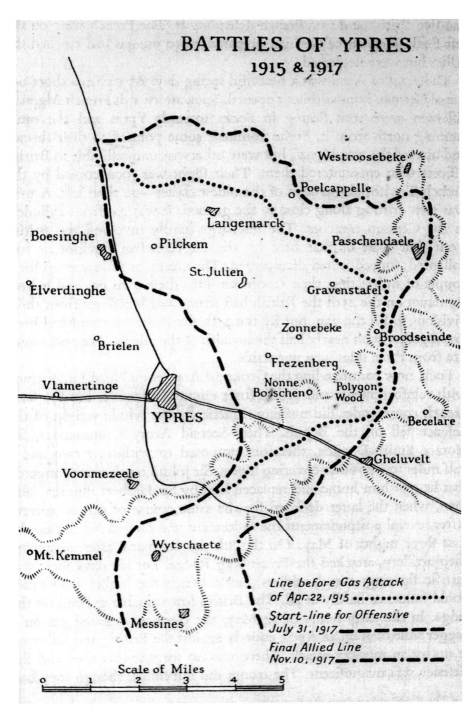

BATTLES OF YPRES
1915 & 1917

Westroosebeke

Poelcappelle

Langemarck

Passchendaele

Boesinghe

○ Pilckem

St.Julien

Gravenstafel

Elverdinghe

Zonnebeke
○

Broodseinde

Brielen
○

Frezenberg
○

Vlamertinge
○

Nonne
Boschen ○

Polygon
Wood

YPRES

Becelare
○

Voormezeele

Gheluvelt

Line before Gas Attack
of Apr. 22, 1915 ••••••••••••••

Mt. Kemmel
○

Wytschaete

Start-line for Offensive
July 31, 1917 ▄ ▄ ▄ ▄ ▄

Final Allied Line
Nov. 10, 1917 ▄•▄•▄•▄•▄

Messines

Scale of Miles

0   1   2   3   4   5

Map of Battles of Ypres, 1915 and 1917. (Cyril Falls, *The First World War* [London, 1960])

Territorials and Colonials, staggering along in awful agony, many falling by the wayside, dying there and then in terrible pain. Across country galloped transport and gun teams, all bent upon putting as great a distance as possible between themselves and that ghastly death cloud.[21]

Fortunately, the Germans did not have enough resources to exploit the 4-mile break in the line, and their troops, who wore no respirators, were not surprisingly afraid of trying to advance quickly. Meanwhile, the magnificent Canadian Division held their ground on the French right, allowing British and Indian reinforcements to be brought up. The enemy was repulsed, some sort of line was formed, and the situation was saved.

As for the 50th Northumberland Division, its artillery units – including Charles and Robert Chapman and the 4th Durhams – arrived in nearby Caëstre on 23 April 1915. With the exception of a field ambulance unit, the division saw no active service in this stage of the battle, and had time to settle down rather comfortably:

Those first billets of ours at Caëstre were all that the heart of a warrior could desire. The officers all had beds and rooms to themselves, or at least not more than two or three to a room, and the men found themselves, in many cases literally, in clover. We fed at the Café Françoise of excellent memory, where the fair Agnes presided with inimitable grace.[22]

However, the luxuries were short-lived, as was the Café Françoise itself, which was shelled out of existence before the end of the war. Records do not reveal the fate of 'fair Agnes'.

On the night of 5 May 1915, Capt. Charles Chapman and Capt. K. Anderson were sent forward to report to the CRA (Commander, Royal Artillery) of the 28th Divisional Artillery, under whom they were to serve for the time being, and shortly afterwards the 4th Northumbrian Howitzer Brigade was ordered to move through Ypres and reconnoitre the position in the area of what became known as 'Hellfire Corner' on the Menin Road. They encountered harrowing scenes:

Old men and women were trudging away from the flame-encircled town, refugees were wheeling their few pitiable effects in barrows and tumbledown perambulators, and little children were clinging in fright to their mothers' skirts … intermingled with ambulances carrying blood-stained men. In Ypres itself, which resembled a huge bonfire, the cathedral was on fire …. (and) shells were bursting everywhere.[23]

On the evening of 6 May the batteries advanced and went into action, being the first Territorial field gunners to take part in the Ypres fighting. Charles' 4th Battery was positioned just north of the Menin Road and 3,000yd east of Ypres when the Germans attacked Frezenberg the following day. The battery nearly ran out of shells, which at this stage of the war were in extremely short supply, amounting on average to no more than three rounds per gun per day across the brigade as a whole. So the battery was instructed to withdraw to the wagon line of its ammunitions column, where it came under intense shellfire for the next fortnight.

Fortunately there was a peaceful interlude, with no German shelling, on Whit Sunday, 23 May, when:

> … the 4th Durham Battery held its first church service in a little ruined cottage where normally Gunner Mackay, of South Shields, exercised his culinary art. Major [Robert] Chapman – the C.O. – read a chapter from his Bible and, after prayers, the hymn "Jesu, lover of my soul" was sung by the assembled company.[24]

During the service, the thoughts of Charles and Robert may well have turned to their brother-in-law Wallace Annand, killed a year earlier in the Gallipoli campaign. The interlude was brief, as the Germans made a heavy gas attack along the divisional front the next day, and the 4th Durham Battery found itself firing at 1,200yd range – nearer the enemy line than any other in the divisional artillery. The 4th Durhams distinguished themselves, and at the end of May the General Officer Commanding the 50th Division, Major-General Sir W.F.L. Lindsay, conveyed to all its ranks his 'keen appreciation of the work done by them during the recent fighting, work which was carried out under very trying and arduous conditions'.[25]

Charles continued to play an important role as Forward Observing (or Observation) Officer, FOO for short. The men undertaking this task with him were usually one or more signallers, equipped with telescopes, flash-spotters and voice tubes. They would go into the front-line area with field telephones and find a location where they could observe and report the effects of their own battery's shellfire. Needless to say, this was extremely dangerous work. During this period news from home travelled slowly, and

Charles and his colleagues would not have known about the Zeppelin (airship) raid by the Imperial German Naval Air Service, in which five high-explosive and incendiary bombs were dropped on South Shields on 15 June. Fortunately damage was slight.

The following day, on 16 June 1915, the 4th Battery was heavily engaged in supporting the 3rd Division's attack on Bellewaarde Ridge near Ypres, which was later officially called the First Battle of Bellewaarde. The brigade's war diary for that day records that 'Capt. C. L. Chapman was recommended for the DSO (Distinguished Service Order) medal for his excellent work as FOO. He sent in many valuable and accurate reports of the enemy's and our own movements.'[26] Charles was also mentioned in a despatch by Field Marshal Sir John French. He did not, in the event, receive a DSO, but the recommendation probably led to him being awarded the Military Cross in the New Year's Honours List of 1916. The 'small operation' to take Bellewaarde Ridge failed. It resulted in the capture of the German front line only, not the whole ridge, and the 50th (Northumbrian) Division alone lost 'about ninety all ranks'.[27]

The brigade was subsequently instructed to move from the Ypres Salient to the Mont Kemmel area, which was 'quiet', but only by comparison with the devastation of recent battles:

> ...although there may have been no attack on, or by, the enemy in pro-gress, the artillery for both sides was seldom silent; snipers were busy, watching like hungry wolves for the thoughtless exposure of heads or bodies; trench-mortar bombs and grenades exploded in the trenches; mining and sapping were going on; mines were 'blown'.[28]

After a month at Kemmel the brigade was in action for three months at Armentières, astride the river Lys on the Franco-Belgian border. During that period, in October 1915, Charles decided – no doubt after much reflection and discussion with his brother and Commanding Officer Robert – that he wanted to have a career in the Army, not as a chartered accountant. So he applied for a permanent commission in the Royal Artillery. It was a very formal, paperwork-heavy, protracted process. Extraordinarily enough, or per-haps simply indicating Army administrative efficiency, the records still exist.

Among the several dozen pages of documents was his original application of 1911 for a commission in the Territorial Force. He was able to answer 'yes' to the first two questions (the second of which exemplified the Imperial

world view of the time): 'Are you a British subject by birth or naturali-
sation?'; and 'Are you of pure European descent?' In the 1915 application
for a permanent commission he had to pass tests of health, horsemanship
and 'moral character'. The medical board found him a fit man, 5ft 9in high,
with a chest girth of 38in, weighing 12 stone. His hearing, teeth and vision
were good. He was 'suitable for a permanent commission in the Royal
Artillery'. As for equestrian skills, Lt Col Stockley, Royal Field Artillery, the
Commander of the 4th Northumbrian Howitzer Brigade, certified that 'I
have seen Capt. C. L. Chapman ride, and am of the opinion that he is an
efficient horseman.' For the moral character test, Charles relied again on
his 1911 application to become a 'Terrier'. His father Henry's close friend,
Alderman Joseph M. Rennoldson, in his role as a Justice of the Peace for
the County of Durham, certified 'to the good character of Charles Lancelot
Chapman for the last nineteen years, i.e. during all his life'.

So far, so good. Even better, Charles was given a quite outstanding
reference from the then Brig. Gen. Herbert Uniacke, General Officer
Commander, Royal Artillery, of the 5th Corps:

> I consider Temporary Captain C. L. Chapman to be exceptionally fitted
> to receive a regular commission in the RFA (Royal Field Artillery) and
> I most strongly recommend him. He is an officer of the very best stamp,
> fitted even now not only to take his place as a Section Commander, but
> actually to command a battery in the field. He is so remarkably qualified
> that I consider his case should be made a special one.

Despite this glowing report from one of the most important artillery
officers of the war, Charles was turned down. The reason for the decision is not clear. Brig. Gen. Uniache's note referred to Charles having
applied for a regular commission immediately on the outbreak of hostilities, 'but nothing was heard of this application, which was forwarded
to the War Office'. The note also hinted that recently recruited younger
officers seemed to be receiving priority, which the brigadier general
thought was unfair. Perhaps his implied criticism hit a raw nerve at the
War Office. Be that as it may, Charles would reapply a year later.

In early December 1915, after a month's rest, the 4th Northumbrian
Howitzer Brigade was moved up again to the Ypres front. Charles' 4th
Durham Battery still had its obsolete and limited-range 15-pounders,
which were outgunned by the German artillery. Only the 1st

Northumbrian Artillery Brigade were fortunate enough, at Armentières, to have been provided with the new 18-pounders and 4.5in howitzers. No wonder, when the orders arrived and the trek back to the Salient began, the comment was 'Well, back to Hell, boys.'[29] The artillerymen knew all too well that the:

> Infantry, magnificent though they were, had but two or three days in (the) front line at a time, and then they were moved back to reserve or to rest, whilst the Gunners were constantly in action, week after week, for four and a half solid months of daily shelling, mud, cold, stink and dirt.[30]

But at least they now had plenty of ammunition.

The sector of the line allotted to the 50th Division ran from south-west of Hill 60, almost to the Menin Road. The artillery batteries' sites were not very far from those they originally held seven months earlier, except that they had subsequently become a mass of pollution and filth. It was difficult, even for military historians, to convey just how awful conditions were:

> Ypres at this juncture beggars description. The area between the shel-tered town and the German trenches to the east of it was scarred and eroded as if blasted by some Titanic fury. Roads were obliterated, blown into nothingness … They had been replaced by a series of duck-boards, sodden with rain and sludge, which spanned the oozing quagmires and linked together the water-logged crumbling craters. The town itself was moribund: nothing moved, nothing lived. The silence was only broken by the sound of interminable gun-fire and the detonation of high explo-sive. Ypres was a charnel-house of horror and devastation.[31]

Charles and his artillery colleagues were heavily engaged in January 1916, again performing with great effectiveness against 'the Bosch', whose guns were far more numerous and much more powerful, and who were now firing 5.9in phosphorous shells. The Commander Royal Artillery of the Division sent a message on 23 January to the brigade commander:

> Will you please convey to Captain Chapman, the BSM (Battery Sergeant Major) and two telephonists of 4th Durham Battery my appreciation of their cool and gallant conduct on the afternoon of 22 January in maintaining the fire of their battery in support of our infantry when the

telephone station was under heavy shell fire. I should like their names noted for a mention in despatches.[32]

In the early months of 1916, there were additional problems for the artillery and infantry summarised laconically in the Divisional General Staff Diary on 18 March 2016: 'Germans held complete command of the air over 50th Divisional front and observed our dispositions at their pleasure.'[33] In April, this air superiority had devastating results for Charles' fellow officers and men in the 151st Brigade: 'With four aeroplanes observing and registering targets the German guns fairly plastered the whole area and the whole of Brigade Headquarters dug-outs at Zillebeke were blown in.'[34] Casualties were severe.

Charles' final war service was not, however, to be with the 4th Durhams, or indeed with the 50th Division. On 14 May 1916 he received orders to return to England to command a second-line battery, and was formally promoted to captain on 1 June 1916. After four months' training he joined the new 529 (Howitzer Battery) of the Territorial Force, as second in command, and sailed with it from Southampton on 2 October, arriving at Havre two days later. He did not, however, return to the 50th (Northumbrian) Division, where his brother Robert was still serving, but was instead posted to the 36th (Ulster) Division. In January 1917 he joined 'D' (Howitzer) Battery of 173 Brigade Royal Field Artillery, a unit of the Ulster Division, and in early March he was made its Commanding Officer and promoted to acting major.

Charles' battery was engaged in artillery support for the meticulously planned attack to capture the long ridge running south from Ypres to Armentières, through the villages of Wytschaete and Messines. The initial aim was to 'straighten out' the Ypres Salient and take the high ground that commanded the British defences and rear areas to the north. The Ulster Division was tasked with taking the strong points of Lumm Farm, and Staenyzer Cabaret, just to the south-east of Wytschaete itself. From those new positions, if successfully captured, Field Marshal Lord Haig planned to launch his 'Northern Operation' – an advance to Passchendaele Ridge, and from there, in conjunction with landings from the sea, to the Belgian coast in order to clear Ostend and Zeebrugge of the highly effective German submarines and surface raiders based there.

Sappers, with help from coal-miners, had dug tunnels to lay twenty-one mines, and the largest concentration of artillery in the entire war had been assembled. The preliminary bombardment of what would become known as the Battle of Messines began on 31 May 1917 and continued for a week. Then, at 3 o'clock in the morning of 7 June:

> …with one monstrous roar, every British gun upon ten miles of front opened fire. At the same time the great semi-circle of mines exploded, spewing up, as it seemed, the solid earth, of which fragments fell half a mile away, and sending to the skies great towers of crimson flame [which were] choked by the clouds of dense black smoke which followed them from their caverns. There came first one ghastly flash of light, then a shuddering of earth thus outraged, then the thunderclap.[35]

The noise of the exploding mines was so loud that it was heard, quite distinctly, in England.

The scale of the resulting devastation was enormous. Some 400 tons of ammonal explosive were used, killing perhaps as many as 10,000 German defenders on the ridge. 'Witnesses reported clods the size of houses thrown up. When the debris settled, the "diameter of complete obliteration" was, on average, twice that of the blast craters themselves, the largest of which measured nearly 100 yards wide and 20 deep.'[36] No wonder the Ulster Division's General Nugent described the scene from his observation post as a 'vision of hell'.[37] The division's infantry assault was then unleased, supported very effectively by its artillery batteries. Indeed, Charles' 173 Brigade succeeded in moving far forward of the original 'No Man's Land'. Within forty-eight hours, despite vigorous resistance by German machine gun units, the British controlled the entire battlefield and had met all their objectives. The fortress of the Messines Ridge, including Wytschaete itself, had been captured. The cost to the division was 700 men killed.

After this exceptionally well-executed battle, Charles had a spell of home leave, between 21 June and 1 July 1917. His father Henry no doubt asked him whether he had had any news about his second application for a permanent commission, which had been submitted the previous November. Charles had heard nothing, and did not know that the application was being viewed favourably. Before the end of July, Charles would be 'Recommended by the Field Marshal Commander-in-Chief British Armies in France, for appointment to a permanent commission in the regular army'. A handwritten note on his application file read 'Selected for RFA. Submit to King'. Charles' dream of adopting soldiering in the Royal Field Artillery as his profession looked as if it were about to come true. It was just a matter of waiting for the final formality of approval from King George V himself, followed by an announcement in the *London Gazette*. Fate, however, had other plans.

Charles had fought with the 50th (Northumbrian) Division in the Second Battle of Ypres, notably at Bellewaarde. Now he was poised to fight with the 36th (Ulster) Division in the Third Battle of Ypres (commonly, but inaccurately, called Passchendaele). On 30 July 1917 the Ulster Division established

HM King George V on Wytschaete Ridge during a tour of the Western Front, 4 July 1917. (© Imperial War Museum [Q 5586])

its temporary headquarters in Poperinghe (seven miles west of Ypres), and the main British offensive began the next day. The headquarters of the brigades were in the 'filth and stenches of Wieltje dug-outs' and conditions both inside and outside were dreadful. The infantry were in action in continuous rain, with mud 18in deep and under continuous fire from howitzers of heavy calibre.

The division was preparing for what would be called the Battle of Langemarck, which started on 16 August. Its battalions were charged with taking the Gallipoli and Schulerfarm strongpoints, and the line between them, but the omens were extremely unpropitious:

> Gas shelling and aeroplane bombing were at their height. The infantry resting in the camps between Vlamertinghe and Elverdinghe had to endure, night after night, the crashing of great bombs among the huts and tents. The casualties to horses were very high, a horse being ten times as vulnerable as a man to bombs. The Casualty Clearing Stations probably suffered higher losses than in any other battle of the war. The counter-battery work was ferocious on both sides. For our batteries

The Third Battle of Ypres: manhandling an 18-pounder field gun through the mud near Langemarck, 16 October 1917. (© Imperial War Museum [Q 3007]).

there was little concealment, and for their guns and teams little shelter. The gunners of the 36th Division, who had been in action … for over a month, suffered from strain and discomfort perhaps even more severely than the infantry on this occasion. And day after day, the rain fell.[38]

After three days of fierce fighting the attack failed: the infantry were exhausted; weather conditions remained atrocious; the German artillery fired from dominant positions and had the greater gun power; the German machine guns in strongly fortified and carefully sited concrete structures ('pillboxes') were highly effective. And, unlike at Messines, preparation had been grossly inadequate. In fact, 'This action was the only attack made by the 36th Division which suffered complete reverse', with heavy casualties.[39]

Artillery fire from both sides continued remorselessly after the infantry attacks had failed, and Charles Chapman was himself very badly wounded, almost certainly by a shell explosion, on 19 or 20 August (the brigade's war diary for this period is missing). He would have received initial treatment at a forward area aid post, then been moved to a dressing station near Ypres itself, probably by motor ambulance. From there he would have been transferred to an ambulance train for the 10-mile journey to 2 Canadian

Casualty Clearing Station at Rémy Farm, Lijssenthoek, south-west of Poperinghe. He died there as a result of his wounds on 22 August 1917, aged 25, and is buried in Lijssenthoek Cemetery immediately adjacent to Rémy Farm. This cemetery developed from small plots in 1914/15 into the second largest military cemetery on the Western Front. Some 9,901 British and Commonwealth servicemen, together with 883 French and German service personnel, are buried there.

Charles' grieving parents, Henry and Dora, would have received some consolation from a letter sent to them in early September 1917 from his former 4th Durham Battery comrades in arms. Each of 'The Old Boys who are left' signed the letter personally.[40] It was rather moving:

Maj. Charles Chapman's gravestone at Lijssenthoek Cemetery, photographed in June 2017, the centenary year of his death. (© Joan Chapman)

To Mr & Mrs Henry Chapman
Seacroft, Westoe
South Shields

4/9/17

We, the remainder of the old Battery, beg to tender our deepest sympathy in the loss of your son, our old Captain. We always followed his movements after leaving us to take command of another Battery, as we were so proud of him. It was with sincere sorrow the boys read of his death in the Shields Gazette, which the Editor kindly sends out to us. He was admired by all ranks for his fearlessness in action, and with him the boys would go anywhere. We will always remember him with regret as a real Englishman and fine Officer who died for his country.

Yours sincerely

The Old Boys who are left

N.C.O's	Gunners	Drivers
BQM Sergt. W. Dunnington	E.H. Whipp	Driver J. Wood
Sgt. H. Urquhart	J. Myers	Dr. C. Scott
Bom. John T. Jackson	W. Common, Cpl.	Dr. J.R. Heywood
Br. R. Spence	T. Martin, Bom	Dr. W. Gracie
Br. W. Martin	T. Thirlwell	J. W. Dougal
Bom. J. Morton	J. Lawson, Gunner	Driver G. Atkinson
F. Wilson, Corp.	G. Dickinson	Driver R. Dodds
J. Lillie, Corp.	C. Wilkinson	Dr. A. N. Anderson
Farr. Q.M.S. A. Robertson	Br. R. Bught	Dr. R. Hush
Bom. T. Miller	Gr. R. Coltman	Dr. M. Robson
Saddler Sergt. T. W. Lyall	W. Little	Dr. J. Hill
Dr. A. Lamb	C. Dunn, Sgt.	F. Robe
Dr. J. Smith	J.C.S. Bullen, Sgt.	J. W. Knight
Corp. C. Napier		
Cpr. Hogan		
Sergt. A. Lain		

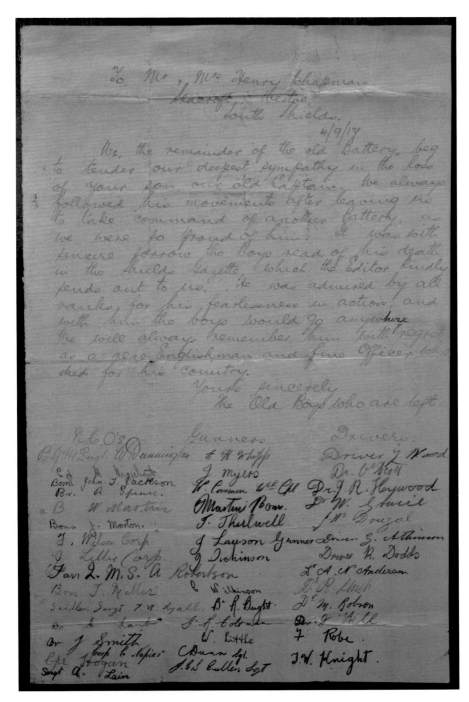

Letter to Mr and Mrs Henry Chapman from 'The Old Boys who are left',
4 September 1917. (Chapman Family Archive)

Dorothy Chapman, Voluntary Aid Detachment nurse. (Chapman Family Archive)

Recruiting poster for Voluntary Aid Detachment nurses. Egypt, where Dorothy Chapman would serve, is highlighted in the top right-hand panel. (© Imperial War Museum [Art. IWM PST 3268])

Dorothy Chapman

Marion Dorothy – always known simply as Dorothy – had to make an important decision in the late spring of 1915. Two of her brothers (Robert and Charles) were artillery officers with the 4th Northumbrian (County of Durham) Howitzer Brigade in Flanders. Another brother (Fred) was a temporary surgeon with the Royal Navy and about to move to the Royal Army Medical Corps. Her brother-in-law (Wallace Moir Annand) had joined the Royal Naval Division and expectations were high that he would soon be involved in the Gallipoli campaign. How could she best contribute to the war effort?

She decided to become a Voluntary Aid Detachment nurse with the Order of St John of Jerusalem, no doubt influenced by Robert, who had just become an Honorary Serving Brother with the Order. Its long and distinguished history could be traced back to the Crusades of the twelfth century, when the Knights Hospitallers of St John of Jerusalem formed a new order, which also comprised priests and lay brethren. Its mission was to provide

nursing and spiritual care with military protection. The order was the first
of its kind, and is seen as the forerunner of military nursing services.

The order was revived in the nineteenth century, and the St John
Ambulance Association was formed under its auspices in 1877, receiving a Royal Charter from Queen Victoria in 1888. Its role expanded
significantly both before and during the First World War. Two years after
the Territorial and Reserve Forces Act of 1907, 'In order to provide a
personnel which would be able to supplement the Military Medical
Organisation of the Territorial Force on home service, the War Office in
1909 issued a "Scheme for the Organisation of Voluntary Aid in England
and Wales".'[41] Under this scheme, which was developed further a year later,
the County Territorial Associations were encouraged to form Voluntary
Aid Detachments, of men and of women. How were they to carry out
this new role effectively in addition to their other home defence responsibilities? The War Office issued clear guidance: County Associations were
'empowered and recommended to delegate the formation and organisation of detachments to the British Red Cross Society'. However, they
had considerable discretion and the guidance explained that a brigade or
county company of the St John Ambulance Association 'may be regarded
as equivalent in every respect to a voluntary aid detachment'.[42]

Each nursing Voluntary Aid Detachment (VAD) was expected to con-
sist of a commandant (man or woman), a quartermaster (man or woman),
a lady superintendent, who should be a trained nurse, and twenty women,
four of whom should be qualified cooks. Volunteers soon became known
as VADs. They were taught first aid and home nursing, on which they were
examined, and many received tuition in hygiene and cookery. They were
supposed to have some hospital experience ('training in an infirmary'),
but in many areas this was not easy to accomplish since VADs were either
not at first taken seriously, or regarded as a threat by the nursing profession, or both. Tyneside hospitals were more welcoming: the Royal Victoria
Infirmary (RVI) in Newcastle 'provided a month's training for VAD nurses
before they took up their formal rotas to supplement the qualified nursing
staff in hospitals'.[43] And given the close links between some of the South
Shields families whose daughters became VAD nurses and the Ingham
Infirmary – Dorothy Chapman's father, Henry, had been Chairman of its
General Committee and was a friend and near neighbour of the President,
Sir James Readhead – it is not surprising that similar training, on the RVI
model, was provided there too.

In the pre-war period it was assumed that the role of the detachments would be confined to home service in the event of an outbreak of hostilities – forming railway rest stations where meals and refreshments for sick and wounded servicemen could be prepared and served, and taking temporary charge of severe cases unable to continue their journey. However, with war looming, there was an order of magnitude change in their responsibilities: 'Detachments were instructed to be ready on mobilisation to set up and staff a sixty-bed hospital. In the summer of 1914, the War Office issued lists of everything that had to be provided including the actual building.'[44] These hospitals were called 'Auxiliary Home Hospitals', and, after the outbreak of war, they were established in all counties, under the control of county

Nursing staff at the Mill Dam VAD Hospital, South Shields, October 1914. (Courtesy and © Patrick Brennan. See also www.donmouth.co.uk/local_history/ VAD/VAD_hospitals.html)

directors for Voluntary Aid Detachments. In October 1914, by which time the scale of voluntary assistance to the sick and wounded had become much greater than anticipated, a Joint War Committee of the British Red Cross Society and the Order of St John of Jerusalem in England was formed, so that resources could be pooled and administration simplified. This committee (which subsequently set up a dedicated Joint Women's VAD Committee) oversaw the activities of the county directors.

The Durham County director, appointed jointly by the Territorial Force Association and the British Red Cross Society, was Col Claude Palmer, fifth son of the Jarrow shipbuilder and businessman, Sir Charles Palmer. He became responsible for twenty-eight hospitals, including the 2nd Durham VA Hospital in Holborn House, Mill Dam, South Shields, the 10th Durham VA Hospital in Jarrow, and the 18th Durham VA Hospital Wing in Hebburn Hall, Hebburn-on-Tyne. There was a certain irony in Holborn House becoming a British auxiliary home hospital at the end of August 1914, since it could trace its origins back to the German Seamen's Mission Committee, set up in 1880 to look after German immigrants in South Shields and German sailors visiting the Tyne. The mission started building Holborn House as a German Seamen's Home in 1909. Once war was declared the mission was closed and the Joint War Committee turned the building into a VAD hospital.

In 1915, Dorothy, having no doubt had training at the Ingham Infirmary, joined the staff of the Mill Dam Hospital, fitting neatly a typical description of a VAD nurse: 'She is the daughter of a clergyman, a lawyer or a prosperous businessman, and has been privately educated and groomed to be a "lady".'[45] As it turned out, these young women made an extraordinarily valuable contribution to the war effort, both at home and, once restrictions were lifted, abroad. The Mill Dam Hospital had fifty beds when it was set up at the end of August 1914, supported by twenty-two VADs from South Shields and Tynemouth. By March 1915 272 patients had been treated. It later expanded to seventy beds. The trained staff were a matron and three sisters, with a visiting masseuse, and five VADs, typically part-time, working in shifts. There were also volunteers in the kitchens, including Dorothy's sister-in-law Hélène Chapman, wife of Robert. The patients came from No. 1 Northern General Hospital in Newcastle (housed in Armstrong College, which had been requisitioned by the War Office) and from local barracks.[46]

After service at Mill Dam Hospital, Dorothy moved to Alnwick. Here, the Duchess of Northumberland's School in Bailiffgate had become the

8/Northumberland VA Hospital. This was transferred to Alnwick Camp in April 1916, and became the Alnwick Military Convalescent Hospital, where Dorothy would have served. It was one of a new wave of military hospitals set up to keep recovering soldiers under military control. Alnwick was for men from Northern and Scottish Commands, men whose homes were in Scotland or who belonged to Scottish regiments from any Command.[47]

Towards the end of 1916, Dorothy decided that she wanted to serve overseas. This had been an option for twelve months or so, since in the autumn of 1915:

> All reservations about sending VADs on active service were swept aside ... anyone who had three months' hospital experience at home, and were twenty-three or over, would have the chance to go abroad – either to hospitals in France or to join the harassed, overworked, trained Sisters and nurses who were struggling to care for the awful flood of sick and wounded from Gallipoli and Mesopotamia in hospitals in the Middle East.[48]

Dorothy's decision may have been prompted not only by the death of her brother-in-law Wallace Annand in Gallipoli, but also by discussions with her brother Charles in the summer of 1916 while he was in England for training as a battery commander before being sent back to the Western Front to provide artillery support for the Messines campaign. In any event, her staging post for service abroad was Lakenham Military Hospital in Norfolk, where she reported for duty sometime after January 1917. This large establishment had been the proposed Lakenham Council School, built by Norwich City Council in 1913 and due to receive its first pupils in August 1914. However, it was requisitioned by the Army Council and, equipped with 100 beds by the Norwich Division of the British Red Cross Society, it opened for the reception of wounded servicemen in November. It served as a military hospital throughout the war.

In the summer of 1917, Dorothy was told that she would be posted to the important military hospital base of Alexandria in Egypt to serve as a nurse in the 'Other Empire Force Voluntary Aid Detachment' at 17th General Hospital. The Order of St John of Jerusalem was very much an international organisation: 'Contingents of V.A.D. men and women come from every corner of the British Empire. Some of the latest Detachments to be utilized at the Front are those supplied from within the Empire of India for service in Mesopotamia.'[49] So it was no surprise that they would also feature prominently in Alexandria, which was the headquarters of Col Sir Courtauld Thomson, the Chief Commissioner of what was laboriously described as the 'British Red Cross and Order of St. John, Malta, Egypt and Near East Commission'.

The journey from Britain to Alexandria was hazardous, to say the least:

> The most usual route was overland to Marseilles and thence by P&O or French Messageries Maritimes; but when the activities of enemy submarines made that route dangerous we sent our personnel across Italy to Taranto, and thence by steamer to Malta, Salonika or Egypt, as the case might be.[50]

Dorothy arrived safely in Alexandria in October, but two months later, several large groups of nurses travelling on the troopship *Aragon* to Alexandria had a traumatic experience. They had travelled via Boulogne and Marseilles, and the *Aragon* called first at Malta on its three-week journey to Egypt. One of the nurses was Sister Burgess whose detailed diary covered the journey. She recounted the final two days:

> Friday, 28 December (1917) left Malta about 4.30 pm yesterday. Feeling rather faint in the evening but went to bed and ate dry biscuits and feel much better this am. Premonition!!
>
> Captain Somerville insists on me wearing his pneumatic waistcoat which is easier to carry than the ordinary lifebelt supplied by the ships. He wouldn't accept a refusal.

> Sunday, 30 December:
> We have been torpedoed this am. Cannot write more just now except that we are safe at Alexandria 21st General Hospital.

Sister Burgess was 'One of many rescued, probably by a trawler, before the torpedoed troopship *Aragon* sank. During the rescue operation the destroyer, HMS *Attack* struck a mine and sank. Over 600 sailors and soldiers were drowned.'[51]

Dorothy found that 17th General Hospital was based in what had been Victoria College before the war. It was a splendid building housing a school run along British 'public school' lines, opened by Queen Victoria's son, Prince Arthur, Duke of Connaught, in 1906. After the outbreak of war in 1914 it was requisitioned by the British High Command and became the headquarters of the Corps Expéditionnaire d'Orient. A few months later it became 17th General (Military) Hospital.[52] This hospital, and the other military hospitals in Alexandria, had played an important role throughout the Gallipoli campaign. At the outset, all casualties were brought by hospital ship to Alexandria – a distance of 700 miles. Initially, conditions in the hospitals were grim, and nurses were faced with daunting challenges, to put it mildly. During the campaign, Sister Cathy Mellor worked at 15th General Hospital in Alexandria, initially on the dysentery ward:

> They lie there in agony, night and day … Great strong men, young, looking as old as men of sixty years. I am not exaggerating at all. Several died while I was there, suffering terribly and conscious up to the last moment. One man from Scotland asked me to write to his mother and say, 'Alex was too weak to write'. That was the only message. It struck me as being just about enough to heartbreak her.[53]

Dorothy served for ten months at 17th General Hospital, from October 1917 to the summer of the following year. The nursing duties were onerous and exhausting, but serious efforts were made to provide opportunities and facilities for leisure and relaxation. In Alexandria – following a successful initiative in Cairo – the Red Cross opened a club for the exclusive use of Military and Red Cross Nursing Sisters and VAD members. Dorothy would have gone there in her Mediterranean Zone VAD outdoor uniform – 'a khaki or white linen jacket and skirt … with a white sola topi or soft panama hat with regulation ribbon and badge, and white or brown shoes and stockings'.[54] At the Nurses' Club in Alexandria, 'Lunches, teas and suppers and beds were provided at prices which compared favourably with restaurant charges.' Elsewhere – and no doubt in Alexandria too – 'Bathing parties and picnics were organised … camels and donkeys being used for transport, and tennis courts were in great request.'[55] Tragically, Dorothy would not have been able to enjoy whatever leisure pursuits were available for very long. Ten months after she arrived in Alexandria she was taken seriously ill, and died on 10 August 1918, just three months before Germany signed the Armistice at Compiègne in France. She was 27 years old. Her service record gives the cause of death as pneumonia, but she was

Dorothy Chapman was buried at the Hadra War Memorial Cemetery, Alexandria. (Commonwealth War Graves Commission)

Dorothy Chapman's headstone at Hadra War Memorial Cemetery. (The War Graves Photographic Project)

almost certainly an early victim of the influenza pandemic ('Spanish flu') which started sweeping through Europe and Africa in June, and which would eventually cause millions of deaths.

Be that as it may, surviving beyond the end of the war on 11 November 1918 was no guarantee of a long and healthy life: 'More than 400 VAD casualties died during or as a result of war service. A few were killed or drowned as a result of enemy action, but most died from exhaustion and/or influenza in the months following the end of the war. Many others suffered long term damage to their health.'[56] Theirs had been a noble and compassionate calling, on an ever-increasing scale. Immediately before the declaration of war, 6,773 women were serving in 241 Order of St John Voluntary Detachments. At the end of the war 24,440 women were serving in 713 detachments. An impressive achievement indeed.

Dorothy was buried at Hadra War Cemetery in Alexandria, close to the 17th General Hospital itself. Her name is also inscribed on the VAD Memorial screen in York Minster to members of the Order of St John and the British Red Cross who lost their lives on active service. This is one of the screens commemorating by name a total of 1,400 women, who are remembered collectively in the Five Sisters Memorial Window in the minster – the only memorial in the country to women of the British Empire who lost their lives during the First World War. Nearer to home, her parents Henry and Dora placed a plaque in her memory in the Church of St Michael and All Angels in Westoe.

Capt. Frederick Ernest Chapman, RAMC

Having qualified as a doctor at Durham University's College of Medicine, Fred Chapman moved to Hartlepool, where he was appointed house surgeon at Hartlepools Hospital in 1912. Immediately after the outbreak of war, on 5 August 1914, he became a surgeon 'for temporary service in His Majesty's Fleet', and was assigned to the steamship SS *Rohilla*. She had been commissioned from the shipbuilders Harland and Wolff of Belfast in 1905 by the British India Steam Navigation Company, and entered service as a passenger ship on the London to Calcutta service at the end of the following year. Her name had an appropriately Indian resonance to it, the Rohillas hailing from Rohilkhand in northern India, which passed to British control after the Mutiny of 1857. Her owners, conscious of a deteriorating climate in Europe, and of increased commercial competition, decided to design *Rohilla* so that she could easily be adapted as a troopship. This turned out to be a wise move sooner than they might have anticipated, since in 1908 she entered service as 'Troopship No. 6', and in 1910 had the distinction of carrying Members of the House of Commons in the Coronation Fleet Review, honouring King George V's accession to the throne.

At the outset of war *Rohilla* underwent a second change of course, becoming a hospital ship. Fred Chapman's medical service on her did not last long, and on 30 October 1914, sailing from South Queensferry in Scotland for Dunkerque to evacuate wounded soldiers, she ran aground on a reef a mile or so east of Whitby, on the North Yorkshire coast. There were eighty-three fatalities out of the 229 personnel on board. The survivors included the captain and all the nurses. The *Birmingham Mail* on 2 November carried the headline, 'Egbaston Doctor's Escape: Swam from the Wrecked Ship'. This was a reference to a Dr Hird, but the report added:

'Dr. F.E. Chapman, the England Rugby international three-quarter, who had volunteered for service, was a surgeon on the ill-fated ship. His name did not appear in the list of the saved.' Fortunately that was not the end of the story, which aroused widespread interest, given Fred's national sporting reputation. A few days later, the *Gloucester Echo* announced that:

> We are glad to learn on enquiry from his brother-in-law, Mr Sidney H. Smith, of Beech Cottage, Amberley [who married Hilda Chapman in 1905], that Dr. F. E. Chapman … was not on the ill-fated hospital ship *Rohilla*, wrecked at Filey. He was transferred to the *Neptune* some months ago, and he is, we are pleased to add, quite safe and well.

Fred's service on SS *Rohilla* could not, luckily for him, have lasted more than a few weeks.

HMS *Neptune* was an altogether different proposition. Built at Portsmouth, she was a Dreadnought-class battleship, heavily armoured and incorporating improvements in gun turret layout and operation. She had been commissioned in 1908 against a background of expanding German shipbuilding, which was causing alarm since Germany was by then providing for 'a vastly more powerful fleet and met our 1908 programme by laying down four keels to our two'.[57] In the event, Britain still had signifi-

HMS *Neptune*, a Dreadnought-class battleship in which Fred Chapman served as a surgeon. (George Grantham Bain Collection, Library of Congress)

cant naval superiority when war was declared, by which time *Neptune* had become the flagship of the Home Fleet. She was then transferred to the newly formed Grand Fleet's 1st Battle Squadron. Fred's period of service with her lasted around eight months, during which time her tasks involved North Sea patrols and training duties. He saw no naval action, and decided to apply to join the Royal Army Medical Corps. On 18 May 1915 he duly became an RAMC temporary lieutenant.

It is not uncommon for RAMC officers' service records to have been destroyed, and unfortunately Fred's no longer exist. However, he did serve initially at Gallipoli, probably arriving there shortly after his brother-in-law Wallace Annand had been killed. He was then transferred to the Western Front, where his brothers Robert and Charles were serving. He was promoted to temporary captain, and was reported in *The Times* of 26 July 1916 as having been wounded. *The Times* provided the further information that he was attached to the Queen's Own Royal West Kent Regiment, which at that time was heavily involved in the Battle of the Somme.

Fred's wounds were not serious, and if he stayed with the Queen's Own he would have been involved in the Somme campaign until November. He was again wounded slightly in February 1917, perhaps during the large raid against the German lines near Givenchy. There is no evidence that he returned to the North East before the end of the war, so he could well have continued his service with the Royal West Kent Regiment on the Western Front at least until the Armistice of November 1918.[58]

In any event, he resumed his medical practice in Hartlepool after being discharged, and was fit enough to play rugby for the Durham County First XV one last time, in November 1919.

Lt Col Robert Chapman, CMG, DSO, Croix de Chevalier

Robert developed a keen interest in artillery as a teenager and a few days after his twentieth birthday, in March 1900, he was commissioned as a second lieutenant in the 3rd Durham, Western Division, Royal Garrison Artillery (Volunteers). His commission, in the penultimate year of Queen Victoria's reign, bore her seal. Four years later he was promoted to captain and acting adjutant. He was clearly an up and coming young officer, and when his unit, in 1908, was renamed the 4th Durham (Howitzer) Battery

Lt Col Robert Chapman. (Chapman Family Archive)

and incorporated into the new 4th Northumbrian (County of Durham) Howitzer Brigade, Royal Field Artillery, Robert was promoted to major and appointed as the battery's Commanding Officer.

The battery, whose role since its formation had been coastal defence, was now to become mobile artillery for a field army. New training was necessary, and the process intensified at camps held in 1908 at Frenchman's Point in South Shields (to which General Robert Baden-Powell, then commander of the Northumbrian division of the Territorial Force, paid a visit) and at Fleetwood and Knott End in 1909. Two years later, in 1911, his younger brother Charles joined the battery as a second lieutenant, and they mobilised together on 4 August 1914. They would be artillery comrades for nearly two years.

A Royal Field Artillery battery such as Robert's comprised almost 200 men at full establishment. The second-in-command was a captain, with three lieutenants or second lieutenants in charge of two-gun sections. Beneath them were a battery sergeant major, a battery quartermaster sergeant, a farrier sergeant, four shoeing smiths, two saddlers, two wheelers, two trumpeters, seven sergeants, seven corporals, eleven bombardiers, seventy-five gunners, seventy drivers and ten gunners acting as batmen (officers' servants).[59]

Robert's battery arrived in Flanders during the Second Battle of Ypres at the end of April 1915, and he would continue as Commanding Officer for two more years before receiving a further promotion. The battery performed exceptionally well in the First Battle of Bellewaarde, in June

The 4th Northumbrian (County of Durham) Howitzer Brigade, Royal Field Artillery, Caëstre, 23 November 1915. From left to right: Back row: Lt J.Y. McLean, Capt. K. Anderson, Capt. C.L. Chapman, 2nd Lt J.G. Rutherford, Capt. Robertson, RAMC, 2nd Lt H. Geipel, 2nd Lt R.C. Smith, Capt. F.M. Armstrong. Sitting: Maj. F.P. Paynter, Capt. A.D. Currie, Lt Col A.U. Stockley, Maj. R. Chapman, Capt. J.R. Crone. Lying: 2nd Lt W.A. Denham, 2nd Lt A.A. Watson. (Chapman Family Archive)

1915, the month in which Robert's brother-in-law Wallace Annand was killed during the Gallipoli campaign. He was mentioned in a despatch from Field Marshall Sir John French and was awarded a DSO (becoming a Companion of the Distinguished Service Order) in the New Year's Honours List of 1916. In the autumn of 1915 the 4th Northumbrian Howitzer Brigade was in action at the French town of Armentières astride the River Lys and close to the Belgian border. Before the war it had been an important industrial centre for the spinning and weaving of flax and cotton, and for bleaching and dyeing. By the end of the war there would be little to see except its ruins.

Robert's 4th Northumbrian Brigade was soon on the move again, returning to the Ypres front in December. Wagon lines for their 1st Northumbrian Brigade comrades were at Ouderdom, some 9 miles behind the guns, a journey that the drivers and teams had to make once, and often twice, a night. This safe distance had its advantages. Ouderdom was:

> … a very nasty little muddy place, which had, however, one redeeming feature, a little hostelry called the 'Trois Amis', kept by a charming lady [known] as 'Fat Madam'. This place was a godsend, and one got there the best cooking in the world, or so it seemed, the toughest A.S.C. [Army Service Corps] steak being somehow reduced to a succulent morsel.[60]

Christmas 1915 came and went, with Christmas Day itself being bitterly cold. The new Expeditionary Force canteen provided welcome variety from the never-ending bully stew, and soon it was time to welcome in the New Year:

> The Batteries saluted the New Year with three good salvoes of H.E. [High Explosive] on the Bosch trenches. Almost every Battery in the Salient adopted the same method of sending their New Year's greetings to Brother Bosch, so that the first minute or so of 1916 was distinctly noisy. The Bosch did not reply, but the morning showed his parapet considerably damaged, and it is more than likely that this unpremeditated and unrehearsed piece of frightfulness did more harm than many of the officially-staged shows in which we indulged from time to time.[61]

In May 1916, immediately after Charles was ordered to return to England to become a battery commander, there was a reorganisation within the

50th (Northumbrian) Division. Robert's unit was renamed 'D' (Howitzer) Battery and transferred to 250 Brigade, Royal Field Artillery. As 'D/250', it would soon face a new challenge – the Somme, known at the time as the great 'Rat Hunt' or the 'Big Noise'. General Haig had three objectives in launching in the summer of 1916 the largest offensive of the war, north and south of the Somme river: 'To relieve the pressure on [the French at] Verdun. To assist our Allies in other theatres of the War by stopping any further transfer of German troops from the Western Front. To wear down the strength of the forces opposed to us.'[62]

The role of the artillery was seen as being pivotal: to destroy the Germans in their dugouts and the barbed wire that protected them before the infantry went over the parapets, and to provide a continual 'creeping' barrage of support once the advances had begun. The theory of the 'creeping' barrage was that:

> … in its menacing advance (it) caught shell holes and other points of cover in no man's land to which isolated units and individuals retired as soon as a bombardment opened. It was like a stream of lava engulfing all in its path between the enemy's first and second lines of defence.[63]

The bombardment of the German lines started on 24 June 1916. It involved 1,500 guns of all calibres, targeting not only the enemy's trenches and the heavy barbed wire entanglements of no man's land, but also his communications and rear defences. The offensive itself began a week later, on 1 July.

Six weeks later, with the battle still in its early stages, Robert's D/250 Battery reached the Somme area after a journey by train from Bailleul to Doullens, then by road to the town of Albert – already badly damaged. The wagon line was left at Bécourt and the battery went into action at Contalmaison on 14 August. Quartermaster Sgt W. Dunnington in Robert's battery described the journey and his first sight of the Somme battlefields:

> During training period we passed through all the small villages immediately behind Albert, whose falling Virgin on the spire we could see in the distance. Our amazement increased as we got nearer the great dumps of ammunition and a string of lorries and wagons filling up. Water tanks, R.E. dumps, everything on a big scale, and troops everywhere. We could

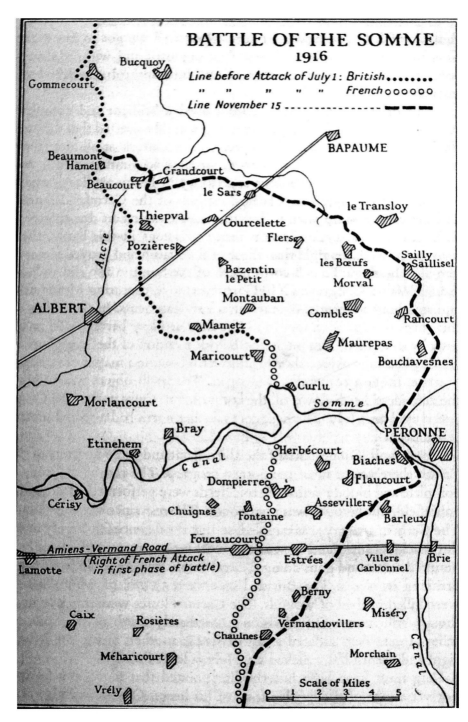

Map of Battle of the Somme, 1916. Amiens lies immediately to the west of Lamotte.
(Cyril Falls, *The First World War* [London, 1960])

hear the roar of gunfire and the usual quaint remarks of our north-country lads. In the pitman's lingo they chaffed each other and said: 'There's a war on here. Aa hope we've got a good cavil', etc. [A 'cavil' was a working place in a colliery, usually allocated quarterly, by lot.]

Arriving in Albert we saw the destruction of the Cathedral as we passed by, and also a few civilian shop-keepers still holding on to their shell-marked houses. Getting out of the town the battle front met our gaze. Never since arriving in France had we seen such scenes. Sausage balloons, both ours and the Germans, in hundreds as far as you could see. Hundreds of our planes, which seemed to have it all their own way, and we witnessed numerous combats. Troops and camps dotted the expanse of the bare hills and valleys. All this we saw as we finally fixed our wagon lines at Bécourt.

The guns, under Major Chapman, went straight into action in what remained of the village of Contalmaison. The gunners immediately began to fix the guns, and at daybreak the next morning we were at it for all we were worth.[64]

The gunners kept at it for a further four long months. By September, 'no words can adequately describe the Somme. For sheer tragedy, wholesale

Horses above their knees in mud pulling an ammunition limber along the Lesbœufs Road outside Flers, November 1916. (© Imperial War Museum [Q 2981])

destruction, the first vision of this ghastly battlefield almost blotted out from one's mind memories of the Ypres salient.'[65] During this month Robert's battery took part in the attacks on Mametz, Bazentin, Martinpuich, High Wood, Le Sars, Eaucourt l'Abbaye and Flers-Courcelette. Heavy casualties were sustained during these actions, with gunners, drivers and horses being killed or wounded in large numbers.

It was at Flers-Courcelette on 15 September 1916 that tanks (known then as 'Land Ships') were used for the first time, on an experimental basis. Since the 50th Division had only two, they had no impact whatsoever on the battle. But they did impress the troops: 'Gasping with astonishment, our infantry watched the tanks move across wire and trenches, knock down buildings, fall upon, and crush out of existence, machine-gun emplacements and generally show the utmost distain for every obstacle encountered during their advance.'[66]

There was very little respite for the artillery. 'Our chief recreations were bathing in Albert – where one's ablutions might at any moment be interrupted by the arrival of a too intimate Bosch shell – de-lousing, harness-cleaning, and being shelled at night.'[67] After a short rest and refitting in October, Robert's D/250 Battery went into action again, the battlefield by then having become a morass in which men and horses floundered helplessly. As for the poor 'Hairies', it was not surprising that so many of them succumbed:

The drivers were really splendid … for their constant efforts to tend and care for their horses. But the thing was beyond any man's capacity. You cannot groom a horse with an inch or two of thick coat all over him, caked up to the trace line with solid mud, and with nothing but a semi-liquid dung heap to stand him on.[68]

Later there was some rather better news, at least for the men:

Major Chapman, of D, looked in [at A Battery, commanded by Second-Lieutenant A.M.G. Trotter, who became the author's godfather] and told us of a good potato field north-east of Flers. This is *bon*, as no potato ration other than dried since coming into action. The morning was spent in looking for a new O.P. [Observation Post] near Gueudecourt, which, of course, meant returning via potato field. O.P. not found. Potato field yes.[69]

An exceptionally cold winter then set in, and the mud turned to ice. Even in southern England skating lasted for three weeks.

The Battle of the Somme continued into the early spring of 1917, when the Germans decided to withdraw several miles to the 'Hindenburg Line', on more favourable and heavily fortified ground. What had been achieved?[70] The battle was certainly the greatest set-piece attack not only of the First World War, but also in British history. Thirteen divisions – some 230,000 men – were involved in it. However, those infantrymen who went over the parapets on 1 July found that the preliminary artillery bombardment of 1.7 million shells had not destroyed the deep German dugouts, and that their 'Maxim' machine gun units remained all too effective. More than 19,000 British soldiers were killed on the first day.

After four and a half months of almost continuous attacks, with sustained artillery support, the capture of ground was minimal. The British Army's total losses were around 500,000, and those of the German Army nearer 600,000. 'But the Somme had, indirectly, ensured that the Germans could not now win – as long as in the meantime the allies did not entirely fall apart.'[71] This was because the Kaiser finally agreed in February 1917 that his U-boats should be allowed to attack all shipping bringing supplies and equipment to Britain, a decision that brought the United States with its huge resources into the war within months.

However, in the spring of 1917 the war was very far from being over. In March the 50th Division moved north to Arras, with Robert now given command of the 250th Brigade RFA with its four batteries (his good friend Major E.A. Angus replacing him at D/250 Battery). Robert was promoted to lieutenant colonel in April, the month in which he was mentioned in despatches (from Field Marshal Sir Douglas Haig) for the second time. His distinguished war service very soon received further recognition. In May he was awarded the Knight's Cross (Croix de Chevalier) of the French National Order of the Legion of Honour (Légion d'honneur).

The Battle of Arras had begun in April as part of the first large-scale Allied offensive of 1917. It lasted for a few months, during which the 50th Division captured Wancourt, and remained in the Arras sector until the early autumn. In October the division, with the 250th Brigade RFA, were ordered to move north to strengthen the Allied forces in the Third Battle of Ypres, which had begun in July, and where Robert's brother Charles had been killed in August.

Château at Querrieu near Amiens, Headquarters of the British Fourth Army, where the French Gen. Robert Nivelle presented Lt Col Robert Chapman with the Croix de Chevalier on 14 February 1917. (Chapman Family Archive)

The 250th Brigade was assigned to the Ypres–Passchendaele sector, facing a nightmarish scene on arrival. Col 'Archie' Shiel was there, and wrote that:

Language fails to picture the Ypres Salient of 1917. No green thing remained, no vestige of house or village church, of chateau or farmstead upon what had once been a fair countryside. All was sunk beneath a sea of black, stinking mud, the roads or tracks across which were discernible only in that they appeared smoother and more like rivers than the rest.[72]

Fifty square miles of slime and filth from which every shell that burst threw up ghastly relics, and raised stenches too abominable to describe; and over all, and dominating all, a never-ceasing ear-shattering artillery fire and the sickly reek of the deadly mustard gas. Such was the inferno into which, after a long journey by train and road, the Colonel [Robert Chapman] led the four Battery Commanders [of the 250th Northumbrian Brigade, RFA] in the early morning of the 23rd October, 1917.[73]

The conditions under which the Northumbrian artillery fought and died were the worst they encountered during the entire war. Everyone who survived had their personal horror stories to recount. A fellow Royal Artillery officer described his all too vividly:

We'd had an awful time getting the guns up the plank road on the Westhoek Ridge – and that was before the worst of the mud. Three weeks later we couldn't have done it at all. It was just sheets of water coming down. It's difficult to get across that it's a sea of mud. Literally a sea. You can drown in it. On the day I reached my lowest ebb I'd gone down from the gun position to meet the ammunition wagon coming up the supply road. It was my job to see that they got the wagons unloaded at the dump and to arrange carrying parties to take the shells and rations up to the battery. Oddly enough it was a quiet afternoon, but they (the Germans) must have seen some movement on the road because just as the wagon came up a heavy shell came over and burst very close. There were six horses pulling that wagon and they took fright at the explosion, veered right off the road and down they went into the mud. We had no possible way of getting them out. In any event they sank so fast that we had no chance even to cut them loose from the heavy wagon. We formed a chain and stretched out our arms and managed to get the drivers off, but the poor horses just sank faster and faster and drowned before our eyes. The wagon and horses disappeared in a matter of minutes. One of the drivers was absolutely incoherent with terror. It was the thought of being drowned in that awful stuff. It's a horrible thought. Anyone would rather be shot and know nothing about it.[74]

Unfortunately, there were other horrible ways of dying apart from drowning in mud:

The Divisional Artillery had a terrible time: 'The enemy's artillery was very active, especially at night when he deluged us with mustard gas. So intense was this gas that everything one touched was infected with it. Nobody had a voice left after the first few days.' The action of mustard gas was insidious: 'We did not at first realize the full danger of this, and just laughed because no one had a voice: but when people began to blister and swell, and two men of my old Battery died horribly from eating bread which had been splashed with this stuff, we got wind up thoroughly. The whole area was tainted: one could touch nothing with safety; even our own doctor, who came to see us, slipped in the mud and was so badly blistered by it that we never saw him again. The gas casualties were bad enough, but oh! the shell casualties were pathetic. I lost many of my greatest friends in the Battery, horribly mutilated in the mud, and towards the end was as near a raving lunatic as possible … Our guns were in the open; the only protection for the gunners the piles of high explosive; and the mud was over everything and tainted with mustard gas.'[75]

The gunners frequently had to spend nights wearing gas masks, sleeping with tubes in their mouths and wire clips on their noses.

The 50th Division, with the 250th Brigade batteries giving the best support they could, was given orders at the end of October 1917 to attack in a north-easterly direction between the southern borders of the former Houthulst Forest (reduced by then to blackened tree stumps) and the Broembeek stream. The attack was wholly unsuccessful, with troops mown down by machine gun and rifle fire. 'Who imagined that the attack could be successful? Only the Higher Command!'[76]

Unsurprisingly, there was little time for '"rest", that most elusive of war time activities'. However, officers did manage to find the time to have a number of good dinners in Poperinghe, and their men had some leave there. Humour kept morale up at nearby Thiembronne, where 'Everything flooded and poisonous, except billet, and *she* was charming.' Col Shiel had a stroke of gastronomic luck there: 'I got a fresh egg for breakfast, as a most confidential hen used to come in at my window, burrow under the bedclothes, and lay an egg in my bed every morning.'[77]

In early November 1917, British and Canadian troops did manage to capture the flattened site of what had been Passchendaele village, enabling Field Marshal Sir Douglas Haig to call off the offensive while claiming success in the ongoing war of 'attrition'. 'The Third Battle of Ypres had cost some 310,000 British and Imperial casualties, with those on the German side in the order of 260,000. The salient had been re-widened by several miles but the advance had not got a yard closer to the Belgian coast.'[78]

Robert Chapman himself received further recognition. In November he was again mentioned in Sir Douglas Haig's despatches, which related to his earlier service at Arras. And in the New Year's Honours list of January 1918 he was created a Companion of the Most Distinguished Order of St Michael and St George (CMG).

His war service was now drawing to an end after three continuous years on the Western Front. On 21 March 1918, the German Army launched an overwhelmingly strong offensive on the Somme along 60 miles of the British front. Within four days the Germans had advanced over 20 miles and captured the important railhead of Albert. All available British units, including the 50th (Northumbrian) Division, were deployed to attempt to stem the advance, but initial counter-attacks were unsuccessful and losses were heavy. The Northumbrians withdrew beyond the Avre River, almost to the gates of Amiens. Robert's brigade, having been withdrawing westwards for several days, set up its headquarters in a village house at Harbonnières (north of Caix) on 23 March. The situation was fast moving and confused:

> Orders came down through the Brigade Office, who passed them on to Batteries. Colonel Chapman, as often as not, was as much in the dark as his Battery commanders. We were constantly in and out of positions, each of which was much like the last, quite in the open, with no cover of any sort, except now and then a bank, behind which one could get.[79]

Robert Chapman's Brigade HQ in Harbonnières, near Caix, south-east of Amiens. (Chapman Family archive)

There was a ferocious German attack on Harbonnières on 27 March, which was repulsed after heavy and courageous fighting, but the brigade headquarters was bombed and shelled all night long. On 28 March the brigade had to retreat further to the south-west, moving into position at Hangard (to the west of Caix) two days later. However, on 1 April it was forced to move again, this time to Gentelles (halfway between Hangard and Amiens itself). The good news was that the British line had more or less stabilised by the end of the first week in April, the Germans had not broken through to take Amiens (a key objective for them) and reserves including Australian troops had arrived. Their support enabled shattered divisions to be withdrawn, and indeed the Northumbrian Division itself received orders to move to Flanders:

> But the artillery of the Division remained behind. When the Great Retreat ended, the 250th and 251st Brigades, R.F.A., found themselves, after many vicissitudes, in the neighbourhood of Gentelles where the gunners stayed until the 8th of April. In front of them there was still a lot of fighting, *i.e.*, attacks and counter-attacks about Hangard Wood as the front line swung backwards and forwards before settling down. In all these actions the Divisional artillery took part, and was heavily shelled, especially on the 4th of April (the Battle of the Avre), when the 250th Brigade suffered a great loss in Lieut.-Col. Chapman, who was hit and wounded very badly in the [left] arm: 'He went home and we saw him no more to our great regret. He had brought the Brigade through many vicissitudes and much hard fighting, with added credit, and we all felt his loss greatly.[80]

The heavy shelling of 4 April also wounded sixteen brigade gunners, and direct hits from German artillery destroyed three of its guns. However, the Great German Offensive on the Somme had been halted, and Gen. Ludendorff had failed to take Amiens. Had he succeeded, communications between the Allied forces on either side of the Somme would have become extremely difficult. Robert was invalided home and the 250th Brigade headed north for Flanders under the command of his replacement, Lt Col F.G.D. Johnston.

Robert was convalescing in South Shields during the summer of 1918 when he was brought news of two tragedies. In June he learnt that the brigade had suffered terribly in the Battle of the Aisne in the Champagne region on 27 May. Casualties were enormous, all guns were lost, and the batteries had to be rebuilt almost from scratch. Then in August he learnt that his sister Dorothy had died from pneumonia, contracted while nursing at 17th General Hospital in Alexandria.

However, the tide was turning against the Germans on the Western Front leading, finally, to the Armistice declared at 11 a.m. on 11 November 1918, seven months after Robert had been wounded. How did the officers and men of the 250th Brigade, still in France and advancing against the retreating Germans, feel? 'Our fellows took the news of the Armistice very calmly. There was very little of the violent ebullition of joy which was seen farther back. The reaction was too great … We were all turned up for a great pursuit, and probably the chief feeling was one of disappointment.'[81]

Soon after Christmas, 'demobilisation' started. Priority was given to miners and other colliery workers, all of whom had left for home by the end of New Year's Day 1919. Officers and men were sent back to England in batches, guns and wagons were removed and horses categorised as either 'Army of the Rhine', 'Disposed of in France or Belgium' or 'sent home'. The process was largely completed by the end of April.

Peace Day celebrations in South Shields, 19 July 1919: the Mayor, Councillor Thomas Sykes, and Lt Col Robert Chapman salute the flag and shout 'God Save the King'. (South Tyneside Libraries)

The brigade's final roll of honour was drawn up: of the twenty officers and 350 other ranks who went out to France and Belgium, eight officers and seventy other ranks (twenty of whom were from the 4th Durham Battery) were killed or died of their wounds. In addition to Maj. Charles L. Chapman, those officers were Maj. Forster M. Armstrong, Lt H.S.T. Bullen, 2nd Lt E.C. Earl, Lt J.L. Gibson, Maj. F.P. Paynter, Lt T.W. Sopwith and 2nd Lt H. Wedell.

Victory had been secured – at an exceptionally heavy price – and it deserved to be celebrated. South Shields held its official peace celebrations on Saturday, 19 July 1919. Lt Col Robert Chapman was deeply involved. He stood next to the Mayor, Councillor Thomas Sykes, to salute the flag and shout 'God Save the King'. And he organised the victory march, with military precision. The *Shields Gazette* announced on 15 July the order for the march. Every organisation whose men and women served during the war was represented, as were volunteers. The list was impressive: nursing sisters, VAD nurses, Wrens, WAACs and WRAF; RN and RNVR; Cavalry and Yeomanry; 4th Northumbrian Howitzer Brigade, RFA (T) Artillery; Royal Engineers; RASC; RAMC; colonial troops; Tyneside Commercials; Tyneside Scottish; Tyneside Irish; Northumberland Fusiliers; 7th DLI (Durham Light Infantry); Infantry and MGC; Volunteers; Royal Air Force; wounded in cars. Bands paraded down the streets. Victory tea parties were held, huge crowds gathered in the Marine Parks, and at 11 o'clock in the evening flares lit up the town for miles around.

Henry and Dora Chapman would have reflected on the day's events with mixed emotions. At last, after four years of carnage, the war was over. But they had lost three talented members of the family, all in their twenties: their son-in-law Wallace Annand at Gallipoli, leaving their widowed daughter Bessie with her 7-month-old son Richard; their son Charles at Ypres; and their daughter Dorothy in Alexandria. Pride in family achievements was matched by sorrow at their losses.

Nevertheless, the war had been won, and justly celebrated. Now came the challenges of the peace.

PART 4

THE INTER-WAR YEARS

7

POST-WAR CHALLENGES

Robert maintained his military activities throughout the inter-war period. In February 1920 he was appointed to command the 3rd Northumbrian Brigade (Royal Field Artillery) of the new Territorial Army. His first task was to build it up as quickly as possible, and his efficiency and enthusiasm created a national record. *Military Intelligence* announced, on 26 July 1920, 'First Territorial Units at Full Strength'. It continued that:

> The distinction has been gained by the 1st and 3rd Batteries (stationed at South Shields and Hebburn respectively) of the 3rd Northumbrian Brigade R.F.A., by being the first Territorial units to reach peacetime strength. Lieut. Col. Chapman, CMG, DSO, TD, who commands the brigade, has received the following telegram from Mr. Winston Churchill [then Secretary of State for War and Air]: 'I send my hearty congratulations to the Officers and Men on being the first units of the new Territorial Army to reach their full strength. This is a fine record.[1]

It was indeed. However, Robert had no intention of resting on the laurels of his distinguished war record and of immediate post-war success with the Territorials. He turned 40 in 1920, he was in his prime and determined to make the most effective contribution he could to local business and public service. He resumed work as a partner in his father's firm, Henry Chapman Son & Co., became a Justice of the Peace for South Shields, a Vice-Lieutenant for County Durham in 1920, and a borough councillor in 1921. He had moved quickly to take advantage of a new municipal opportunity. He and his wife, Hélène, lived on the outskirts of South Shields, at Harton, just a mile from his parents' house in Westoe. Following a corporation-sponsored Act of Parliament, Harton was to be incorporated into the borough in November 1921, with three new councillors. Robert decided to stand, was duly elected and took his seat in the splendid Town Hall, completed a decade earlier and described by Nikolaus Pevsner as 'the most convincing expression in the county of Edwardian prosperity'.[2]

The extended borough had a population of 118,631, which turned out to be its all-time peak. The new council comprised fifteen aldermen and forty-five councillors, including Robert and his two fellow members from Harton. The composition of the council was broadly representative of the town's various trades, industries and professions. Butchers and licensed victuallers led the way, with nine councillors between them, followed by two miners and three miners' check-weighmen. From the maritime sector there was a tug owner, boat builder, ship repairer, master mariner, pilot, and Alderman Robert Readhead ('gentleman' and prominent member of the shipbuilding family). From industry came an ironfounder, riveter, plater, driller and crane-man. Two builders and a builders' merchant were from the construction sector. As for tradesmen, there were two drapers, a tailor, two grocers and a jewel-ler. The professions fielded two medical practitioners, and a dental surgeon, chemist, architect, land agent, house agent and chartered accountant – Robert Chapman himself. It was an all-male council. The first female councillor, Mrs. E. Thorpe, won Tyne Dock for the Labour Party in 1927, and there were never more than two women on the borough council in the following decade.

The council's statutory responsibilities had grown dramatically since the beginning of the century, and it now faced huge challenges in hous-ing, public health and education. Robert was voted on to the Finance Committee, Town Improvement Committee, Watch Committee (respon-sible for the police and courts), Parliamentary Trade and Commerce Committee, and Education Committee. He remained on those commit-tees throughout the 1920s. It soon became all too apparent to Robert and his fellow councillors that the town, and indeed Tyneside as a whole, also faced serious economic problems, which the war had temporarily masked. The local economy was highly dependent on a few industrial sectors – coal mining, iron and steel, engineering and shipbuilding – and heavily reliant on export markets. Continued success and prosperity would be dependent on a high volume of international trade, and also on price and product competitiveness. Danger signals had been observed before the war. They would soon be flashing with increasing frequency.

South Shields Town Hall and clock tower, 1910, described by Nikolaus Pevsner as 'the most convincing expression in the county of Edwardian prosperity'. (South Tyneside Libraries)

Meanwhile, at a national level, 'A million (demobilised) men found that their old jobs had either disappeared or were held by someone else – usually a woman, or a man who had escaped conscription.'[3] Lloyd George's Coalition Government, re-elected in December 1918, had taken decisive action. Building on the radical foundations of the pre-war National Insurance Act, it had given every member of the fighting forces below commissioned rank a free unemployment Insurance policy, which entitled him to benefit while he was seeking work. A similar scheme was then devised to cover civilians who had been employed in war work, excluding women, despite the fact that trades unions were pressurising employers to dismiss female war workers so that men could have their jobs back. By the end of 1920 the scheme was extended further to include all manual workers, except for agricultural labourers and domestic servants.[4]

At a local level, South Shields did what it could to provide jobs on its new public works projects. In 1921 it set up an Unemployment Committee, with the borough engineer instructed to find work for 'suitable necessitous cases' selected by the manager of the town's Labour Exchange 'irrespective of whether they were ex-service men or not'. Labour Exchanges had been set up in 1908 under Winston Churchill as President of the Board of Trade, and had an uphill struggle in seeking to match jobs and skills. The borough engineer reported back that he had found jobs for up to 300 unemployed labourers on four projects: a new housing estate in Cleadon; the proposed Robert Readhead Park, in memory of the famous shipbuilder (which was later opened by his son, Alderman Robert Readhead, in 1923); the North Marine Park extension; and the construction of a light railway between South Shields and Jarrow (subsequently abandoned).

On the housing front, Lloyd George had promised, before the December 1918 General Election, 'To make Britain a fit country for heroes to live in'. The following year Dr Christopher Addison – a well-known social reformer who became Minister of Health – secured the passage through Parliament of the Housing, Town Planning etc. Act 1919. Known as the Addison Act, it placed on local authorities, for the first time, 'the duty of surveying the needs of their districts with regard to houses and of making and carrying out plans for the building of these houses'.[5] Ministry of Health approval was required before specific municipal schemes could proceed, and, once approved, the Treasury would subsidise all costs in excess of the product of a penny rate.

South Shields Council was all too well aware that much housing in the borough was thoroughly unfit for ordinary folk, let alone for heroes. It reported to the Ministry of Health in October 1919 that 4,200 new working-class dwellings would be required over the following three years.[6] With commendable foresight, the council had purchased a large tract of land on its southern fringe – the Cleadon Park Estate – and it now secured Ministry of Health approval for its development. The foundation stone for what became known as the Cleadon Park Housing Estate was laid in November 1920. In the following year, under the South Shields Corporation Act 1921, the estate (together with parts of Harton, Boldon and Whitburn) was included within the borough's extended boundaries. Housing construction soon started in earnest, and over the following decade the council would build 1,528 homes on the estate. It was just as well that the borough had moved so quickly to secure Ministry of Health approval, because, on Treasury cost-cutting advice, the subsidy provisions of Addison's Act were terminated by the Government in July 1921.

Cleadon Park Housing Estate: The Ridgeway, 1930s. (South Tyneside Libraries)

In the same year, the national Census of 1921 demonstrated all too clearly appalling conditions in the existing housing stock. The population of South Shields, before the post-Census boundary extension, had grown to 116,635, of whom 41,681 (36.5 per cent) were found to be living in overcrowded accommodation. Dwellings were at that time defined as 'overcrowded' when more than two people were living in one room. South Shields and Tyneside generally were in fact severely overcrowded by national standards. In the remainder of England and Wales, only two small areas (in London) had an overcrowding rate of more than 30 per cent of households.[7] In South Shields, as elsewhere on Tyneside, 'The oldest and worst slums are to be found, as a rule, clinging along the steep banks above the river, or jammed in among warehouses and works on the bank itself. Many of these are half ruinous, with tortuous staircases, and with poor water supply.'[8] The reference to 'poor water supply' was an understatement in South Shields, where only half of all properties had water closets in 1926 (a lower percentage than most Tyneside boroughs). This nevertheless represented an improvement on the situation a decade earlier since 'Earth or pail closets were the prevailing type of accommodation in most areas right up to the period of the [First World] War.'[9]

As for the supply of new housing, between 1919 and 1927 some 2,000 homes for the working classes were provided in the town, 1,450 of them by the borough council itself. A small contribution to working-class housing had also been made by 'private enterprise' of 370 dwellings, which received 'state assistance', and another 300 were completed without such subsidy. In short, by the end of the 1920s there had been significant progress on the housing front. However, a huge amount remained to be done, especially on slum clearance, which – with very strong support from Robert – would become a borough council priority in the following decade. Meanwhile, economic conditions in 1921 were rapidly deteriorating into a depression whose severity would have profound consequences for South Shields and other Tyneside authorities, not only for the remainder of the 1920s, but also for much of the 1930s. Demand was falling, prices were rising, and wages in many sectors were not keeping pace with increased living costs. As a result industrial disputes were widespread.

In the coal industry, where 11 per cent of all Tynesiders were employed as miners, matters came to a head with a strike in April 1921. The Government, fearing a combined strike from the 'Triple Alliance' of miners, railwaymen and transport workers, had set up a Defence Force. As soon as the miners' strike started Robert returned to full-time military

Boldon Colliery: Harton Coal Co. Ltd photo from *South Shields Industrial and Commercial Official Handbook*, 1929. (South Tyneside Libraries)

Boldon Colliery Young Miners, 1923. (South Tyneside Libraries)

service as commander of the 1st Northumbrian Brigade RFA, which had quickly been incorporated into the Defence Force. One of its batteries was stationed in the City of Durham, 'armed and horsed'.[10] In the event, the miners did not receive support from the other two unions. The strike was called off after the Government declared a state of emergency and Robert relinquished his Defence Force commission at the end of August 1921. He returned to his role as lieutenant colonel, commanding what had become the 74th Field Regiment (RFA) of the Territorial Army.

The underlying problems of the coal industry remained. Rival sources of coal production on the Continent led to severe falls in exports, while lower levels of local consumption caused by the depression made a serious situation even worse. With labour comprising a high proportion of total costs, it is not surprising that there were bitter disputes over pay and hours, leading to the miners' prominent role in the General Strike of 1926, where their action accounted for 90 per cent of the total days lost during the industrial dispute. Stanley Baldwin, who had become Conservative Prime Minister in 1924, 'sat out the miners' strike until they were starved back, on the owners' terms, after a siege of six months'.[11] Unfortunately, the market for coal continued to deteriorate.

The human cost was a remorseless rise in unemployment, soon leading to job losses of around 20 per cent of all coalfield workers.[12] The impact on County Durham parliamentary elections in 1931 would be profound.

It was not just the coal industry that was affected by the depression. Shipbuilding was particularly badly hit, all the more painfully after a decade of growth leading up to the First World War, when 'Tyneside became a huge arsenal and dockyard'.[13] The post-war situation at first looked rosy, since the Armistice led to a two-year trade boom, with British shipbuilding producing an all-time record of 2 million gross tons of shipping in 1920. This extraordinarily high output amounted to 35 per cent of the world total, and nearly half of it – 948,000 gross tons – was launched in the North East.[14]

South Shields' yards had made a significant contribution to these output figures. During the First World War, John Readhead & Sons had come under Admiralty control. In addition to constructing twenty 'tramps' (merchant vessels for general cargo), the yard built *Oletta* – its first, and last, deep-sea refuelling tanker – and three fast 'P'-class submarine chasers. A total of thirteen ships was built for the Government. James Readhead ran the yard, and was knighted in 1922, by which time the depression was

SS Floristan, built in 1928 by John Readhead & Sons Ltd for the Strick Line. (South Tyneside Libraries)

biting. Indeed, given deteriorating trading conditions and the decline in naval shipbuilding, the company did pretty well throughout the 1920s, launching some three dozen 'tramps', with a good spread of clients, nationally and internationally. The yard built four of them for Walter Runciman's Moor Line in Newcastle, five for P&O (which had taken over its long-standing client, Hain, in Cornwall), four for the Strick Line in London, and a further four for companies in Dunkirk and Bilbao. However, the early 1930s would be a very different story.[15]

Three, much smaller, South Shields yards made it through the First World War, but did not survive the depression of the 1920s. J.T. Eltringham & Co. Ltd, an audit client of Robert Chapman at Henry Chapman Son & Co., acquired Charles Palmer's Shipbuilding and Iron Company's yard at Willington Quay, Howden, on the north bank of the Tyne, in 1912. With Durham Walter Fitzgerald as chairman, the company moved from South Shields to its new site in 1914. There was more than enough war-time work from the Admiralty to keep the yard going. It built fast patrol boats, the minesweeper *Harrow* and small 'tramps' – some thirty ships in all. However, the company did not emerge from the war in a strong financial position, and underwent a restructuring in 1919, relaunching itself as Eltringham's Ltd. Although it then completed a further thirteen ships, the severe recession of 1922 was too much for it, and the company sank without trace.[16]

J.P. Rennoldson & Sons had a long-established reputation for their screw tug boats. The founders' sons, Joseph and Charles, ran the South Shields business together very successfully for thirty-five years, from their father's death in 1878 to 1913. For unrecorded reasons – perhaps after a blazing fraternal row – Charles then launched out on his own. The original company, under Joseph, continued building screw tugs throughout the First World War from its four-berth yard. *George V* was launched for service on the Tyne, and a series of salvage tugs was built for Dover Harbour Board and for Mersey Docks and Harbour Board. In total, two dozen vessels were launched during the war. The company then completed a further sixteen ships between 1919 and 1926, when it too fell a victim to the depression. No ships were built subsequently, and the yard finally closed a few years later.[17]

For his part, Charles Rennoldson opened his new, well-equipped, Lawe Shipyard in South Shields in 1913, trading as Charles Rennoldson & Co. He quickly built up a diversified business, with orders for coasters, a small passenger tender for P&O, a twin-screw tug and salvage steamer, followed by two minesweepers and a pair of ice-breakers for Russia. He secured orders for colliers in 1919 and 1920, but he died in 1924, having launched four dozen vessels in nine years. No further ships were built after his death, and his yard had also closed by the end of the decade.[18]

Writing about shipbuilding and ship-repairing on Tyneside in the year before Charles Rennoldson's Lawe Shipyard closed, Henry Mess noted the 'unprecedented severity of the depression' and concluded that 'it is necessary to ask whether the limitation of naval armaments and the growth of foreign-shipbuilding have not brought about a permanently changed situation'.[19] It certainly looked that way with the percentage of unemployed insured workers in Tyneside's shipbuilding and ship-repairing industries standing at the frighteningly high figure of 61 per cent at the end of 1926.[20] A full answer would take many years to emerge, but when it did it would be devastating for South Shields and Tyneside shipyards.

Meanwhile, Robert was becoming very involved with the council's education service, which was expanding to meet growing statutory requirements. In addition to the main committee, Robert was a member of sub-committees responsible for Secondary and Technical Education, Medical Inspection of School Children, the Open-Air School, and Finance and Works. He was also on the Committee of Managers of one of five Schools Groups (his Group II was responsible for half a dozen schools), and a Committee 'Manager' of Westoe Secondary School. He was a council representative on the 'Statutory Body of Managers of Voluntary Schools', his school being Harton St Peter's Church of England School. He was already closely involved with St Peter's, having been vicar's warden since before the First World War. As if this was not enough in what would soon become a quite exceptionally busy life, further educational appointments followed. When his father, Henry Chapman, retired as a governor of South Shields Boys' High School, he was soon replaced by Robert, who had been educated there himself. By the end of the decade he would be chairman.

The new housing estate of Cleadon Park needed educational provision for the children of incoming families. An infants' school accommodating 350 children was built in 1924, and a year later the Cleadon Park Open-Air School was completed. 'Delicate children' were sent there for varying periods, and 'children found in the schools who are partially sighted, are sent to a special school at Cleadon Park where the system of education

Sunday School Union, Good Friday 'Procession of Witness' reaches the Market Place, South Shields, 1924. Robert Chapman was a devout man who had been 'Vicar's Warden' at St Peter's Church, Harton, since before the First World War. (South Tyneside Libraries)

The Open-Air School at Cleadon, from *South Shields County Borough Council 1835–1935: A Hundred Years of Local Government*, 1936. (South Tyneside Libraries)

is specially adapted to their requirements'.[21] These were important projects for the Education Committee, which formed a Cleadon Park Estate Sub-Committee in 1925 (Robert became a member), and slotted the new infants' school into its Schools Group II (on whose committee Robert sat). His interest in education, and the cost-effectiveness of its provision, would receive national attention in the 1930s.

The Local Government Act 1929, introduced in the final year of Stanley Baldwin's Conservative Government, extended still further the responsibilities of county councils and of county borough councils such as South Shields. Its provisions, and in particular central government's control over them, would prove to be highly controversial and unpopular, as Robert Chapman and his fellow councillors would soon find out. Until the passage of the 1929 Act through Parliament, the administration of the Poor Law for the relief of poverty had been the responsibility, not of local authorities, but of independent Poor Law Unions controlled by 'guardians'. Over many decades the South Shields Poor Law Union had 'displayed skilful management in the provision of services for the relief of the poor which combined local discretion with a general acceptance of central authority principles'. Administration was characterised by 'An awareness of local conditions, an understanding of the plight of the able-bodied unemployed, and a sympathy for those who were unable, from whatever cause, to care for themselves.'[22]

The 1929 Act brought with it significant new challenges. It transferred the administration of the Poor Law from Boards of Guardians to local councils, who would also take over the physical assets and staff of the Poor

Law Unions. Councils were also required to set up new Public Assistance Committees, to be responsible for 'relief' (financial support) to the able-bodied destitute, and to those unemployed persons who had exhausted their entitlement to benefits under the National Insurance scheme. The new responsibilities would come into effect on 1 April 1930, and under the Poor Law Act of that year 'Poor Law relief' was formally renamed 'public assistance'.

South Shields Borough Council had to produce, in a short period of time, an 'administrative scheme' for the transfer, which was subject to Ministry of Health approval. And a new Public Assistance Committee had to be set up, taking into account the 1929 Act's requirement that two-thirds of its members must be councillors and that 'the remaining members are to be appointed from outside, some of whom are to be women'.[23] The committee's composition clearly was important, as highlighted in a letter of November 1929 to the council from the Secretary of the National Conference of Friendly Societies. He drew 'attention to the desirability of co-opting upon the Public Assistance Committee shortly to be appointed by the Council, a proportion of men and women who, by reason of their Friendly Society Work and Associations, have a close and direct experience of the lives and the social needs of the population within the Borough'.[24]

The council made its decision later in November. There would be twenty-four members of the committee, of whom sixteen would be councillors (the maximum permitted). Of the remaining eight non-council members, at least two would be women. Voting papers were circulated and Robert was one of the councillors elected. As to the occupations and social background of the fifteen other elected members, two were 'gentlemen' (men of independent means), three were house, estate or land agents and two were miners. There was also a director, a builders' merchant, a manager, a licensed victualler, a schoolmaster, a boot and shoe dealer, a secretary and a riveter. In short, as with the council as a whole, there was a reasonable cross-section of South Shields society.

The eight non-council members (five male and three female) were almost certainly all selected after an internal process of 'soundings'. Of the men, there were two 'gentlemen', a colliery manager, a shipyard manager (who had been a member of the Poor Law Union Board of Guardians), and a Post Office official. As for the three women, two were extremely closely connected to new committee members: one was the wife of Alderman Curbison, and the other was Robert's wife, Hélène, always described as Mrs R. Chapman. She had been a volunteer in the Forces' canteen and at the Mill Dam Hospital in the First World War, and in 1920 had become the District Commissioner of the South Shields Girl Guides Association. She would soon expand very considerably the range of her voluntary activities. Meanwhile, she was also active politically as president of the Conservative Association Ladies' Section of the Houghton-le-Spring 'Division' (parliamentary constituency). This would turn out to be a very significant position when the next General Election was called.

At the first meeting of the new Public Assistance Committee on 9 December 1929, Robert was appointed chairman, and a decision was taken to admit the press to meetings after 1 April 1930, when its statutory powers were to come into effect, and when the Poor Law Union's assets (including the Harton Institution – the former workhouse – children's homes in Cleadon known as Cottage Homes, offices in Barrington Street, and staff) would formally be transferred to the council. After the transfer was completed, the council undertook an operational review. The Public Assistance Committee reported to the council in September 1930 that it had determined its 'relief' scales and issued accompanying guidance for District Relief Committees (the term 'relief' remaining very much in use, despite officially renamed as 'assistance'). These scales of financial assistance were so important locally that they were published in full in the annual pocket diaries issued to councillors. The Public Assistance Committee was also appraising a scheme to extend the use of the Harton Institution's hospital block so that it could become 'a Hospital for the use of the inhabitants (of South Shields) generally, under the Public Health Acts'.[25] This scheme went ahead the following year, subsequent reports referring, separately, to Harton Institution and to Harton Hospital (which would become South Shields General Hospital before the end of the decade).

In October 1930 Robert and Hélène were reappointed to the committee for a further year and Robert remained chairman. In its quarterly report to the end of December, against a backdrop of continually rising unemployment and a 'Relief Regulation Order' from Government, which encouraged training and local employment initiatives, the borough engineer and the 'Master of the (Harton) Institution' had formulated 'a scheme of work and training for the benefit of able-bodied men in receipt of public assistance'. The works (which the report was careful to note 'would not otherwise be undertaken or ordinarily carried out under contract or usual trade conditions') were mostly proposed to be carried out at the Harton Institution and involved field drainage, road making and levelling land, including the making of a 'Bowling Green for the use of the Mentally Defective Patients'. Additionally, in response to the Relief Regulation Order's requirements and in liaison with the council's Education Department, 'suitable classes for providing training and instruction for the younger men up to 35 years, who are in receipt of out-relief' (i.e. they were not living in the institution) were to be set up.[26]

In any one week in the final quarter of 1930, the committee was providing 'Out-relief' to around 2,800 people (some 1,400 cases), and 'emergency' relief to a further 200 to 400. The 'Indoor Poor' being provided with residential accommodation totalled just under 1,000 people, of whom around 570 were housed in the Harton Institution, 125 in children's homes and 218 ('persons of unsound mind') in mental hospitals. Total costs of public assistance were running at around £4,000 per month. With unemployment continuing to rise steeply, these costs would soon be absorbing a third of the council's total income from rates.

The following year, 1931, would bring about decisive political change at national government level, in County Durham constituencies, and for Robert personally. The May 1929 General Election had resulted in the defeat of the Conservatives, Stanley Baldwin having been replaced as Prime Minister by Ramsay MacDonald, Labour Member of Parliament for Seaham in County Durham (who had previously been Prime Minister in the short-lived Labour Government of 1924). In South Shields the formerly safe Liberal seat was narrowly won by Labour for the first time, the new MP being Chuter Ede.

The new Government, which did not have an overall majority, faced formidable problems, which became even more acute after the Wall Street crash in the autumn of 1929: a contraction in world trade highlighting Britain's weakened competitive position; a major recession; and unemployment soaring at a frightening rate. Nationally, the unemployment level stood at around 7 per cent of the insured workforce in 1929. There were 1.5 million unemployed by January 1930, and 2.5 million by the end of the year – around 15 per cent of the workforce.[27] The problems were all too obvious, but the solutions far from self-evident. John Maynard Keynes, who chaired the committee of economists of the Economic Advisory Council that MacDonald had set up, advocated a series of measures in the autumn of 1930, including tariffs on imports (not then supported by the Government) and public works. The Government was not able to formulate a clear strategy, and meanwhile kept in place so-called 'transitional benefits' aimed at assisting insured workers whose benefits had run out and who would otherwise have had to apply for relief to local authority Public Assistance Committees.

In March 1931, the Government set up a Committee on National Expenditure chaired by Sir George May, secretary of the Prudential Assurance Company. Its report at the end of July predicted an enormous £120 million Government deficit and recommended, among other draconian measures, 20 per cent cuts in unemployment benefit. MacDonald and his Chancellor briefed the Opposition parties, the Cabinet could not agree on the way forward, and so MacDonald tendered the Labour Government's resignation on 24 August, accepting King George V's commission to form a National Government, in which he remained Prime Minister.

The new Government's September budget raised taxes and proposed cuts in public salaries and 10 per cent off all unemployment benefits (not the 20 per cent proposed in Sir George May's report, but still very substantial). These proposals had an immediate impact on the South Shields Public Assistance Committee. In its report to the council of 25 September 1931, the committee referred to the Ministry of Health Circular 1222 of 11 September, which required that administrative economies be made. The committee sought the council's approval to a range of cost-reducing measures, including significant salary decreases for staff: a 10 per cent reduction in the superintendent relieving officer's salary, and a 5 per cent cut in the salaries of the four relieving officers. In addition, the Medical Officer of Health's salary was to be reduced from £800 to £600, and the matron's salary from £180 to as little as £100. These proposals were bitterly opposed by staff and their unions, and the committee decided to put forward amended proposals to the council, in its end of year report. It duly did so, proposing that the Medical Officer of Health's salary be reduced 'only' to £700, and the matron's by 10 per cent to £162.

Meanwhile, momentous events were unfolding. There was a Sterling crisis in September 1931 and by the end of the month Britain had left the Gold Standard. The immediate result was a sharp devaluation of the pound against the dollar, accompanied, however, by restored international confidence. Ramsay MacDonald started preparing the ground for a snap General Election to provide him with a popular mandate, and announced on 5 October that it would take place on 27 October, just three weeks later. He made it clear that he was standing again as the

National Government candidate, fully supported by the Conservatives and by nearly all Liberals. However, the Labour Party was now bitterly opposed both to the National Government and also to MacDonald, who was expelled from its membership.

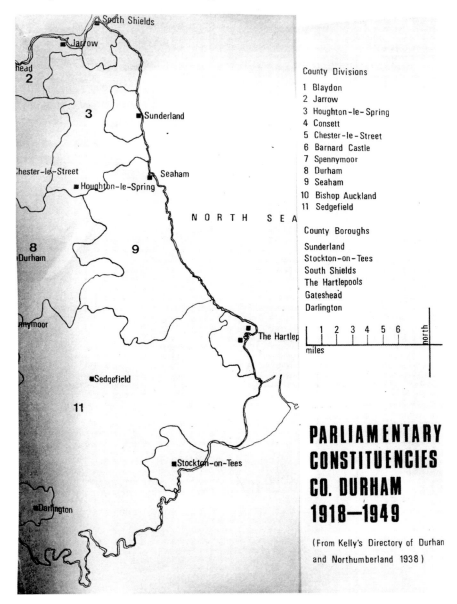

County Divisions

1 Blaydon
2 Jarrow
3 Houghton-le-Spring
4 Consett
5 Chester-le-Street
6 Barnard Castle
7 Spennymoor
8 Durham
9 Seaham
10 Bishop Auckland
11 Sedgefield

County Boroughs

Sunderland
Stockton-on-Tees
South Shields
The Hartlepools
Gateshead
Darlington

PARLIAMENTARY CONSTITUENCIES CO. DURHAM 1918–1949

(From Kelly's Directory of Durham and Northumberland 1938)

Extract from map of parliamentary constituencies in County Durham, from *Kelly's Directory of Durham and Northumberland*.

Preparations for the election started immediately in County Durham's seventeen parliamentary constituencies (eleven county 'divisions' and six county boroughs). Both Harton Ward in South Shields (where Robert was a borough councillor), and *Undercliff*, Cleadon (where Robert and Hélène were now living), were in the Houghton-le-Spring division. Shaped like a jigsaw puzzle piece, its boundaries touched those of South Shields, Jarrow, Gateshead, Chester-le-Street, Seaham and Sunderland. Labour had won the seat in 1918, and at all four of the General Elections in the 1920s – in 1922, 1923, 1924 and 1925.

Robert was asked by the Houghton-le-Spring Conservative Association to allow his name to go forward as their candidate. Despite the long odds against being elected as a Member of Parliament, Robert must have thought hard before making his decision, because the 'Moderate Party' (comprising Conservatives and Liberals) on South Shields Borough Council had voted to nominate him as the next Mayor, whose twelve-month term of office would begin in November. In the event, and rather at the last minute, he did agree to put his name forward. And on 12 October, just a fortnight before the General Election on 27 October, the Executive Committee of the Houghton-le-Spring Conservative Association met in Sunderland to decide on Robert's candidature. In his supporting address to the meeting, the association's chairman 'spoke of the service the colonel had already rendered to his country, and described him as a financial expert and a great authority on local government. Men of his stamp were wanted in Parliament to protect industries that needed protection, and to improve the commercial conditions of the country.'[28]

Robert's wife, Hélène, president of the ladies' section of the association, was then asked to say a few words. She:

> … thanked the meeting for the kind welcome given to her husband. 'I think', she added, 'it is really my fault he is here this evening. He was rather inclined to say "No" until this morning. I said to him, I would very much like you to stand, because I know the women of Houghton-le-Spring will support you in every possible way, and he promised he would.[29]

In his address to the Executive Committee, Robert covered themes that would be expanded during the campaign – restoring confidence, protective tariffs, getting men who were 'on the dole' (receiving unemployment benefits) back to work, and economy in the administration of public services. The formal motion to adopt him as their parliamentary candidate was carried unanimously.

In seeking a mandate from the electorate, Ramsay MacDonald's own National Labour Manifesto, *An Appeal to the Nation*, emphasised that 'In these days of transition and uncertainty we must all pull together, and by our co-operation now, strive to put a new spirit of energy and hope into our people.'[30] At constituency level the strategy was to ensure as far as possible that Conservatives and Liberals did not stand against each other and so split the anti-Labour vote. MacDonald himself wrote to Robert on 14 October emphasising that:

> The arrangement we have come to is that none of the [National] Party leaders should be expected to support directly candidates belonging to other Parties. The amount of confusion and weakness which would arise if that were done, believe me, would on the whole have a very bad effect.[31]

In Houghton-le-Spring, the Liberals had been in second place to Labour in the 1929 General Election, but they did not have an obvious candidate in 1931, and so they decided not to contest the seat. This led to the position MacDonald wanted to see – a straight fight between the National Party (represented in this case by Robert as a Conservative) and Labour, represented by the sitting MP, Robert Richardson, a miner's check-weighman.

Robert and his supporters entered the fray with energy and enthusiasm. He arranged to speak at twenty-two public meetings throughout the constituency, and further afternoon and open-air meetings were added to the schedule during the campaign fortnight. Venues included a school at Boldon Colliery and the Miners' Welfare Hall at Herrington Burn. The chairman of the divisional Liberal Association – which supported the National Government – predicted that he would have a rough time in some of the colliery villages, to which Robert replied, 'I am not afraid of going into the pit villages. I have been in more awkward spots than that!'[32] No doubt he was referring to three years' service – alongside many miners – on the Western Front in the First World War.

The election manifesto of the sitting MP, Robert Richardson, told voters that 'At the request of organised Labour in the Division I am again offering myself as candidate for the constituency which I have had the honour of representing in every Parliament since the year 1918 when Houghton-le-Spring first declared in favour of Labour and Socialism.'

Col R. Chapman, General Election
manifesto, 1931. (Chapman Family
Archive)

Robert Richardson, General Election
manifesto, 1931. (Chapman Family
Archive)

He said that 'The so-called National Party is asking for a "free hand".
The Cabinet has no definite policy to put before the country, and the
people are to be asked to give a blank cheque. This is an insult to the intelligence of the electors.'

The key issue was indeed one of trust. Robert's manifesto asserted that
'the National Government has already inspired confidence without panic
or collapse – it has stopped borrowing, imposed economy and balanced
the budget. The confidence that has been retained must be maintained.' On
the campaign trail he emphasised that 'I am the standard-bearer of Ramsay
MacDonald, who for 40 years has done more than any man alive for the
working man. I believe today that his policy is the only one to save us.'[33]

It was the Labour Party which had most of the specific policy proposals. Richardson's manifesto stated clearly enough that 'socialism provides the
real solution to the evils resulting from unregulated competition on the one
hand and the domination of vested interests on the other'. He supported

nationalisation of the mines and public ownership of the land to solve the problems of the agricultural industry, adding that 'The Banking and Credit system of the country must be brought under public control.' His manifesto stated that 'The cuts in Unemployment Benefit, reduction in Wages, and other so-called economies were introduced on the pretence of preserving the Gold Standard. Now that this has been abandoned, what justification is there for the continuance of the attack on the workers' standard of living?'

Robert's manifesto retorted that the Socialist Cabinet, following Sir George May's Committee on National Expenditure, and the continuing flow of money abroad, had 'prepared draft proposals to balance the Budget – including cuts in the pay of the Army and Navy, Teachers, Police, Civil Service, and in Unemployment Insurance Benefits'. However, most of the Cabinet 'shirked their unpleasant duty of enforcing economy and resigned. The leaders of the Conservative and Liberal parties at once joined the Prime Minister and the National Government was formed. Confidence abroad appeared to be restored and fresh credits of £80,000,000 were obtained in the United States and France.'

At constituency level it was the unemployment figures that were so damaging to Labour. As Robert's manifesto pointed out, 'when the Socialists assumed office in June, 1929, the number of unemployed was 1,100,125. On August 24th, 1931, when the Socialist Government resigned the figures were 2,813,163 – a record of total failure almost resulting in the collapse of the Nation.'

Interestingly enough, given its interventionist nationalisation proposals, Labour supported free trade. Richardson's manifesto stated that:

> Tariffs will make living almost impossible. Protection is utterly useless as a remedy for our present ills. It has been tried in other countries and proved a failure. The conditions in America and Germany where there are millions of unemployed on the verge of starvation is sufficient proof of this. The Tory Party wants full-blooded Protection, including taxes on foreign food-stuffs, but all experience shows that Food Taxes are paid by the consumer.

As an example, he said that bread was significantly more expensive in such 'Protectionist Countries' as France, America and Germany than it was in Great Britain.

Robert's views were essentially pragmatic: 'I am not a tariff reformer, a Protectionist out and out, as some people are trying to make out. I do not know sufficient about them, but I do consider that everything should be inquired into.'[34] Houghton-le-Spring being essentially a mining constituency, he illustrated his point by referring to:

> … the coal industry … [which] in this part of the country largely depended on export to Continental countries. But within the last five or six months Germany, France, Belgium and Spain had decreed that not a ton was to be imported without a licence, and what was worse, they had reduced the amount of coal which they allowed to be imported. Germany had a large number of unemployed miners, and a large amount of coal above bank, and France had reduced the amount of coal allowed in from foreign countries by 20 per cent. During the past three years England had been exporting to France a million tons a month, so that there was a reduction of 200,000 tons a month, or 2½ million tons a year.[35]

'This was where a tariff might help', he continued:

> If this country had had a tax on luxuries (he had earlier mentioned champagne, silks and jewellery) could it not have said to the French, 'we will take off the tariff on the luxuries if you let in our British coal'? I only give you that as an example of how tariffs may be used as a source of barter.[36]

This was in line with his election manifesto, which referred to Mr Baldwin (Leader of the Conservatives) advocating a tariff 'as the quickest and most effective weapon not only to check excessive imports but to enable us to induce other countries to lower their tariff walls'.

The South Shields and Sunderland newspapers, strong supporters of the National Government, gave minimal coverage not only to Richardson's public meetings, but also to the important issue of women's votes. It was only two years earlier, before the 1929 General Election, that there was a full democratic franchise with all women over the age of 21 being eligible to vote. In Houghton-le-Spring this had nearly doubled the number of female electors, and in 1931 there were 29,436 female voters, a few hundred more than the 28,849 males on the electoral register.[37] Robert's wife Hélène and supporters from the constituency Women's Conservative Association worked hard to win these female votes. *A Word to Women* pamphlet was distributed widely, urging support for Robert Chapman and the National Government in the following terms:[38]

Houghton - le - Spring Parliamentary Division.

GENERAL ELECTION, 1931.

A WORD TO WOMEN.

Is there a woman who doesn't want to be out of debt?

Is there a woman who doesn't long to feel that she and her husband, even by stinting and scraping, are paying their way.

What woman wouldn't give her all to see her home secure, her husband in regular work, and that little over each week which makes all the difference between a comfortable life and the misery of debt?

Under the Socialist Government this country has been spending more money than it could get from its people and then borrowing to spend still more. It was heading straight for bankruptcy.

What would any woman do in similar circumstances? She would cut down her expenses and live within her means.

That is what the National Government has had to do to save the country.

Now it wants to make things better by building up the country's trade, putting people back to work, and bringing back prosperity.

They want YOUR HELP in this splendid task.

VOTE FOR CHAPMAN

and Support the

National Government.

Published by C. H. LANE, Bridge Street, Westminster.
Printed by JOHN B. BOWES, LTD., Feakle Street, Newcastle upon Tyne.

A Word to Women: National Government General Election pamphlet, 1931. (Chapman Family Archive)

As reported by the press, the Houghton-le-Spring election campaign was not the rowdy affair that had been predicted. The *Sunderland Echo* covered a meeting held at Boldon on 21 October:

> ... in a hall where the feeling towards the National cause was about 50–50. He [Robert Chapman] was accorded a very fair hearing. One of the written questions handed to him read: 'Nationalists are Tories. If a skunk changes its name will it smell just the same?' Col Chapman's reply was, 'If my questioner mixes with skunks he will know better than I do' – a direct hit which was greeted with applause.'[39]

The following evening, four days before the election, Robert spoke at the Temperance Hall, Silksworth. 'There were present in force Socialists and Liberals, who went prepared to scoff but remained to cheer. There was not a single interruption as for more than half an hour Col Chapman pleaded for country to be put before party.'[40]

On the day before the election, a meeting for women was held in the Barnes Institute, Whitburn. The *Shields Gazette* reported that:

> Mrs Chapman appealed to the women to support her husband and vote for him. When her husband was adopted as the National candidate he said the Houghton-le-Spring division was a very hard nut to crack, but she felt that the nut had now been cracked and that the Kernel (Colonel) would be taken out and put at the top of the poll.[41]

Fortunately, if there were any more laboured puns like this one, they were not reported. In the evening Robert spoke for the final time at the Majestic Ballroom in Houghton-le-Spring: 'I think I am the most fortunate candidate in England today, because on my platforms I have had life-long Liberals and there has been a large body of good, sound Labour opinion in my audiences.'[42] Would this all-embracing message be enough to get him elected?

On the morning of the Election Day, on 27 October, the *Newcastle Journal's* headline was 'Socialist Majority Fading'. It reported that:

> The contest in the Houghton-le-Spring Division has been one of the most quietly contested in the North. That is not to say that the campaign has lacked keenness; even the socialists admit that Colonel

Robert Chapman is proving the strongest opponent ever put up in the division … Mr. Robert Richardson, the Socialist candidate, has talked until he has no voice left, and yet he is seeing his big majority slipping away day by day. This fight will be the closest in the division for many years.[43]

There was frenetic activity on polling day itself. Miners going to work were among the first to visit the polling stations, and Robert Chapman had 150 cars bringing supporters to vote. The *Shields Gazette* reported that polling 'was much heavier during the earlier part of the day than in past elections. An average of about 20 per cent had voted at the forty-one polling stations throughout the scattered constituency by noon.' Robert was upbeat: 'Everywhere I have been I have had enthusiastic receptions. Last night it was almost like a royal procession when I travelled from one great meeting to another at Houghton, Fence Houses, East Boldon and Harton.'[44] The counting of votes did not begin until 9.30 a.m. the following day and the result was declared in the afternoon. Robert had won by 3,000 votes, polling 25,549 votes to Robert Richardson's 22,700.

As the *Shields Gazette* reported, 'It was regarded as one of the greatest achievements of the elections, representing a turn over of over 17,000 votes in a constituency which was strongly entrenched in labour interests, almost to the extent of invincibility.'[45] In the 1929 General Election Robert Richardson had had a majority of 14,800 over his Liberal opponent. One of the first of numerous telegrams received by Robert Chapman came from the Conservative leader: 'Warmest congratulations on your splendid victory. Stanley Baldwin'. Ramsay MacDonald wired a message of 'best congratulations'.

As it turned out, the 1931 election result nationally, and in County Durham, was a landslide in favour of the National Government. In the House of Commons it now had 521 MPs (Conservatives, 473; National Liberal, thirty-five; National Labour, thirteen). Labour was decimated, with its MPs reduced from 287 in 1929 to just fifty-two. The historian A.J.P. Taylor's view was that 'The voters judged in simple terms. Labour had run away; the National Government had faced the crisis. Electors responded to an appeal for disinterested sacrifice, as the young men had done over Belgium in 1914.' And, 'On a more prosaic level, the Liberal vote mattered most. Some three million Liberals, who had no longer a candidate of their own, presumably voted solid for Conservatives.'[46] This

"St. George and Merry England!"
Once made the welkin ring.
This one also slew a "dragon"—
Cheers for Robert of Houghton-le-Spring!

Sunderland Echo, December 1931, cartoon of 'dragon' slayer 'Robert of Houghton-le-Spring'. (*Sunderland Echo*)

undoubtedly happened in County Durham, where no Liberals opposed Conservatives, and vice versa. Labour lost fifteen of the seventeen constituencies in the county, and even Ramsay MacDonald himself was far

Harcourt Johnstone, BA (Oxon), MP, who won South Shields for the Liberal Party in 1931. (South Tyneside Libraries)

from unscathed. He was indeed re-elected at Seaham as the National Labour candidate. However, having been ejected from his party, he was up against a left-winger, William Coxon, as the official Labour Party candidate selected by the constituency. MacDonald's majority was cut from 29,000 in 1929 to 6,000 in 1931 – a very strong warning from his previously loyal electorate.[47] Nevertheless, he was back in the House of Commons as Prime Minister.

In South Shields itself, the Conservatives supported the Liberal candidate, Harcourt Johnstone, who secured a 10,000 majority over the sitting Labour MP, Chuter Ede, in a straight fight. In Jarrow, the Conservative candidate, W.G. Pearson – a former Mayor – defeated the sitting Labour MP, R.J. Wilson, in another straight fight. And in Stockton-on-Tees the future Conservative Prime Minister Harold Macmillan, who had lost to Labour in 1929, won the seat in 1931, yet again in a straight fight.

Robert travelled to London for the swearing-in ceremony as a new MP at the House of Commons on the afternoon of 4 November. By 11 p.m. he was back in his constituency, celebrating his success with 300 dancers at the Victory Ball in Ryhope. The next twelve months would be frenetically busy, because he was now also certain to be elected Mayor of South Shields at the upcoming meeting of the borough council.

8

MAYOR AND MAYORESS OF SOUTH SHIELDS

Robert was about to embark on the busiest period of his life, juggling the responsibilities of representing his constituency at Westminster with mayoral duties in South Shields. At his first council meeting after his Houghton-le-Spring success, he was given a very warm welcome: 'The members of the Council with few exceptions, rose in their seats and heartily cheered the new Member of Parliament.'[1]

Robert was formally elected Mayor and chief magistrate of the borough on the morning of 9 November. Appreciative speeches were made, Alderman E. Smith noting that:

> The appointment is unique in the history of South Shields – that of having a Member of Parliament as its Mayor. And Col. Chapman is a man we can look up to with respect and admiration He has a strong personality and is never afraid to voice his convictions, even when he knows he will be in the minority.

He added, in good humour:

> He has a great helpmate – I nearly said General – in Mrs. Chapman who is beloved by all who are privileged to know her. Her cheerful, fascinating personality, and her kindness of heart has made her name a household word. I know of no lady who could carry out the multifarious duties of Mayoress with greater grace, ability and satisfaction.

Robing the new Mayor, 9 November 1931. Left to right: Alderman E. Smith, the Mayor (Col R. Chapman, MP), Mrs Watt, Councillor C. Henderson (Deputy Mayor), Mr G. McVay (Mayor's secretary), Alderman G. Druery. (South Shields Museum & Art Gallery, Tyne & Wear Archives & Museums)

This speech received 'loud applause'.[2]

A Mayor during this period occupied the most important elected position in a local authority. In Robert's case, he was an ex officio member of all the standing committees of the council. He was chairman of the Public Assistance Committee, the Unemployment Special Committee, and the Watch Committee. He also remained on key sub-committees – Town Planning, Housing, and Education Finance and Works and had recently been appointed a Durham County Justice of the Peace in addition to his long-standing borough JP's role.

After being elected Mayor on 9 November, and formally invested with the robes and chain of office, Robert made his inaugural speech to the council. Some of it must have been considered controversial. He presented a detailed analysis of the hugely increased responsibilities thrust upon municipalities by Acts of Parliament over the previous decade, which had been accompanied by substantial increases in their capital expenditure and sinking fund charges. He conceded that 'some brake has been put upon capital expenditure during the past three years, but we have still the responsibility of dealing with the slums in front of us, a responsibility which should have been tackled before instead of pouring out so many hundreds of thousands of pounds upon roads and the seashore'.[3] Given his views on the borough's difficult financial situation, he advocated 'an entire cessation from capital expenditure for twelve months' except for slum clearance and the rehousing of affected families. He also believed that economies could be made in day-to-day expenditure on education without reducing the standard of education provided, a theme to which he would return in the House of Commons.

He continued that:

> … no town in England has suffered more from the aftermath of war, many industries have closed without others being opened out to take their place, our population has decreased from 118,599 in 1921 to 113,452 in 1931. Many have gone, perforce if you will, to other parts in search of livelihood, but it is a sign that the spirit of independence and self-preservation burns strongly within them.

The most important task was to attract industry and trade to the town. 'South Shields has many inducements to offer – lower rates than neighbouring towns, efficient transport by rail, river and sea, cheap power, light and fuel, and abundance of willing skilled and unskilled labour at hand.'[4]

After Robert's speech, the members of the council and senior officials repaired to the Royal Hotel for the Mayor's luncheon, where economy was certainly not on the menu. After a choice of kidney soup or chicken broth came steamed halibut with egg sauce. The main course was roast beef or roast gosling, with a choice of apple tart, milk pudding or stewed fruit for dessert, followed by cheese and biscuits. Everyone present was in a jovial mood. Robert welcomed his principal guest from the business community, Sir James Readhead, and hoped that his shipbuilding firm would have continued success and be able to find more employment for the men of South Shields. To his fellow councillors he said that 'It might be that in the Council chamber they were sometimes far apart, but even though they differed on points of view, after all they loved each other. (Applause).'[5]

In proposing a toast to 'His Worship the Mayor', Alderman J.R. Lawson, JP, said he was confident that Col Chapman would be able to fulfil the duties both of Mayor and Member of Parliament. Equally, turning to the

Mayoress, he said that 'Mrs Chapman's energy and ability were such that she would be able to combine the duties of Mayor and Mayoress at the same time. (Laughter).' The town clerk, Mr J. Moore Hayton, thanked councillors for their appreciation of the work of officials, and quoted amid laughter the couplet that runs:

To our virtues ever kind;
To our failings ever blind[6]

Armistice Day, 11 November 1931. The scene during the two minutes' silence at the War Memorial, Westoe. (Inset top): The Rev. H.G. Hastings Shaddick, who conducted the service and the Mayor (Col R. Chapman, MP) who spoke. (Inset bottom): Sounding 'The Last Post'. (*Shields Gazette*)

Robert's schedule in South Shields continued to be busy throughout the month. On Armistice Day, 11 November, he attended an 11 a.m. open-air service at the war memorial in Westoe, where the surrounding streets were packed out, and laid a wreath of poppies on behalf of the South Shields branch of the British Legion, where he was president. Later he visited the South Shields High School, where he was an old boy and had become chairman of the governors. He spoke on the meaning of Armistice Day, emphasising 'the responsibilities of the rising generation in connection with the maintenance of peace'. The *Gazette* reported that:

> South Shields today kept faith in common with the rest of the nation, and throughout the Empire, with its heroic dead. In every street and avenue, in every workshop and office, in its institutions, and its day schools, and in the privacy of the home itself, the sacred Two Minutes' Silence was kept.[7]

A few days later came 'Mayor's Sunday' on 15 November. A long procession passed from the Town Hall to King Street and to St Hilda's Church in the Market Place. Two dozen organisations were represented, including the 74th Northumbrian Brigade RFA, the Royal Naval Volunteer Reserves, the 1st Durham Cadet Battalion, the Veterans' Association, the Volunteer Life Brigade, the South Shields Pilots, the Boys Brigade, Sea Scouts and Boy Scouts, River Tyne and Borough Police, tramwaymen, the Ingham Infirmary, the Merchant Service Guild, the Chamber of Commerce and Grocers' Association, the Master Builders Association, aldermen, councillors and officials, justices and – for the first time – the headmaster, staff and boys of the High School.

The sermon was given by the Rev. Hudson Barker, Vicar of St Hilda's, on the text of 'Having on the Breastplate of Righteousness' (from the Epistle of Paul the Apostle to the Ephesians, Chapter VI, verse 14). The sermon ranged widely, applying the wisdom of St Paul to a Christian life and to problems in contemporary South Shields, 'where there is so much to be done towards the reconditioning of slum property'. He concluded by saying:

> Mr. Mayor, one word to you personally … Perhaps the most important office you will hold, among all those in the coming year, is that of Chairman of the Public Assistance Committee. What a lamentable task is likely to lie before that Committee, in the coming days, when for the unemployed, there will be an increasing difficulty of facing the barbaric music of poverty and penury. I wish greater co-ordination could exist between this Committee and the Labour Bureaux than has existed heretofore. All this will claim all the courage you possess, all the wisdom which God gives you, and above everything else all the fullest sympathy and wide considerateness which lie in your heart. May you wear always the 'Breastplate of Righteousness'.[8]

The Rev. Barker's strong and heartfelt message on 15 November 1931 could hardly have been better timed. The newly elected National Government, with its 521 MPs, faced by only fifty-two Labour members, was determined to reduce the budget deficit of £120 million. One of the largest areas of public expenditure was unemployment benefit, where 'transitional payments' to 400,000 of the 2 million unemployed no longer eligible for insurance benefits were costing the Government around £30 million annually. The decision was made to cut by 10 per cent the benefits payable to these long-term unemployed.[9] On 12 November 1931, just three days before the Rev. Barker's sermon, the Government announced that it was reintroducing 'the twenty-six-week time limit for insurance benefits consigning those who had exhausted their entitlement (and were therefore claiming transitional benefit) to means-tested payments from local authority Public Assistance Committees'. These committees would have to apply a means test of the income and possessions of all co-residing relatives.[10] This became known as the Household Means Test.

South Shields had not only a legal obligation to implement Government policies, but also a duty to its ratepayers to keep close control of costs, at a time when there were around 15,000 unemployed in the town. The borough council and adjoining authorities were faced with an intractable problem: 'The greatly increased relief expenditure imposed by the inter-war depression involved costs which could not be sustained by the limited local resources.' Put another way, 'there was no correlation between population, the extent of social problems and the income enjoyed by local authorities'. For example, later in the decade, Newcastle, with a population of 290,000, raised £10,000 as its 'product of a penny rate', whereas South Shields, with a population of 111,000, raised only £2,000.[11]

Robert was re-elected as chairman of the Public Assistance Committee (PAC) for the third year running, and would remain in the role for three further years. Hélène also sat on the committee throughout this period, and was vice-chairman of the Cleadon Cottage Homes Sub-Committee. With 7,000 cases being handled by the PAC, these were very hot seats indeed, especially since the Household Means Test and its application aroused bitter and lasting resentment in the North East and well beyond. This would soon be reflected in a huge march on the Town Hall. Meanwhile, Robert was targeted by a witty anonymous satirist:

Our P.A.C. is quite unique,
You surely must agree,
It's ruled by only two old lads,
Or possibly by three.

There's Chapman with his titles long,
the Chairman of the Band,
Who hopes by his reduction song,
To make a better land.

'The poor should not be poor at all'
He, in his anger cries,
'Success is e'er within the call
'Of everyone who tries.'

'I dine each day upon the best,
'And care not for the cost;
'On grapes and tender chicken-breast
'No pleasures have I lost.'

'But as for Poor Law Officers,
'There surely is no doubt,
'Nine Bob a week is quite enough,
'For food to make them stout.'

'My salary I cannot gauge,
'It comes from many sources,
'But laundry scrubbers at a quid,
'Should feel as strong as horses.'

The Echo Thompson comes along
And says 'I think so too'
'This waste has gone on far too long'
'We'll see what we can do!'

And so they did, at what a cost,
The whole town wants to know
Their case, e'er tried was surely lost,
And now they're lying low.

ANON.[12]

Robert undoubtedly dined 'upon the best'. But he certainly was not 'lying low'. 'I take off my hat,' he said at the annual dinner in December 1931 of the Royal British Legion's South Shields branch:

> ...to all the people who are unfortunate in having to come in front of the Public Assistance Committee to have their unemployment benefit determined. We have got through nearly all the cases, and when we read of disturbances in other parts of Tyneside and the country, I think we can be satisfied that the people here do appreciate the difficulties, and that they are prepared to face them, hoping that by that [sic] they will more readily come to better times.[13]

However, there were strong dissenting views, and they were about to be aired. On 6 January 1932, some 15,000 to 20,000 men and women marched through the streets of South Shields accompanying a deputation – supported by Labour councillors – to the council meeting that evening. Robert was then in effect wearing three hats – as Mayor, chairman of the PAC, and MP for a constituency adjoining South Shields. He would need all his diplomatic and people skills to navigate through what could become a very tense situation. Organised by the South Shields Labour Party and the Trades and Labour Council, the marchers included representatives of Miners' Lodges from Boldon, Harton and Marsden – all of which were in Robert's Houghton-le-Spring constituency. Also represented were the Boilermakers' Society, the Municipal and General Workers' Union, the Amalgamated Engineers' Union, the Iron Founders' Union and several women's labour organisations. According to the *Shields Gazette*, the demonstration, accompanied by well-known colliery brass bands, 'was one of the most imposing ever seen in the borough', with the growing crowd outside the Town Hall finally estimated as between 20,000 and 25,000'.[14] The newspaper gave the background. Apparently a deputation had wanted to discuss its grievances with the Public Assistance Committee, but on the advice of the town clerk, this request had been refused. This refusal had triggered the march. The town clerk gave the same advice to the council as a whole, but this time, in a delicate balancing act, Robert recommended to the council that, in these exceptional circumstances, it should receive the deputation. This was duly agreed.

As a result, the situation was soon defused. Robert read out a letter from Mr E.A. Gompertz, secretary of the South Shields Labour Party and

Trades Council (who would soon become a prominent borough councillor) simply asking the council to support their request to be able to put before the Public Assistance Committee various anomalies and grievances relating to transitional payments in particular. The deputation withdrew briefly from the council chamber, and Robert put a resolution to his colleagues that the Public Assistance Committee be requested to receive the delegation. This was carried unanimously. Afterwards Mr William Blyton, Chairman of the Harton Miners' Lodge, reported the successful result of the deputation's request to his members, commenting on the Mayor's courtesy and help in smoothing over a potentially difficult situation. Mr Blyton continued that he was well aware that the Public Assistance Committee (PAC) did not have the power to abolish the means test, 'but they had power to make their scale commensurate with the generous treatment that obtained in the Durham County Council area', which included nearby Whiteleas and Marsden.[15]

The PAC heard the deputation on 27 January 1932, and Robert took upon himself the responsibility of recommending that the committee could not support the deputation's various detailed requests. He said that it would be entirely against the law to continue benefits at the same level once men had passed from ordinary (insurance) benefit to transitional benefit. It would not be reasonable to ignore savings altogether, but he quite agreed that it would have been better if the Government had given the PACs more detailed instructions on how far savings could be ignored. He added that the committee had recently made their scale of relief a little more generous. The committee duly turned down the deputation's requests.

RELIEF OF UNEMPLOYED.
MAXIMUM SCALE OF INCOME.

1.—SCALE.—That, as a general rule the grant of relief to Unemployed Persons or their Dependants (except in special cases referred to below) shall not exceed the following amounts per week, viz:—

Head of House (Man or Woman) ..14/-
Wife (living with husband) 6/-
Man, Wife, and one child.......... 22/-
   ,,   ,,   two children........ 24/-
   ,,   ,,   three children 26/-
   ,,   ,,   four children 28/-
   ,,   ,,   five children........ 30/-
Single Adults (in Lodgings) 13/3
       ,,   ,,   (with Friends) 10/-
together with an additional allowance, where necessary in respect of rent, not exceeding the amount of rent actually paid, and in no case to exceed 3/3 per week.

2.—INCOME.—That in fixing the amount of relief all income (subject to statutory limitations) shall be taken into account except as follows :—
(1) Family Earnings—
(a) Wife—the first 10/-
(b) Children 14 to 17 years of age   Sons.   Daughters.
                                    1st 10/-   1st 8/-
              18 to 21 ,,   ,,   1st 12/6   1st 10/-
              over 21   ,,   ,,   1st 15/-   1st 12/6

56

'Relief of Unemployed: Maximum Scale of Income': extract from South Shields borough councillors' pocket diary 1931/32. (South Tyneside Libraries)

Robert – who was clearly widely respected throughout the borough – had handled a very difficult issue fairly and skilfully. No similar demonstrations were held again in South Shields. However, a few months later violence broke out across the river in North Shields in very similar circumstances. Tynemouth Borough Council had given a warning that it was not its policy to meet a deputation accompanied by a demonstration. A very large crowd – 'thousands of people' – nevertheless processed to the PAC offices, with 'Down with Means Test' banners. Missiles were thrown, shop windows were broken, street skirmishes took place, the police charged with drawn batons and arrests were made.[16]

The South Shields deputation had referred to the more generous benefits paid by the Durham County Council Public Assistance Committee. They were, in fact, becoming notorious and the county had been in serious conflict with the Ministry of Labour for two years. Robert predicted in his Houghton-le-Spring constituency that the county council would back down and 'administer the Means Test as other authorities are having to administer it. The alternative is that there will be commissioners in this county, and do you think these people will have Government officials administering transitional benefit?'[17]

In fact, the county council remained intransigent, and before the end of 1932 its Public Assistance Committee was indeed replaced by Government-appointed commissioners. They found lax administration:

> Their elected predecessors had been refusing only about 1 per cent of applications for relief and had been paying out maximum levels of relief in the case of 92 per cent of applicants, with only 7 per cent at lower levels, which scarcely suggested any punctilious regard for the existing regulations. The new authority embarked upon a careful review, while claiming to be completely fair, as a result of which the proportion of cases allowed full benefit was reduced to 70 per cent, reduced benefit was given in 23.5 per cent of cases and 6.5 per cent of cases were disallowed.[18]

The North-Eastern Public Assistance Committees had come together a year or so earlier in Newcastle to consider a uniform scale for the administration of transitional payments, and South Shields had put forward a suggested model scheme. But the 'Durham County Public Assistance Committee was in a state of eruption over the whole business' and the idea was not pursued. Each PAC was left to its own devices.[19] In 1932 the Ministry of Health took the initiative and convened a conference of Tyneside local authorities with the objective of securing greater uniformity in benefit levels for able-bodied persons, and a new scale was drawn up. South Shields approved it in principle and under its provisions would have increased its payments to a married couple by just over 10 per cent. In the event, several neighbouring Public Assistance Committees were not in favour of the new uniform scale, which was therefore not implemented in South Shields. It was understandable that an under-resourced authority like South Shields should, with Robert's strong support, try to keep council rates as low as reasonably possible. Total rates in 1931/32 were 11s 4d in the pound, of which around one third (3s 9½d) was for public assistance – a very significant proportion. Rates per head of population were £2 3s 10d, broadly similar to those across the river at Tynemouth, and among the lowest in the county.[20]

On becoming Mayor, Robert had made it clear that a key task for the council was to improve housing conditions. Slum clearance, in his view, should have been carried out more extensively in previous years, and was now a priority. Displaced residents would need new housing, and it was the borough's responsibility to ensure that it was provided. At the same time, he personally wanted to make a contribution to housing supply in

New road and housing at Quarry Lane on the edge of the Cleadon Park Estate, 1930s. Harton pit in centre background. Adjacent land was sold by Robert Chapman to the Sutton Dwellings Trust. (South Tyneside Libraries)

the town, and he also had proposals for national policy changes that he would share with his council and parliamentary colleagues.

He was an active housing developer himself, and had acquired significant land holdings both in South Shields and in the surrounding area. In the spring of 1932 he sold to the Sutton Dwellings Trust, at the very substantially discounted price of £4,000, 33 acres of land near Cleadon Hills, then just outside the municipal boundary. The trust was a national housing association, based in the south, which had already built a scheme in Newcastle. To be laid out on garden city principles, the proposal was to build 350 rented dwellings for workmen 'of the cottage type, consisting of living rooms, sculleries, separate bathrooms, and chiefly with two or three bedrooms'. The houses would have large gardens, there would be ample open spaces, 'and as local labour will be largely employed, a substantial instalment of men will be taken off the books of the Labour Exchange'.[21] The *Shields Gazette* was enthusiastic: 'A piece of good fortune has fallen to South Shields in the way of a big housing scheme. It is a stupendous effort in private enterprise which has been brought about on the initiative of the Mayor of the borough, Colonel Chapman CMG, MP.'[22]

The Mayor and Sir Hilton Young, Minister of Health, crossing the river, 15 September 1932. Sir Hilton's responsibilities included housing. (South Shields Museum & Art Gallery, Tyne & Wear Archives & Museums)

Later in the mayoral year, Sir Hilton Young, Minister of Health – who also had responsibility for housing and for the work of Public Assistance Committees – visited South Shields to survey housing conditions. He met tenants on the council's new Egerton Road housing scheme and was then shown round the borough's largest housing estate, Cleadon Park. No doubt Robert pointed out the adjoining site that he had very recently sold to the Sutton Dwellings Trust and told him that the job opportunities there would be for local unemployed men. The minister had already been informed that there were 15,300 unemployed borough residents, representing the horrifically high figure of '50 percent of employable persons' (a higher percentage than in Gateshead or Tynemouth, which was the minister's next port of call).[23] Sir Hilton 'complimented South Shields on the work being done in respect to housing, especially bearing in mind the necessary economy that needed to be practised throughout the country'.[24]

Supporting charitable, as well as municipal, activities was an important part of a Mayor and Mayoress' year. Hélène played a prominent role in

The Mayoress, Mrs R. Chapman (centre), with the Westoe Road Baptist Fraternity who 'entertained poor children to tea' in December 1931. Their president, Mr Ernest Bailey, is on the Mayoress' right. (South Shields Museum & Art Gallery, Tyne & Wear Archives & Museums)

numerous annual balls and dances, Christmas treats, bazaars, sales of work, and other charitable events. Her energy and enthusiasm were infectious. On 2 December 1931, for example, she stood in for the Marchioness of Londonderry (whose train from London was delayed) and unofficially opened the afternoon bazaar and sale of work of the Houghton-le-Spring Conservative Association in Sunderland's Alexandra and Edward Halls. Two hours later, Lady Londonderry – whose family home was Wynard Park in the south of County Durham – arrived and declared the bazaar officially open. In the evening, Hélène attended the annual ball of the South Shields borough police, whose 200 guests in the King's Hall made it one of the largest balls of the year. She left early to present the prizes at another event – the South Shields Pals annual dance in the Majestic Ballroom. The Pals' evening was in aid of the South Shields Shoeless Children's Fund, whose secretary and treasurer was the chief constable and which had been set up at the very end of the nineteenth century. In 1931/32 the fund issued to 'necessitous children' in the borough 4,109 pairs of boots or shoes, and stockings to go with them.

The Mayoress, Mrs R. Chapman, received 800 'callers' at her 'At Home' reception in the Town Hall on 10 December 1931. On her right is the Deputy Mayoress, Mrs C.A. Henderson. (South Shields Museum & Art Gallery, Tyne & Wear Archives & Museums)

A week later, on 10 December, came what the *Shields Gazette* called 'the greatest of all social functions of the civic year in South Shields – the Mayoress' "At Home" in the stately apartments of the Town Hall'. The *Shields Gazette* reported that:

> ... the embellishments were on a scale of unusual spectacular magnificence, the elaborate [floral] scheme having been carried out in exceedingly good taste and artistry under the direction of the head gardener of the West Parks, Mr. William Thompson. Over 700 plants were used and a light orchestra discoursed sweet music.[25]

For her 800 afternoon 'callers' who paid their respects, Hélène wore a rather elegant outfit, described in minute detail by the *Shields Gazette*:

> ... the Mayoress chose for her reception gown a Worth model copied in shagreen romaine [silk with a grained texture] with long tight-fitting sleeves, and gracefully swathed skirt cut in diagonal lines, with a rich velvet band of the same soft shade as the sole ornamentation. Her matching felt hat, one of the newly tilted mushroom shapes, was tightly rolled off the head on the right side and softened with a band of curled ostrich feathers.[26]

The entire ensemble was made by Fenwick, the renowned department store in Newcastle.

Since, on their invitations, 'callers' were 'kindly requested to leave their cards in envelopes', the *Shields Gazette* devoted several columns to listing the names of those who had attended. Guests had come from far and wide, and included numerous civic dignitaries: the Lord Mayor and Lady Mayoress of Newcastle, and the Mayors and Mayoresses of Morpeth, Blyth, Tynemouth, Wallsend, Stockton and Middlesbrough. Further columns described the 'Dresses of the Lady Helpers'. These included the Mayoress' mother-in-law – readers were told that Mrs Henry Chapman had generously paid for the whole event – and Robert's sister Miss Ethel Chapman, who 'looked extremely nice in beige printed marocain' (a crêpe fabric made of silk or wool).[27] The reception rooms, looking splendid with their thirty-year-old, 25ft palms and elaborate floral displays, were open to the public the following day thanks to the 'kindly thought' of the Mayoress. On departure all visitors were politely encouraged to consider giving contributions for the benefit of the Ingham Infirmary, which was still going strong, as were its annual ball, by then in its fifty-third year, and separate children's ball. The Mayoress attended both of them.

Robert and Hélène were determined to launch an initiative that would help ease the day-to-day sense of boredom and purposelessness of the unemployed in the town ('to prevent both physical and moral deterioration'). So Robert set up a working committee to take forward his idea of providing recreational and educational opportunities for the unemployed in church halls and other buildings, and also through outdoor activities. This became known as the Mayor's Scheme for Unemployed Recreation and, as usual, Robert led from the front. He owned a building in the Laygate area of the town called Zion Chapel, which had belonged to the Methodists, and he offered it rent free as the first dedicated recreation centre. The churches responded well, and the halls of St Paul's, St Michael's, St John's and St Bede's were made available for the initiative. The Rotary Club gave its full support, and its chairman, Councillor W.R. Bell, also chaired the Mayor's Scheme. For outdoor recreation, the council agreed to make available bowling greens in the parks, the South Shields Cricket

Unemployed men renovating the Zion Hall recreation centre before the visit of the Prince of Wales on 27 April 1932. (South Shields Museum & Art Gallery, Tyne & Wear Archives & Museums)

The Bishop of Durham, The Right Reverend Hensley Henson, inspecting allotments run by unemployed men based at Zion Hall. (South Tyneside Libraries)

Club made its cricket field available, and the YMCA allowed its field at Harton to be used for cricket, bowls and quoits. An expanded allotment scheme, strongly supported by Robert, was launched. Robert and Hélène opened the gardens of their house at *Undercliff*, Cleadon, on two after-noons a week with the head gardener, Mr Sidney Snelling, available to offer advice in the kitchen garden or elsewhere.

Robert had learnt that the Prince of Wales, in his role as patron of the National Council of Social Service, was travelling to Newcastle to address the Tyneside Council of Social Service, on the theme of 'The National Opportunity – A Fresh Call for Service', on 27 April 1932. Although the formal programme for the visit had already been arranged, Robert cor-responded with Sir Godfrey Thomas, the Prince's equerry at St James's Palace, to see whether the Prince could fit in a brief visit to South Shields. The *Shields Gazette* ran the story 'Prince on Tyneside – Hopes of Visit to Shields' for several days until the good news was received that the Prince of Wales would be able to make a short 'informal' visit to the town on the morning of 27 April. He would be able to visit the recreation centre at Zion Hall (the renamed chapel), whose activities tied in rather neatly to the theme for his Newcastle speech of 'mutual helpfulness and individual effort'. The visit was a great success, and the Prince learnt that between 1,500 and 2,000 men visited the centre every day. In addition to a recreation room for playing games of cards, draughts and chess, with plenty of reading material, there was a workroom for carpentry and shoe repairing. Lectures also took place, and a Zion Hall orchestra had been formed. Robert's initiative had taken off, and indeed a positive report on it as a model scheme for replication nationally was sent to London by the local Labour Exchange manager and circulated to Cabinet ministers.

The Prince also paid a brief visit to the Mission to Seamen's Institute, where he was introduced to Sir James Readhead. Asking him when his firm had last built a ship, the rather depressing answer was eighteen months earlier. The Prince then talked to seamen in the recreation room, Mr Miles Toale, an able seaman, telling him that he had last been in a ship a year ago. Another seaman, Mr J. Gray, told the Prince that things were very hard for unemployed men.[28]

Times were also very hard for the wives and partners of more than 14,000 unemployed men, and for the 958 women and girls on the lists of the town's Labour Exchange. Hélène, as Mayoress, now followed in Robert's footsteps and formed a women's section of the Mayor's recreation and educational scheme in June 1932. This was the South Shields Women's Mutual Service Club, formed in St Michael's Church Hall in South Westoe, which had been made available by the Rev. H.G. Hastings together with the church's putting green and tennis court. Hélène opened the club at the end of June, and its governing committee included Miss MacFadyen, the women's officer of the Labour Exchange, and unemployed women and girls (150 of whom were at the opening). Equipped not only with ping pong table, books, magazines and parlour games but also with typewriters and sewing machines, it was soon offering instruction from volunteers. Singing lessons were also given and within a few months girls from the club put on a very successful concert, with the Zion Hall Band lending instrumental support.

It was now high summer, bowls tournaments were in full swing and soon townsfolk would be enjoying themselves at a memorable outdoor event, where brass bands would complement numerous other attractions. This was the eightieth Annual Show of the Durham County Agricultural Society, where Robert, in yet another of his roles, was president. Held on the August Bank Holiday in Cleadon Park, countryside activities came to town and were appreciated by more than 7,500 visitors. There were

The Mayoress, Mrs R. Chapman, about to bowl the first wood in the South Shields Ladies' Bowling Festival in North Marine Park, July 1932. (South Shields Museum & Art Gallery, Tyne & Wear Archives & Museums)

The Mayor (Councillor Robert Chapman, MP) presenting the cup to members of the Boldon Colliery Brass Band, winners of the brass band contest at the Durham County Agricultural Show, Cleadon Park, 1 August 1932. (South Shields Museum & Art Gallery, Tyne & Wear Archives & Museums)

entries, to be judged in the Showyard during the day, for horses, ponies, cattle, sheep, pigs, goats, dogs, poultry and rabbits – 1,450 in total. *Shields Gazette* readers were told that the entries for cattle included 'fine animals of the Shorthorn [whose "home" was Durham] Ayrshire, Guernsey, Aberdeen Angus and British Friesian Breeds'.[29] In his luncheon speech, Robert recalled that it was twenty-seven years since the show had last visited South Shields, and he highlighted current issues affecting the agricultural sector and steps the Government was taking to assist. For example, there had been dumping of potatoes from the Continent because the Germans and French were stopping the importation of Dutch and Belgian potatoes. Following recent Acts of Parliament, import duties had been raised very substantially, to £1 a ton. That, said Robert, 'would give the farmers the opportunity to get £7 an acre more for their potatoes'.[30]

In the afternoon there were sheepdog trials in a special enclosure, with the brass band competition getting under way. There were plenty of other attractions – an equitation display by the Mounted Wing of the Royal Corps of Signals from Catterick Garrison in Yorkshire, 'horse leaping', pony racing and musical chairs on horseback. In the early even-

The South Shields branch of the British Legion being inspected by the Mayor after the memorial service in St Stephen's Church, 6 November 1932. (South Shields Museum & Art Gallery, Tyne & Wear Archives & Museums)

ing there was an auction of the pig, sheep and beast used in the weight guessing competition, generously donated by the South Shields Butchers' Association. Robert subsequently offered two fat lambs for sale to benefit the Ingham Infirmary, which received a total of £14 from the auction. Finally, it was announced that Boldon Colliery had won the brass band competition. All in all, a thoroughly enjoyable day out.

The mayoral year was drawing to a close. Remembrance Sunday on 6 November would see Robert and Hélène perform, very willingly, their final duties as Mayor and Mayoress. A few days earlier, Robert had launched an appeal to employers as Mayor and Chairman of the South Shields King's Roll Committee to do their best to take on one or more unemployed disabled ex-servicemen, of whom there were 40,000 in the country and 245 in South Shields. Having been badly injured in the Great War himself, this was a cause dear to his heart: 'The men for whom I now appeal are looking for help in the hour of their need. In the hour of our national crisis these men offered all they could give, and now suffer from a permanent disablement, and a sacrifice of the many advantages of life.'[31] On Remembrance Sunday itself, Robert and Hélène attended a British Legion Memorial Service in St Stephen's Church.

On 9 November Robert was succeeded as Mayor by the Labour Party's unopposed nominee, Councillor George H. Linney. There were warm words of praise for Robert and Hélène's contribution during the mayoral year, words that went far beyond a polite vote of thanks. Alderman Smith said that 'Colonel Chapman had satisfied everyone in the town by the way in which he had guided its affairs. He had controlled the Council in a masterly and impartial manner. He had worked double time all the year.'

'With regard to their beloved Mayoress', he continued, 'she had carried out her work to the great advantage of the town … (Her) gracious smile and winning ways had captivated the heart of South Shields.'[32]

Hélène also received several letters extolling her praises in verse, and the *Shields Gazette* received a letter from 'H.B.M.', a resident of Cleadon Estate, who, 'though no public correspondent', wrote that 'She is beloved by all and sundry, and I do hope that … she may be endowed with strength to still go on with the good work she has commenced.'[33] As it turned out, Hélène was fortunate enough to be able to continue her voluntary activities for a further thirty years.

9

PARLIAMENT AND THE 'SPECIAL AREAS'

Robert somehow managed to juggle his parliamentary duties with his mayoral and wider South Shields responsibilities, though the combination was exhausting. He was almost certainly the only MP in the 1931 Parliament to have the additional responsibilities of a municipal Mayor. Having survived successfully all the engagements in the North East and in London that were crammed into the first three months of his new roles, he received in February 1932 a flurry of invitations to rather grand 'At Home' events within walking distance of Westminster. The first of these was from the Marchioness of Londonderry, who was entertaining guests in early February 1932 at her husband's magnificent London home, Londonderry House on Park Lane. She was the leading political hostess of the day, and had a close friendship with the Prime Minister, Ramsay MacDonald, who appointed her husband Lord Londonderry Secretary of State for Air, but was criticised, as a Labour politician, 'for making the aristocratic Londonderry House the social centre of his government'.[1]

The following month Robert was invited to a soirée hosted at 4 St James's Square by the society hostess Viscountess (Nancy) Astor, who had been elected as Conservative MP for Plymouth Sutton in 1919, when her husband succeeded to his father's viscountcy. Then followed invitations from the 'Prime Minister and Miss MacDonald' – Sheila MacDonald, acting as hostess for her widowed father Ramsay – at 10 Downing Street, and from Mrs Stanley Baldwin next door at No. 11, where her husband was ensconced as Lord President of the Council (in effect Deputy Prime

Minister) in the National Government. Networking was important, especially for a newly elected MP, and it probably helped Robert to pursue in Parliament his three principal interests – education, housing and unemployment. He was able to bring to bear in a remarkably effective way his experience in South Shields and Tyneside on the evaluation and formulation of national policy in Westminster.

Education was one of the areas where a balance – not easy to achieve – had to be struck between the costs of expanding statutory requirements and the resources available locally. Robert, both as Mayor and as a long-standing member of the South Shields Education Committee (chairing its Finance and Works Sub-Committee), believed strongly that economies could be made in day-to-day expenditure without reducing the standard of education provided. This was a theme he pursued energetically and in fact his maiden speech in the House of Commons, on 18 April 1932, was a contribution to the debate on the Board of Education financial estimates. Some of his remarks and comparisons were controversial, made in the context of cutbacks in expenditure across the board by the National Government. He referred to 'a great outcry by the teachers with regard to the 10 per cent cut in salary' (Sir George May's Committee on National Expenditure had recommended 20 per cent), but pointed out the benefits they received, including generous pensions of 50 per cent of their salaries at the end of their careers. Their annual contributions while working were only 5 per cent, and local ratepayers also contributed 5 per cent.[2] He did not think that teachers had any cause to complain.

He then drew attention, in considerable detail, to the variation in the cost of education in different areas, a theme which – across all council services – would receive ever-increasing attention in later decades from central government as well as from local authorities themselves. He gave as an example the average expenditure per child in elementary schools. Nationally it was £13 2s, in Bradford £15 15s, and in South Shields £9 15s. Bradford fared badly on another comparator, the cost of 'special services', including nursery schools, physical training, feeding of children and medical inspection, where the national average was 16s. In West Hartlepool, in County Durham, it was just over 6s, and in Bradford it was £2 6s. He felt that an inquiry would be justified to ascertain why Bradford was so much more expensive, and meanwhile gave his view that 'this variation in the cost has arisen through the system of percentage grants. If we had a block grant system, there would not have been the same encouragement for local authorities to be extravagant.'[3] Warming to his theme, Robert turned to loan charges. He highlighted administration and inspection and made 'a point on which I think I shall have the support of the National Union of Teachers'. Leicester, for example, spent 16s per child on this item, London £1 6s and South Shields 5s. He observed that 'Many local authorities have an inspectorate of their own, but I cannot see why the inspectors of the Board of Education and the head teachers are not sufficient to manage education.'[4]

Finally he turned to South Shields with its 114,000 inhabitants, 14,000 of whom were unemployed, and gave an example of how careful economies could benefit both employed and unemployed workers. The council had succeeded in reducing the rates from 19s 6d in the pound in 1920/21 to 10s 6d in 1932/33. As a direct result, the borough had reduced by 25 per cent the rent on a four-roomed house. In short, 'We have done much for the workman who is in employment, and much more for the unemployed, by keeping down the cost of education and the rates, and so lowering rents.'[5] The *Shields Gazette* reported his speech, and his closing remarks that emphasised the borough had 'always received good reports from the Board of Education, and, if academic success is any guide … in the school certificate examination our secondary scholars during the past four years have had a percentage of passes of 90 against 66 for the rest of the country'.[6]

After his speech, Robert sent a telegram from the House of Commons to Hélène with the brief message, 'Jumped the hurdle. Well received. Rob.' The thought-provoking speech did not, however, meet with universal acclaim. A correspondent, 'G.S.', wrote to the *Shields Gazette* on 21 April, challenging some of Robert's statements as 'weak and erroneous'. For example, 'In elementary schools, parents, children and teachers alike are continuously concerned about winning of scholarships into Secondary Schools, since South Shields does not offer a sufficiently large number of free places to supply all the meritorious [applicants]. Hence good results.'[7] Robert did not reply to this letter, and correspondence from his supporters and detractors rumbled on for months. However, an already planned new secondary school would open in the borough a few years later.

Robert, as an exceptionally able chartered accountant, was thoroughly at ease with figures. He had a gift both for high-level financial overview and for detailed analysis, and he could apply these skills to policy areas that were important to him, including financial administration, education and housing. Later in the year, on 7 December 1932, Robert spoke in the housing debate at Westminster, in the presence of the minister, Sir Hilton Young. As we have seen, Robert strongly supported municipal and state financial assistance for slum clearance, and shared with members the recent success of South Shields in building new three- and four-room houses that were let at rents of between 4s 5d and 5s 7d per week, which people who live in 'distressed areas' – whether in work or on the dole – could afford to pay.

He then put forward an imaginative and carefully costed proposal for a substantially expanded housing programme. He was certain that private enterprise, which had built 800,000 houses since 1919 with no subsidy – as compared with 1 million houses built with subsidy – could make an even greater contribution to increasing the supply of new housing for sale. The question was simply and solely one of interest rates. Currently, building societies in Newcastle, for example, were making loans on four-room houses at an interest rate of 5 per cent. He explained in great detail that if the Government were to make housing loans available to the building societies at 3.5 per cent, the total costs to their borrowers of repayments, rates, repairs and insurance on a £350 loan (the typical cost of a new four-roomed house) would be 10s per week, representing a saving of around 25 per cent when compared to a loan at 5 per cent. This would allow the societies a reasonable margin for their working expenses, as he knew from personal experience of running a society (the South Shields Commercial Permanent Building Society) for many years.

Robert then showed, again in meticulous detail, how a Government loan of £100 million would finance the construction of 300,000 houses at £350 each, assuming land costs at a maximum of £400 an acre, and associated transaction costs of £10 million. Assuming that 80 per cent of the cost of housebuilding was labour, and that wages were £3 per week, 24,000 man weeks would be available, equivalent to a full year's work for 480,000 men – substantially more than the 300,000 unemployed men in the building trade at the time.[8] Robert added that there would be very large financial benefits for the state: 'each unemployed man on the "dole" or "transitional payments" costs not less than £50 a year, so every 100,000 put into employment would not only save the State £5,000,000 but by their [insurance] contributions would add to the Unemployment Fund about £1,000,000 a year'.[9]

Robert spoke again on housing in a Ministry of Health debate in July 1933, fully supporting Sir Hilton Young's slum clearance proposals, and recalling the Minister's visit to Tyneside and 'how much struck he was with the horror of the conditions' in the slum houses. Robert confirmed, from South Shields' experience, that 'the removal of people from the slums into new housing estates [was] beneficial in every way', both for the families rehoused and for the men out of work in the building trade. Robert pointed out that on Tyneside 70 per cent of ship repairers, 40 per cent of miners and 50 per cent of seamen were out of work, as were 22.5 per cent of men in the building trade – 'the one industry in which the Government can really help to get some unemployed back to work' through an expanded housing programme.[10] Robert also predicted, correctly – no doubt also from his experience at the South Shields Commercial Permanent Building Society – that the demand for owner-occupation from the working classes was potentially enormous ('it has scarcely started'), held back for the time being only by the limited supply of low-priced small dwellings. He tried again to drum up support for his idea of Government raising a large loan at 3.5 per cent, this time of £75 million for houses to be let by municipalities and housing trusts. Again, the figures and benefits were laid out in great detail. His ideas for raising large sums of money to be on-lent to building societies or to a range of housing providers were not implemented. Perhaps they were too far ahead of their time. Decades later very similar ideas would receive significant financial support from Government.

Nevertheless, the Government did continue to support slum clearance through the housing subsidy system, and South Shields embarked on a

Slum clearance properties: 27–29 Lower Thames Street, 1931. Photo by James Henry Cleet for South Shields Borough Council. (South Tyneside Libraries)

Slum clearance programme: 12 Mitre Street, 1932. Photo by James Henry Cleet for South Shields Borough Council. (South Tyneside Libraries)

major programme. The borough's survey completed in 1933 showed that there were about 2,000 dwellings, housing some 8,000 people, in need of demolition, which was planned over a three-year period. Within five years, most housing in the riverside areas had been demolished, together with other unfit housing – 2,790 homes in all.[11] In the inter-war period as a whole, the council built 4,280 homes, the North Eastern Housing Association built 650, and the Sutton Dwellings Trust 350 (on land sold to the Trust by Robert). A total of 17,800 residents were housed, of whom 11,664 were from clearance areas. The last estate to be built in the 1930s was at Horsley Hill, with 608 houses.[12]

Robert's final speech in Parliament had been in 1933 – a year of some good news for South Shields, but of dreadful news for neighbouring Jarrow. The good news was that Readhead's, the only surviving shipbuilding firm in the town, had won its first new order in two years, prompting the council to write a letter of congratulations to Sir James. The order had come just in time, as after the completion of two vessels for the ship owner Frank C. Strick in 1931, the whole workforce, except for the apprentices, was laid off. Grass was soon growing on all three shipways at the West Docks yard. However, Sir James then decided to take the risk and build a 'speculation' ship, at an extremely slow pace in order to keep costs down. This was the ship, of 8,400 tons deadweight, that he sold, during its construction in 1933, to the Bank Line. The *Shields Gazette* reported that there would be work for several hundred men, including platers, riveters, angle-smiths, carpenters and painters: 'Many of the firms' workmen will now be able to come off the "dole", and once more ply their craft with pleasure and profit to themselves.'[13] The ship was named *Tynebank* and launched in 1934.

Readhead's was just about keeping its head above water in exception-ally difficult times. Tragically, the same could not be said about Palmer's shipyard in neighbouring Jarrow. The company was in severe financial dif-ficulties, but managed to complete its 109th warship, HMS *Duchess*, which was launched – appropriately enough – by the Duchess of York in the summer of 1932. Palmer's now desperately needed another Admiralty order to keep afloat. It was unsuccessful, and the result was by then inevi-table: the yard closed in the summer of 1933. The cumulative effect of job losses in the town was catastrophic. Ellen Wilkinson, who would become the town's MP at the next General Election, wrote:

> Jarrow in 1931–33 was utterly stagnant. There was no work. No one had a job, except a few railwaymen, officials, the workers in the co-operative stores, and the few clerks and craftsmen who went out of the town to their jobs each day. The unemployment rate was over 80 per cent. 'Six thousand are on the dole, and 23,000 on relief out of a total population of 35,000', was the estimate given at the time by the Medical Officer of Health.[14]

As if the closure of the shipyard was not painful enough, within a year it had been sold, at little more than scrap value, to National Shipbuilders Security Ltd, a company that had been set up by prominent shipbuilders, with Government support, to purchase redundant or obsolete yards, thereby rationalising over-capacity and strengthening the financial posi-tion of NSS ship owners' own interests. The scheme was, as it turned out, a failure at national level, and for Jarrow, 'The irony was that in a shortage of tramp (cargo) shipping eighteen months later, British orders were under-taken by Belgian yards at cut prices, because they had bought first-class machinery at Palmer's sale for the price of scrap.'[15]

Not surprisingly, initiatives to alleviate the impact of unemployment at both local and national level remained a priority in the winter of 1933 and throughout the following year. In November 1933, a new council was elected in South Shields. The 'Moderates' (councillors who would almost certainly have voted Conservative or Liberal in national elections) remained in control, with thirty-five seats, the remaining twenty-five being won by socialists, who were steadily increasing their representation on the council. Robert retained, for one final year, his chairmanship of the Public Assistance Committee, and also became chairman of the Development

Special Committee, charged with revitalising important riverside sites following the council's successful slum clearance programme.

These were two important roles to which Robert devoted a significant amount of energy, in addition to his parliamentary duties. In December 1933, the council received a deputation from the South Shields Winter Relief Campaign Committee, led by the Rev. George King, a local Methodist minister. The deputation asked for extra winter relief at the rate of 3s for each adult and 1s 6d for each child, and demanded the abolition of the means test. The Rev. King said that he had come 'because his duty pledged him to be concerned not only with the spiritual but the physical condition of the men and women around. He was appalled at the need present in the town.'[16] These proposals were supported in a formal 'motion' by two socialist councillors, and it was left to Robert to reply that 'South Shields had the most generous scale of relief in the North East. No one would say that any scale gave unfortunate people anything but a mere existence, but to take action along the lines suggested would mean about £25,000 a year out of the rates.' As for the means test, 'it was a political question which neither the Council nor the Public Assistance Committee had anything to do with'.[17] In the event, the motion on increased winter relief rates was defeated by the narrowest of margins (by twenty-seven votes to twenty-six).

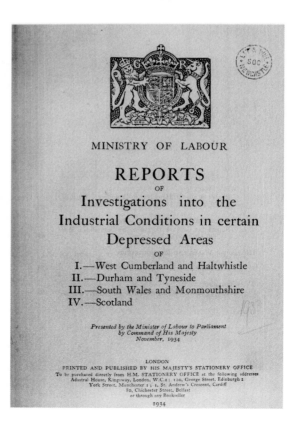

MINISTRY OF LABOUR

REPORTS
OF
Investigations into the
Industrial Conditions in certain
Depressed Areas
OF
I.—West Cumberland and Haltwhistle
II.—Durham and Tyneside
III.—South Wales and Monmouthshire
IV.—Scotland

*Presented by the Minister of Labour to Parliament
by Command of His Majesty
November, 1934*

LONDON
PRINTED AND PUBLISHED BY HIS MAJESTY'S STATIONERY OFFICE
To be purchased directly from H.M. STATIONERY OFFICE at the following addresses
Adastral House, Kingsway, London, W.C.2; 120, George Street, Edinburgh 2
York Street, Manchester 1; 1, St. Andrew's Crescent, Cardiff
80, Chichester Street, Belfast
or through any Bookseller

1934

Ministry of Labour *Reports of Investigations into the Industrial Conditions in certain Depressed Areas*, 1934. Capt. Euan Wallace, MP, wrote the report on Durham and Tyneside. (HMSO)

Ramsay MacDonald's Government was well aware that local authorities in the North East and elsewhere had the greatest difficulty in coping financially with the impact of large-scale unemployment. Painful decisions had to be made – such as refusing an increase in winter relief rates or increasing borrowing with its adverse long-term impact on ordinary ratepayers. In 1934 the Government took action on two related fronts: it launched through the Ministry of Labour, 'Investigations into the Industrial Conditions in Certain Depressed Areas', which included County Durham and Tyneside; and it announced plans to centralise most of the burden of administering and paying out unemployment benefit. Capt. D. Euan Wallace, MP (Civil Lord of the Admiralty), was appointed to report on the industrial situation of shipping, shipbuilding, ship-repairing, marine engineering and coal mining in Durham and Tyneside. Robert's Special Development Committee moved quickly to secure borough council approval for an industrial development scheme on cleared riverside land, to be submitted to Capt. Wallace for potential financial assistance.

Capt. Wallace visited the North East in June 1934, holding a series of meetings with Tyneside local authorities, including South Shields, and with the Tyne Improvement Commission. His report was produced very quickly and, backed up with detailed statistical analysis, made compelling reading. While in County Durham and Tyneside as a whole the numbers of unemployed had fallen since 1932, there were black spots including Jarrow and Bishop Auckland where a majority of insured workers were unemployed. In South Shields itself (where he 'was very impressed by the progressive outlook of the Corporation'[18]) there were 13,000 unemployed people, representing 31 per cent of insured workers, one of the highest ratios among Tyneside authorities. He made the important observation that:

> ... prolonged unemployment is destroying the confidence and the self-respect of a large part of the population, their fitness for work is being steadily lost and the anxiety of living always upon a bare minimum without any margin of resources or any hope of improvement is slowly sapping their nervous strength and their powers of resistance.

He concluded that 'Durham and Tyneside can only escape from the vicious circle, where depression has created unemployment and unemployment intensified depression, by means of some positive external assistance.'[19]

There were a dozen recommendations in Capt. Wallace's wide-ranging report, several of which could, if implemented, benefit South Shields. The most important was grant-in-aid for a major redevelopment at Jarrow Slake (immediately upstream of the borough's boundary) to provide facilities for larger ships than current docks could handle. Grant-in-aid was also proposed for a road tunnel under the Tyne between North and South Shields. He also recommended the formation of an Industrial Development Company for Tyneside (one of whose responsibilities could be to clear derelict factory sites), 'some measure of unification' of the thirteen mostly small Tyneside municipalities, and the appointment of a commissioner 'to co-ordinate all activities in connection with Government schemes for the rehabilitation of the area'.[20] Although there was no specific proposal for grant-in-aid for the South Shields riverside scheme, Robert Chapman was cautiously enthusiastic about Capt. Wallace's report: 'His proposals are sound, bold and far-reaching, and while it is unlikely the Government will accept the whole of them there are none that would not ultimately prove beneficial to the district.'[21]

The Government's encouraging response was the Special Areas Act, passed in November 1934 following Capt. Wallace's report. It implemented one of his major recommendations, the appointment of a commissioner for the Special Areas of England and Wales (Scotland was given its own commissioner), and it very tentatively supported another. This was the key recommendation of financial assistance: the Treasury would support the work of each commissioner with a budget of £2 million annually. This was certainly very small beer indeed, but it turned out to be an important milestone in regional development policy making and grant support.

The Government appointed Malcolm Stewart as the Special Areas' Commissioner for England and Wales, and Robert lost no time in promoting the cause of South Shields. The commissioner visited the town on 4 January 1935, where he met Robert, the town clerk (Harold Ayrey) and the borough engineer (John Reid). He was shown the riverside development plan, which proposed a new deep water quay and associated industrial and commercial redevelopment. He familiarised himself with the site, walking through Thames Street, Thrift Street, Wapping Street and Ferry Street, remarking encouragingly that the scheme 'would be an amazing improvement'.[22] After the meeting and site visit, Robert hosted a lunch at *Undercliff* for Malcolm Stewart, who might well have confirmed informally his support for the £260,000 scheme. In any event, Robert, as chairman of the Development Special Committee, reported on progress to the council on 3 April 1935. The Commissioner for the Special Areas had agreed to a grant of £60,000 towards the redevelopment, and had indicated that the borough should apply to the Minister of Transport for grants towards the cost of its new roads. Robert recommended that the council should proceed on this basis, applying to the Minister of Health for borrowing approval to finance the remaining net costs, and this was readily agreed.

The overall objective for the scheme was to transform the rather desolate area between The Lawe (overlooking the mouth of the Tyne) and the Market Place, which would be connected by a new riverside road. Old riverside buildings and works would be demolished, a new deep water quay (first proposed forty years earlier) would be built, and the adjacent ballast hill behind the important local businesses of Brigham and Cowan's ship-repair yard and the Tyne Dock Engineering Company would be levelled, enabling their docks to be expanded. Six months later, the first stage of the scheme, which had attracted funding through the Special Areas' Commissioner, was formally inaugurated by the Mayor, Alderman J. W. Watson. The grant was enough to cover the costs of the new road and retaining wall from Pilot Street (near The Lawe) to Mile End Road, the levelling of the ballast hill, the extension of the existing railway line to the river, the demolition of redundant buildings and associated land acquisition. Robert, as chairman of the Development Special Committee, stressed how important the scheme was as a good 'shop window' for attracting new industries, and expressed optimism that the Ministry of Transport would fund the new road's extension to the Market Place. However, he cautioned that the provision of the quay (at £100,000 of total estimated scheme costs of £260,000) 'is a longer matter, but the Committee are proceeding with the preliminaries and the taking of soundings so that our engineers can get out their plans'.[23]

The Government had taken the first steps towards a grant-assisted policy to alleviate unemployment in the depressed areas. It also introduced an Unemployment Bill in the autumn of 1933 to centralise the administration and payment of unemployment benefit, thereby reducing the financial burden shouldered by local authorities. One of its additional provisions was a special grant of £300,000 for the 'distressed areas', to reduce the cost of public assistance. This was discussed in the committee stage of the Bill – a marathon twenty-three-hour sitting on 13 and 14 December. Several MPs from southern constituencies, including Croydon, wanted to reduce this amount, which sparked a lively response from County Durham MPs, including Samuel Storey (Conservative) from Sunderland, Jack Lawson (Socialist) from Chester-le-Street, and Robert from Houghton-le-Spring.

Robert had expected opposition from MPs for constituencies such as Croydon. He drew attention to the 'awful distress there has been in County Durham for the past ten years', and specifically to the overall unemployment rate of 42 per cent in South Shields, compared to 6.6 per cent in Croydon, adding that juvenile unemployment in neighbouring Jarrow stood at an almost unimaginable 98 per cent. He concluded that 'They in the North-Eastern areas thanked the Government for this Bill. He would have been more glad if the Chancellor had seen his way to take over the whole burden of the able-bodied unemployed, but at the same time he was gratified for the £300,000 which he had granted.'[24] He supported the proposed grant assistance even though South Shields, as a result of 'careful administration', would not be classified as a distressed area for the purposes of this piece of legislation, and therefore would not benefit from it.

The Unemployment Act 1934 finally reached the statute book in June. Its radical administrative provision was to set up a new national Unemployment Assistance Board with responsibility for determining payments to almost all unemployed people. It would have its own offices and staff throughout the country, leaving local authority Public Assistance Committees with a very small residual role (which included payments to those unemployed who worked on their own account, such as small tradesmen, commission agents, hawkers and news vendors).

Somewhat ironically, given its much-reduced importance, Robert was outvoted for the role of chairman of the South Shields PAC in November. He was unable to be present at the meeting due to commitments in London, but secured the most votes among three contenders (the other two being Aldermen Druery and Linney) at what turned out to be the first round. It was then pointed out that Robert, with eight votes, did not have an overall majority (Aldermen Druery and Linney securing six and four votes, respectively), and that there should be a second round. Alderman Linney then stood down, and Alderman G. Druery – also from the Moderates Party – secured eleven votes to Robert's nine, and was duly elected chairman. On the face of it, this looked like a mini-coup within the Moderates' camp. In any event Robert's wife Hélène lost no time in resigning from the committee, tactfully citing 'an increasing number of public and social engagements', and 'on the advice of her doctor'.[25]

She did, however, continue to take a very active interest in the council's Cottage Homes at Cleadon, including hosting their events at *Undercliff*.

If the Government thought that the 1934 Act was 'job done', it would soon have a rude awakening. In early January 1935 the Unemployment Assistance Board published its financial assistance rates, which were soon found in many cases to be lower than those of the Public Assistance Committees. This led to widespread protest, demonstrations and marches. In an ominous development for his own political future, when Prime Minister Ramsay MacDonald visited Newcastle on 16 January he was greeted at the station by shouts of 'Judas' and 'traitor' and 'down with the means test'. He had to be escorted by the police to the hall where he was speaking, with hundreds of protesters in the streets outside. There were also large demonstrations and marches in North Shields, Felling and Gateshead – but none in South Shields itself.[26] The Government quickly took action to try to defuse the situation, with the passage through Parliament of the Unemployment Assistance (Temporary Provisions) Act 1935 – soon known as the 'Standstill Act'. This suspended the UAB's scales for two years and allowed unemployed applicants to receive the old PAC or the new UAB rates, whichever were higher. This was a messy compromise and, not perhaps surprisingly, 'unemployment assistance entered upon two years of administrative waste, confusion and chaos'.[27]

There were certainly protests in Robert's Houghton-le-Spring constituency. On 3 February 1935 the men's section of the Boldon Labour Party and the local lodge of the Durham Mineworkers' Association organised a 'mass demonstration' that was attended by councillors, ex-Labour MPs and lodge officials. An ad hoc 'United Conference' of organisations in Boldon Colliery then wrote to Robert to ask him to do his best to have the Unemployment Assistance Act withdrawn. He replied that he could not agree to this request, but he did support the Government's suspension of regulations (i.e. of the financial assistance rates) made under it. Robert clearly thought that the Government's Unemployment Assistance Board had unwittingly created a complete mess, since he added that:

> It is not the intention of the Act that thousands of people should be sentenced to starvation. The object is quite the reverse. I do not in any way believe in breaking up of family life and I trust that when the new regulations are issued the Board will see that they are administered in a reasonable and sympathetic manner, and not in the manner which has

caused so much hardship in many thousand determinations which have been made since the 7th January.[28]

Robert was all too well aware of the strength of feeling against the means test throughout his constituency. He would, before the year was out, suffer its impact personally.

In the early summer of 1935 there was some badly needed light relief. On 6 May, the Government gave King George V the special honour of a Jubilee, and a national holiday, to celebrate the twenty-fifth anniversary of his reign. Robert and Hélène played a leading role in making the day as memorable as possible. The grounds of *Undercliff* were opened to the public, with the proceeds of a sixpenny admission charge going to the Ingham Infirmary. But the big event was in the evening. A few years earlier, Robert had bought Cleadon East Farm and Sunniside Farm, which included Cleadon Hills, which were within easy walking distance of *Undercliff*. Robert opened them to the public, having encouraged the South Shields Boy Scouts to build a 30ft beacon (one of a coastal chain celebrating the Jubilee) on the highest point, with a Union Jack fluttering from a flagpole nearby.

Thousands of people went up to the hills, awaiting the crucial moment of 10 p.m., when, 'By means of an accumulator, a length of cable and a fuse, Col Chapman fired the beacon, a burst of flame at the topmost point appearing noiselessly and then developing into a fierce crackle as the dry gorse bushes were licked by the flames', which eventually leapt 70ft into the air. The huge crowd joined in the singing of the National Anthem and 'gave three lusty cheers from the hilltop for the King, three for the Queen, then the Prince of Wales and finally for Col. Chapman'.[29] At 11 o'clock the Union Jack was hauled down and a solitary bugler sounded the Last Post. All in all, a splendid way to celebrate a Jubilee.

In London there were several large events. St Paul's Cathedral led the way with 'A Form of Prayer and of Thanksgiving to Almighty God for the protection afforded to The King's Majesty during the Twenty-five years of his Auspicious Reign'. This was followed on 9 May by a very tightly organised 'Presentation of Addresses to His Majesty George V by Both Houses of Parliament' in Westminster Hall. Robert attended as an MP, and listened to addresses by the Lord Chancellor and by 'Mr. Speaker' from the House of Commons, to which His Majesty graciously replied. Seating arrangements in the Hall took careful account of appropriate protocol.

Robert and Hélène's invitation from the Lord Chamberlain to a ball at Buckingham Palace on 14 May 1935. (Chapman Family Archive)

On one side of the Royal Dais sat 'Indian Princes and Representatives of UK Legislatures', and on the other 'Dominion, Indian and Colonial Representatives'. Invitees were advised that 'No artificial heating can be provided in the Hall and ladies whose seats are near the north door are warned that the temperature may be low.'[30]

Not every London event was sedentary. 'Commanded by Their Majesties', Col and Mrs R. Chapman were invited by the Lord Chamberlain to a ball at Buckingham Palace on 14 May. Hélène had been presented at court by the Duchess of Devonshire the previous year, but this was the first Court Ball invitation they had received. 'The keynote [for the 2,000 guests] will be informality. Dancing – waltzes, fox-trots and polkas are the only dances on the programme – will begin as soon as the royal procession has entered the ballroom and the King and Queen have taken their seats on thrones on a dais.'[31] A week of enjoyable Jubilee celebrations was now over, and Robert returned – hopefully with his spirits lifted – to the political fray.

In June 1935, Ramsay MacDonald, whose political influence was by then exhausted, swapped offices with Stanley Baldwin, who had served

The *Newcastle Journal* reported on 11 June 1934 that 'Mrs Chapman, wife of Col R. Chapman, CMG, DSO, MP of Cleadon, presented at last night's Court by the Duchess of Devonshire, wore a striking gown of pale azalea pink satin and net, beautifully embroidered in a rose design of palest pink crystal and diamante. Her satin Court train was winged with net, and outlined with rich embroideries to match her gown. She wore an ostrich feather fan of a deeper tone. By Fenwick'. (*The Newcastle Journal*/Chapman Family Archive)

under him as Lord President of the Council. The change reflected the Conservative majority in the National Government and, as the new Prime Minister, Baldwin lost little time in going to the country to consolidate his position and secure a mandate for rearmament. Parliament was dissolved on 25 October, and the General Election fixed for 14 November. Once the election campaign started, rearmament and foreign policy were pushed into the background. 'The electors showed little interest in these questions, and the arguments of the rival parties at best cancelled out. Housing, unemployment and the special areas were still the dominant themes.'[32] This time, Robert would be in the firing line, and he knew it.

One of the principal reasons for Robert's success in 1931 had been the agreement between the Conservatives and Liberals in the National Government not to stand against each other. This had benefited both parties in the eleven County Durham constituencies (called 'divisions'), and together they had taken eight seats from Labour. The new Conservative MP for Barnard Castle, Cuthbert Headlam, recalled in his diary entry a farmers' dinner in Sunderland where he 'sat next to Chapman who seems a very decent fellow, a cut above most of our Durham MPs. He is all out for the "National Party" idea – mainly because he considers that unless he can retain Liberal support he cannot hold his seat.'[33] Unfortunately for Robert there was no such general agreement at national level in 1935. In his Houghton-le-Spring constituency, the Liberal Association's members dithered for a week before deciding not to put forward a candidate themselves. However, unlike in 1931, they were divided and did not come out in favour of Robert, leaving it to individual members to make up their own minds on which candidate to support.

The Labour Party had voted in a new parliamentary candidate to fight Houghton-le-Spring. This was William J. Stewart of Boldon Colliery, an unemployed miner, Durham County councillor and Methodist lay preacher. It soon turned out that some prominent local Liberals had signed nomination papers for him, and others – including Sir Hedworth Williamson of Whitburn Hall near Sunderland – for Robert. The prospect of Liberal votes being split between the two candidates was not a good omen for Robert.

Just as the campaign was starting to warm up, Robert had to deal with criticism from an unexpected quarter – from no less a personage than the national President of the Conservative Party, Lord Stonehaven. In South Shields, instead of again supporting the Liberal MP Harcourt Johnstone against the Labour candidate and former MP, Alderman Chuter Ede, the Conservatives had decided to field a National candidate, F.A. Burden. This meant that there would be a three-way contest, significantly reducing the chances of either Johnstone or indeed Burden himself winning the seat. Robert must have been furious with this decision, not least because Harcourt Johnstone had discouraged the Liberal Association in Houghton-le-Spring from fielding its own candidate. He soon made his views known because when J.H. Thomas, the Dominions Secretary in the National Government, visited South Shields to speak in support of F.A. Burden, Robert refused an invitation to appear on the platform with them. This was reported in the *Shields Gazette*, and led to Lord Stonehaven writing sternly to Robert expressing 'surprise' at his decision.

Robert was unrepentant, the *Shields Gazette* reporting that he 'holds that a division (constituency) should have been selected for Mr Burden where he would have had a straight fight with Socialism, instead of having a division where a Liberal who was a member of the last Parliament

VOTE FOR
CHAPMAN

Polling
Day:
November
14th

THE NATIONAL CANDIDATE

_{Printed by The Northern Press Ltd., Harrington Street, South Shields, and Published by C. J. Archer, 1, Viewforth Terrace, Fulwell, Sunderland.}

Robert's 1935 General Election poster.
(Chapman Family Archive)

was standing'.[34] Unsurprisingly, Burden was not a happy man, particularly given Robert's prominence in South Shields. When a questioner at a meeting started to ask him a question, 'Col. Chapman has referred ....', he interrupted by saying, 'If you refer anything about Col. Chapman to me, it is like holding a red rag to a bull.'[35] Party politics did not prevent Harcourt Johnstone from supporting Robert and criticising Lord Stonehaven's intervention. 'I think it is rather a singular way to treat a loyal Conservative Member of Parliament, who has often had the courage to take an independent line in the House of Commons, and who in this case too, has had the courage to say what he thinks.'[36] Robert made no further comments about the South Shields contest. He had his hands more than full in Houghton-le-Spring. The coal industry, unemployment and the means test were the key issues, particularly at the thirty or so public meetings he attended.

The candidates' manifestos did range more widely, over both foreign affairs, including armaments, and home affairs – housing, education, social services, agriculture and transport. On rearmament, Robert said that the Navy needed modern ships: most of our battleships were thirty years old. Moreover, Germany was spending £800,000,000 in a single year on rearmament:

PARLIAMENTARY ELECTION.

POLLING DAY,
THURSDAY, 14th NOVEMBER, 1935.

HOUGHTON-LE-SPRING DIVISION.

Yours sincerely,
W. J. STEWART.

_{Printed and published by Thos. Summerbell, 10-11 Green Street, Sunderland.}

William Stewart's 1935 General Election manifesto. (Chapman Family Archive)

… the whole of industry was mobilised for war, submarines were exercising in the Baltic, every youth was being trained, while the air force was being developed at great speed. If England is strong, and known to be, there will be peace; but if England is weak, and thought to be, there will be war.[37]

William Stewart's manifesto commented that the Government's:

… feeble policy on Collective Security frustrated all attempts to achieve a reduction of Armaments, and stimulated the 'Arms Race'. The Labour Party regards war as senseless and wicked, a blasphemy against the human spirit. It believes that the only guarantee of Peace lies in the development of a co-operative world Commonwealth.

Issues of war and peace, in 1935, did not ignite voters' passions. There was extensive press coverage of the campaign, but very few references to any debate on rearmament in public meetings. The shipyards were certainly all in neighbouring constituencies, but Houghton-le-Spring's northern boundaries did abut those of Gateshead, Jarrow, South Shields and Sunderland with their badly suffering, or closed, shipyards. Robert set out his robust personal view at a meeting in Cleadon Park, South Shields:

The main cause of unemployment on Tyneside was the desire and yearning of this country for disarmament. If we had continued to build battleships, not only for ourselves but for all the nations of the world as we did before the war, there would not have been unemployment in this part of the country.[38]

He had, in his very first campaign speech in Houghton-le-Spring itself, referred to disarmament and unemployment, 'but repeatedly there were cries of "Tell us about the Means Test. Never mind about more battleships, tell us about how we are going to get our bread and butter".'[39]

Robert turned to housing policy and progress, an area where his knowledge was deep and interest passionate, and where the National Government's record was starting to look good, certainly in comparison to the Labour Government's performance in 1929–31. His manifesto pointed out that the National Government was now building 320,000 houses annually (compared with 178,000 p.a. in 1929–31); 80,000 slum houses

The STORY of the POSTERS

A General Election always produces a crop of posters—and promises. It is easy enough to make these promises, but the only ones worth while are those that are kept. See for yourself how the Socialist Government in 1929-31 failed to live up to its poster promises. On the other side see how the National Government's promises have been fully redeemed.

SOCIALIST POSTERS

[GENERAL ELECTION, 1929]

GREET THE DAWN: GIVE LABOUR ITS CHANCE

Labour had its chance and failed utterly. Instead of "greeting the dawn," the country was faced with a nightmare of depression and brought to the verge of bankruptcy.

Why I am voting LABOUR

LABOUR WILL USE ITS POWER
To secure to every member of the community the Standards of Life and Employment which are necessary to a healthy independent and self respecting existence.

And what happened in fact? Nearly 2 million workers lost their jobs and wages fell steadily.

MEN & WOMEN WORKERS YOUR CHANCE AT LAST!

THE WORKS ARE CLOSED! BUT THE BALLOT BOX IS OPEN

VOTE LABOUR IN YOUR OWN INTERESTS!

Under the Labour Government industry was brought almost to a standstill—hundreds of factories closed down and exports were halved.

NATIONAL GOVERNMENT POSTERS

[GENERAL ELECTION, 1931]

"BOOM ALONG" TO BETTER TIMES

VOTE for the NATIONAL GOVERNMENT

Better times are with us to-day. Four years steady work under National Government has restored confidence and put the country on the high road to prosperity.

"Mates! help me get a job."

VOTE FOR THE NATIONAL GOVERNMENT

In the past four years over a million more workers have got back into employment and wages have started rising again for the first time since 1927.

BRING BACK THIS SIGN

HANDS WANTED APPLY WORKS MANAGER

VOTE FOR THE NATIONAL GOVERNMENT

This sign has come back. Factory output in this country to-day is breaking all records. Exports have risen by over £30 millions and are still on the upgrade.

[P.T.O.

General Election campaign 1935: The Story of the Posters: Vote National. (Chapman Family Archive)

 Under the Labour policy of free imports Britain was the dumping ground of the world and it was the foreigner who was getting the work while unemployment in this country soared sky high.

 One of the first acts of the National Government was to impose tariffs which reduced the import of foreign goods by over £150 millions. These goods are now being made by British workers who are " punching-in " at the factory instead of being " knocked out " by the foreigner.

 What a charter ! Under the Socialists thousands of acres of land went out of cultivation, thousands of farm hands lost their jobs. In 1931 agriculture was threatened with complete collapse.

 The farming industry has been protected from foreign dumping and has been placed permanently on the road to recovery. Wheat acreage has been increased by a half and farm workers' wages to-day are the highest ever recorded.

 And what was the result ? Overseas trade fell by £2 millions a day — unemployment rose by 2,000 a day. Nothing but depression and crisis !

 And no wonder ! What is more, he is going to vote for the National Government again because he knows that it delivers the goods.

FOR PEACE, PROGRESS AND SECURITY
VOTE NATIONAL

Printed and Published by McCorquodale & Co. Ltd., St. Thomas's Street. London, S.E.1.

No. 3545. *November, 1935*

General Election campaign 1935: The Story of the Posters: Vote National. (Chapman Family Archive)

were being cleared each year (7,000 p.a. in 1929–31); and the Housing Act 1935 required local authorities to 'abolish overcrowding for good and all' (there had been no Government action at all, he said, on overcrowding in 1929–31). He took the trouble to produce a special flyer for the residents of the Sutton Estate near Cleadon Park: 'It was through my efforts that the Sutton Dwellings Trust were persuaded to come to South Shields to develop their Estate and provide so many houses at low rents (which) were made possible because I assisted the Corporation and the Sutton Dwellings Trust to acquire the land cheaply.'

So far as the mining areas in his constituency were concerned, 'He hoped that the Government's plan of reconstruction would include small houses for aged miners and that these miners, many of whom had no chance of starting work again, would be given pensions to allow them to live in the comfort which they deserved.'[40] Here he touched on a key issue in the campaign – unemployment in the coal industry and what the Government was, or was not, doing about it. In the decade to 1934, the North East coalfield as a whole lost around 50,000 jobs, or 20 per cent of its total employment. Coal exports were much lower, as was the demand from local industries hit hard by the depression:

> These blows fell heaviest on the older and less efficient collieries, and the loss of employment and income was most severe in areas where the cost of production had risen with the working-out of the most accessible and easily extracted seams of coal, as in many of the older Durham pits.[41]

Collieries in Houghton-le-Spring were badly affected, and indeed 20 per cent of the insured population in the district were unemployed (of whom 60 per cent had been unemployed for more than a year).

Robert advocated several measures to help the mining industry: a subsidy for export coal; a price rise to electricity and gas undertakings and to other coal-using industries; and the encouragement through cheap loans (as already applied to railway improvements) of new plants in the Special Areas for obtaining oil from coal, which would lead to more employment and better wages for miners. None of these proposals was at that time on the Government's agenda. As for the Government's current financial support, 'The Commissioner for the Special Areas [Malcolm Stewart] had put forward schemes which would have helped the County, but he had not been given any money with which to put the schemes into operation.'[42] Robert was no doubt referring to a proposal originally floated in Capt. Euan Wallace's report to finance new 'trading estates', but no details of this potentially important initiative would emerge until after the General Election.

Meanwhile, Robert was faced with exactly the same situation as Cuthbert Headlam, the Conservative MP in the adjoining constituency of Barnard Castle, who had also been elected in 1931: 'No one can honestly say that conditions have improved in the mining areas under the National Government ... The Means Test, and nothing but the Means Test, is the issue in these parts for this election.'[43] The points Robert made seemed reasonable enough: the Labour Government of 1929–31 had introduced it; it was necessary to have some form of means test (he highlighted the case of an unsuccessful applicant to the South Shields Public Assistance Committee who turned out to have investments of £3,000 and an income of £3 a week); and Part II of the Unemployment Act of 1934 had increased benefit levels.[44]

Nevertheless, Robert did not mention the means test specifically in his election manifesto, unlike William Stewart who said that its 'harsh cruelties ... are a disgrace to our National Life'. Rather, Robert focused on the reduction in the number of unemployed (900,000 fewer since 1931), emphasising that in August 1935 there were 10,424,000 in employment, 'a larger number than had ever before been employed in the history of this country'. He did add that 'unemployment is unfortunately still a heavy burden', as indeed it was in Houghton-le-Spring.

Robert received a stormy reception at a meeting of miners and their wives in Ryhope, where 'the crowd took up the strains of "The Red Flag"',[45] and he was howled down as he tried unsuccessfully to address a meeting at the Herrington Burn Miners' Welfare Hall. These were isolated incidents, from which William Stewart, through his agent, quickly dissociated himself: 'If rowdyism does occur, we very much regret it, because we both believe that everyone should have a fair hearing.'[46] As for William Stewart's own campaign, the North Mail reported that he 'is having splendid receptions in his tour of the principal polling areas ... and at an open-air meeting at Houghton-le-Spring yesterday, he had the support of the local branch of the National Unemployed Workers' Movement'.[47]

Robert, who stated publicly that his views 'are just as far from the extreme Tory as from the extreme Socialist', received a letter of support from the National Liberals' leader, Sir John Simon, who hoped that he would have the fullest support of Liberal voters in the constituency.[48] The Hon. Walter Runciman, prominent Liberal MP and President of the Board of Trade, who had been at South Shields Boys' High School with Robert, wrote encouragingly: 'Let me say that if I were a voter in Houghton-le-Spring I would (as a Liberal) plump for you. And as I have had a lifelong knowledge of you, I would know that I was voting for a straight and patriotic candidate.'[49]

In the event, the cards were stacked too heavily against Robert. A crowd of some 3,000 people was waiting outside the Newbottle Street Council School in Houghton-le-Spring when the result was announced on 15 November. On a high turnout of 82 per cent, William Stewart had polled 30,665 votes against Robert's 22,990, giving the Labour candidate a decisive majority of 7,675 votes. Robert congratulated William Stewart and said:

> I hope that at the end of four or five years Mr. Stewart will have the pleasure of coming back to Houghton-le-Spring to see many more people living in better conditions, and a vast number of men returned to work. I hope that better times will prevail, and that much of the unhappiness which is unfortunately present in many homes, will turn to brightness. Though you have turned me out this time, I shall be glad at any time to do all I can for any of you.

Robert's comment to the *Northern Echo*'s journalist was simply: 'I think that the conditions in the mining industry and the Means Test have influenced the electors on this occasion.'[50] They certainly had.

At Westminster, Stanley Baldwin's National Government was re-elected with a commanding majority. It had 429 MPs in the new Parliament, of whom 387 were Conservatives. Labour had done much better than in 1931. They now had 154 MPs, a hundred more than in 1931, but the Liberals were down to just twenty-one MPs. This was the beginning of a two-party system, with the Conservatives in an unassailable position for, as it turned out, the next decade.

Robert was not alone in losing his seat. Labour regained the eight County Durham 'divisions' lost in 1931, and Ramsay MacDonald himself was a further and spectacular casualty. Continuing to stand as a National Labour candidate at Seaham, he was trounced by Emanuel (Manny) Shinwell, the official Labour nominee, who secured a massive 20,000 majority. In South Shields, Robert's fears proved fully justified. The Conservative candidate

Chuter Ede, MP for South Shields, 1935. (South Tyneside Libraries)

F.A. Burden polled 10,784 votes, not far off Harcourt Johnstone's 12,932. However, this split 'anti-Labour' vote enabled Chuter Ede, with his 22,031 votes, to win back the seat that he had originally won by just forty votes in 1929. He would represent the borough in Parliament for the next fifteen years. And in Jarrow, Ellen Wilkinson won the seat for Labour from the incumbent Conservative MP, W.G. Pearson.

Robert may have been 'turned out', as he put it, of Houghton-le-Spring, but he had plenty on his plate in South Shields and County Durham. In 1930 he had become chairman of the General Committee of the Ingham Infirmary in Westoe, where his father Henry had at various times been honorary auditor, governor and chairman himself. December 1935 was a red letter day for the Infirmary, which originally opened in 1873. Its president, Sir James Readhead, opened a new wing with a golden key presented to him by the scheme's architects. The total cost when fitting out was completed would be £60,000, of which nearly £50,000 had, Robert reported, already been raised. The extension would house an additional fifty-nine beds – bringing total accommodation to 183 beds – as well as a new operating theatre, out-patients' department, and further accommodation for nurses. A 'new electrical department will contain apparatus for radio therapy, radiography and electro therapy'.[51]

Ellen Wilkinson, MP for Jarrow, 1935. (South Tyneside Libraries)

The Infirmary had an inclusive governance structure, which included 'Workmen Governors'. Subscriptions from workmen were important for the infirmary's finances, and so Robert:

> ... referred to the hopes of further work for the West Docks (Sir James' shipyard) and said that the Ingham Infirmary had a pecuniary interest as the sums contributed by the workmen when the docks were working had at present to be made up by subscriptions and contributions from other sources.[52]

The new year of 1936 would turn out to be one of generational transition nationally, and for Robert personally. In January, the popular King George V died at the age of 70, his successor, King Edward VIII, ascending the throne aged 41. *Shields Gazette* readers were reminded that three years earlier, as Prince of Wales, he had visited the town 'in connection with his investigation into social services on Tyneside. He inspected the Zion Chapel Unemployed Workmen's Recreation Centre placed at the

Opening of the Ingham Infirmary extensions, December 1935. Front row from right to left: the Mayor (Councillor Edmund Hill), Mrs Hill, Col Robert Chapman, Sir James Readhead, the matron (Miss A. Lowe), Lady Readhead. (South Tyneside Libraries)

disposal of the men by the Mayor (Col. R. Chapman).'[53] The following month, in February, Robert himself had a bereavement when his father Henry died at the ripe old age of 85. He had been fortunate enough to have lived through the years of South Shields' economic growth, sharing in its prosperity through the businesses he founded. However, he and Dora (who would die two years later) had also suffered pain and anguish as parents who had lost a son, a daughter and a son-in-law in the First World War. Among the 200 mourners at St Michael's Church in Westoe were representatives of all the main businesses, sporting clubs and voluntary organisations in the town.[54]

These voluntary organisations included the Boys' High School, which the borough council had purchased in 1908 and where Robert himself had been actively involved for many years. As chairman of the Education Finance and Works Sub-Committee, Robert had, with South Shields' MP Harcourt Johnstone, successfully lobbied the Board of Education in London to approve the construction of a new High School for Boys, which would also incorporate all the pupils from Westoe Secondary School, on a splendid 14-acre site in Harton. The new school was opened later in 1936 – the year in which the school leaving age was raised from 14 to 15 – by the Bishop of Durham, Dr Hensley Henson. Robert, as chairman both of the governors and of the Old Boys' Association, must have been very proud of the new establishment, built to accommodate 550 pupils. Its collegiate layout housed sixteen classrooms, chemistry, physics, and biology laboratories, libraries, art and music rooms. There were also four football pitches and a cricket pitch. In Robert's words, 'Ample playing fields have been provided on the site, as I believe that all schools should have proper provision for the children to take healthy exercise.'[55] The *Shields Gazette* summed up the positive mood at the opening ceremony, reporting that the new premises had been described as 'the finest school building controlled by a municipality north of London'.[56]

Robert remained deeply involved with borough council development activities, and – although no longer an MP – with Government 'Special Areas' policies throughout the North East. In February 1936 he publicly expressed admiration for the work of Malcolm Stewart, the Special Areas' Commissioner, whose second report proposed that a 'trading estate' be set up to attract new industries and jobs, and that a North-Eastern Housing Association be set up to build working-class houses, thereby relieving councils from having to make a financial contribution towards them. Robert wished, however, that the Special Commissioner had more powers (and no doubt a much larger budget).

In March 1936, Malcolm Stewart announced that he had indeed approved the setting up of North Eastern Trading Estates Ltd:

> The object of the company will be to acquire a suitable site in the North-Eastern special area, and to develop that site by the construction of roads, railway facilities, the provision of power in the form of gas, electricity, steam or hot water, and the construction of factory buildings so as to provide all reasonable facilities required by industrialists engaged in starting fresh enterprises.

He added that the North East did not have any trading estates, and there was growing demand for the facilities they could offer.[57] The company's capital would come from the Special Areas Fund, and its activities – including selecting a site from a shortlist of six with the assistance of the North-East Coast Development Board – would be controlled by a board of eight directors. The chairman would be Col Appleyard, managing director of the Birtley Company, iron founders and engineers, and the directors would include Robert himself (now also an alderman of South Shields Borough Council), Viscount Ridley (chairman of the North-Eastern Housing Association) and William Westwood (president of the Engineering and Shipbuilding Trades Federation).

Col Appleyard made it clear that:

> The intention of the company is to disturb the balance of economy in the North-East, so that the prosperity of the area does not depend entirely on one section of industry. We are concerned more with a long-term policy extending over 10 to 20 years and by bringing new industries into the North-East, put the eggs of prosperity into more than one or two baskets. We have had strong assurances that the North-East will benefit from the Government's extended armaments programme. That is excellent and will do much to relieve immediate unemployment. The function of the trading estate is, however, to ensure that prosperity becomes a normal and continuing state.[58]

The *Sunday Sun* commented that as the new enterprise 'is the first attempt to promote private industrial undertakings with public money, the formation of the company has aroused considerable national interest. (Its) success or failure may have far-reaching effects on future official policy.'[59] Indeed it would, happily as a major success story.

The worst of the recession was now over, although improvement nationally was very much stronger than in the North East. The famous Jarrow march of October 1936 to the Houses of Parliament, dignified and disciplined as it was, took place against a background of staggeringly high unemployment. Of 8,000 former workers in its shipyards and steelworks, only 100 were still employed in 1936.[60] The march had cross-party support within Jarrow Borough Council, and a conference of all Tyneside local authorities agreed to launch a petition to support the town's demand for work. The petition was duly presented to the House of Commons, with a few supportive questions asked by north-eastern MPs, including Chuter Ede of South Shields. It would soon influence still further the development of Government policy towards the distressed areas.

Also at Westminster, a potential constitutional crisis was developing, as it became clear that King Edward VIII intended to marry the already once

Jarrow crusade, 1936: Ellen Wilkinson, MP, in the front row of marchers en route to London. (South Tyneside Libraries)

divorced Mrs Wallis Simpson just as soon as she had obtained a divorce from her second husband. The crisis was averted by his abdication on 11 December 1936, in time for wits in South Shields to write in their Christmas cards:

Hark the Herald Angels sing
Mrs. Simpson's pinched our king.[61]

The new King was his brother Albert, Duke of York, who took the title of George VI.

The New Year would bring good news for South Shields and Tyneside. Serious rearmament was now well under way and business confidence in the economy was growing. These positive trends were reflected in the strength of the Readhead shipyard's order book, which for many decades had been a key economic indicator in the town. Two cargo-liners, *Armanistan* and *Baltistan*, had been ordered the previous year from Strick

Line and were completed in 1937. Then came orders for nine more cargo-liners, four more for Strick Line and five for Bank Line. Future expansion potential was gained by the acquisition of Smith's Docks Company's adjacent dry docks, and by the end of 1939 both the shipyard and Readhead's repair yard would be working at full capacity.[62]

Meanwhile, significant changes were under way within the borough council. In November 1937, after twenty-six years of administration by the Moderates, Labour gained control for the first time. The new regime flexed its muscles by voting off all Moderate members – including Robert as former chairman – from the Development Special Committee. His considerable success in that role would, nevertheless, receive further recognition before long.

Robert now became very active on the civil defence and Territorial Army fronts. In March 1938, the month in which Germany annexed Austria, he called for more volunteers to become 'air raid precaution workers' and the following month he repeated his appeal, contending that 'Even the most confirmed pacifist could not raise any objection to them.'[63] His wife Hélène became an air raid warden (as a 'precaution worker' was soon renamed), as did Robert himself in May – the first member of the council to do so. The council set up an Air Raid Precaution (ARP) Sub-Committee, whose initial preparations – including identifying sites for the storage of 120,000 civilian gas masks and large supplies of sand bags – displayed a distinct lack of commitment to the task in hand. Robert criticised the sub-committee in no uncertain terms. He said that they had failed 'to show any real interest and to point out to the townspeople the urgency of the situation – and their responsibility [to volunteer as air raid wardens]'.[64] Fortunately, the council soon became much more proactive. In October, Robert was appointed Chief Air Raid Warden, and the Mayor wrote to the *Shields Gazette* saying that with its population of 114,000, the Government's recently inaugurated Air Raid Protection Services calculated that 3,400 volunteers would be needed. With 1,800 already in place, he appealed for 1,600 new volunteers to come forward.[65]

Hélène, for her part, took up the new role of centre leader for South Shields Women's Voluntary Service for Civil Defence. She and her committee would be responsible for the organisation of women volunteers as air raid wardens, nurses, cooks, motor drivers, canteen drivers 'and in all other capacities for which women are most suited'.[66]

Robert, by now honorary colonel of 74th (Northumbrian) Field Regiment, Royal Artillery (Territorial Army), and vice-chairman of the Durham County Territorial Army and Air Force Association, did everything he could to encourage young men to volunteer. Some employers in the county, notably Associated Breweries in Sunderland, were very supportive, with 95 per cent of employees under 30 having joined Territorial Army units or the Army or Navy Reserves. The company was praised by General Sir Walter Kirke, Director-General of the Territorial Army, at an event in December, at which Robert proposed the toast of 'The Territorial Army', giving examples of units in County Durham that had doubled in numbers in just twelve months. He observed that:

> The recent crisis brought forward many men who did not before recognise their responsibility. Many who hoped to be officers have gone into the ranks and it seems to me, in these democratic days, that it would be an advantage if every man had to serve in the ranks – and attend one training in the ranks – before he could take a commission.[67]

The new Team Valley Trading Estate from the air. (Roland Park, reproduced in S. Middlebrook, *Newcastle upon Tyne* [Newcastle upon Tyne, 1950])

Robert also recommended, as a way of building up a reservoir of potential future recruits, that the Commanding Officers of all units should have a company of cadets – under the command of a retired officer – attached to them. Meanwhile, foreseeing the likely need for a much greater number of trained servicemen, he joined the Territorial Association's committee campaigning for a period of compulsory National Service.

These civil defence and Territorial activities sat alongside the major contribution he was making as a director, and soon to be chairman, of North Eastern Trading Estates Ltd. The company, set up by the Special Areas' Commissioner, had chosen the Team Valley near Gateshead as the site of its first 'trading estate', a ground-breaking national initiative that received £2 million in grants under the Government's Special Areas Fund. Plans were drawn up by the well-known architect Bill (later Lord) Holford in the summer of 1936. In addition to providing completely new infrastructure for the huge site – its central artery called 'Kingsway' was 2 miles long – plans included the construction of factories and other industrial units. This major work programme proceeded at a fast pace, and the first unit was occupied in October 1937 by Orrell and Brewster Ltd, haulage contractors. Speedy development paid off, since the industrial estate was soon benefiting from the financial provisions of the 1937 Special Areas (Amendment) Act, which authorised the Treasury to make loans to firms moving into the depressed areas, and the Special Commissioner to give them incentive payments to do so.

The Team Valley hit the headlines on 22 February 1939, when King George VI, accompanied by Queen Elizabeth, performed the trading estate's formal opening ceremony. A banner that proclaimed 'A hundred new industries join in loyal greetings to Your Majesties'[68] highlighted the extraordinary progress already made, thanks to Special Areas funding and the trading estate's management team. These new industries were employing more than 7,000 workers at the time of the royal visit. Robert attended the opening, and the special luncheon for the King and Queen that followed it.

South Shields was also fortunate enough to receive royal attention. The King and Queen visited the new municipal clinics, 50 per cent of whose total cost of £14,000 had been met by the Commissioner for the Special Areas. They were welcomed by a choir of 150 school children – who had been given a day's holiday – and by the Harton Colliery Band. A Guard of Honour was in place, 'composed of nurses and staff drawn from the various hospitals and services in the Borough'. The building's facilities were extensive, with specialist clinics for maternity and child welfare, for schools ('for the treatment of defects found at the medical examinations in schools') and for tuberculosis. There were also three dental surgeries and a 'light clinic', where 'a modern apparatus is installed for the treatment of rickets, skin diseases, etc'. The staff of forty-five included six doctors (three men and three women), fifteen midwives, ten health visitors, three dental surgeons and four nurses. Between them they saw some 16,000 patients, who collectively had made 77,000 'attendances' during the previous year.[69] In short, the clinics offered an impressive multi-disciplinary, community-focused range of services.

On the following day, the King and Queen visited another new trading estate, St Helen Auckland, which had opened on a 22-acre site. They were welcomed by Robert in his capacity both as a director of North Eastern Trading Estates Ltd, which had constructed the industrial facility, and also as a director of the South West Durham Improvement Association Ltd. This association had been set up in 1937 under the chairmanship of Lord

King George VI and Queen Elizabeth visit the new trading estate at St Helen Auckland, February 1939. Col Robert Chapman is on the Queen's right. (*Northern Echo*)

Barnard against the background of declining employment in the local coal pits, with a mandate to acquire and restore derelict industrial sites. King George and Queen Elizabeth visited the two completed factories, occupied by Ernest and Henry, button makers, and by Bond Moulding and Engraving Company. They were told that when the remaining three factories were completed, occupied and in full production, there would be employment for 800 people on the estate.

The royal visit to Tyneside and County Durham was a great success, and Robert received an appreciative message from the King (through Lord Londonderry, the Lord Lieutenant of County Durham, who had been 'commanded by His Majesty' to send it to Robert):

> Please convey to the people of Durham our warmest thanks for their friendly welcome in all parts of the County that we have visited. We have been very glad to have this opportunity of seeing what is being done to assist those who are suffering the great misfortune of unemployment. We come away deeply impressed by the courageous spirit so clearly prevailing even among those who have been for long periods without work and we should like to send them a message of encouragement and hope for a better time to come.

The letter was sent on behalf of 'George R.I.', that is to say *Rex et Imperator*, King and Emperor.[70]

Further recognition of achievements in South Shields came in the summer, when Capt. Euan Wallace, Minister of Transport and author of the influential Government-commissioned report of 1934 into industrial conditions and unemployment in County Durham and Tyneside, revisited the town and officially opened the River Drive bridge. This was a key element of the 35-acre riverside redevelopment scheme, with a new road from the Market Place crossing the bridge and linking up with the northern end of Mile End Road. A further new section to Pilot Street joined Harbour Drive and led to the Coast Road to Sunderland. The borough council had been very successful with Government funding, since the Special Areas' Commissioner had met two-thirds of the costs of land acquisition and construction, including a railway extension to the site, and the Ministry of Transport had contributed 50 per cent of the costs of the new bridge and roadworks. All in all, the Government had met £125,000 of the scheme's total costs of £200,000. In addition to its £75,000 contri-

View from Heugh Street of the River Drive Bridge under construction. It was opened by Capt. Euan Wallace, MP, in August 1939. (South Tyneside Libraries)

bution, the council itself intended to finance 215 flats and four shops at a cost of £127,000.

Robert gave a speech in which he thanked Capt. Wallace for his financial support as minister, adding that he must be delighted to see that so many of the proposals in his 1934 report had already been realised. Robert gave several examples: the formation of an Industrial Development Company (now set up); the establishment of trading estates (North Eastern Trading Estates Ltd had already brought 120 factories to Tyneside); the acquisition (with the aid of Government grants) of Tyne Dock by the Tyne Improvement Commission from the LNER railway company, with a further £1 million to be spent on improving its amenities; the acquisition for new industry of Palmer's yard in Jarrow (where a new steelworks was under construction); and the setting up of the North-Eastern Housing Association.[71] Robert mentioned Capt. Wallace's recommendation for a road tunnel linking South Shields and North Shields, expressing confidence that, as Minister of Transport, he would support a tunnel with an entrance not far from the town. The tunnel was certainly built – but after a delay of three decades.

Robert was starting to become rather disillusioned with the politics of the borough council. It had decided to finance the 215 new flats on the riverside scheme itself, with financial support from the rates, rather than approach the North-Eastern Housing Association, whose schemes required no local authority contribution. He objected to the all-Labour composition of a new three-member committee formed to take over municipal administration in the event of war, and he also objected to the council's appointment of a number of young men of military age to home service Air Raid Precaution (ARP) posts, and pointed out that one member of the new 'committee of three' was also of military age. This prompted the Labour leader, Councillor Ernest Gompertz, to retort that his party would not stand for industrial or military conscription. Robert walked out of the council meeting in disgust, and soon afterwards resigned from the post of chief air raid warden. The *Shields Gazette* tactfully reported that Col Robert Chapman 'is unable to give as much time to the office as he thinks it deserves'.[72] He was replaced by Maj. H.L. Todd.

Robert was watching the international situation with growing alarm. Speaking at a conference in Newcastle in April 1939, a month after Hitler invaded and annexed Czecho-Slovakia, he referred to the annexation of Austria the previous year, and continued:

> The occupation of Czecho-Slovakia and later the seizure of Memel [on the Baltic coast of Lithuania] had made it clear that Herr Hitler's ambition was not satisfied and that he was willing to break his pledged word without hesitation in an endeavour to see the fulfilment of his scheme for a mighty dominion from the North Sea to the Black Sea and perhaps even beyond that.[73]

After these prescient remarks, he continued that to meet the threats of the dictators (Hitler and Mussolini, who had recently invaded Albania), 'the policy of a peace bloc must be pursued, and in addition to Poland, Rumania and Greece, Russia had also to be persuaded to join in. Russia is deeply affected by the Nazi ambition ... [and] it is Germany who threatens the peace of the world – not Russia.'[74]

Robert called for more volunteers, stressing that:

> ... the call of the Field Army must come first. Wars are not won by remaining on the defensive. We must have the 250,000 Territorials now

asked for and we must have them quickly. Northumberland and Durham require between 15,000 and 20,000 – they are there and I urge each one of you to see that they are obtained without delay.[75]

He reported a month later that his call for recruits had had such an excellent response that both the 74th Field Regiment, RA, and the 389th Company, 47th (Durham Light Infantry) Anti-Aircraft Battery R.E. were up to war establishment. However, there were still vacancies with the Northumberland Hussars, the Second Line Durham Light Infantry (the Tyneside Scottish) and with the Royal Engineers in Sunderland.

In May 1939, under the headline 'Civil Defence in Shields: Many Avenues of Service Open to Women', Hélène, who was centre leader, Women's Voluntary Service for Civil Defence, set out the volunteering opportunities available in auxiliary nursing, first aid posts, hospital supplies and in the transport department. Cooks, domestic workers, cyclists, messengers, telephonists and switchboard operators were all needed, too.

Few now doubted that war was on the way, and in August events started to move quickly. The Nazi–Soviet pact was followed by the 25 August Anglo-Polish treaty of mutual assistance. On 1 September German troops crossed the Polish frontier and its aeroplanes bombed Warsaw. A British ultimatum demanding the withdrawal of German troops was delivered to the German Government at 9 a.m. on 3 September. No reply was received before the ultimatum expired at 11 a.m. Britain immediately declared war, as did France in the late afternoon. The Second World War had begun.

10

UNDERCLIFF

'The happiest place on Earth', Ada C. Brown, 1931

Undercliff from the lake, 1932. (*Shields Gazette*/Chapman Family Archive)

By the outbreak of the Second World War, Robert and Hélène had been living at *Undercliff* in Cleadon for sixteen years. They purchased the house from the Allison brewing family in 1922, and moved in on Saturday, 24 March 1923, a date recorded inside Hélène's meticulously kept visitors' book. The house still stands, splendidly situated beneath Cleadon

Hills on the road to Whitburn and the sea. Set in secluded grounds of 10 acres, mostly enclosed by a traditional wall of locally quarried stone, it was built in the middle of the nineteenth century. In the authoritative architectural series, *The Buildings of England*, it is described as 'A fine classical brick house' probably built between 1853 and 1856. The south façade, overlooking the garden, is 'divided into three bays by brick pilasters', all windows having stone surrounds. The rooms on the south side – drawing room, morning room and dining room – all have 'fine plasterwork'.[1]

Robert and Hélène moved in with their two sons, Robin and Nicholas, then aged 12 and 9 respectively, and a staff of twelve indoor and outdoor servants, as they were described at the time. Robert, whose left arm was badly injured in the First World War, was not able to drive, and so a chauffeur was an essential member of the staff. He engaged Benjamin (Ben) Ward, who, with the rank of sergeant, had been his batman in the 4th Durham Howitzer Battery during the war. No doubt encouraged by Robert, Ben continued to serve as a part-time Territorial artillery volunteer until the late 1920s, when he re-enlisted for a further four years as a volunteer Trooper with the Northumberland Hussars Yeomanry, also a Territorial Army regiment.[2] He would remain at *Undercliff* for more than thirty years.

The house was ideal for entertaining, and Robert and Hélène hosted dinner parties, weekend house parties and dances with great gusto. Being able to entertain guests in some style became increasingly important as Robert's local and national political roles expanded in scope alongside his and Hélène's numerous charitable commitments. They got off to an impressive start, putting up sixty house guests between the end of March and December 1923 – family, friends and visitors attending local functions. Mabel Paynter, widow of Maj. F.P. Paynter, a comrade in arms of Robert in the 4th Northumbrian Howitzer Brigade RFA (T) who was killed in the war, stayed on 27 March. Guests were obliged to sign the visitors' book on departure, and encouraged to make comments about their stay. All were appreciative; many were witty. Mabel wrote, 'I am the first guest that Rob and Hélène have had in "Undercliff" and feel very honoured. Many happy years to them both.' They would, as it turned out, be fortunate enough to have forty happy years together in the house, Mabel Paynter becoming Hélène's best friend and a frequent visitor over that period. After her next visit in May, she commented on an 'exhausting afternoon coping with Hélène's "at home" guests! Everything in apple-pie order.'

Family members stayed many times during the next few years. Hélène's father, James George Macgowan, had retired from the oil company he managed on the Champs-Elysées in Paris, and now lived with his wife, Jenny, in York House, overlooking Kensington Gardens in London. They had visited battlefield sites with Robert and Hélène in 1920, including the farmhouse that had been Robert's brigade headquarters at Harbonnières near Amiens. James must have felt the need to keep his French going, commenting in the visitors' book, '*Qu'il est dur de quitter une maison où on est si bien reçu*' (it's hard to leave a house where one is so well looked after'). His sister Ann Macgowan, who had moved from Stirling to Riding Mill in Northumberland, described 'A topping weekend with much reminiscing, despite the host's shaking of cushions' (shaking or 'plumping' cushions to restore their shape at the end of an evening was an essential drawing room task).

On her departure Jenny Macgowan, Hélène's mother, doubtless recalling her Scottish childhood, expressed the earnest wish, 'May a mouse ne'er get into your meal barrel.' Later in the decade, as a widow, she signed herself 'Grand'Mère', which is how Robin and Nicholas always described her, and she recorded '*une bonne visite, le beau temps et la vraie hospitalité*'. Hélène's sister Isabelle (Lady White after her marriage to Sir Dymoke White, who had estates in Hampshire and Norfolk) was a regular guest, often with her husband. She commented that 'a thing of beauty is a joy for ever'. For his part, Dymoke wrote simply 'an oasis' – the precise phrase he used when the author asked him, thirty years later, what he thought of *Undercliff*.

Robert's family, mostly living nearby, were well represented as house guests. His mother, Dora, and sister, Ethel, lived in Westoe, and his aunt, Elizabeth Chapman, from 1 Challoner Terrace in South Shields, recalled, 'Every comfort and great kindness.' His brothers stayed occasionally. Hal, an architect living in Westoe Village, had returned from London for a house party: 'bacon and eggs at 5.30 after a night in the train, most welcome!' was his appreciative comment, not necessarily shared by the cook or parlour-maid who served him breakfast at dawn. Laurence, who studied at Durham University and became an agricultural chemist in Pamilola in Upper Assam, stayed one December, on home leave. He may or may not have had a good time: 'Drunk every night' was his visitors' book comment. Sadly he had multiple health problems and died in Scotland during the Second World War. Robert's widowed sister, Bessie Annand, who had married Lt Cdr Wallace Annand – killed in the Gallipoli campaign a year after their wedding – frequently came to stay from Westoe with her son

Richard (Dick) Annand. As he was a 10-year-old, his mother may well have fed him his visitors' book line: 'But the glory of the garden lies in more than meets the eye.'

Some of Robert's military friends seemed almost as close as family. Graham Angus and Charles Brims from the 74th (Northumbrian) Field Brigade RA (Territorial Army) were frequent visitors. Maj. E.G. Angus, MC, TD, became Commanding Officer of the 4th Durham (Howitzer) Battery in South Shields, living with his wife Bridget at Wylam-on-Tyne in Northumberland. Brevet Lt Col C.W. Brims, CBE, MC, TD, became the Commanding Officer of the 1st Durham (Hebburn) Battery. A few months after Robert and Hélène moved in, there was a military reunion. Charles Brims wrote, 'After a gorgeous banquet at Headquarters where we celebrated Ypres, Armentières, Somme, Arras and Wancourt(!)[3] we have returned sober and happy to sleep peacefully at Undercliff, and this morning the sun rose on a vision of shingled beauty!'

Many other friends who had shared experiences in the 50th (Northumbrian) Division came to stay. They included Brig. Gen. Cyril Eustace Palmer, CB, CMG, DSO, a professional soldier who lived with his wife Nina at the Manor House in Bedale, North Yorkshire, and Brevet Col F.R. Archie Shiel, DSO, TD, managing director of South Garesfield Colliery, and his wife Inez, from Leazes Hall, Burnhopefield in County Durham, who were all regular visitors. Archie Shiel had kept detailed war diaries, which described all too evocatively life on the Western Front, and which were quoted widely by military historians.[4] Audrey Sebag-Montefiore, whose husband Lt Col Eric Sebag-Montefiore had fought with the Durham Light Infantry, was another visitor with links to the 50th (Northumbrian) Division.[5] Wartime allies from France also unwound in *Undercliff*, no doubt helped by Hélène's fluent French. A 'Capitaine Instructeur à l'Ecole Spéciale Militaire' at St Cyr commented that if he had not already been an anglophile he would have become one after the hospitality he had received ('*Si je ne l'étais pas déja, l'hospitalité que j'ai reçu ici me rendrait anglophile*').

An Army chaplain who became well known on the Western Front, 'Philip Clayton, alias Tubby of Toc H', as he described himself in the visitors' book in April 1926, had by then become a national figure. 'Tubby' Clayton, instructed by his senior chaplain, Rev. Neville Talbot, opened *Talbot House* in 1915 at Poperinghe near the Ypres salient in Belgium. Robert later visited this very popular 'Every Man's Club', a rest-house for all soldiers, regardless of rank, which became known as TH or Toc H in Morse signallers' code. After the war 'Tubby' became vicar of All Hallows by the Tower and founded the Toc H movement for service in the community, which expanded rapidly in Britain and beyond. The South Shields branch had been set up two years earlier 'and there was tremendous jubilation over the coming of their great leader', as 'A Shieldsman's Diary' later recorded:[6]

> The meeting I attended in the church hall of St. John's Presbyterian was a delightfully unorthodox affair. There was no stage setting, no platform ceremony, no oratory. When the sturdy, rubicund Tubby appeared on the scene the boys were in full song with the 'Blaydon Races' [often described as the 'Geordies' National Anthem']. That and another song, 'Keep yer feet still, Geordie, hinney' captivated him on the spot, and they were sung in Tyneside halls wherever he was a guest. He gave us an encore and another and we sang it to him with gusto, to his manifest delight. It was a memory to take away from his Tyneside visit.[7]

On leaving *Undercliff*, 'Tubby' wrote in the visitors' book, 'This is without doubt Interpreter's House with the Chamber called Peace, and windows towards the sunrise', a clear reference to an episode in John Bunyan's *The Pilgrim's Progress*, where Interpreter's House is a place 'for rest and instruction'.[8] In the book, the pilgrim Christian departs saying, 'Here I have seen things rare, and profitable … let me be/Thankful, O good Interpreter, to thee.'[9] Encouraged by 'Tubby' Clayton, Robert supported the South Shields branch, which initially ran a boys' club and worked with blind people. He later helped expand its activities, became president and donated a chapel to a new Toc H house in Westoe Village in memory of his brother and sister, Charles and Dorothy, who died in the First World War.

Meanwhile, the situation in the coal industry was deteriorating rapidly. On 24 and 25 April 1926 the well-known industrialist Sir Alfred Mond, MP (later Lord Melchett), Chairman of Amalgamated Anthracite Collieries in Wales, and the creator of Imperial Chemical Industries, came to stay. Despite his best efforts, he was not able to avert the miners' strike, which commenced on 1 May and was quickly followed by the nine-day General Strike. The miners held out for six months,[10] an *Undercliff* guest in October commenting that 'The warmth of my hosts' hearts made up for no coal.'

Professional friends from South Shields were also in evidence at *Undercliff*, notably the solicitor Victor Grunhut, often with his son Stephen. Victor had, like Robert, been at South Shields Boys' High School and a volunteer with the 4th (Durham) Howitzer Battery before the war. He became a ubiquitous figure in South Shields' legal and social life, crossing the river each day from his home in Tynemouth to reach the offices of his firm, Grunhut, Grunhut and Makepeace. He and Robert worked together on numerous transactions. As a house party guest for the Ingham Infirmary Annual Ball in 1927, he wrote in the visitors' book, 'Infirmary Ball – Hélène outshone them all'. Also from Tynemouth came Shannon and Daphne Stevenson, who became good friends of the Chapman family. Shannon, a sub-lieutenant in the Royal Navy on the China station, had left the service to work in his family's business, the Northern Press, owners of the *Shields Gazette*. When he stayed at *Undercliff* he was a recently appointed trainee manager, a decade later becoming director and general manager.[11]

In the summer of 1929 Dorothy, Countess Haig, the widow of Field Marshal Lord (Douglas) Haig, drove down from Scotland to stay at *Undercliff*. During the war she had been appointed a 'Lady of Grace' of the Order of St John of Jerusalem and had worked with the Red Cross.

Opening of the North East Coast Exhibition, Newcastle upon Tyne, 1929. It attracted more than 4 million visitors. (*Newcastle Chronicle*, reproduced in Sir Arthur Lambert's *Northumbria's Spacious Year 1929* [Newcastle 1930])

In 1926 she had founded 'Lady Haig's Poppy Factory' in Edinburgh to offer disabled veterans employment making remembrance poppies for the Royal British Legion's yearly appeal. She and Robert attended the annual church service for its South Shields branch, where he was president.

Some three dozen house guests stayed between May and October 1929 and were lucky enough to have the opportunity of visiting the North East Coast Exhibition of Industry, Science and Art on the Town Moor in Newcastle. Held five years after the British Empire Exhibition in London, its advertised purpose was 'to show to the Country, and to the World at large, the many and varied products of its Yards, Factories and Workshops', based on modern science and business organisation. 'Not only from every district in the Homeland, but from every part of the Empire and her dominions overseas, exhibits will be drawn to bring hundreds of thousands of visitors a startling realisation of the amazingly rapid march of progress in all lands which fly the British flag.'[12]

The exhibition was an impressive achievement. Erected within sixteen months, there were three huge 'palaces' – for industry, engineering and the arts – and a festival hall, all designed in an art deco style by Stanley Milburn of the well-known Sunderland architects W. and T.R. Milburn. These buildings were complemented by separate pavilions for women (with continuous displays of arts and crafts), for artisans and for the Empire Marketing Board (whose slogan was 'Empire buyers are Empire builders'), and by an amusement park and a stadium that could house 20,000 people.

The Prince of Wales opened the exhibition on 14 May, emphasising that its aim was to 're-vitalise existing industries', and that 'To restore our

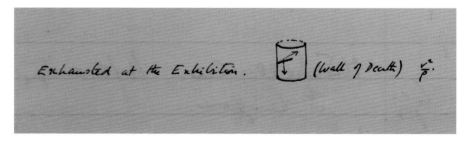

Undercliff visitors' book: diagram by house guest Alan Robson, senior mathematics master at Marlborough College, showing the forces acting on a motorcyclist riding the 'Wall of Death' and consequent centripetal acceleration. (Chapman Family archive)

economic prestige we need courage and imagination – courage in ruth-
lessly scrapping all methods of machinery that do not come up to the
most modern standards, and imagination in exploring every commercial
avenue overseas.'[13] These challenging words during an increasingly severe
depression did not prevent over 4 million visitors from having a thoroughly good time, their spirits lifted by the music from forty brass bands,
including from Marsden, Harton and St Hilda's Collieries. The very popular amusement park had a number of special attractions – a great water
chute, a Himalayan railway, an African village and a wall of death. One
of the *Undercliff* house guests was Mr Alan Robson, senior mathematics
master and teacher of Robin and Nicholas at Marlborough College. He
commented, 'Exhausted at the Exhibition', and provided a rather neat diagram and formula explaining the physics behind the newly introduced
wall of death entertainment (in which motorcyclists ride safely along the
vertical inside wall of a large drum-shaped wooden structure, thanks to
centripetal force).[14]

There was further entertainment for house guests even closer to home.
The Sunderland Empire, also designed by W. and T.R. Milburn and
founded by Richard Thornton who was born in South Shields, put on a
variety show, *The Five O'clock Girl*, which Robert and Hélène's niece, the
20-year-old Kay Smith, went to see at the end of October. The show had
been transferred from the London Hippodrome with a large cast of dancers and singers, and some catchy tunes. This prompted Kay to write in the
visitors' book, no doubt humming the tune as she did so, 'Are you one of
the Empi-r-r-re gurls?'

After six years at *Undercliff*, and with the North East Coast Exhibition
in full swing, Robert and Hélène decided it was time to commission a
comprehensive 'inventory and valuation' for insurance purposes. It was
completed in September 1929 by the London firm of Chinneck, Gardner
& Corbet, and its sixty-six pages included 'furniture, linen, wearing
apparel, furs, wireless installation, consumable stores, gun, silver, plated
items, cutlery, old Sheffield plate, china, glass, books, ornamental items,
contents of outbuildings, pictures, trunks, household equipment, etc'.[15]
Sixty-six detailed pages later came the bottom line: the total valuation was
'Six thousand, seven hundred and thirty pounds, six shillings'.

We can see from the inventory that, after being greeted at the front
door, guests would enter the outer hall, which was furnished in oriental style. It had a Chinese florally decorated umbrella stand, an 'eight-day

striking grandfather clock, circa 1700' in a red lacquer case decorated with a Chinese landscape, a red lacquer table, a suit of Japanese armour and a Japanese bronze gong. A stag's head on the wall was a helpful reminder to guests that they were, in fact, not far from Scotland.

Maj. James Stuart, County Down 86th Regiment of Foot, by John Knox, 1809. (© Joan Chapman)

Proceeding through the 'Lounge Hall' with a Tudor-style baronial feel to it, but comfortably furnished, and with a large painting of Aethelbert, King of Kent, receiving St Augustine giving a brief opportunity for spiritual reflection, guests were ushered into the drawing room. In this very light, south-facing room, mahogany dominated the furniture – chairs, chests of drawers, oval and octagonal top tables, coffee tables, folding card tables, and a 'square top urn table', not to mention a torchère with fluted columns and the frame for an eighteenth-century mirror. Even the 'Columbia grafonola' phonograph record player was on a mahogany table. The major exception was the 'Bechstein grand pianoforte, No. 88482', which was elegantly housed in a rosewood case. Persian rugs covered the wooden floor and an Asiatic touch was provided by a tiger skin and a leopard skin, both hunting trophies of Robert's brother Laurence in Upper Assam. The walls were hung with family and other portraits, including a fine 1809 painting of James Stuart, a major in the County Down 86th Regiment of Foot. Very proud of her Scottish ancestry, he was Hélène's great-great-uncle.

Sumptuous meals were served in the dining room, whose Georgian mahogany dining table could seat comfortably a dozen guests. On the walls were portraits of Hélène's maternal great-grandparents William Mills, merchant, ship owner and a Lord Provost of Glasgow, and his wife Mrs William Mills (née Janet Stuart). Painted in 1837, its artist was Sir Daniel Macnee, an eminent and fashionable portrait painter who became president of the Royal Scottish Academy. He had been apprenticed in Glasgow to John Knox, who painted the portrait of Maj. James Stuart. These paintings had all hung in Hélène's parents' home in Paris.

Guests would not have entered the adjacent pantry with its double-door, floor-to-ceiling silver safe, whose deep blue velvet-lined shelves contained some 300 items of table silver alone, many from the early 1800s, with Glasgow and Edinburgh marks. They would have been a fitting accompaniment to the 101-piece Doulton dinner service.

William Mills, merchant and ship owner, Lord Provost of Glasgow, 1834–1837, by Sir Daniel Macnee. (© Joan Chapman)

Nor would guests have seen the kitchen where copper utensils were still the order of the day for cookers, dishes and preserving pans. The larder contained an ice safe, a meat safe and five pickling pails. Housemaids' tasks would have been eased by the latest 'Northern' electric sweeper. Beyond the kitchen was the servants' hall with its table, eight chairs and boot cupboard, and a staircase leading to the cook's bedroom

Janet Mills, by Sir Daniel Macnee, 1837. (© Joan Chapman)

and one shared maids' bedroom with four iron bedsteads, dressing tables, chairs and gas heater. Next door was the maid's bathroom.

There was no shortage of sleeping accommodation for family and guests on the first floor, reached by an impressive dog-leg staircase with an elaborate cast-iron balustrade.[16] Robert and Hélène each had their own, interconnecting, bedrooms. Hélène slept in some style in her 5ft 6in wide mahogany four-poster bedstead, its top panel adapted for an electric light and silk shade. On top of the bed's thick hair mattress was a spiral spring mattress, with a down (feather) bolster and quilt. Her bedspread, hangings, pelmet and valance were all 'en suite' in blue damask. Robert was comfortable in his 4ft mahogany bedstead with a panel top and end, its domed centre decorated with oval herringbone inlay. Their 'personal wardrobe' was also valued, Hélène's at £400, excluding her hugely expensive 'Persian lamb coat, mink cuffs, collar and facings, lined silk', valued at £330, substantially more than the £200 valuation of Robert's entire wardrobe.

Robin and Nicholas, at the time, shared a bedroom and had their own large and well-furnished sitting room, with a French rosewood and an oak pedestal writing desk, and bookcases containing some 500 volumes ('Miscellaneous literature, including classics, history, encyclopaedia, biography etc'). The room was adjacent to the servants' wing, to which, however, there was no access at first-floor level. It had varied views, at one end overlooking the stable yard, and at the other the rose garden and conservatory.

The pace of entertaining, both indoors and in the gardens, stepped up in the 1930s. In the summer of 1931 the game of 'Murders' was introduced at *Undercliff*, and much fun was had by all. In June guests felt a tremor while the game was in full swing, enabling them to write in the visitors' book, 'A marvellous week-end. Midnight shocks to order (a local earthquake) and a murder on every floor, was provided by my charming hosts', and 'I murdered her and it quaked in the night'. Visitors were invariably appreciative, Ada C. Brown from Cornwall, on her sixth visit shortly afterwards, writing 'The happiest place on Earth'.

The gardens, which had welcomed fêtes and other events throughout the 1920s, really came into their own in Robert's mayoral year of 1931/32, when he also became MP for Houghton-le-Spring. He was now juggling duties in the constituency and in Westminster as well as in South Shields, and must have been relieved when the summer recess came, enabling him to enjoy garden parties and fêtes at *Undercliff*. At the beginning of July 1932 the *Shields Gazette* ran a well-illustrated article on 'The Glory of the Garden – A visit to the Mayor's Home'. The reporter was 'Joan' and she started her flowery description by the lakeside at the southern end of the garden. 'A fairy rockery spreads along one bank: its smooth stones come down in terraces to the water; its flowers are sweeter than life itself. Red of rock plants, green of lake rushes, delphiniums blue burn there in glory.'[17]

She wound her way up the woodland path, then through 'lovely lawns, terraces and a flower garden path' before arriving at the rose

Undercliff rose garden with whalebone arch, 1932. (*Shields Gazette*)

Sidney Snelling, head gardener at *Undercliff*, judging chrysanthemums at a flower show in Sunderland, 1939. (*Sunderland Echo*)

garden, where 'A Whale's jaw bone, grown over with dark ivy, guards the entrance. In olden days these whalebone arches were quite common near seaport towns, but now seem rather quaint.' She stepped down into the rose garden itself, 'where the roses round the arbour here look so neat. I think the gardener must have run round and pinned them all in place before we came.' She was very complimentary about the head gardener, Mr Sidney Snelling, who had worked at *Undercliff* since 1923 and was well known in horticultural circles in South Shields and Sunderland. Joan waxed lyrical: 'He is really a wonderful person, not only a gardener but an artist too.' Mr Snelling told 'Joan' that his main work was 'in the potting sheds and hothouses',[18] which were in the walled garden just beyond the rose garden. Here, in addition to all the vegetables and fruit cages – loganberries were a speciality – the walls hosted espaliered apple and pear trees. From the hothouses came grapes, figs and white flesh peaches, which were a real delicacy then and for many years afterwards.

A few days after Joan's visit came the YMCA fête, a well-established event in the social calendar. Its numerous attractions were advertised in the *Shields Gazette*: a wrestling exhibition by the South Shields police, dancing displays, a gymnastic display by YMCA members, 'a Farcical Sketch by the Royal Repertory Company', sideshows and stalls. Even better, special buses would be laid on to leave the town centre every five minutes, dropping visitors at 'the beautiful grounds of *Undercliff* which alone are worth the entrance fee (6d) and will be flood-lighted in the evening' when there would be dancing to music by the Royal Artillery Band (74th Field Brigade, RA).[19] Rather cleverly, the organisers had also managed to attract 'Wireless Advertising': after the local Newcastle news, the BBC gave details of the event.

The fête was opened by Hélène's sister, Isabelle (Lady White) from Hampshire, and she was welcomed by Robert, who sat on the YMCA's National Council and was president of its North Eastern Division. He reminded the fête's visitors that the YMCA had been established in the Market Place in 1851, that their huts had been havens of rest for 'Tommies' after their return from First World War trenches, and that the association had now put its hall, buildings and field at the disposal of the unemployed. Men without jobs put on popular displays of boxing and self-defence. Two thousand tickets for the event were sold, 300 visitors attended in dull weather, and a total of £300 was raised for the YMCA.

Summer fêtes at *Undercliff* were popular events throughout the 1930s. (Chapman Family Archive)

Two months later in Robert's mayoral year, on 16 September 1932, there was great excitement on Tyneside: Naval Week had begun, with the arrival of HMS *Malaya*, a 27,000-ton battleship originally built by Armstrong, Whitworth & Co. at Walker-on-Tyne in 1916, immediately joining the Grand Fleet and taking part in the Battle of Jutland. After a formal welcome by the Lord Mayor of Newcastle and the Mayors of all the Tyneside boroughs, there was a busy programme of events for *Malaya*'s Captain Guy Halifax and 200 of his petty officers and men (out of a total crew of over 1,000). A 'Divine Service' was held in South Marine Park, with over 10,000 people in the congregation. The Harton Colliery Band played the four hymns, which very appropriately included 'Eternal Father, strong to save' with its refrain, 'O hear us when we cry to Thee/For those in peril on the sea'. The celebrations in the park, which culminated in a splendid fireworks display, were described by a correspondent to the *Shields Gazette* as 'probably the most inspiring and most successful function ever held in Shields'.[20]

The following afternoon, Robert and Hélène hosted a garden party at *Undercliff* in honour of Capt. Halifax and his officers. This was a huge event, with more than 500 guests to be fed and watered. All Tyneside's civic dignitaries were there, from the Lord Mayor of Newcastle down-

Capt. Guy Halifax of HMS *Malaya* with Robert and Hélène, who hosted a garden party at *Undercliff* for 500 guests in his honour during Tyneside Naval Week, September 1932. (*Shields Gazette*)

stream to the Mayor and Mayoress of Tynemouth, together with their town clerks and – in the case of South Shields – all council members. The *Shields Gazette* meticulously listed the names of each and every guest, with all prominent local families represented, including Annands, Armstrongs ('with a bevy of pretty daughters'[21]), Brighams, Edwardses, Flaggs, Gowanses, Grants, Grunhuts, Readheads, Rennoldsons, Scotts and Stevensons. The MPs for Jarrow and Tynemouth (W.G. Pearson and Irene Ward) were present, and the Church was well represented by the Lord Bishop of Durham and his wife, Mrs H. Henson, the Rev. and Mrs Hastings Shaddick of St Hilda's, South Shields, the Rev. and Mrs Robson of All Saints' Church, Cleadon, and half a dozen other vicars. The Chapman family itself was there in strength – Robert's parents Henry and Dora, brother Dr Fred (the former international rugby player), sister Ethel, sons Robin and Nicholas, who 'assisted in the entertaining', and nephew Dick Annand.

Sporting activities in the grounds included tennis, organised by Robert and Hélène's elder son, Robin, then captain of the first team at Corpus Christi College, Cambridge. 'Joan', the *Shields Gazette* columnist, noted that the Misses Readhead – daughters of Sir James and Lady Readhead – 'were much in demand on the tennis courts, where the officers thoroughly enjoyed themselves'.[22] As ever at *Undercliff* garden parties, music was played in the open air by the band of the 74th Northumbrian Field Brigade, RA (TA), where Robert would soon be appointed honorary colonel. 'A large marquee was erected in the grounds, and the delicacies of the table were generously dispensed by Messrs. Tilleys of Newcastle. Floral decorations were carried out on a scheme of great lavishness and good taste.'[23] In short, a great party on dry land for Captain Halifax and officers from *Malaya*.

The following evening there was a final Naval Week event – a dinner and social evening for some 200 petty officers and men from *Malaya* at the King's Hall in South Shields. In his after-dinner speech, Robert said that it was unfortunate that due to the depression there were so many 'tiers' of idle tonnage (steamers) on the river, and no spare berth for *Malaya*. As a result she had had to moor out to sea beyond the piers, and bad weather had prevented thousands of Tynesiders from going on board her. However:

> One thing which would always be remembered to the credit of the crew of the *Malaya* was the day [Sunday] which they set apart for the unemployed men of Tyneside to pay them a visit. Happily that was a day not affected by the adversities of the weather, and many took advantage of their kindly invitation and found real enjoyment in the visit. Every one of us are grateful for that expression of your sympathy towards a splendid body of men who are passing through the trials of these unfortunate times.[24]

Members of the South Shields Women's Mutual Service Club attend 'Serving the Soup' at Zion Hall, 15 November 1933. On the cook's right is Mrs Lawlan, Mayoress, with Hélène Chapman standing behind her. On the cook's left is Mrs Linney, former Mayoress. (South Tyneside Libraries)

The problems faced by the unemployed were never far from the forefront of Robert's mind.

Throughout the 1930s Robert continued to give strong support to the South Shields Unemployed Recreation and Education Committee, where he had become president after founding it at Zion Hall during his mayoral year. For her part, Hélène remained a very active supporter of its sister organisation, the South Shields Women's Mutual Service Club. With support from churches, the Rotary Club and the borough council, the committee expanded its range of activities for the unemployed very substantially. It opened a soup kitchen, which provided meals for 300 at a penny or twopence a head, an occupational centre in Bolingbroke Street (which produced 1,200 toys for poor children at Christmas 1933) and a physical training centre whose activities included boxing. Its orchestra was now complemented by a male voice choir. The allotments scheme, very dear to Robert's heart – he promoted it not just in South Shields but also in Sunderland – continued to expand. A special committee, whose secretary was Sidney Snelling, the head gardener at *Undercliff*, oversaw its activities, which included an annual show for flowers and vegetables.

A South Shields Unemployed Drama Group was also formed. Its production of *Babes in the Wood* was warmly received in January 1934 by a full house in Zion Hall. The *Shields Gazette* reported that the huge audience 'had apparently come expecting a rather amateurish effort and were astonished at the high talent and polish displayed by the unemployed in their pantomime effort'.[25] Robert, always keen to maintain close links with Government, had sent an invitation to Sir Henry Betterton, Minister of Labour, who sent best wishes for the production and for future activities by and on behalf of the unemployed in the town.

In the summer, the gardens of *Undercliff* hosted an open-air production of *The Merchant of Venice*, described as a 'Pageant Play'. The Unemployed Occupational Centre made the stage settings, and the production included the Unemployed Male Voice Choir and Orchestra. An audience of 500 people attended on 31 July, and the performance was judged a great success, with members of the South Shields Women's Mutual Service Club cast as 'Attendants to Portia' (the heiress in the play). However, a tragedy unfolded just a hundred yards from the stage. *Undercliff*'s grounds were floodlit with the lake 'illuminated with coloured lamps'. During their installation one of the swans bit a live cable and was killed instantly, leaving 'a widow

Members of the cast of the South Shields Unemployed Drama Group's open-air production of *The Merchant of Venice* at *Undercliff*, 1934. (South Tyneside Libraries)

and a large and young family who were last night swimming about in rather a disconsolate manner'.[26]

Hélène remained totally committed to numerous charitable activities in South Shields, having recently also become vice-president of the Ingham Infirmary and Chairman of the South Shields Nursing Association (to whom she had donated a fully furnished house in Westoe Village, to double as their headquarters and as a nurses' home). She enjoyed entertaining at *Undercliff* and also social events in London as an MP's wife. A confident and striking woman, now aged 48, she decided it was a good time to have her portrait painted, and the end wall of the drawing room, next to her Bechstein piano, would be the ideal place to hang it.

Whom should she choose to paint it? She was well aware that all the portraits in *Undercliff* – of her Macgowan great-grandparents and Stuart ancestors – had been painted by Scottish artists, so a talented Scottish portraitist already established in fashionable society would be ideal. She chose Cowan Dobson, whose extensive list of patrons north and south

Cowan Dobson's portrait of Hélène Chapman, 1934. (South Shields Museum & Art Gallery, South Shields, UK. © Tyne & Wear Archives & Museums/Bridgeman Images)

of the border included Lady Lauder, the Countess of Weir, the Duke of Argyll and, displayed at the Royal Academy's 166th Exhibition in May 1934, Earl Beatty, Admiral of the Fleet. At the end of June the painting was finished, and the society magazine *The Tatler* published an arresting photograph of 'Mrs. Robert Chapman and her Portrait by Mr. Cowan Dobson', who also appeared in the image. The magazine, perhaps unsurprisingly, rated the portrait 'a big success for the former Scottish artist'[27] (by then living mostly in England). It was soon hanging in the *Undercliff* drawing room.

Napoleon Bonaparte's instruction to pay the grenadiers of the 19th Brigade, Cairo, 1799. A gift in 1934 to Robert from his close friend South Shields solicitor Victor Grunhut, conveying his grateful feelings for 'loyal and true friendship over so many years'. (© Joan Chapman)

Robert did not commission a portrait, but a few months later he received the gift of an unusual manuscript from his great friend Victor Grunhut, which was also given prominent wall space in the drawing room. This was an instruction, signed by Napoleon Bonaparte in Cairo during the Egyptian campaign in 1799, that overdue monthly payments be made to the grenadiers of the 19th Brigade.[28] This interesting historical document was accompanied by a handwritten letter from Victor that included a rather moving paragraph:

> No money, even if I had it, could purchase a gift which could convey to you my grateful feelings for your loyal and true friendship over so many years which has never failed. Time is passing – for me more rapidly than for you – may our friendship ever continue unbroken until it must give place to the inexorable hand of Time.[29]

As it turned out, this special friendship did continue unbroken until Victor's death a quarter of a century later.

The drawing room's generously proportioned windows had wonderful views of the terrace, lawns and grounds, which continued to be well trodden by appreciative visitors throughout the summer months, the 1930s being the glory years of fêtes and galas. Numerous charities benefited, mostly locally based such as the Ingham Infirmary (where Robert was chairman of the governors), the YMCA and Cleadon Cottage Homes (for orphans). Occasionally the net was cast wider, with a major event for the Northumberland, Durham and Newcastle Eye Hospital extensions' appeal fund, opened by its president, the Dowager Viscountess Allendale.

Robert was a devout man, a church warden at All Saints' Cleadon, a member of the Durham Diocesan Conference and Board of Finance, and a supporter of a wide range of church groups. Several fêtes were held in aid of the Methodist Overseas Missions and the Havelock Street Salvation Army Corps. All visitors commented on the beautiful grounds, formal gardens and hothouses, still presided over by the head gardener, Sidney Snelling. He had a nasty shock in July 1939, when in a violent thunderstorm a flash of lightning hit rainwater running down the *Undercliff* drive just 10ft away from him. He was lucky to escape with a mildly scorched face.

The last fête of 1939 was on 31 August, in aid of the Sunderland YMCA. It was opened by Sybil, Lady Eden, a 'Lady of Grace' of the Order of St John of Jerusalem, and mother of Anthony Eden, MP, soon to be Foreign Secretary in Winston Churchill's government. Her theme was that 'As a nation we have strayed far from our Christian principles.' Having warmed to it, she concluded that 'the world was looking to England for an example'.[30] Four days later, on 3 September, England did show by shining example that, whatever the cost, it intended to make a principled stand against the forces of evil.

PART 5

THE SECOND WORLD WAR AND BEYOND

11

THE SECOND WORLD WAR, 1939–45

Shortly after Prime Minister Neville Chamberlain declared war on 3 September 1939, sirens in London sounded their first air raid warning. It was a false alarm: no bombs fell then, and it would be nine months before the first German bomber targeted South Shields. At the time, however, given the importance of the Tyne for shipbuilding and armament manufacturing, it was vitally important to be prepared for an imminent attack. South Shields Borough Council stepped up the implementation of previously prepared plans and was soon operating on a well-organised wartime defensive footing.

There were two special meetings of the council in September, with Robert present at both. The decision was taken that the Air Raid Precautions (ARP) Committee, set up eighteen months earlier and renamed the Emergency Committee, should be granted exceptional powers to act on behalf of the council on all matters of Civil Defence, except those relating to the police and fire services, which would continue to report to the Watch Committee. The scale of the Emergency Committee's task was daunting, since there should have been over 3,000 male and female 'authorised personnel' (excluding reserves) to deliver the wide range of Civil Defence services – air raid wardens, first aid parties, first aid posts, drivers and attendants for ambulances, rescue parties, decontamination squads (the use of gas, as in the First World War, was widely expected), and report and control centres.

Women air raid wardens entering a gas van during training in South Shields, 1941.
(South Tyneside Libraries)

However, the report from the four councillors on the Emergency Committee to the council in October pointed out that just over half of the 3,000 'authorised personnel' (the number deemed necessary by the Home Office) were available for duty at any one time, because of the limited number of volunteers who had come forward and been trained in ARP duties prior to the emergency, a failure that Robert had highlighted publicly. Urgent steps were being taken to reduce the shortfall. By December there were 191 full-time wardens (almost a full complement), 6,000 arch-shaped Anderson shelters built from prefabricated steel sections for individual households, public shelters for 5,000 residents (including in subways in the Market Place and Westoe) and communal shelters, where Anderson shelters could not be provided, for 3,500 (around one third of the target). Supporting the main control room and report centre in the Town Hall, with its staff of twenty, were five decontamination depots, four first aid party depots and six first aid posts acting as bases for 112 first aiders (eighty-four women and twenty-eight men). Public buildings were protected by more than 600,000 sandbags.

There was good news to report to the council in December 1939. There had recently been a formal visit to the borough by Wing Commander

Hodsell, Inspector General of Air Raid Precautions, who 'expressed his satisfaction with all branches of the local organisations and tendered his congratulations to the Officers in charge of the various services on the state of preparedness which had been attained'.[1] It might still have been the 'phoney war' on Tyneside for a few more months, but the borough was living up to its proud motto of 'Always Ready'.

For the armed forces, however, it was certainly no longer a 'phoney war', reservists and volunteers having been called up several months earlier. Robert Chapman's nephew Dick Annand, whose father Lt Cdr Wallace Annand had been killed at Gallipoli when Dick was 7 months old, joined the Royal Navy Volunteer Reserve's Tyne Division on leaving Pocklington School in North Yorkshire. After a brief and not very happy spell in the south with the National Provincial Bank, he took his Uncle Rob's advice to embark on a military career. He returned to the North East and, through the Supplementary Reserve, joined the 2nd Battalion of the Durham Light Infantry (DLI), known as 'The Faithful Durhams' since the 1760s.

They were soon on the move. Before the war, the Government had promised the French that the Army would provide a British Expeditionary Force on their left wing along the Belgian border in the event of a German attack, mirroring undertakings given in the First World War. The DLI's 2nd Battalion was the first to cross the Channel, on 25 September 1939, as part of 6 Brigade of 2nd Division. For all troops, not just the handful who as teenagers had fought in the First World War, the journey past its battlefields and cemeteries towards Belgium must have evoked very mixed emotions. On 21 December, Dick Annand sent a 'Best Wishes for a Merry Christmas and a Happy New Year' card to Robert and Hélène at *Undercliff*. The card's address was simply 'France', which was good enough for Censor No. 780 to give the envelope a stamp of approval. In fact, the battalion was by then in its final concentration area on the Belgian frontier.[2]

Most of what was an exceptionally cold winter was spent in trying to improve the frontier's defences, which were almost non-existent except for a few French pillboxes built in 1937. The French felt very safe behind their Maginot line, and ignored the possibility of an attack from the west of it. For their part, the Belgians had refused to allow the Allied armies to construct a defensive line deep inside their territory in case it provoked a German attack.

This unpropitious situation did not prevent the DLI from generously offering technical support to other regiments:

'B' Company of the 2nd Battalion, Durham Light Infantry, working on fortifications in France, 1940. (David Rissik, *The DLI At War: The History of the Durham Light Infantry 1939–1945* [Durham, 1953])

A party of two NCOs and twenty-four other ranks under the command of 2/Lt Richard Annand, all of whom were skilled miners having worked in the north-east coalfields, was sent to the 2nd Battalion The Buffs (Royal East Kent Regiment) to assist in the construction of defences in their sector.[3]

By this time Dick Annand had been nicknamed 'Jake' after a 'can do' cartoon character of the time, 'because whenever his platoon created a defensive position he would take off his coat, roll his sleeves up, and dig with his troops – those great miner-soldiers'.[4]

Despite these best efforts, the defences would prove to be woefully inadequate for the onslaught they would soon face. On 9 May 1940 the Germans invaded Holland and Belgium, and by the evening Winston Churchill had become Prime Minister. Two days later, at dusk on 11 May, the DLI's Second Battalion moved off in troop-carrying transports to take up positions on the River Dyle, some 15 miles south-east of Brussels. The battalion, headquartered at La Tombe, was instructed to hold a section 2,000yd in front of which, along its whole length, ran the river and a rail-

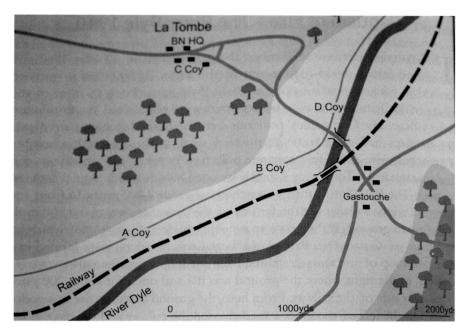

Map of the 2nd Battalion's positions on the River Dyle, Belgium, May 1940.
(Courtesy Harry Moses, author of *For Your Tomorrow* [Durham, 2012])

way line. On the other side of the Dyle were thickly wooded, steeply rising hills, ideal for offensive action. The battalion's four companies spent the next two days digging in, 'D' Company – which included Dick Annand – being responsible for covering the bridge over the railway and river. Company commanders thought that they probably had ten days to prepare for an attack, presumably not knowing that by the evening of 13 May the Germans had already punched a gap 50 miles wide in the French defences and had advanced 60 miles beyond the original front.

Just twenty-four hours later, on 14 May, the Germans advanced on to the forward slope of the high ground facing the waiting Durhams, who had blown the bridge over the river a few hours earlier. The following day the Germans attacked in earnest, mortar barrages accompanying fierce attempts to bridge the river and get their tanks across. But, thanks very largely to Dick Annand's bravery, they were unsuccessful:

> Annand's command of the platoon holding this vital position had been outstanding throughout. Twice the Germans tried to cross the demolished bridge. Twice he personally repulsed them. During the previous

morning they had got a bridging party into the sunken bottom of the river and when the ammunition had run out, he himself ran forward across the open, oblivious of mortar and machine-gun fire, and dispersed the German party with grenades which he carried in a sandbag. He killed some twenty Germans before he was wounded; but after rejoining the platoon he had his wounds dressed and remained in command.[5]

His courageous counter-attacks did not end there. The following evening the Germans launched another assault, and Dick Annand again went forward, stood on the parapet of the bridge, tossing grenades that forced them to retreat, taking heavy casualties. His platoon sergeant, Terry O'Neil, said later:

> Mr. Annand came to me at platoon headquarters and asked for a box of grenades as they could hear Jerry trying to repair the bridge. Off he went and he sure must have given them a lovely time because it wasn't a great while before he was back for more. Just like giving an elephant strawberries. I don't suppose he knows the meaning of the word 'fear'.[6]

The battalion could not hold the line indefinitely against the Germans with their heavy armour, backed up by Stuka dive-bombers, and the order came to withdraw. After Dick Annand had brought his platoon out safely, he discovered that his batman, Private Joseph Hunter from Sunderland, had been wounded, was unable to walk and had been left behind:

> Despite his own wounds sustained in the previous days' fighting, Dick returned again, found a wheelbarrow, lifted Hunter into it and wheeled him to the rear until their way was barred by a fallen tree. Now without the strength to lift, he left Hunter in an empty trench and set out to find help. He collapsed from exhaustion and loss of blood shortly after finding his company HQ position abandoned.[7]

Fortunately, he was was found by retreating comrades. The advancing Germans captured Joseph Hunter and sent him to a Dutch hospital where, sadly, he died of his wounds.

Dick Annand himself was evacuated to No. 17 Field Hospital at Étaples next door to Le Touquet on the Normandy coast, where on 20 May he wrote, with typical modesty and understatement, to Robert:

Dear Uncle Rob, This is just a line to let you know I'm quite O.K. It is difficult to know just what one can tell you with all this censoring business, but I think it's alright to say that I've had a go at the Bosches and that they've also had a go at me with the result that I'm writing this in a hospital camp miles behind the line amid glorious summer weather! The wound is not serious. A bit of a mortar bomb.[8]

The letter was never finished. The Germans continued their rapid advance and the field hospital at Étaples was evacuated on 21 May. Dick Annand was fortunate not to have become a prisoner of war. A few days later he was across the Channel and in a Portsmouth hospital, from which he telegrammed Robert on 26 May, 'wound progressing favourably'.

What he did not know was that after his evacuation from the River Dyle area, the 2nd Battalion retreated towards the coast, making a last stand at St Venan on the River Lys where it was almost completely wiped out. Its survivors managed to reach Dunkirk, embarking for England just before the Belgian forces capitulated on 28 May. However, the Germans had been held up long enough for 340,000 men, comprising almost the entire British Expeditionary Force, to be taken from Dunkirk to England under Operation Dynamo – a miraculous recovery of manpower after a devastating defeat. Dick Annand did not recover fully from his injuries. His hearing was very badly affected and within two years he would be almost completely deaf. The result was a medical downgrade and departure from his beloved battalion. However, new opportunities would open up for him, to be grasped with great determination and success.

Meanwhile, in August 1940, while the Battle of Britain was being fought with growing intensity, his heroism received national recognition. He was awarded the Victoria Cross for what was cited as 'most conspicuous gallantry', becoming one of the first Army VCs of the war. Local and national newspapers carried the story in great detail, the *Daily Sketch* informing its readers that the 25-year-old 'Wheelbarrow VC is 6 ft Tynesider'.[9] Congratulations to Dick himself and to Robert and Hélène at *Undercliff* flooded in before his investiture at Buckingham Palace during an air raid alert. South Shields Borough Council's Mayor, Alderman W.L. Pearson, hosted a civic reception in his honour shortly afterwards. November was also a special month for Dick: South Shields made him an Honorary Freeman of the Borough, and on the following day he travelled to London where – in St George's, Hanover Square, during another air raid alert – he

Robert and Hélène in the library at *Undercliff* receiving congratulations on their nephew Dick Annand's VC, August 1940. (*Daily Mirror*)

Wedding of Lt Richard Annand, VC, and Miss Shirley Osborne, St George's Hanover Square, London, November 1940. (*Westminster Press*)

married Shirley Osborne, a volunteer driver with the London Auxiliary Ambulance Corps.

By the time of their wedding in November 1940, the Battle of Britain had been won and the worst of the Blitz was over. Even though London and the South East had borne the brunt of the German attacks, Tyneside did not escape unscathed. In June the first bombs had been dropped on South Shields, and July had seen the first major raid, in broad daylight, on the Tyne, during which heavy anti-aircraft guns had brought down one enemy plane. The following month had been critical for the area, not that it was widely appreciated at the time. On 15 August the Luftwaffe had launched major raids, escorted by Messerschmitt Bf 110s, on Yorkshire and Newcastle, but the RAF had destroyed a substantial number of their planes, and the guns of Anti-Aircraft (AA) Command had shot down two bombers and five escorting fighters.[10] This 'Battle of Tyneside' had barely affected the urban population. In South Shields 'many people had very little idea how momentous an occasion it was. The roar of planes and heavy gun-fire were heard; there were occasional glimpses of aircraft attacking or taking evasive action, but bombs were only dropped in the harbour, on the cliffs and at sea',[11] and there were

Wedding of Maj. Robert (Robin) Chapman and Miss Barbara Tonks, Warwickshire, January 1941. 'The bride wore a grey-blue dress. Her bouquet was of orchids' (*Shields Gazette*). Barbara said she would have felt very uncomfortable wearing a traditional white wedding dress because of her hospital work as a Red Cross nurse following the bombing of Coventry. (Chapman Family Archive)

no casualties. The Luftwaffe carried out a few attacks in the remainder of 1940, a ceiling at *Undercliff* being brought down by a high-explosive (HE) bomb that fell on a nearby field in October, but the Germans never again launched such a massive raid on Tyneside.

Robert's elder son, christened Robert but always known as Robin, kept up the family's long 'gunner' tradition, his grandfather Henry having joined the Third Durham Artillery volunteers in the 1860s. Robin had been commissioned into the Territorial Army (TA) in 1933, serving with the 51st Heavy Anti-Aircraft (HAA) Regiment in London, where he was studying to become a chartered accountant. He returned north in 1939 and transferred to the 63rd (Northumbrian) HAA regiment based in Sunderland, which he found 'very much more efficient' and where – having received a call on 24 August to report for duty immediately – he spent the first three months of the war 'sitting at gun sites close to *Undercliff*'.[12] He was moved 'as a learner' to 30th Anti-Aircraft Brigade in Newcastle, and then in January 1940 he was transferred back to London, becoming a senior general staff officer at the headquarters of AA Command in Stanmore, Middlesex. In November he was promoted, becoming the youngest major in the command, serving with the 1st Anti-Aircraft Corps, which covered southern England and South Wales.

Robin was fortunate in his London posting, which gave him the opportunity to be 'best man' at a close friend's wedding in the summer of 1940. There he met a very attractive bridesmaid, Barbara May Tonks, and a hectic autumn courtship ensued. No time was lost in the uncertain climate of war, and in January 1941 they were married at Henley-in-Arden, Warwickshire. Barbara had been born in Ceylon, where her father ran a tea estate and where her parents were obliged to remain for the duration of the war. So she was 'given away' at her wedding by her uncle Peter Parsons, who bred racehorses at a nearby stud. At the outbreak of war she had become a Voluntary Aid Detachment nurse with the British Red Cross Society (a 'Red Cross nurse'), serving at Stratford-upon-Avon Hospital. This had been one of the receiving hospitals for civilians injured in the German bombing attacks on Coventry two months earlier, described as 'the first, vicious "all-in" blitz on Britain – a prolonged intensive attack on a limited area of about three square miles'.[13] It was a harrowing experience that she never forgot. Nor did AA Command, which was experiencing serious teething problems with radar and only managed to 'down' two enemy bombers during the attack.

Tyneside's own anti-aircraft defences continued to be improved, at least numerically. When war was declared, thirty heavy anti-aircraft guns protected the river, the total rising to forty-six guns by early 1941, comparable to the level of defences in another important shipbuilding area, the River Clyde in Scotland.[14] In and around South Shields itself searchlight sites had been, or soon would be, installed at Hebburn, Harton, Frenchman's Bay, Cleadon, Whitburn and Fulwell. Before the year was out these defences would soon be severely challenged by the Luftwaffe.[15]

The Germans had done their homework in reconnaissance missions, and had detailed maps of the Tyne at South Shields and Tynemouth. The main targets were shipyards, ship repair facilities, power stations, armament factories (mostly further upstream) and timber yards. A post-war company brochure from John Readhead & Sons Ltd displayed a September 1940 Luftwaffe map that showed not only their own shipyard (including sheds and slipways) but also the premises of Middle Docks, Tyne Dock Engineering Company, Brigham and Cowan and Smith's Dock Company among others. The Luftwaffe chose 9 April 1941 for a raid by seventy bombers, whose flares lit up the whole area. The timing was perfect because the aircraft carrier HMS *Illustrious*, built by Vickers-Armstrong, was on the Tyne, and the cruiser HMS *Manchester*, laid down by Hawthorn Leslie at Hebburn before the war, was waiting in Jarrow Slake to escort her on her next mission.

As it turned out, neither ship was hit, but the Luftwaffe's careful mapping was not in vain. Their forty or so high-explosive and 6,000 incendiary bombs that fell on South Shields caused major fires at Readhead's yards (which also suffered structural damage), at the west side of Tyne Docks, the Middle Docks, the Tyne Dock Engineering Company, Brigham and Cowan's stores shed and at Wardle's timber yard. A Satan bomb of 1,800kg – one of the largest bombs dropped so far in the war – was found unexploded in commercial premises in Templetown. Fortunately, the Bomb Disposal Section defused it. The raid had also caused substantial damage to houses in the town, resulting in twenty-two fatalities, and seventy-six injured.[16] Fifty people were rendered homeless or evacuated, including Robert's aunt Elizabeth Chapman from Challoner Terrace, which suffered severe bomb damage, as did adjacent Anderson Street. She was lucky enough to be taken by Robert and Hélène to *Undercliff* to recover from the ordeal. Had the Luftwaffe caught *Illustrious* and *Manchester* as they steamed out of the Tyne soon afterwards with their combined crews of 2,000, there would have been a national disaster.

Both Robert and Hélène were exceptionally busy with war effort commitments. Before the outbreak of hostilities, Hélène had been appointed South Shields Centre Leader for the Women's Voluntary Service (WVS), which formed part of the Air Raid Precautions (ARP), or Civil Defence, operation in the borough. By the end of September 700 women had enrolled as volunteers. It became a highly efficient organisation, whose separate departments included Hospital Supplies (where more than 100 volunteers worked at its Westoe Road depot making blankets, operation shirts, bed jackets, stockings, bandages and other items for the Ingham Infirmary, the Red Cross and the Missions to Seamen Institute), Transport (forty women drivers available for the fire service in an emergency), Publicity and Propaganda (including an 'anti-gossip' campaign with posters urging 'no careless talk'), and Evacuation. The WVS throughout the North East provided 'sterling service ... particularly after an air raid when they ran clothing distribution and rest centres for those "bombed out". They kept mobile canteens open 24 hours a day, every day of the year, throughout the war.'[17]

WVS services after air raids would again be badly needed in South Shields in the autumn of 1941. Meanwhile, a fortnight before the major Luftwaffe attack on 9 April, Hélène had received, in strict confidence, a letter from R&W Hawthorn Leslie & Co. Ltd asking her 'if she would be kind enough to launch a warship from their Hebburn Shipyard on Thursday 10th April, about 2.45 p.m.'. The letter explained that:

The Admiralty have particularly asked us to have all Warships correctly named, even though we are at war, but, combined with that request, we have been instructed that the event should not in any way be made public and that the name of the ship and date of launch should be kept secret. I feel sure that you will appreciate the necessity for these instructions at the present time, and forgive us for arranging a very quiet and simple ceremony, realising none the less, as we do, how anxious the Royal Navy is to have its ships launched in the traditional manner.[18]

The warship was the destroyer HMS *Pathfinder*, and her launch duly took place the day after the major air raid of 9 April, German bombers fortunately having failed to find her. Hélène gave the traditional naval salutation: 'I name this ship *Pathfinder*. May God guide her, and guard and keep all who sail in her.' After the launch came the final fitting out and the tests and trials of her equipment. Officers and key ratings gradually joined the ship, praised

The destroyer HMS *Pathfinder* launched by Mrs (Hélène) Chapman at Hawthorn
Leslie's Hebburn shipyard, April 1941. (© Imperial War Museum [ADNO 8722])

the standard of workmanship and 'could not have wished to meet a more
friendly and co-operating firm than Hawthorn, Leslie's, who have for so
many years been renowned for their ship and engine building'.[19]

A year later the final sea trials were concluded and the formal hand-
over of the ship from Hawthorn Leslie's took place. The process was
extraordinarily unbureaucratic: 'Acceptance from the builders is a very
simple matter: it involves no more than the Captain's signed receipt for
one destroyer, typed on an ordinary sheet of paper.'[20] The Commanding
Officer was Capt. Edward. A. Gibbs, who later recalled that:

> I look on the *Pathfinder* as the best of the many good ships I have served in.
> She was nearly always at sea or at short notice for steam, which grievously
> cut our opportunities for maintenance; but whatever calls were made on
> her hull, engine and equipment, she rose to the occasion every time. And
> more than that, she was a joy to handle – she was more nearly human than
> any other ship I've known. There was another side to her too – she was a
> lucky ship [losing only one life during her wartime service].[21]

His was an informed view, having served with *Pathfinder* in battles to pro-tect Atlantic and Malta convoys and becoming the first naval officer to win three bars to his Distinguished Service Order medal. Hélène Chapman's good wishes at the launch had been more than fulfilled.

Wartime challenges were far from over. In June 1941 Germany invaded Russia, with which Churchill immediately forged an alliance, expressing total solidarity in the war against Hitler. It was hoped that the Luftwaffe's new priority would be to support the advancing German armies, and that the risk of large-scale air raids on England, including on Tyneside, would be much reduced. America, under President Roosevelt, sought to avoid direct involvement in the war, although specialist anti-aircraft 'observers' from the USA had been providing significant and much-appreciated tech-nical and other assistance to AA Command since the previous autumn.

For their part, pro-British Americans were giving substantial help on a voluntary basis and, through Robert and Hélène and their son Robin, County Durham became the beneficiary of generous philanthropy from East Coast America. While at Corpus Christi College, Cambridge, Robin had struck up what became a close friendship with Dick Hollister, whose father George Hollister was a stockbroker in New York, and he had stayed with their family in Connecticut. George wanted to demonstrate positive support for the British war effort and, together with 174 fellow students in the Class of 1896 at Yale College (later Yale University), subscribed for an ambulance to be sent to 'Colonel Robert Chapman, *Undercliff*, Cleadon, near South Shields' through the British-American Ambulance Corporation. Unfortunately, although the ambulance was known to have arrived safely in England, it did not reach Robert. An appeal for informa-tion in the British press elicited a not altogether helpful report in the *Daily Mail* on 17 March 1941: 'A driver in the Royal Artillery informed *The Daily Mail* yesterday that the ambulance was doing good work at a mili-tary hospital, though the censorship forbade him to go into any details'! Robert, a Royal Artillery man himself, must have been furious.

Greatly to their credit, George C. Hollister and his Yale classmates of 1896 responded by subscribing for a second ambulance, which happily was not purloined on the way to *Undercliff* and arrived safely in July. Robert, who was now chairman of the Durham County Territorial and Air Force Association as well as County Welfare Officer, formally presented the vehicle on the drive outside the entrance porch to representatives of the British Red Cross Society and of the St John Ambulance Brigade for their

American ambulance donated by the Class of 1896 at Yale College outside *Undercliff*, July 1941. Left to right: Col Robert Chapman, Maj. Robert (Robin) Chapman and his wife Barbara, Hélène Chapman, Nicholas Chapman. (James Henry Cleet)

use in South Shields and Sunderland. Hélène attended the event as both deputy president of the Durham County Branch of the Red Cross and also vice-president of St John Ambulance Brigade's South Shields Nursing Division (the two organisations having set up a joint committee at county level for their work during the war). It was a happy family occasion: both Robin and Nicholas were there. Robin had travelled up from his AA Command posting in the south, and Nicholas was on leave from Accra in what was then the Gold Coast (Ghana after independence). He was a senior civil servant, instructed by the Colonial Office to remain in West Africa for the duration of the war.

Hélène sent a warm letter of thanks to George C. Hollister, which was published in the Yale alumni magazine. She added that:

America has been magnificent and we have received endless gifts from the Red Cross in the way of clothes and food … the quantities have been so tremendous that we are almost overwhelmed. The clothing from America is under my supervision as head of the Women's Voluntary Services for South Shields and we have distributed it equally in various centres of the town so that should we have a bad air raid everything is organised for the welfare of the people.[22]

The preparations of the WVS and of all Civil Defence services would soon be severely tested. Just two months after the arrival of the ambulance came the heaviest bombing raids of the war. On 30 September 1941, the electric power station was hit, causing an immediate blackout in the town, Middle Docks was damaged, the Whitehill Point ferry was sunk, the Harton Dye Works was wrecked, gas and water mains burst, roads and railway lines were blocked, damage to residential properties was extensive, and many graves in St Hilda's churchyard were 'disturbed'. In Barrington Street the *Shields Gazette* offices received a direct hit, and the printing department was wrecked. Henry Chapman Son & Co.'s offices across the road at 14 Barrington Street – where Robert was by then the senior partner – suffered roof damage.

Worse was to come. As the well-known local historian and official war photographer Amy Flagg reported:

> Tired workers had not had sufficient rest nor had essential services been fully restored when, on Thursday October 2, the Luftwaffe carried out an even more intensive and determined raid. In the short space of an hour and a quarter many parts of the town suffered from indiscriminate bombing, and the Market Place was rendered almost derelict by High Explosive (bombs) and resultant fires.[23]

At daylight on Friday morning, she observed that:

> … the Market Place looked like the ruins of Ypres; nothing could be seen but broken buildings; the square was littered with debris and a tangle of fire hose; all the remaining windows in St. Hilda's church were shattered, the roof dislodged and the old stone walls pitted and scarred with shrapnel. The Old Town Hall suffered heavy interior harm and none of the business premises was left intact.[24]

In other areas of the town, the newly constructed power house at Brigham & Cowan's dock was destroyed, and one side of the Tyne Dock

The *Shields Gazette* defiantly flies the Union Jack after its Barrington Street printing works and offices suffered a direct hit by heavy-calibre bombing on 30 September 1941. The attack also caused damage to the roof of Henry Chapman Son & Co.'s offices on the opposite side of the street. (South Tyneside Libraries)

'The Market Place looked like the ruins of Ypres' after bombing on 2 October 1941. (South Tyneside Libraries)

Bombing of the Tyne Dock Engineering Company's repair yard on 2 October 1941 wrecked the side of the dry dock and lifted the 570-ton SS *Southport* off her keel blocks. (South Tyneside Libraries)

Engineering Company's dry dock was wrecked, the force of the explosion lifting the 570-ton SS *Southport* off the keel blocks and depositing her on the other side of the dock. The ARP Rescue Service received badly needed assistance from services in Gateshead, Sunderland and Newcastle. In total some 240 houses, offices and shops were destroyed and a further 1,900 or more were damaged. Two thousand people were made homeless, including – for the second time – Robert's 87-year-old aunt Elizabeth Chapman from Challoner Terrace, who died at *Undercliff* six months later. Taking the two major raids together, there were eighty-six fatalities, with a further 168 residents seriously injured.

Not knowing that the most intensive air raids of the war were over, the town's Civil Defence services remained on constant alert. However, in December it was clear that a tragic event on the other side of the world would at some stage bring huge benefits to Britain. The Japanese attacked the American fleet in Pearl Harbor, sinking most of it, and Hitler followed by Mussolini declared war against the United States in support of their Japanese ally. America was now in the war and the outcome would surely be eventual victory for the US and its allies, even if the timing and cost could not be foreseen. Meanwhile, December 1941 also brought good news on the family front to Robert and Hélène. Their elder son Robin's wife, Barbara, gave birth to a baby boy – David Robert Macgowan. They were now proud grandparents for the first time.

Much of Hélène's prodigious energy continued to be deployed through the WVS in South Shields, with wider county-wide responsibilities through the Red Cross. Robert remained a borough alderman throughout the war, and he had been appointed to the prestigious position of High Sheriff of County Durham for 1940/41. Nominated by the sovereign, the key element of what had become a largely ceremonial role was to support the Royal Family, the judiciary, the police, local authorities, church and faith groups and the voluntary sector. In June 1940, following established tradition, he attended the Summer Assizes at the courts in Durham, where cases were heard by two judges from 'His Majesty's High Court of Justice' in London.

Robert's links with voluntary organisations were exceptionally strong, and when as High Sheriff he was asked in July to address the annual meeting of the Durham County Nursing Association, with its 180 trained nurses in 120 districts, he proposed the post-war provision of nurses' homes in each district. He pointed out that:

… the services of the nurses would be more needed as the result of the war because many men would return home suffering from wounds and ill-health, and that the nurses would be able to discharge their duties more effectively if they had comfortable cottages wherein to rest at the end of the day's labours.[25]

The proposal was warmly received and was another example of Robert's long-term support for service personnel re-entering civilian life. A substantial amount of his time and energy was now being spent on his voluntary roles, notably as County Welfare Officer for the armed services, supporting servicemen and service women (for example in the Auxiliary Territorial Service and Women's Auxiliary Air Force) stationed in Durham. By the spring of 1942 he had been carrying out this role for two and a half years and it had developed considerably in scope during that period.

The War Office defined the key task of 'Local Army Welfare Officers' (LAWOs), of whom there were over 700 nationally – including County Welfare Officers such as Robert – as being:

… to get in touch with commanding officers in their locality and in cooperation with voluntary organisations and other bodies in the area, provide what assistance they could in terms of securing amenities and recreational facilities for the troops [there were around 1.5 million troops stationed in Britain throughout the war], as well as giving advice on personal problems.[26]

This was a very broadly defined brief, but once the War Office had set up a Directorate of Welfare, monthly memoranda of directives and advice were sent out to Welfare Officers. The War Office was concerned both about the 'deplorably large proportion of officers who fail to care properly for their men's welfare and to inspire their men's respect',[27] and, relatedly, about the problem of boredom, for example in anti-aircraft batteries with their small detachments often in isolated areas.[28]

A number of important morale-boosting initiatives were launched. One of these was to supplement the canteen provisions of the NAAFI (the Navy, Army and Air Force Institutes), whose resources could not meet all the demands of the expanding armed services at home and abroad and whose premises soldiers often found rather institutional, with a network of additional facilities:

These were run by such bodies as the Women's Voluntary Service, the YMCA (Young Men's Christian Association), the Salvation Army, the Church Army and Toc H (these organisations coming together with other philanthropic agencies that had a religious background to form the Council of Voluntary War Work – CVWW). The canteens were supervised by Local Army Welfare Officers and the emphasis was placed on the creation of a real home atmosphere.[29]

Robert had supported Toc H for many years, and its founder 'Tubby' Clayton had stayed at *Undercliff* in 1926. As County Welfare Officer and High Sheriff, Robert had been present at the opening of Talbot House, a Toc H rest and recreational centre for the Army, Navy, Air Force and Merchant Service men at *Westoe Grange*, in May 1940. Hélène had performed the opening ceremony, remarking that she had visited the original Talbot House in Flanders (at Poperinghe) and had been very impressed by its simplicity as a haven of rest, shelter and peace. She added that the new Talbot House, with its homely atmosphere, was well equipped with a canteen, lounge, reading room, bedrooms and warden's quarters. It brought back happy memories for her, as it was where she had first met Robert before the First World War while staying in the house, then in private ownership, with her school friend from Scotland, Bessie Gowans. She and Robert made a personal contribution to the new centre by endowing a chapel on the top floor in memory of his brother, Maj. Charles Chapman, MC, and his sister, Marion Dorothy Chapman, VAD nurse, who died during the First World War, in 1917 and 1918 respectively.

In addition to his County Welfare Officer duties, Robert was also president of the YMCA's North-Eastern Area of Durham, Northumberland and North Yorkshire. He devoted a substantial amount of his time to this role, chairing monthly meetings of its War Emergency Committee and using his contacts to help bring many projects to fruition. The provision of canteens for the troops, and for new RAF stations, was the core activity, and when Robert opened a new facility at his old stomping ground of Houghton-le-Spring in November 1939 he was able to report that since war had been declared twenty-two new canteens had been opened in the three counties, with another eighteen in the pipeline. At Houghton itself, in addition to the canteen serving refreshments, there was accommodation for reading, writing and games and a large room with a platform and piano, ideal for entertainments.

In South Shields there were weekly concerts for servicemen at the YMCA's premises in Fowler Street, lively affairs with tap dances, solos, chorus items and impromptu community singing. The building also offered 'showerbaths' to the troops, who could enjoy billiards, table tennis and other games, the facilities being open not only on weekdays but also on Sundays from 2 p.m. to 9 p.m. In response to an appeal in the *Shields Gazette* by Councillor Edwin Thompson, YMCA Secretary, around 100 people had expressed their willingness to entertain to tea small parties of troops stationed in the district. As one prospective host wrote, 'I am only doing what was done for me in the last war. I will never forget the YMCA's great kindnesses.'[30]

There were a substantial number of new RAF air stations being built in the North East and demand for facilities was high. At RAF Usworth, located between Washington and Sunderland in County Durham, there was a joint YMCA and YWCA (Young Women's Christian Association) project with a new canteen (run by WVS volunteers) and recreation hut,

The Bishop of Durham, Dr Alwyn Williams, and Col Robert Chapman, Durham County Welfare Officer for the armed services, at the opening of the new YMCA/YWCA canteen and recreation centre at RAF Usworth, County Durham, 2 January 1941. (*Northern Echo*)

whose official opening ceremony on 2 January 1941 was performed by the WAAF (Women's Auxiliary Air Force) Officer Commanding in the presence of the Bishop of Durham, Robert himself and other dignitaries.

Mobile canteens were a key element of the YMCA's service. In County Durham by mid-1941 there was a canteen in nearly all its fourteen welfare districts, many funded by private donations from local and international bodies. The well-known Sunderland brewers, Messrs Vaux, had donated two, and the Hong Kong Rotary Club and the USA War Relief Society had each funded another. In what surely must have broken all speed records, it was reported to a meeting of the North Eastern Division's War Emergency Committee:

> ... that at the urgent request of the Ministry of Food and the Port Regional Officer, Mobile Canteen Services had been made available at an hour's notice on Sunday 17th May to troops on dock service, and had continued daily for 17 days. Nearly 10,000 teas and meals had been served and warm thanks had been expressed by the Authorities for the efficiency of this service.[31]

Equally warm thanks for services rendered through more than 100 canteens in Durham and Northumberland by the end of 1942 were received from their diverse range of users, including the 10th Armoured Corps, the 54th Division, AA Command, the Border Regiment, and RAF Balloon Command. It was not just teas and meals that had been on the move. There were also three mobile libraries operating in County Durham, funded by private donations including from Robert's wife Hélène for the service operating in the south of the county. Each library was stocked with 600 volumes of fiction and general literature.

Robert presided over an extraordinarily effective YMCA war effort. His complementary role as County Welfare Officer for the armed services had also received wide acclaim. However, he had used his discretion to make one particular decision that proved to be highly controversial. This was whether cinemas in South Shields should be open to the troops on Sunday evenings. The passing of the Sunday Public Entertainments Act in 1932 had delegated decisions to local authorities, subject to safeguards against excessive working hours for staff and to a charitable levy being imposed on the takings.[32] In South Shields itself, the borough council had approved an application in November 1933 from the manager of the

Palace Theatre in Frederick Street 'to open the theatre for the purpose of a cinematograph performance on Sunday the 10th of December in aid of the St. Hilda Lodge Aged Miners' Christmas Treat Fund'.[33]

A new wartime application for Sunday opening sparked a controversy played out over a six-month period, with Robert in centre stage. As reported in great detail in the *Shields Gazette*, the commander of local troops had asked Northern Command (the 'Competent Military Authority') to sign a certificate requesting the borough council to authorise the opening of cinemas on Sunday. This certificate had been submitted to the council and before the application was formally considered letters of objection had been received from six different societies together with a petition signed by 1,200 people on behalf of twenty-six churches and chapels. Robert, in his role as County Welfare Officer, had taken the view that there was no need for Sunday opening for the 100 soldiers posted to the town, since they were off duty twelve hours a day and had access to six cinemas, open six nights a week within a quarter of an hour of their billets. He had accordingly asked the 'Competent Military Authority' to withdraw the application certificate, informing the council that he had done so. The application was duly withdrawn, but the council subsequently discussed the principle of Sunday opening for the troops, approving it by a substantial majority (twenty-nine votes to nine against).

The next step was a resolution of the council, moved by Councillor A.E. Gompertz, a prominent member of the controlling Labour Party, criticising both the 'Competent Military Authority' and Robert Chapman, as an alderman of the council and a member of the Moderate Party, over his role in effecting the withdrawal of the certificate. After a bad-tempered debate, in which Robert said that he had acted perfectly properly and would not consult the council about his actions for the welfare of the troops ('you have nothing whatever to do with what I do as County Welfare Officer'), the motion was very narrowly carried, by seventeen votes to sixteen with three members abstaining.[34]

Robert remained County Welfare Officer and an alderman for the remainder of the war, and beyond. He also somehow found time for additional responsibilities, becoming chairman of the Durham County Cadet Committee, which encouraged young men to join the armed forces. Hélène was equally interested in developing the potential of young people, as president of the newly formed Girls Training Corps. At a meeting for parents and guests, she said that the two-year training course 'was designed not only to prepare the girls for the women's services, but to make them useful citizens of the world of the future'.[35] Opportunities in the services included not only the Women's Royal Naval Service and the Women's Auxiliary Air Force, but also the Auxiliary Territorial Service (ATS), attached to the Territorial Army. ATS women's role in AA Command, for example, became increasingly important as 'mixed' heavy anti-aircraft batteries of men and women were formed. On 8 December 1941, 'It was a mixed battery at Newcastle that gave the girls their first taste of blood … they behaved like a veteran party and shot an enemy plane into the sea.'[36]

Sporadic air attacks on South Shields itself continued. In April 1942 four large bombs were dropped on Westoe Village, one of them in the grounds of *Seacroft* where Robert grew up, fortunately failing to explode. The last bombing raid was in May 1943, when a number of galvanised metal canisters also fell on to the town and on to Cleadon Hill behind *Undercliff*. Robert and Hélène were given one of them, which contained a German propaganda leaflet pronouncing, 'Here is the reason why the British Government says nothing about the shipping losses. It knows that to be told the truth about the state of the battle of the seas would shake the belief of every Englishman in British naval supremacy and ultimate victory.'[37] The four-page leaflet listed the names of 412 ships, amounting to 29 million tons, said to have been sunk over the previous two years, though four of them were actually in the Tyne at the time of the raid.[38] Merchant shipping losses had certainly been very severe indeed – at times catastrophic – and censorship prevented their publication in any detail. However, the German propaganda 'drop' was rather late in the day, as the

UXB (unexploded bomb) at *Seacroft* Westoe, where Robert Chapman grew up, 15 April 1942. (South Tyneside Libraries)

Keeping up morale: King George VI at John Readhead & Sons' shipyard, April 1943. The yard built aircraft engine repair ships and coastal tankers to support the Normandy landings. (South Tyneside Libraries)

summer of 1943 saw the tide turn decisively against the U-boats, thanks to the deployment by the Americans of numerous destroyers for convoy protection and to the redeployment of significant numbers of British bombers for escort duties.

Shipbuilding output on the Tyne at South Shields was not severely affected by the German air raids before 1943, and in the final two years of the war not at all. As a result, the yards' contribution to Admiralty orders and to merchant shipping was very substantial. At Readhead's, thirty-one cargo ships were built with carrying capacity of 307,000 tons. Two coastal tankers, *Chant 60* and *Chant 61*, were commissioned by the Admiralty to carry oil in bulk to support the Normandy landings and the Navy also ordered two aircraft engine repair ships, HMS *Moray Firth* and HMS *Beauly Firth*. As for the dry docks, they:

> … were hardly allowed a moment to breathe. Victims of E-Boat Alley, such as the colliers *Wandle* and *Firelight*, were both entirely rebuilt about their fore-ends; torpedo damage and the devastation of a direct hit in the engine room were repaired on the banana carrier *Eros*; dry dock work for naval vessels also formed part of a continuous programme.[39]

Hawthorn Leslie, at its Hebburn shipbuilding yard and St Peter's Marine Engine Works, also made an outstanding contribution to the war effort.

Hélène Chapman had launched HMS *Pathfinder* under conditions of strict security in 1941. The ship was one of sixteen flotilla leaders and destroyers launched at Hebburn, together with one aircraft carrier, three cruisers, two fast minelayers, two gun boats, three transport ferries and fourteen landing craft. The yard had built the first tank landing craft in the world, and production was stepped up at short notice in the run up to D-Day. These forty-one naval vessels had carrying capacity of 91,000 tons, in addition to which the yard built 142,000 tons of merchant shipping, mostly tankers.

The firm was proud of its record of having played a leading role in carrying out the final instruction in Winston Churchill's famously stirring commands of 1940: 'Fill the Armies, rule the air, pour out the munitions, strangle the U-boats, sweep the mines, plough the lanes – build the ships.'[40] Hawthorn Leslie's impressive record was not confined to shipbuilding. In its yards it carried out conversions, repairs, refits and underwater work to 112 merchant ships and to 121 warships, including to the famous HMS *Kelly*, torpedoed near a German minefield, successfully repaired but eventually sunk by a 1,000lb bomb in the Battle of Crete. These shipbuilding and repair achievements required a substantially increased workforce: the 4,000 employees at the outbreak of war rose to 6,600 at peak production. They were all very lucky: despite 252 air raid 'alerts', not a single bomb was dropped on the shipbuilding yard throughout the war.

Robert and Hélène were equally lucky at *Undercliff*. Although not itself a military target, there were Anti-Aircraft Command batteries nearby, and bombs had been dropped on Cleadon Hills and in Cleadon village itself. Fortunately, collateral damage to the house was confined to blown-out windows and a collapsed ceiling. The war did, however, have a significant impact on the gardens, since within a few months of it being declared, Mrs Robert Chapman, as Hélène was always described in the press, was 'setting a good example in the "Dig for Victory" campaign. The beautiful lawns of the grounds of her home are being ploughed up for vegetable cultivation.' The *Shields Gazette*, while applauding this 'National Service', permitted itself a touch of nostalgia: 'There must be few women who do not know of the charity *fêtes* and garden parties held on the *Undercliff* lawns amid gay summer flowers and trees, and feel a touch of regret that until the war is over, at least, such events in this setting are out of the question.'[41] This was certainly true, but the change of use increased the production of vegetables and what became a market garden operation benefited local traders and residents, as did the sale of pigs from the large piggeries beyond the kitchen garden.

More mouths needed to be fed in *Undercliff* itself. Once Robin had been posted to coastal batteries in the South East, Barbara moved into the house with their baby son David, where they were joined by the author following his delivery in a home birth on 24 August 1944. There were some staff changes, too. Sidney Snelling, the head gardener, had retired and his successor, Fred W. Knaggs, made a success of the expanded vegetable growing project. Robert, always encouraging employers to take on disabled ex-servicemen, himself took on as gardeners in 1943 two former soldiers who had been badly injured, one having lost a leg and the other an arm. Benjamin Ward, Robert's batman from the First World War, who had continued voluntary service with the Territorials in the inter-war period, remained chauffeur/handyman in *Undercliff* Cottage, and a key member of the staff. He and his wife had two sons, both of whom also fought in the armed forces. One had been killed serving in Sicily in 1943, and the other, RAF Sgt Alexander Ward – whom Robert had before the war employed as an articled clerk in his chartered accountancy office – was awarded the Distinguished Flying Medal after a bombing raid on Germany in which his plane was badly damaged but managed to limp home, crash landing near the coast.

The head housemaid, Elizabeth Brady – always known as Lizzie – also had a distinguished war record. She had been one of the very first of the *Undercliff* staff, starting as a 25-year-old in July 1923. In September 1940 she had volunteered for service with the WRNS, the Women's Royal Naval Service, or Wrens as they were usually called. After a successful interview and intelligence test, almost certainly at the Turk's Head Hotel in Newcastle,[42] she was posted briefly to HMS *Condor*, a Royal Naval Air Station at Arbroath in Scotland. Wrens were not permitted to serve at sea, but – somewhat counter-intuitively – all shore stations were nevertheless designated by the Royal Navy as ships. Her next posting was to HMS *Jackdaw* in Fife, followed by a brief spell at HMS *Victory III* in Oxfordshire, and then by two and a half years at HMS *Kestrel*, the RNAS station at Worthy Down near Winchester. Now with the rank of 'Leading Wren' she took the opportunity of seeking further promotion, and passed a selection course to become a petty officer in 1944, by which time the number of Wrens had grown to 75,000, from a standing start at the outbreak of war. Her final posting was to HMS *Cochrane* at the Rosyth naval base, from which she was released from service five months after the end of the war.[43] Lizzie subsequently rejoined the staff at *Undercliff* as cook and, after several breaks, was still working there twenty years later.

The war was far from over when Lizzie Brady had become a Wren petty officer in the summer of 1944, but it was about to enter a decisive phase. In South Shields a 'Salute the Soldier' campaign, to raise £500,000 in national savings to equip two battalions of the Durham Light Infantry and the 74th Field Regiment, Royal Artillery (where Robert was honorary colonel), began on 27 May. Lt Richard Annand, VC, was present at the opening march past of men and women of the armed services and Civil Defence services, and he gave a short speech during the interval of a military concert at the Odeon Regal Theatre the following day.

A few days later, in the King's Birthday Honours List, Robert received the award of a CB, becoming a Companion of the Order of the Bath, recognising his public service as chairman of the Durham County Territorial and Air Force Association. The *Newcastle Journal* listed his numerous other voluntary appointments and business directorships, including of the Newcastle and Gateshead Gas Company, George Angus & Co. Ltd, and Manchester Dry Docks Co. Ltd. He received further national recognition in the New Year's Honours List, being appointed CBE (a Commander of

Mobile 3.7in anti-aircraft guns of 219 HAA battery, Royal Field Artillery (Commanding Officer Maj. Robert (Robin) Chapman) at Mushroom Farm Camp, Wethersfield, Essex, November 1943. (Photographic News Agencies Ltd)

the Order of the British Empire) for his role as acting chairman of North Eastern Trading Estates Ltd, providing a further opportunity to attend an investiture with Hélène at Buckingham Palace.

Their son, Maj. Robert (Robin) Chapman, had been transferred from Anti-Aircraft Command headquarters in London to be Commanding Officer of 219 HAA Battery, which moved between sites in Essex, Kent and Sussex before settling down near Southwold in Suffolk. If the North East was, by 1944, experiencing only sporadic air raids, the South required a substantial build-up of anti-aircraft defences to support Operation Overlord (the proposed second front in Europe) and to minimise damage from an expected surge of German attacks. AA Command agreed to deploy 1,094 heavy anti-aircraft guns out of its total of 2,800, potentially leaving the North dangerously exposed to renewed raids.

On D-Day, 6 June 1944, the Allies landed in Normandy, and a week later the second Battle of London began, this time against German V1 flying bombs. Vividly described as 'the first battle of the robots',[44] it lasted nine long months. Fortunately there had been very significant technical advances in anti-aircraft defences, and a major contribution from the USA in the supply both of manpower (additional AA batteries for London) and of guns and equipment, including the latest SCR 584 radar. Together they had a substantial impact on the eventual victory over the V1. As for its much more formidable successor, the V2, General Montgomery's 21 Army Group overcame their launching pads in Holland at the end of March 1945 before they were able to wreak complete havoc in London and beyond.

The war in Europe was now nearly over. By the end of March, the Americans and British had crossed the Rhine. On 28 April Mussolini was shot and two days later Hitler committed suicide. On 7 May the Germans surrendered at General Eisenhower's headquarters. The following day the Russians in Berlin ratified the agreement and Winston Churchill announced victory in the House of Commons. In South Shields, there was a thanksgiving service at St Hilda's Church, a reception by the Mayor and Mayoress, and dancing to bands in the parks. At its meeting on 6 June the council resolved to 'offer devout thanks to Almighty God on the victorious conclusion of the war against Germany'. Heartfelt congratulations were respectfully tendered to His Majesty King George VI 'on the glorious achievements and fortitude of His Majesty's Forces', and the council placed on record 'its deep and lasting gratitude to the members of the

Armed Forces of our Empire and of the Allied Nations, and also to the men of the Merchant Navy, for the magnificent part they have played in the achievement of victory'.[45] In September, after the Japanese surrender, the Air Raid Precautions Emergency Committee was disbanded. The war was now well and truly over, and South Shields could take pride in its contribution to eventual victory. Now, for the second time in three decades, came the challenge of the peace.

12

ROYALTY AND RECOGNITION

A new chapter in Robert's life opened in June 1946 when *The Times* announced that 'The King has approved the appointment of Colonel Robert Chapman to be Vice-Lieutenant of the County of Durham, to act for his Majesty's [Lord] Lieutenant during his absence from the county, sickness or other inability to act.'[1] The Lord Lieutenant was the Marquess of Londonderry, who was now living at his Mount Stewart estate in Northern Ireland, having become severely incapacitated after a gliding accident the previous year. He was in no position to carry out any duties in Durham from his Wynyard Park estate in the south of the county.

The duties of a Lord Lieutenant, as the sovereign's representative, included escorting visiting members of the Royal Family, supporting the armed services and civic and voluntary activities in the county. Robert was soon busy with the most enjoyable task of escorting the 21-year-old Princess Elizabeth on her visit in October 1947 to St Mary's College and Finchale Abbey Training Centre for the Disabled in Durham.

To an enthusiastic welcome of cheering and flag-waving, not least by the 3,000 school children on Palace Green between Durham's Norman cathedral and castle, Princess Elizabeth first visited the old St Mary's College where she met the principal, Miss M.B. Fergusson, and had coffee with students. After a thirty-minute conducted tour of the cathedral by the dean, with a melodious background of choristers singing in the choir, she laid the foundation stone of the new St Mary's College, and gave a

Princess Elizabeth enjoying a joke with Dr J.F. Duff, Warden of the Durham
Colleges, as she walks through the grounds of St Mary's College escorted by
Col Robert Chapman, Vice-Lieutenant of County Durham, 24 October 1947.
(*Sunderland Echo*)

rather good address 'in a fine and well modulated voice'. Praising the plans
for the new building, she said that:

> It is now fifty years since women first entered the University. They did
> so in the teeth of strong prejudice, and at Durham and elsewhere they
> must often have had to accept living conditions to which no man would
> have submitted. (Laughter). There can be no thinking people in this
> country who do not wish to see the advantages of a University educa-
> tion extended as widely and as soon as possible.[2]

Characterising a university as a 'place of light, liberty and learning', the
princess added that:

Women have moved far in this century. Nobody will deny the splendour of their part in the war, or underestimate the work they are doing in every aspect of our national life, but if we are to maintain this high tradition, which is none the less noble for being new, we must not forget that before all else we are women; that if we have established our rights we have, in so doing, multiplied our duties.[3]

Multiple duties the princess certainly had, having already been introduced to more than fifty people by the end of her visit to St Mary's College.

After a luncheon hosted by the University of Durham in the hall of Durham Castle, Princess Elizabeth was driven to Finchale Abbey Training Centre for the Disabled, where Robert had been chairman of the management committee since its foundation in 1943. No doubt he had been pivotal in securing her visit. The princess inspected the 'roll of honour' recording the names and case histories of the 400 disabled men who had already secured employment through training received at the centre in welding, plumbing, carpentry, boot and shoe making, tailoring and watch

Princess Elizabeth opens the new wing of Finchale Abbey Training Centre for the Disabled with Col Robert Chapman, chairman of the Management Committee, 24 October 1947. (Chapman Family Archive)

and clock repairing, and learnt that around half of the 100 current train-
ees were ex-servicemen. She chatted to them, formally opened the new
extension and said:

> Today, when there is so much to give us anxiety, it is good to speak
> of something which can arouse nothing but enthusiasm. Thanks to
> the generosity of private charity [Robert had briefed her on Sir John
> Priestman's founding donation], the unstinted support of the Ministry of
> Labour, and the tireless work of the Committee, Finchale Abbey today is
> a high expression of our social development.[4]

Presented with a gold-mounted pen supplied by J. Grant & Sons, the well-
known South Shields goldsmiths and silversmiths, the princess was driven
away after what for her must have been an exhausting day, however exhilarating for all who met her and for the crowds who cheered her on.

Robert's Vice-Lieutenancy role would continue for a further decade.
In February 1949 Lord Londonderry died at his home at Mount Stewart
in County Down, and a memorial service was held in Durham Cathedral,
which Robert and Hélène attended. King George VI appointed as the new
Lord Lieutenant Mr J.J. Lawson, MP. 'Jack' Lawson was a remarkable man.
He had started work as a 12-year-old down the mine at Boldon Colliery,
won a scholarship to Ruskin College, Oxford, returned to mining, entered
local Labour Party politics, and in 1919 became MP for the Chester-
le-Street division of County Durham, a seat he held for thirty years. He
stepped down on being appointed Lord Lieutenant in 1949, and was created a peer, taking a seat in the House of Lords with the title of Lord
Lawson of Beamish. Robert was quickly re-appointed Vice-Lieutenant.

Another royal engagement was soon in prospect when it was announced
that Princess Marie Louise would be visiting the North East in October,
and would be opening a new YMCA centre in Sunderland. An extremely
active 77-year-old, she was a granddaughter of Queen Victoria who in
the 1890s had had a disastrous marriage to Prince Aribert of Anhalt in
Germany. The marriage was eventually annulled by his father, and she
returned to England. She never remarried, devoting the rest of her life to a
wide range of charitable causes, including the YMCA. The princess's visit
was particularly memorable for Robert and Hélène. Not only did Robert
play a central welcoming role as Vice-Lieutenant, but he remained closely
involved with the YMCA as president of its North Eastern Division.

Princess Marie Louise with Robert and Hélène at *Undercliff*, where she stayed when opening YMCA centres in Sunderland and Gateshead, October 1949. (*Shields Gazette*)

Hélène, for her part, must have been very excited because Princess Marie Louise would be staying at *Undercliff* during her three-day tour. She would have her own en suite accommodation and separate sitting room on the first floor, and a new specially ordered Axminster carpet had been laid on the staircase and landing in her honour.

The visit was a great success. The princess opened the new YMCA centre in Sunderland, designed by the well-known local architect and friend of Robert, Stanley Milburn, with grace and enthusiasm. She referred to the warm-hearted friendship she had always found in the North East, recalling happy memories of her previous visit to Sunderland twenty years earlier. She stressed that 'The work of the YMCA is far-reaching. It is not only represented by hostels and rest camps – it is a world-wide movement [in seventy-five countries] – establishing friendship and fellowship which is so lacking in these days.'[5]

Robert's own speech emphasised that the YMCA's work was certainly extensive in the North East itself, with twenty civilian centres, eight centres for His Majesty's armed forces, twenty-six hostels for agricultural workers, a dedicated study centre and a large holiday camp. After a tour of the new building the Mayor and Mayoress of Sunderland (Alderman and Mrs Jack Cohen) accompanied the princess to – but, presumably in line with municipal etiquette, no further than – the borough boundary with South Shields. There she transferred to Robert and Hélène's car for the final mile to *Undercliff*.

The following day the princess visited the newly completed Gateshead YMCA centre, *Sutherland House*, named after its generous benefactor Sir Arthur Sutherland, a prominent ship owner who was president of the Newcastle and Gateshead Chamber of Commerce. Refreshed by a cup of coffee and rye bread – instead of tea and white bread, by special royal request to the kitchen staff – she returned to *Undercliff* for a good night's rest. The following morning she signed the visitors' book on a page entirely devoted to her and took the train back to London. Her future Christmas cards were always given pride of place on the Bechstein grand piano in the drawing room. Grandmother did have a soft spot for a princess.

Earlier in 1949 Robert had played his part in an important celebration in South Shields – the centenary of the *Shields Gazette*, whose proud boast was 'Britain's oldest provincial evening newspaper'. In a packed Hedworth Hall, messages of greeting were read out on behalf of the King, the Duke of Edinburgh and of the town's long-standing MP, Chuter Ede, who was Secretary of State for Home Affairs in the Attlee Government and unable to be present. Alderman Longstaff, deputising for the first woman Mayor of South Shields, Alderman Mrs M.J. Peel, who was unwell, proposed the toast of the chairman, directors and staff of the *Gazette*. Shannon Stevenson, director and general manager of the *Gazette*'s owners, the Northern Press, in proposing a toast 'to the guests', said that the occasion was also his family's centenary in newspapers. He added that 'Colonel Chapman's family and mine have enjoyed a friendship which has extended over most of that time and through several generations. So I welcome him here not only as a distinguished member of the community, but as an old family friend.'[6]

Robert's response on behalf of the guests was an impressive historical review of the borough where:

> … generation after generation of Shieldsmen have read with eager interest [the *Gazette*'s] true record of local news and particularly does this apply to the large seafaring community who live in this, the largest dormitory

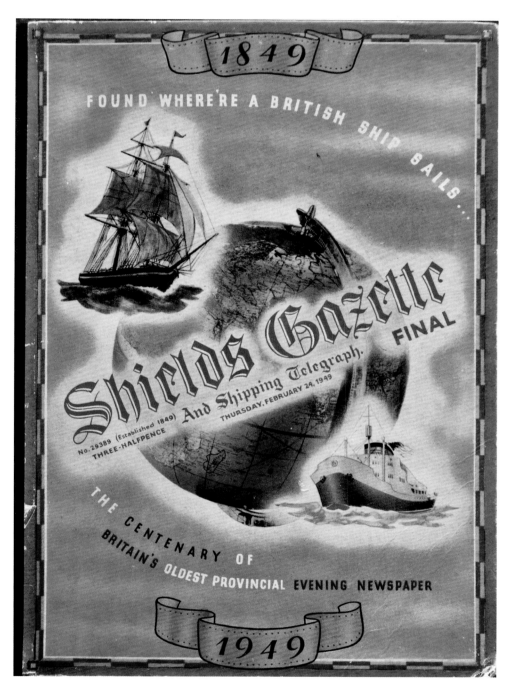

The *Shields Gazette*, Britain's oldest provincial evening newspaper, celebrated its centenary in 1949 with a special publication. (*Shields Gazette*)

town for seafarers in the British Isles. Declaring that *The Shields Gazette*
was a saga of the Stevenson family and at the same time a history of South
Shields ...[7]

Robert praised Shannon Stevenson's great-grandfather James Stevenson,
who founded the Jarrow Chemical Company and then the *Gazette* in
1849, and his son James Cochran Stevenson, who took over the *Gazette*
and represented the borough in Parliament for twenty-seven years: 'he
was a remarkable man and one of the greatest, if not the greatest of our
townsmen'.[8] Robert added that J.C. Stevenson was the first Freeman
of the Borough, and among the guests in Hedworth Hall was the latest
Freeman, (his nephew) Capt. R.W. Annand, VC, a grandson of Robert C.
Annand, managing director of the Northern Press for several decades. Also
in the audience was Robert's elder son, Robin.

Robin was by now well established as a partner with Robert in Henry
Chapman Son & Co., chartered accountants, and was following in his

Proud grandparents at a family gathering in *Undercliff*'s drawing room, early 1950s.
Front row, seated: David (left) and the author. Centre row, left to right: Hélène,
Barbara, Robert with granddaughter Elizabeth on his knee. Back row: Shirley and
Dick Annand, and Robin. (Chapman Family archive)

father's public service footsteps as a Justice of the Peace and Territorial Army officer. He had recently been promoted to lieutenant colonel and appointed Commanding Officer of 325 Light Anti-Aircraft (LAA) Regiment, Royal Artillery (TA) in Sunderland, maintaining South Shields links as honorary treasurer of the town's branch of the Royal Artillery Association. He and his wife Barbara also lived in Cleadon and were now the proud parents of Elizabeth (born in 1946), whose elder brothers David and the author had been born during the war. Robert and Hélène were devoted grandparents whose *Undercliff* doors and grounds – soon to become a wonderful adventure playground – were permanently open for the family.

There was a pre-Christmas celebration at *Undercliff* in December 1949 when Robert and Hélène's younger son, Henry James Nicholas (Nick), announced his engagement. A colonial civil servant, he was Deputy Finance Secretary to the Gold Coast (now Ghana) government. His fiancée was Anne Barbara Croft, secretary to the Colonial Secretary in Accra, and daughter of Sir William Croft, chairman of the Board of HM Customs and Excise. They were married two months later. There was another family celebration with the announcement in the New Year's Honours of 1950 that Robert had received a knighthood. His voluntary work as chairman of Finchale Abbey Training Centre for the Disabled was specifically mentioned in the citation, and newspaper articles covered his numerous other public service activities, including with North Eastern Trading Estates.

Robert had become chairman of North Eastern Trading Estates in 1944 after five years as acting chairman, and he worked tirelessly to promote new light industrial development in the region. He and his colleagues had been fortunate in having a ministerial champion for their cause in Hugh Dalton, MP for Bishop Auckland in the south-west of County Durham. In 1942 Dalton had become president of the Board of Trade in Churchill's Coalition Government, and he was the only Cabinet Minister who represented a constituency in what before the war had been called a 'Distressed' or 'Special' Area. Dalton was determined to gain powers to influence employers' decisions on locating new factories to benefit what he renamed 'Development Areas'. The result was his Distribution of Industry Bill, which received its formal First Reading in the House of Commons in February 1945.[9] A month later he visited the North East, inspecting sites in South Shields (where the welcome party included Robert in his capacity as a borough alderman) and Jarrow. He was upbeat about his parliamentary Bill, stressing that 'The Government will have power to acquire land and build factories itself and be able to finance development of trading estates', and – music to Robert's ears – 'the North-East Trading Estate Co. will be undertaking greatly increased responsibilities on behalf of the Government in the North-East region'.[10] Dalton added that he hoped that the Board of Trade would soon be able to establish a new trading estate on the boundaries of the two boroughs. This would become the Bede Trading Estate, with the capacity to create 4,000 new jobs.

The Distribution of Industry Bill only just made it, enacted on 15 June 1945, the very day on which Parliament was dissolved before a new General Election took place. Under this ground-breaking legislation, the Board of Trade took over the powers of the pre-war Special Area Commissioners and was enabled to buy land, reclaim derelict land, and build factories in the Development Areas, and make loans to industrial estate companies (the rebadged 'trading estate' companies).[11] In the North East the Development Area was extended to include Teesside in the south and the city of Newcastle itself in the north.

The new General Election took place in July 1945, with Clement Attlee winning for Labour a commanding overall majority of 146 seats. Hugh Dalton – to his surprise – was appointed Chancellor of the Exchequer, and was succeeded by Sir Stafford Cripps at the Board of Trade. This change required new targeted lobbying, and in September Robert secured a meeting with Sir Stafford, who followed it up with a positive letter to Robert: 'I was most grateful to you and Colonel Methven [General Manager] for arranging the very interesting, and I hope fruitful, meeting with the Directors of the North Eastern Trading Estates.'[12] Fruitful it certainly was: the Board of Trade approved the new Bede Trading Estate, and Sir Stafford himself visited it on a whistle-stop tour in December 1946 with Robert and director colleagues, meeting the Mayor of Jarrow (Alderman J. Hanlon, who was already negotiating an extension of the estate), the Mayor of South Shields (Alderman Malcolm M. Barbour) and other dignitaries. The first factories, including the engineering works of Barker Perkins and the lock and key makers Mullins, were soon up and running.

Robert continued as unpaid chairman of the board of North Eastern Trading Estates until 1948, standing down when Harold Wilson, who had become President of the Board of Trade the previous year, decided to appoint a full-time salaried chairman, S.A. Sadler Forster, formerly

Regional Controller of the Board of Trade in Newcastle. The achievements in the first decade of the company's life had been impressive, and
continued to be so. By the time Robert retired as a director of the board
a decade later on its amalgamation into the English Estates Corporation,
North Eastern Trading Estates was responsible for thirty-eight industrial
estates and sites, on which 317 companies occupied 12,500,000 sq ft of
factory space and employed 59,000 people (18,000 on the original Team
Valley Estate in Gateshead).[13] Its property assets were valued at around
£19 million.[14] A success story indeed.

The year 1950 was a bumper one for celebrations, personal and civic.
On 1 March, the *Shields Gazette* asked rhetorically, 'Where are the boys
of the Old Brigade?', and answered that the veteran officers of 274 Field
Regiment RA (TA) were dining together at the Drill Hall in Bolingbroke
Street, South Shields, in honour of Col Robert Chapman's fifty years of
service with the Volunteer and Territorial Forces, and on his relinquish-
ing his appointment as honorary colonel.[15] The Commanding Officer,
Lt Col J. Wadham Grant, recalled that Robert had received his first commission in the 3rd Durham Volunteer Artillery in 1900, when Queen
Victoria was on the throne, and he had served under four kings subsequently. The War Office had granted him special permission to hold the
rank of honorary colonel for four days beyond his 70th birthday – the
usual retirement age, which Robert would reach on 3 March – so that he
could complete exactly fifty years' service.

The veterans had a jolly good dinner, and reminiscences flowed freely.
Robert recalled that in the early days of mobilisation for the First World
War, a young Territorial officer (might it have been Robert himself or his
officer brother Charles?) needed ammunition for his unit in South Shields.

> With difficulty he commandeered one or two lorries and with the driv-
> ers went to Fenham Barracks in Newcastle. The regular Army units
> badly needed transport and when the Terriers [Territorials] drove into
> the Barracks the 'old sweats' decided to augment their Motor Transport.
> Drawing a revolver, the TA officer shouted: 'Either you let me out of
> here with the ammo, or I'll shoot.' He got his ammunition.[16]

There were later reminiscences from 'other ranks'. Former battery sergeant Maj. Dunnington, DCM, recalled his First World War experiences
in a full-page article in the *Shields Gazette*: 'The team spirit fostered by

Major R. Chapman (as he then was) brought all ranks together like brothers and whatever we took up we worked like one man.' He added that 'When both Col. Chapman and I were wounded in action at Hangard on 4 April 1918, Col. Chapman was then acting Brigadier General, and I can say on behalf of the men that are left he was a leader of men and got things done.'[17]

Civic celebrations were major events in 1950, the council's centennial year. It honoured with the freedom of the borough two regiments – the Durham Light Infantry and 274 Field Regiment RA (TA) itself – together with the town's long-serving Member of Parliament, J. Chuter Ede, and five distinguished Shieldsmen. These were Lord Wright (sponsored by Robert), who had become an Appeal Court judge, the shipbuilder Sir Amos Ayre, the veteran *Shields Gazette* journalist R.P. Fernandes, Alderman Edward Smith and Alderman C.H. Smith.

John Readhead & Sons' 8,200-ton cargo liner *Armanistan* commissioned by the Strick Line. It was completed in 1949 and was then the largest vessel ever built in South Shields. (South Tyneside Libraries)

The South Shields Centenary publication, produced by the borough council, reviewed '100 Years of Progress'.[18] Shipbuilding and repairing remained an important industry for the town, whose population of around 109,000, though growing since the war, remained below the levels of the 1920s and '30s. Nevertheless, 5,000 men were still employed on the waterfront, half of them with John Readhead & Sons – the only shipbuilder left in the town. The remainder worked for ship-repairing firms – Middle Docks & Engineering Company (under Sir Lawrie Edwards), Brigham & Cowans, Tyne Dock Engineering, Anthony Proud and T.R. Dowson. A further 5,600 men were employed in mining, the pits having been nationalised in 1946. Two years later work had started on a new mine at Westoe.

The town was still largely dependent on these traditional industries but making strenuous efforts to diversify. *The South Shields Centenary* pointed out that:

Today South Shields has a greater variety of industries than ever before. They include a wireless component factory, clothiers' factories, cleaning and dye works and the manufacture of hardware, slippers and electric batteries. All are flourishing and providing more and more employment.

A number of firms and financial organisations founded in the nineteenth century were also still going strong, including J. Barbour & Sons at 5 Market Place with its large mail order business and 'world-wide reputation',[19] the Trustee Savings Bank (on whose management committee Robert sat) and the South Shields Commercial Permanent Building Society, where Robert and his son Robin were joint secretaries.

The South Shields Centenary also reviewed progress and key events in education, housing, health and sport. On the further education front it looked forward to the establishment of the South Shields Marine and Technical College 'in which the famous Marine School founded by Dr. Winterbottom [where Robert had been joint Secretary in 1902–47] will play a prominent part and yet retain its world famous reputation with all seafaring folk'. The publication took pride in the borough's record on housing and redevelopment from 1921, when the first council houses were built on the Cleadon Park Estate. By 1950 some 6,600 homes had been completed, 2,000 of them since the war. The publication recorded the huge advances made in the field of public health. The National Health Service had been set up, and the South Shields District Hospital Management Committee was now responsible for the hospitals, including the Ingham Infirmary, where Robert had been chairman of the governors from 1930 to 1945.

There was an upbeat summary of the development of sporting activities, including rowing, swimming, running, cycling, bowling and sea angling. The review noted that the South Shields Cricket Club was also celebrating its own centenary and that it had in 1919 amalgamated with the Westoe Lawn Tennis Club and Westoe Rugby Football Club. Robert's father Henry had been the first president of the enlarged club, and on his death in 1936, Robert had succeeded him, and was still president twenty-five years later. Looking to the future, the *Centenary* noted that the new Gypsies Green athletics stadium near the South Beach was nearly completed, and that cricket, football and hockey pitches were planned in the Temple Memorial Park, whose 170 acres had been donated to the borough by the Church commissioners in 1947 as a lasting memorial to those men and women of the town who had laid down their lives in the Second World War.

Robert had now been on the council for thirty years, a councillor from 1921 to 1936, and an alderman since then. He should probably have stood down when he came up for re-election in 1952 – as he subsequently conceded – but he again put his name forward, only to be defeated, the Labour Party securing a commanding majority in the council chamber. He was now reducing other activities, but not yet his beloved YMCA. Meanwhile, Hélène seemed to be on permanent over-drive. Among numerous roles, she was chairman of the South Shields Nursing Association, local president of the Royal British Legion's Women's Section, vice-chairman of the Ingham Infirmary, president of the South Shields Shoeless Children's Fund and president of the British Red Cross Society in County Durham.

Appointed as a Justice of the Peace in 1936, she became president of the North East branch of the Magistrates' Association in 1952. Never afraid to tackle a difficult subject, her presidential address to the Northern Provincial Conference at Otterburn Hall in Northumberland asked the question, 'Should magistrates send mothers to prison for child neglect?' The answer was nuanced, and she reminded her audience that alternatives were a fine or a probation order. Nevertheless, the law permitted a sentence of six months' imprisonment, in support of which:

We may feel that the offence well merited it. We know that in prison she will have regular habits, which will be physically beneficial [and there were also now] courses of treatment in which housewifery and mother-craft were taught. A prison sentence, nevertheless, involves the breaking up of the home and building this again on release is sometimes beyond the mother's poor capacity. Contact would have to be made with the family to build up decent conditions to which the prisoner could return. After-care was required if the training received in prison was to be put to practical use on release.

She concluded that 'without these provisions, training in prison is about as useful and as dangerous as an operation without convalescence'. In short, a custodial sentence was only likely to be effective if accompanied by a rehabilitation programme on release.

The summer of 1953 was memorable for royal events. First came the excitement of the Coronation in June of the 27-year-old Queen Elizabeth II. Then just a month later, to the great pleasure and pride of Hélène, who was Durham County president of the British Red Cross Society, came a visit to the county by the Princess Royal. She was Mary, Countess of Harewood in Yorkshire, the only daughter of King George V, who had been elevated to the title of Princess Royal back in 1932. She was the devoted Commander-in-Chief of the Red Cross, and she had lunch at *Undercliff* with Hélène and Robert on Sunday, 19 July before travelling to Durham City to present the county branch with its first colours at a special service in the cathedral. She was greeted with a fanfare by the trumpeters of the First Battalion, the Durham Light Infantry and the colours (composed of the Union Jack and

Lady (Hélène) Chapman, Durham County president of the British Red Cross Society, handing over to the Princess Royal (on the right) the ambulance she had donated in July 1953. The Princess Royal then presented it to Lt Col R.M. Percival, the county director, on the left of the photo. (© *Shields Gazette*/JPI Media Ltd)

the Red Cross flag) were dedicated by the Dean, the Very Rev. John Wild, to the memory of the former county director, Mrs W.A. Ellis.

After the service, attended by a congregation of some 2,000, evenly split between Red Cross invitees and the general public, the Princess Royal inspected a 600-strong parade of uniformed members and cadets on Palace Green. To the evident delight of Hélène, she formally handed over to Lt Col R.M. Percival, the Red Cross county director, an ambulance that had been donated to the branch by Hélène herself. The princess then addressed the parade, congratulating them on their achievements in reinforcing the medical services of the Crown, which included providing 800 volunteers for the National Hospital Service Reserve, and assisting at 161 sessions of the Blood Transfusion Service, which resulted in 16,000 donations of blood. She praised the society's pioneering venture of a mobile library taking books to remote sanitoria and to the homebound, and its work with over 3,000 disabled civilians and ex-servicemen, carried out jointly with St John Ambulance.[20]

A few days later Hélène received a personal letter from the Princess Royal (signing herself 'Mary') thanking her and Robert for their hospitality at *Undercliff*, adding that 'It was such a pleasure to me to be able to accept the ambulance you have so generously presented to the Durham Red Cross.'[21] Robert and Hélène celebrated the success of the event with a trip to London with their sons Robin and Nick, and daughters-in-law Barbara and Anne. They all attended a garden party in Buckingham Palace – one of the first of the new Queen's reign.

A long, cold spell followed Christmas, and when Hélène was interviewed about her garden at *Undercliff* in April 1954 by the *Newcastle Journal* for a feature article, 'two swans stood disconsolate on the frozen lake … and all around lay the white mantle of winter'. The grounds of the house were described as sloping 'towards the south-west, and south-eastwards the sea glints in the distance. A belt of trees, their branches stark against the sky, shelter the house on three sides and in the background the rocky Cleadon Hills bear the buffets of the withering North-East winds.'[22]

Hélène recalled in the article that:

> … when my husband and I came here in 1922, we felt we had found an ideal home in an ideal setting. Before the war, knowing the great demand there would be for food, we ploughed up a large part even of the lawns, and during the war we provided a great deal of bacon for the area.

Undercliff resplendent, early 1960s. (© Peter S. Chapman)

Winter scene at *Undercliff*: view from the frozen lake, early 1960s.
(© Peter S. Chapman)

A hundred or so pigs were still kept and the estate was run partly as a market garden – almost a small farm – although the primary purpose was to make the home and garden as self-supporting as possible. She added that:

> I was born and brought up in France, where much is made of little. For instance, they never throw away the water in which vegetables are boiled. It all goes into the stock. English people tend to use too much water, but vegetables should be cooked in very little. Another tip, with which all keen gardeners will fully agree, is first to use all edible scraps for feeding poultry and other livestock, and then to throw all suitable household waste on the compost help to rot, so that the goodness taken out of the soil is returned to it.

Ducks, geese and hens were kept, Hélène commenting that:

> Some people are afraid of duck eggs, but providing the ducks are kept clean I think they are perfectly safe. I prefer them to ordinary hens' eggs. There is nothing like a boiled duck egg, and they make very good cakes, sauces and so on. Of course they should always be well cooked.

The whalebone arch casts a long shadow over the snowy rose garden towards the conservatory on the kitchen garden wall. *Undercliff*, early 1960s. (© Peter S. Chapman)

Hélène extolled the virtues of jam-making and preserving and bottling fruit and vegetables to ensure a winter reserve when things were scarce. 'One secret of gardening is "beating the season", and making ends meet in the sense of spinning out production to last the year round. This of course can only be done successfully with the aid of greenhouses, the gardener's magic doorway to a better climate.' Flowers from greenhouses or garden adorned the house all year round, and the *Newcastle Journal* reported that Mr F.W. Knaggs, the head gardener, had just carried a glowing pink azalea into the drawing room. Daffodils and red, white and violet primulas were among the flowers in full bloom in the greenhouses, and conservatory plants included 'a Passion flower which blooms over a long period, but whose individual blooms lasted only one day'. Figs, grapes and peaches were also produced in abundance.

Fred W. Knaggs, head gardener, with Caroline Chapman on 'Dolly', 1963. (Courtesy Caroline Steane)

Hélène described one unique feature of *Undercliff* – the 16ft-high wall surrounding the fruit gardens:

The base of the wall is hollow, and years ago, when coal was cheap and plentiful – and good – hot air used to flow along inside it, from a furnace, to ward off the frost in the critical blossom-setting season [of pear and apple trees espaliered on the wall], in the same way as the Romans used to warm their luxury villas in ancient Britain.

The article concluded that in the summer the grounds remained as popular as ever for fêtes, with the beautiful rose garden entered through an archway made from a whale's jawbone found on the shore of nearby Seaburn and used traditionally as a 'wishing gate'.

Robert loved pottering about in the grounds of *Undercliff*, and was still active in his external commitments as Vice-Lieutenant of the county, and president of the YMCA's North Eastern Division. In November he returned to his old stamping ground of Houghton-le-Spring to preside at the opening by Viscount Lambton, MP, of the new YMCA. In giving the vote of thanks, Robert showed that he had lost none of his self-deprecating sense of humour. He said, amid laughter, that he had enjoyed rather a chequered career in Houghton:

> The first time I came was in the late 1890s as a [rugby] footballer, and the game was very rough. I seemed to be the culprit so far as the crowd was concerned and I had to be escorted from the town. I returned in 1931 and was welcomed with open arms [becoming the Member of Parliament], but that did not last long and they soon got back to the roughness again. [Robert had been defeated at the 1935 election.][23]

He finally retired from his YMCA role in 1956. At a special event held in his honour at Gateshead he said that 'As I look back on a connection with this association extending over 35 years I am convinced that the opportunities for service and Christian witness by the YMCA are as wide and challenging as they have ever been.'

Nevertheless, he was upbeat about the future:

> Circumstances change, but each generation has its own contribution to make, and as we look at the younger men and boys typified by the representatives at the [recent YMCA] celebrations in Paris, I feel that those now retiring from active service can rest content that the ideals of service and self-sacrifice are in safe hands.[24]

Meanwhile, Robert's own 'Christian witness' continued as a member of the National Assembly of the Church of England, and as a Church commissioner.

Robert received one last honour. In 1958 he was created a baronet 'for political and public services in the north of England', which were related in great detail by the regional press. As the *Gazette* noted, 'he has lived all his life in the district and regards himself, first and foremost, a Shieldsman'.[25] The *Gazette* also pointed out that since a baronetcy was a hereditary title, it would in due course be inherited by his son, Lt Col Robin Chapman. The Honours Committee in London would have been aware that Robin himself was following in his father's footsteps on a wide number of fronts. He was a Justice of the Peace, a Vice-Lieutenant of the county, a member of the Durham Diocesan Conference and Board of Finance (where he would later become chairman), a governor of the United Newcastle Hospitals, a board member of Finchale Abbey Training Centre and of two 'approved schools', president of the South Shields Boy Scouts Association and honorary treasurer of the county branch. For twenty years a partner in Henry Chapman Son & Co., he would shortly become president of the Northern Society of Chartered Accountants. An active member of the Conservative Party, though without parliamentary ambitions, he was chairman both of the Jarrow Conservatives and of the Northern Counties Provincial Area of the Conservative and Unionist Association.

Robert and Hélène had the good fortune to be hale and hearty enough to celebrate their Golden Wedding Anniversary at *Undercliff* the following year. Champagne was still flowing in the drawing room when the housemaid Lily Shepherd entered, announcing, 'Dinner is served, My Lady.' The family processed formally – two by two, arm in arm, led by Grandmother and Grandfather – through the inner hall, past the library and into the dining room. At the table, their sons Robin and Nick with their wives Barbara and Anne were joined by Hélène's brother-in-law and sister, Sir Dymoke and Lady White, who had travelled up from Salle Park in Norfolk. From Durham came their nephew, Dick Annand, accompanied not only by his wife Shirley but also by an early 18mm film camera to record the occasion. Three of the four grandchildren (David, Elizabeth and the author) were present with 4-year-old Caroline snug in her bed upstairs. It was a memorable evening, evoked from time to time in later years through Dick Annand's flickering film.

The following morning, in pale November sunshine, the family posed for photographs on the garden steps outside the library, the set-

Golden Wedding Anniversary, 1958: family group at *Undercliff*. Front row: Robert, Caroline, Hélène. Second row, left to right: Nick and Anne Chapman, Barbara Chapman and David, Lady White (Hélène's sister Isabelle), Elizabeth. Back row, left to right: the author, Sir Dymoke White, Robin Chapman. (Chapman Family Archive)

ting for countless fête openings over the decades. The staff were brought together for their photograph: Lizzie Brady the cook, Nellie Stott and Lily Shepherd, housemaids, were all there. Between the three of them they had worked at *Undercliff* for seventy-six years. It was a happy household: Lily told the author on more than one occasion that 'Your Gran has been like a mother to me.' The head gardener for seventeen years, Fred W. Knaggs, was there with his three under-gardeners and the 'pig man'. Together with the chauffeur Mr Robert Gawthorpe, the third maid and a laundry woman, there were eleven staff in all.

Robert and Hélène would no doubt have counted their blessings – not one of his ten brothers and sisters was still alive in 1959. For her part, Hélène recalled, for the benefit of the *Newcastle Journal*, their wedding in Scotland in 1909, which:

… went famously. A gorgeous day, a ceremony without a hitch and off we went on our honeymoon in Italy, Switzerland and then Paris. But our guests stayed on in Stirling for two days. A big roller skating rink had just been opened there and it was quite a novelty in those days, so they made the most of it.[26]

The highlight for Robert of the following year – and one of his last public engagements – was the centenary of the Territorial Army's 274 (Northumbrian) Field Regiment, Royal Artillery. The oldest member of the regiment, he and Hélène attended the centenary ball at the Bolingbroke Drill Hall in March, and the parade in May in Bents Park, where thousands watched in bright sunshine as a twelve-gun salute was fired. A message of congratulation was read out from the Queen as Captain General, Royal Artillery, and reinforced in the address of the inspecting officer, Maj. Gen. Lord Thurlow, General Officer Commanding 50th (Northumberland) Infantry Division (TA). With 500 members, 'Your strength is now higher than that of any Territorial regiment of artillery in Northern Command, and perhaps in the whole country.'[27]

Golden Wedding Anniversary, 1958: staff at *Undercliff*. Front row: Hélène and Robert. Middle row, left to right: Nellie Stott and Lily Shephard (housemaids), Eleanor Smith, Lizzie Brady (cook), Jane Armstrong. Back row, left to right: Aubrey James, Robert Gawthorpe (chauffeur), Jessie Lambert and William Burrows (gardeners), Wilfrid Murphy (pigman), Fred Knaggs (head gardener). (Chapman Family Archive)

In January 1961, Brig. O.F.G. Hogg published his *The History of the 3rd Durham Volunteer Artillery, now part of the 274th (Northumbrian) Field Regiment, RA (TA) 1860–1960*. Robert wrote the foreword:

> My family has been associated with the Regiment throughout the century and I have held a commission for 60 years since 7 March 1900. [*The History*] is a tribute to all who have served in the Regiment and an encouragement to all who are now serving or may serve in the future. The Regiment was never stronger in numbers nor more efficient than it is today. The story it tells will inspire future generations of Shieldsmen to follow in the steps of their fathers and be 'Always Ready' [the town's motto] to defend this old country of ours. God bless all who are now serving and who may serve in the future.[28]

The following month the *Shields Gazette* published the First World War reminiscences of James Sambrooks, DCM, MM, Croix de Guerre, always known as 'Sammy', who had served at Ypres and on the Somme with the 4th Durham Battery of the 4th Howitzer Brigade. Recalling his

The High Sheriff of Durham, Lt Col R.M. Chapman, precedes Justice Thesiger (left) and Justice Havers as they leave Durham Castle for Assize Sunday service in the cathedral, 30 January 1961. On the right is Bandsman James Gallagher of South Shields, from the 274 (Northumbrian) Field Regiment RA (TA). The banner on his trumpet displays the Chapman family coat of arms. (© *Northern Echo*)

old Commanding Officer, Major (now Colonel Sir Robert) Chapman, Sammy said:

> He was the straightest man I ever knew ['straight' in the sense of straight-talking and honest]. Physically he stood – or rode – ramrod stiff; mentally, he saw only the task in hand, everything else was either directed towards the main cause or pushed into the background. He was absolutely unswerving in purpose.[29]

Robert continued to take pride in the achievements of his son Robin, who had become High Sheriff of County Durham. A twelve-month appointment, the role was largely ceremonial, but with significant opportunities to promote and support civic and voluntary organisations. Traditionally linked to the administration of justice, one particularly enjoyable duty in 1961 was to escort the judges presiding over the Assizes (court cases)[30] in Durham Castle across Palace Green to the cathedral for a special Assize Sunday service. Robin, in Territorial officer's uniform, sword sheathed, was accompanied by his chaplain, the Rev. Harrison Thornton, Vicar of All Saints' Church Cleadon, and by two trumpeters from 274 Field Regiment RA (TA) in South Shields. Their duty was to sound a silver fanfare announcing the judges' entrance into the cathedral. The trumpets originally belonged to Robert, who had been High Sheriff twenty years' earlier, and from them hung armorial banners displaying the Chapman family coat of arms.

The Bishop of Durham, Dr Maurice Harland, preached the sermon, reported in some detail in the *Northern Echo*. He emphasised that:

> … punishment must seek to restore and repeal, and that it must never be vindictive or cruel. He added that punishment was a just deterrent and that without it there would be a rule of terror. It was a good thing that we did not indulge any longer in public executions.[31]

Robin would certainly have agreed: one of a High Sheriff's rather gruesome traditional duties was to be present at all executions. A few months later, in the Queen's Birthday Honours of June 1961, Robin received further recognition: he was appointed CBE (Commander of the Order of the British Empire) 'for political and public services in the North of England'. He would soon extend those services, becoming honorary colonel of 463 Regiment Light Anti-Aircraft (TA), in Sunderland.

Robert was increasingly housebound, but he did make two further trips to London for special occasions. His voluntary work with welfare services was well known and in October 1961 he attended a reception in the Mansion House, London, made available by the 'kind permission' of the Lord Mayor, Sir Bernard Waley-Cohen. The reception was to celebrate, 'in the gracious presence of Queen Elizabeth The Queen Mother', the opening of the new National Headquarters of Family Service Units. Their high-profile president, who had sent out the formal invitation, was the Hon. Sir David Bowes-Lyon, younger brother of the Queen Mother. The charity had branches throughout Britain, all with a commitment to family casework, stressing that 'children's needs are best met within the family, and only by helping parents to provide adequately for their children, will there be good outcomes for the whole family'.[32]

Robert had now stepped down from chairing the management committee of Finchale Abbey Training Centre for the Disabled, where his nephew Capt. Richard Annand, VC, continued as personnel officer after more than a decade's service. In 1962 the *Evening Chronicle* featured his career under the banner, 'The wheelbarrow V.C. dedicated his life to others.' Those 'others' were disabled ex-servicemen and civilians, 3,000 of whom had passed through the centre, nearly all into employment. 'Dickie Annand' was clearly totally committed, but remained 'bashfully modest' about his work: 'Every disabled man who goes to Finchale is interviewed immediately by Captain Annand. The ex-DLI officer watches every man's progress, helps him with personal problems, and at the end of the course works with the Ministry of Labour to find the men employment.'

Annand's own hearing disability remained very severe but had not prevented him taking on the chairmanship of the Hard of Hearing Association's Vocational Committee. His motto was 'Keep smiling and help yourself: never give up.'[33]

Twenty-two years after it was awarded, Richard Annand's VC captivated the imagination of an up-and-coming generation. 'The Wheelbarrow Hero' was featured on two colourful pages in *The Victor*, whose 'exciting pictures tell the stories in the star picture paper for boys'. Well researched and illustrated, the comic strip told its young readers that 'One of the most gallant actions of the last war took place in Belgium, when Second Lieutenant Annand of the Durham Light Infantry made this amazing rescue of a wounded man under heavy fire.' Despite a fierce defensive action and the lobbing of numerous grenades into the Germans' position, the DLI was

'The Wheelbarrow Hero' in *The Victor*, 24 January 1962 (front page).
(Used by kind permission of D.C. Thomson & Co. Ltd)

'The Wheelbarrow Hero' in *The Victor*, 24 January 1962 (back page).
(Used by kind permission of D.C. Thomson & Co. Ltd)

forced to withdraw. 'Sorry, Sir, but your batman was left behind,' Annand was told. 'I'm going back for him,' he replied. Annand 'found a wheelbarrow and loaded the wounded soldier into it. Under heavy fire and suffering from loss of blood, he stumbled across No-Mans-Land and brought his batman back. He was awarded one of the first VCs of the war.'[34]

On 13 July 1962, Robert and Hélène enjoyed their last 'Afternoon Party in the Garden' of Buckingham Palace, just four days before Dick and Shirley Annand attended another garden party there, this time solely for holders of the Victoria Cross and George Cross. Award holders included veterans of the First World War, and invitees travelled from Australia, Canada, Denmark, India, Jordan, Pakistan and the United States. In the evening Dick Annand attended a dinner given by the Lord Mayor of London.

In September one of Robert's oldest friends and colleagues, Victor Grunhut, died at the ripe old age of 92. Like Robert, he had been educated at South Shields Boys' High School, and they had both served with the 50th (Northumbrian) Division on the Western Front in the First World War. Victor had founded the law firm of Grunhut, Grunhut and Makepeace in 1893, and had practised as a solicitor until he was 90. He was a regular guest at *Undercliff* over forty years. Robert was not well enough to attend his funeral, but he and Hélène were present in the South Shields magistrates' court where a special tribute was later paid to Victor.

Robert celebrated his eighty-third birthday quietly with the family at *Undercliff* in March 1963. Arrangements were being made for the annual garden fête, and readers of the *Shields Gazette* were given advance notice later in the month that Dame Irene Ward, MP for Tynemouth, would open the Jarrow Conservative Association event on 15 July. The previous year's fête had attracted more than 1,500 people, *Undercliff* providing an idyllic setting. 'The terraced gardens, facing the sun and sheltered from the wind, are perfect for the marquees and side-shows.'[35]

The fête was, as usual, a great success. Robert was too ill to attend, but Hélène and Robin managed to appear happy and relaxed for the press cameras. On 24 July the *Sunderland Echo* reported that Robin and Barbara's elder son David, now aged 21 and studying for a commerce degree at McGill University in Montreal, was home on four months' vacation. His 17-year-old sister Elizabeth was also home, having just completed three months studying art at Le Fleuron, a finishing school

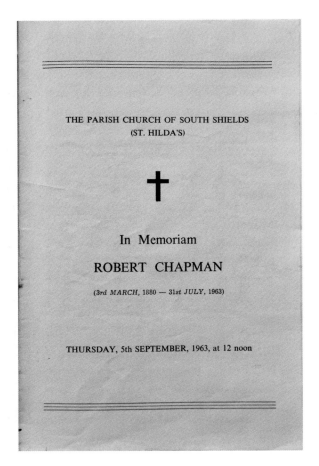

THE PARISH CHURCH OF SOUTH SHIELDS
(ST. HILDA'S)

✝

In Memoriam

ROBERT CHAPMAN

(3rd MARCH, 1880 — 31st JULY, 1963)

THURSDAY, 5th SEPTEMBER, 1963, at 12 noon

More than 600 people attended Robert Chapman's Memorial Service at St Hilda's
Church in September 1963. (Chapman Family Archive)

in Florence. 'During her last two weeks in Italy, she went on a camping
holiday with her 19-year-old brother, Peter, who has also arrived back
in England after spending some time in South Africa'[36] before going up
to Trinity College, Cambridge, in October. Robert would have been
very pleased to see his grandchildren one last time. He died at *Undercliff*
a week later, on 31 July 1963.

A memorial service was held on 5 September in St Hilda's, the parish
church of South Shields, where Robert's grandfather, Robert Chapman,
JP, had been a select vestryman and church warden a century earlier.
More than 600 people from all walks of life in South Shields, County
Durham, Newcastle and Northumberland listened to a tribute from the

Robert Chapman in military uniform, 1930. (Chapman Family Archive)

Rt. Rev. H.E. Ashdown, Bishop of Newcastle. 'It is my humble duty,' said the bishop:

> ... on behalf of our whole community, the Church and countless asso-
> ciations of men and women – not least in the youth services – to express
> our debt to a most distinguished life of public service to the nation and
> the North-east, and for an example of unremitting endeavour to further
> the good of all.[37]

The Armistice hymn, 'O Valiant Hearts', one of Robert's favourites, was sung:

> O Valiant Hearts, who to your glory came
> Through dust of conflict and through battle-flame;
> Tranquil you lie, your knightly virtue proved,
> Your memory hallowed in the Land you loved.[38]

Tributes to Robert flowed in, numerous obituaries were published and letters of condolence to Hélène, Robin (now Sir Robin) and Nick arrived daily.[39] They all emphasised the exceptional breadth of Robert's contribution, in war and peace, in South Shields, County Durham and London. He followed proudly in the Tyneside footsteps of his father and grandfather, displaying selfless commitment and unwavering determination to do everything in his power to help the community. He had been, in the words of South Shields' own motto, 'Always Ready'.

NOTES AND REFERENCES

Part 1: South Shields and the Tyne

1   Matthew Stainton's poem, of which these are the opening lines, was first published on 24 February 1868 and reproduced in the *Shields Daily Gazette and Shipping Telegraph* exactly twenty years later, on 24 February 1888. He had an iron foundry in South Shields, was a Poor Law guardian, a borough alderman and Mayor in 1856/57 and again in 1876/77.

1 The Transformation Begins

1   George B. Hodgson, *The Borough of South Shields* (Newcastle upon Tyne, 1903, reprinted by South Tyneside Libraries, 1996), p. 138.
2   See David Dougan, *The History of North East Shipbuilding* (London, 1968), p. 23 (quoting Hodgson, op. cit.).
3   Thomas Salmon, *South Shields: Its Past, Present and Future!* (South Shields, 1856), p. 18.
4   Hodgson, op. cit., p. 298.
5   Hodgson, op. cit., p. 298.
6   Hodgson, op. cit., p. 299.
7   Hodgson, op. cit., p. 324.
8   Norman McCord, *North East England: An Economic and Social History* (Batsford Academic, 1979), p. 51.
9   McCord, op. cit., p. 37.
10   Ian Whitehead, *Lest We Forget – The Miners' Bond*, www.durhamrecordsonline.com, 1997.
11   The mine, originally called St Hild's, became known as St Hilda's. I shall refer to it by the latter name, except where a contemporary quotation mentions 'Saint Hilda Pit' or 'St. Hild's'.
12   Salmon, op. cit., p. 35.
13   McCord, op. cit., pp. 42–3.
14   Hodgson, op. cit., p. 368.
15   For the full story see Hew Stevenson, *Jobs for the Boys* (London, 2009).
16   McCord, op. cit., pp. 52–3.

17 L.T.C. Rolt, *George Stephenson and Robert Stephenson: The Railway Revolution* (London, 1962), p. 263.
18 Hodgson, op. cit., p. 385.
19 *The Gazette Jubilee: Fifty Years of Progress – An Interesting Review, Editorial Reminiscences* (South Shields, 1899), p. 7.
20 Hodgson, op. cit., p. 393.
21 Hodgson, op. cit., p. 152.
22 Hodgson, op. cit., p. 167.
23 See Pamela Mawson, *Poor Law Administration in South Shields, 1830–1930* (MA Thesis, University of Newcastle upon Tyne, 1971), p. 36.
24 Mawson, op. cit., p. 40.
25 See Alan Johnson, *The Marine School of South Shields with introductory biographical notes on the founder, Dr. Thomas Masterman Winterbottom* (Washington, Tyne & Wear, 2010).
26 Hodgson, op. cit., p. 152.
27 Hodgson, op. cit., p. 155.
28 Salmon, op. cit., p. 60.
29 Salmon, op. cit., p. 60.

2 A North-Eastern Powerhouse

1 It was in *The Gazette Jubilee: Fifty Years of Progress – An Interesting Review, Editorial Reminiscences* (South Shields, 1899) pp. 5–6, that the then editor Charles B. Grubb 'imagined' the town centre as it was fifty years earlier.
2 Quoted in K.B. Smellie, *A History of Local Government* (London, 1968), p. 30.
3 Smellie, op. cit., p. 31.
4 George B. Hodgson, *The Borough of South Shields* (Newcastle upon Tyne, 1903, reprinted by South Tyneside Libraries, 1996), p. 180 et seq.
5 *The South Shields Centenary, 1850–1950: One Hundred Years of Civic Progress* (Town Council of the County Borough of South Shields, 1950), unpaginated. The newspaper is referred to throughout this book as the *Shields Gazette*, its later title.
6 *The South Shields Centenary*, op. cit.
7 Thomas Salmon, *South Shields: Its Past, Present and Future!* (South Shields, 1856), p. 10.
8 Salmon, op. cit.
9 Salmon, op. cit., p. 66.
10 Hodgson, op. cit., p. 193.
11 For the full story, see Brig. O.F.G. Hogg, *The History of the 3rd Durham Volunteer Artillery, now part of the 274th (Northumbrian) Field Regiment, RA (TA)*, (South Shields, 1960).
12 R.W. Johnson, *The Making of the Tyne* (London, 1895), p. 14.
13 Johnson, op. cit., p. 67.
14 Johnson, op. cit., p. 69.
15 Hodgson, op. cit., p. 334.
16 Richard E. Keys, *Dictionary of Tyne Sailing Ships* (Newcastle, 1998), p. 3.
17 Johnson, op. cit., p. 77.
18 Johnson, op. cit., p. 79.
19 Johnson, op. cit., pp. 80–1.
20 Johnson, op. cit., pp. 91–2.

21 Norman McCord, *North East England: An Economic and Social History* (Batsford Academic, 1979), p. 144.
22 Hodgson, op. cit., p. 201.
23 Keys, op. cit., pp. 1 and 28.
24 Keys, op. cit., p. 1.
25 Keys, op. cit., p. 1.
26 Sir Walter Runciman, Bart, *Before the Mast – and After: The Autobiography of a Sailor and Shipowner* (London, 1924), p. 39
27 Quoted in Runciman, op. cit., p. 155.
28 Keys, op. cit., p. 10.
29 Sir Walter Runciman, Bart, *Collier Brigs and Their Sailors* (London, 1926), p. 124.
30 J.G. Kohl, *Russia: St. Petersburg, Moscow, Kharkoff, Riga, Odessa, The German Provinces of the Baltic, The Steppes, The Crimea and The Interior of the Empire* (London, 1842), p. 185.
31 Kohl, op. cit., pp. 185–6.
32 Keys, op. cit., p. 46.
33 Runciman, *Collier Brigs and Their Sailors*, pp. 165–6.
34 Runciman, *Collier Brigs and Their Sailors*, pp. 173–4.
35 Keys, op. cit., p. 49.
36 Runciman, *Collier Brigs and Their Sailors*, pp. 23 and 84–5.
37 Keys, op. cit., p. 9.
38 Keys, op. cit., p. 13.
39 Keys, op. cit., p. 13.
40 Tyne Commission, *Proceedings*, quoted in Graeme J. Milne, *North East England, 1850–1914: The Dynamics of a Maritime-Industrial Region* (Woodbridge, UK, 2006), p. 83.
41 Johnson, op. cit., pp. 115-6.
42 Runciman, *Before the Mast – and After* (London, 1924), pp. 198–9. In this book he also recounts his three-year stint as a South Shields councillor, 1890–93.
43 Hodgson, op. cit., p. 198.
44 Dorothy Davis, *A History of Shopping* (London, 1966), p. 255.
45 Davis, op. cit., pp. 260–1.
46 Davis, op. cit., p. 261.
47 T. Brown, *Reminiscences of South Shields* (Shields Gazette, 1919), p. 30.
48 Brown, op. cit., p. 33.
49 David Wyn Davies, *Owen Owen, Victorian Draper* (Gwasg Cambria, undated), p. 21.
50 Milne, op. cit. (Woodbridge, 2006), p. 130.
51 W. Clark Russell, *The North-East Ports and Bristol Channel* (Newcastle upon Tyne, 1883), pp. 24–5.

3 Full Steam Ahead

1 G.M. Young, *Portrait of an Age: Victorian England* (Annotated edition by George Kitson Clark, Oxford University Press, 1977), p. 87.
2 See *Centenary of the Shields Gazette, Eighteen Forty-Nine to Nineteen Forty-Nine* (South Shields Public Libraries, 1949).
3 Glen Lyndon Dodds, 'William Brockie – his life and times in South Shields and Sunderland', *Durham County Local History Society Journal*, Number 83, September 2019, p. 82.

4   Brian Mains & Anthony Tuck, *Royal Grammar School Newcastle Upon Tyne: A History of the School in its Community* (Oriel Press, 1986), p. 99. This extract includes a quotation from Newcastle Central Library's publication, *Facts and Scraps*, viii (1862–65), p. 802.

5   Maberley Phillips, *A History of Banks, Bankers and Banking in Northumberland, Durham and North Yorkshire* (London, 1894), p. 116.

6   Norman McCord, *North East England: An Economic and Social History*, pp. 60–5.

7   Hartley Withers, *National Provincial Bank, 1833–1933* (London, 1933), p. 69.

8   See Sir Harold Howitt, *The History of The Institute of Chartered Accountants in England and Wales* (London, 1966).

9   Chapman Fletcher & Co. *Agreement of Partnership*, Chapman Family Archive.

10 See Amy Flagg, *Notes on Westoe II: The Village Houses and Some of Their Occupants* (South Shields undated, probably 1955), p. 82.

11 Dorothy Fleet, *Westoe: A History of the Village and its Residents* (Harton Village Press, 2019), pp. 184–5.

12 Aaron Watson, *South Shields: A Gossiping Guide* (South Shields, 1892), p. 26.

13 Howarth, 'Gender, Domesticity, and Sexual Politics', in Colin Matthew, editor, *The Nineteenth Century – The British Isles: 1815–1901* (Oxford, 2000), pp. 182–3.

14 Janet Howarth, op. cit., p. 183.

15 Jacqueline Beaumont, 'Dorothea Beale', in H.C.G. Matthew and Brian Harrison, editors, *Oxford Dictionary of National Biography* (Oxford 2004), vol. 4, p. 511.

16 See Elizabeth H. Shillito, *Dorothea Beale* (London, 1920), p. 64.

17 Dorothea Beale, *Literary Studies of Poems, New and Old* (London, 1902), p. 13.

18 I am grateful to Mrs Rachel Roberts, College Archivist, Cheltenham Ladies' College, for kindly providing me with all available records on Ethel and Hilda Chapman and for the photograph of the CLC Guild's production of *Dante* in July 1900. She also kindly referred me to Dorothea Beale's *Literary Studies*, op. cit.

19 See www.cheltladiescollege.org/about-clc/history-of-college

20 Elizabeth Raike, in her biography *Dorothea Beale of Cheltenham* (London, 1908) was dismissive of these lines: 'Flippant scholars might echo the words of Punch, "How different from us, Miss Beale and Miss Buss!" But in the sense in which the words were intended, this was not true in either case. Suffice it to say, that Dorothea Beale knew what it was to be admired, loved, even for a short time engaged to be married' (p. 61).

21 Elizabeth J. Morse, 'Dame Louisa Innes Lumsden', in H.C.G. Matthew and Brian Harrison, editors, *Oxford Dictionary of National Biography* (Oxford, 2004), vol. 34, p. 763.

22 Kate Perry, 'Dame (Jane) Frances Dove', in H.C.G. Matthew and Brian Harrison, editors, *Oxford Dictionary of National Biography* (Oxford, 2004), vol. 16, p. 752.

23 I am grateful to Jane Claydon, Archivist, St Leonards, for kindly providing me with all available records on Dora Elizabeth and (Marion) Dorothy Chapman, Hélène and Isabelle Macgowan, and Bessie (Elizabeth) Gowans, and for the house photographs.

24 Louise Innes Lumsden, *Yellow Leaves* (Edinburgh, 1933), p. 81.

25 I am grateful to Mike Todd, who set up the excellent historical website www.boyshighschool.co.uk for permission to use information on it, and for the additional information he provided in correspondence. The account that follows of the history of the South Shields High School, and the attendance details of the seven Chapman brothers, is largely drawn from that information.

26 Rev. Alfred J. Church, *Heroes and Kings: Stories from the Greek* (London, 1890), pp. 230–1.

27 *Articles of Agreement*, Chapman Family Archive.

28 The Holy Rood is the Cross of Jesus, or a representation of it. 'Rude' is an archaic form of Rood.

29 I am grateful to Neil Dickson, Assistant Archivist, Stirling Council Archives, for information on East Church and for retrieving the report in the *Stirling Observer*.

30 Boddy, *The Building Societies* (Macmillan, 1980), p. 7.

31 *Royal Commission on Friendly and Benefit Building Societies*, 2nd Report, Parliamentary Papers, vol. XXVI (HMSO, 1872), quoted in Boddy, op. cit., p. 7.

32 Martin Boddy, op. cit., p. 8.

33 Boddy, op. cit., pp. 9–10.

34 E.J. Cleary, *The Building Society Movement* (London, 1965), p. 118.

35 Boddy, op. cit., p. 10.

36 Cleary, op. cit., p. 143.

37 Antoninus Samy, *The Building Society Promise: Access, Risk and Efficiency 1880–1939* (Oxford, 2016), p. 57.

38 Samy, op. cit., pp. 61–3.

4 Business and Community Leaders

1   'Westoe is a pleasant village situated about a mile south of South Shields … From its proximity to South Shields and other large centres of industry in the neighbourhood, many of the principal residents belong to the mercantile classes', *Christie's Directory for Newcastle, Gateshead, North and South Shields and Sunderland* (1876/77).

2   This account draws heavily on Hew Stevenson, *Jobs for the Boys* (London, 2009), and on Francis Goodhall, 'Stevenson, James Cochran', in H.C.G. Matthew and Brian Harrison, editors, *Oxford Dictionary of National Biography*, vol. 52 (Oxford, 2004), pp. 583–4.

3   Stevenson, op. cit., p. 248. For a full account of all the houses in Westoe, see Dorothy Fleet, *Westoe: A History of the Village and its Residents* (Harton Village Press, 2019).

4   George B. Hodgson, *The Borough of South Shields* (1903; reprinted by South Tyneside Libraries, 1996), p. 204.

5   This and the following quotations are from Stevenson, op. cit., pp. 114–15.

6   Hodgson, op. cit., p. 325.

7   Nikolaus Pevsner, *The Buildings of England: County Durham* (revised by Elizabeth Williamson, New Haven and London, 2002), p. 423.

8   Norman L. Middlemiss, *British Shipbuilding Yards, Volume 1: North-East Coast* (Newcastle upon Tyne, 1993), pp. 104–6.

9   Hodgson, op. cit., p. 326.

10 Amy C. Flagg, *Notes on the History of Shipbuilding in South Shields 1746–1946* (South Tyneside Borough Council Library Service, 1979), p. 228.

11 Flagg, op. cit., p. 226.

12 Hodgson, op. cit., p. 215. Hodgson also details the controversy in the town as to the respective roles of William Wouldhave and Henry Greathead in the lifeboat's design.

13 William Richardson, *History of the Parish of Wallsend* (Newcastle upon Tyne, 1923), p. 315.

14 See Sir Walter Runciman's fascinating autobiography, *Before the Mast – and After* (London, 1924). Brief quotations in the following paragraphs are from this book.

15 Runciman, op. cit., Part VII, Chapter I, 'Municipal Life – A Merry Interlude'.

16 Runciman, op. cit., p. 256.

17 Obituary of J.H. Morton in the *Journal of the Royal Institute of British Architects* (London, 1923), pp. 596–7.

18 Obituary of J.H. Morton, op. cit., p. 596. Hodgson, op. cit., pp. 457–9, gives an account of Freemasonry in South Shields.

19 See Maurice Milne, *The Newspapers of Northumberland and Durham* (Newcastle upon Tyne, c.1965), p. 129. A fuller account is given by Aaron Watson in *A Newspaper Man's Memories* (London, no date), pp. 46–7.

20 *Shields Gazette and Shipping Telegraph: The Centenary of Britain's Oldest Provincial Evening Newspaper, 1849–1949* (South Shields, 1949).

21 *Shields Gazette and Shipping Telegraph Centenary*, op. cit.

22 Stevenson, op. cit., p. 327.

23 Milne, op. cit., p. 155.

24 Stevenson, op. cit., pp. 328–32.

25 Stevenson, loc. cit.

26 I am indebted to Julia Carnwath, whose husband Dr Tom Carnwath is a great-grandson of Dr Joseph F. Armstrong, for information on the Armstrong family.

27 Hodgson, op. cit., p. 231.

28 Amy Flagg, *Notes on Westoe II: The Village Houses and Some of their Occupants* (South Shields, c. 1955), p. 73 et seq.

29 Hodgson, op. cit., p. 448.

30 Hodgson, op. cit., p. 231.

31 Hodgson, op. cit., p. 448.

5 Sporting Lives

1 See Ian Whitehead, *The Sporting Tyne* (Gateshead, 2002), p. 21, and *James Renforth of Gateshead: Champion Sculler of the World* (Newcastle upon Tyne, 2004).

2 Eric Halladay, *Rowing in England: A Social History* (Manchester, 1990), p. 17.

3 See Whitehead, *The Sporting Tyne*, op. cit., pp. 18–20.

4 A wherry was a clinker-built vessel used to carry coal and other materials.

5 Whitehead, *James Renforth of Gateshead*, op. cit., pp. 129–30.

6 Aaron Watson, *A Newspaper Man's Memories* (London, c.1925), p. 36.

7 *Newcastle Daily Chronicle*, 30 July 1870.

8 *Newcastle Daily Chronicle*, 20 July 1872.

9 *Newcastle Daily Chronicle*, 20 August 1872.

10 *Newcastle Daily Chronicle*, 20 August 1872.

11 Whitehead, *The Sporting Tyne*, op. cit., p. 11 and p. 4.

12 Whitehead, *The Sporting Tyne*, op. cit., p. 30.

13 Norman McCord, *North East England: An Economic and Social History* (London, 1979), p. 188.

14 I am indebted to Michael A. Lyon of Westoe RFC who wrote *The Chapmans: A Short Account of a Westoe Family*, and, in 1999, a detailed note on Fred Chapman's

playing career. See also W.N. Dodds, *A History of Westoe Rugby Football Club, 1875–1975* (South Shields, *c.*1977).

15 Phil McGowan, *One of Us: England's Greatest Rugby Players* (Amberley, 2015), p. 131.

16 See C. Berkeley Cowell and E. Watts Moses, *Durham County Rugby Union, 1876–1936* (Newcastle upon Tyne, 1936).

17 U.A. Titley and Ross McWhirter, *Centenary History of the Rugby Football Union* (London, 1970), p. 122.

18 Tony Collins, *A Global History of Rugby* (London, 2015), pp. 206–7. Collins paints a dismal picture of the then current controversy over whether the payment of expenses to players on international tours breached amateur principles.

19 Phil McGowan, *Doing their Duty: How England's Rugby Footballers Helped Win the First World War* (London, 2017), pp. 88–9.

20 *The Times*, 17 January 1910. Under the RFU scoring system at the time, five points were awarded for a converted try (rather confusingly simply called 'a goal'), three points for a penalty goal, and three points for a try (i.e. unconverted).

21 *The Times*, op. cit.

22 *The Times*, op. cit.

23 Michael A. Lyon (see ref. 14).

24 Titley and McWhirter, op. cit., Part II. Biographies.

25 Arthur Morton, *A History of Westoe Lawn Tennis Club, 1880–1980* (South Shields, *c.*1980), p. 3.

26 Op. cit., p. 6.

27 Op. cit., p. 8.

28 Clive Crickmer, *Grass Roots: A History of South Shields Cricket Club, 1850–1984* (South Shields, 1985), p. 42.

29 Morton, op. cit., p. 15.

30 Morton, op. cit., p. 15.

6 War on all Fronts, 1914–18

1 Wallace Annand, *Adjutant's Diary*, Collingwood Battalion, 3 April–8 May 1915. Annand Family Archive.

2 Op. cit.

3 H.M. Denham, *Dardanelles: A Midshipman's Diary 1915–16* (London, 1981), p. 88.

4 Denham, op. cit., p. 91.

5 Allan Mallinson, *Too Important for the Generals: How Britain Nearly Lost the First World War* (London, 2016), p. 102.

6 Stanley Geary, *The Collingwood Battalion, Royal Naval Division* (Hastings, no date, but before end of the First World War), p. 9.

7 Loc. cit.

8 Loc. cit.

9 Peter Hart, *Gallipoli* (London, 2013), p. 245.

10 Hart, op. cit., pp. 245–6. The quotation is from Imperial War Museum *Sound* (J. Murray, AC8201, reel 9).

11 Geary, op. cit., final page (not numbered).

12 Hart, op. cit., p. 252.

13 For historical background and a detailed account of the 4th Northumbrian Brigade in the First World War, see Brig. O.F.G. Hogg, *The History of the 3rd Durham Volunteer Artillery, now part of the 274th (Northumbrian) Field Regiment, RA (TA), 1860–1960* (South Shields, 1960).

14 Hogg, op. cit., p. 42.

15 A phrase in a commissioned report by Chris Baker of 'Fourteeneighteen research' (Milverton Associates Ltd). He provided invaluable information on Maj. Charles Chapman, and indeed on all the family members in this chapter.

16 A limber is the detachable front part of a gun carriage, consisting of two wheels, axle, pole and ammunition box (*OED*).

17 Hogg, op. cit., p. 45.

18 Hogg, op. cit., p. 45.

19 C.H. Ommanney, *The War History of the 1st Northumbrian Brigade RFA (TF)*, (Newcastle upon Tyne, 1927), p. 21.

20 This and the following quotation are from Everard Wyrall, *The Fiftieth Division, 1914–1919* (first published in 1939; republished by The Naval and Military Press, 1999), pp. 7–8.

21 Wyrall, op. cit., pp. 7–8.

22 Ommanney, op. cit., p. 22.

23 Hogg, op. cit., p. 47.

24 Hogg, op. cit., p. 49.

25 Hogg, op. cit., p. 50.

26 The National Archives (ref. WO-95-2820-1), *50th Division: 4th Northumbrian BDE, became 253 RD BDE RFA, APR 1915–NOV 1916*.

27 Wyrall, op. cit., pp. 86–8.

28 Wyrall, op. cit., pp. 86–8.

29 Hogg, op. cit., p. 50.

30 Ommanney, op. cit., p. 53.

31 Hogg, op. cit., pp. 51–2.

32 The National Archives, op. cit.

33 Wyrall, op. cit., pp. 117–18.

34 Wyrall, op. cit. pp. 117–18.

35 Cyril Falls, *The History of the 36th (Ulster) Division* (Belfast, 1922), p. 90.

36 Mallinson, op. cit., p. 247.

37 Falls, op. cit., p. 90.

38 Falls, op. cit., p. 113.

39 Falls, op. cit., p. 120.

40 The original letter is in the Chapman Family Archive.

41 *Reports by the Joint War Committee and the Joint War Finance Committee of the British Red Cross Society and the Order of St. John of Jerusalem in England on Voluntary Aid Rendered to the Sick and Wounded at Home and Abroad and to British Prisoners of War, 1914–1919* (HMSO, 1921), p. 189.

42 *Reports by the Joint War Committee*, op. cit., p. 190.

43 Neil R. Storey and Fiona Kay, *Northumberland and Tyneside's War* (Stroud, 2017), p. 102.

44 Mary Ingham, *Tracing Your Service Women Ancestors* (Barnsley, 2012) p. 48.

45 Lyn Macdonald, *The Roses of No Man's Land* (Revised edition, London, 2013), p. xi.

46 Information helpfully provided by Sharda Rozena of St John Ambulance, St John's Gate, London EC1M 4DA.

47 See Storey and Kay, op. cit., p. 106, and *The Long, Long Trail: The British Army in the Great War of 1914–1918*, www.longlongtrail.co.uk.

48 Macdonald, op. cit., p. 116.

49 Thekla Bowser, *The Story of British V.A.D. Work in the Great War* (Facsimile reprint, London, 2003), pp. 274–5. The book was originally published in 1917.

50 *Reports by the Joint War Committee*, op. cit., p. 102.

51 Anne Powell, *Women in the War Zone* (Stroud, 2013), pp. 357 and 388. A longer description of this tragic event can be found in Macdonald, op. cit., pp. 259–62.

52 Samir Raafat, *Victoria College – Educating the Elite, 1902–1956*, www.egy.com/victoria/96-03-30.php.

53 Macdonald, op. cit, p. 123.

54 Ingham, op. cit., p. 58. A sola topi was an Indian sun helmet made from the pith of an East Indian swamp plant, the sola.

55 *Reports by the Joint War Committee*, op. cit., pp. 409–10.

56 Ingham, op. cit., pp. 58–9.

57 Oscar Parkes, *British Battleships* (London, 1957), p. 508.

58 For a detailed regimental history, see C.T. Atkinson, *The Queen's Own Royal West Kent Regiment, 1914–1919* (London, 1924).

59 I am grateful to researcher Chris Baker (www.fourteeneighteen.co.uk) for this and much other helpful information (see ref. 15).

60 Ommanney, op. cit., p. 55.

61 Ommanney, op. cit., p. 58.

62 Wyrall, op. cit., pp. 135–6.

63 Hogg, op. cit., p. 55.

64 Quoted in Wyrall, op. cit., pp. 137–8. Battery Quartermaster Sgt W. Dunnington was one of the signatories of the letter of condolence sent by 'the remainder of the old Battery' to Mr and Mrs Henry Chapman in September 1917, following the death of Robert's brother, Maj. Charles Chapman.

65 Wyrall, op. cit., p. 139.

66 Wyrall, op. cit., p. 148.

67 Ommanney, op. cit., p. 118.

68 Ommanney, op. cit., p. 129.

69 Ommanney, op. cit., p. 132, quoting from the war diary of Col N.L. Parmeter.

70 The following brief summary is based on Mallinson, op. cit., pp. 206–29.

71 Mallinson, op. cit., p. 228.

72 Col Shiel of the 50th (Northumbrian) Division, quoted in Ommanney, op. cit., p. 171.

73 Ommanney, loc. cit.

74 Lt J.W. Naylor, Royal Artillery, quoted in Lyn Macdonald, *They Called It Passchendaele* (London, 1978, Second Impression 1979), p. 188.

75 Col Shiel, quoted in Wyrall, op. cit., p. 248.

76 Wyrall, op. cit., p. 244.

77 Ommanney, op. cit., pp. 179–80.

78 Mallinson, op. cit., p. 259.

79 Ommanney, op. cit., p. 195.

80 Wyrall, op. cit., p. 305. This quotation includes an extract from C.H. Ommaney, op. cit.

81 Ommanney, op. cit., p. 243.

7 Post-War Challenges

1   O.F.G. Hogg, *The History of the 3rd Durham Volunteer Artillery, 1860–1960* (South Shields, 1960), p. 65.
2   Nikolaus Pevsner, *County Durham*, revised by Elizabeth Williamson (New Haven and London, 2002), p. 419.
3   Robert Graves and Alan Hodge, *The Long Week-End: A Social History of Great Britain 1918–1939* (London, 1940), p. 27.
4   Graves and Hodge, pp. 27–8 and 44–5.
5   Fred Berry, *Housing: The Great British Failure* (London, 1974), p. 35. A financial analysis of the Addison Act and subsequent legislation is provided by A.A. Nevitt in *Housing, Taxation and Subsidies* (London, 1966).
6   Henry A. Mess, *Industrial Tyneside: A Social Survey* (London, 1928), p. 79. Henry Mess was director of the Bureau of Social Research for Tyneside, and later became the director of the Tyneside Council of Social Service.
7   Mess, op. cit., pp. 69–80.
8   Mess, op. cit., p. 95.
9   Mess, op. cit. p. 95.
10 Hogg, op. cit., p. 65.
11 Peter Clarke, *Hope and Glory: Britain 1900–2000* (London, 2004), p. 141. A.J.P. Taylor's comment was that the miners 'had to accept longer hours, lower wages, and – worst of all – district agreements. Nothing was done to reorganise or to improve the industry.' See his *English History 1914–1945* (Oxford, 1965), p. 248. The appalling conditions and dangers faced by pitmen down the mines in South Shields is well described in Joseph Robinson, *Tommy Turnbull: A Miner's Life* (Stroud, 2007).
12 See Norman McCord, *North East England: The Region's Development, 1760–1960* (London, 1979), p. 216.
13 Mess, op. cit., pp. 42–3.
14 David Dougan, *The History of North East Shipbuilding* (London, 1968), pp. 136–7.
15 Norman L. Middlemiss, *British Shipbuilding Yards, Volume 1: North-East Coast* (Newcastle upon Tyne, 1993), pp. 106–7.
16 Middlemiss, op. cit., p. 135. See also www.tynebuiltships.co.uk/Eltringham-History.html.
17 Middlemiss, op. cit., p. 137. See also www.tynebuiltships.co.uk/RennoldsonJP.html.
18 Middlemiss, op. cit., p. 137. See also www.tynebuiltships.co.uk/RennoldsonC.html.
19 Mess, op. cit., p. 55.
20 A. Mess, op. cit., p. 55.
21 South Shields County Borough Council, *1835–1935, A Hundred Years of Local Government* (South Shields, 1935), p. 51.
22 Pamela Mawson, *Poor Law Administration in South Shields, 1830–1930* (MA thesis, University of Newcastle upon Tyne, 1971), p. 198.
23 South Shields Corporation, *Minutes of Proceedings, vol. 68, July–December 1929*, p. 174.
24 South Shields Corporation, op. cit., p. 938.
25 South Shields Corporation, *Minutes of Proceedings, vol. 70, July–December 1930*, p. 616.
26 South Shields Corporation, *Minutes of Proceedings, vol. 71, January–June 1931*, pp. 101–2.
27 For a fuller account, see Peter Clarke, *Hope and Glory: Britain 1900–2000* (London, 2004), Chapter 5, 'Economic Blizzard'.

28 As reported in *Shields Daily Gazette*, 13 October 1931.
29 Ibid.
30 Quoted in Maureen Calcutt, *Parliamentary Elections in County Durham 1929–1935* (M. Litt. thesis, University of Newcastle upon Tyne, 1973), p. 115.
31 Chapman Family Archive.
32 *Shields Daily Gazette*, 17 October 1931.
33 *Sunderland Echo*, 23 October 1931.
34 *Shields Daily Gazette*, 22 October 1931.
35 Ibid.
36 Ibid.
37 Calcutt, op. cit., pp. 243–4.
38 Chapman Family Archive.
39 *Sunderland Echo*, 22 October 1931.
40 *Sunderland Echo*, 23 October 1931.
41 *Shields Daily Gazette*, 27 October 1931.
42 Ibid.
43 *Newcastle Journal*, 27 October 1931.
44 *Shields Daily Gazette*, 27 October 1931.
45 *Shields Daily Gazette*, 28 October 1931.
46 Taylor, op. cit., p. 325.
47 There were eleven county 'divisions': Blaydon, Jarrow, Houghton-le-Spring, Consett, Chester-le-Street, Barnard Castle, Spennymoor, Durham, Seaham, Bishop Auckland and Sedgefield. Labour lost all of them except Consett and Spennymoor (Ramsay MacDonald as the National Labour candidate for Seaham defeating William Coxon, the official Labour Party candidate). Of the six county boroughs (Sunderland, Stockton-on-Tees, South Shields, The Hartlepools, Gateshead and Darlington), Labour won five in the 1929 election, and lost them all in 1931. The Hartlepools returned a Conservative MP in both 1929 and 1931. Full details can be found in Calcutt, op. cit.

8 Mayor and Mayoress of South Shields

1   *Shields Daily Gazette*, 29 October 1931.
2   *Shields Daily Gazette*, 10 November 1931.
3   Ibid.
4   Ibid.
5   Ibid.
6   Ibid.
7   *Shields Daily Gazette*, 11 November 1931.
8   Chapman Family Archive.
9   Stephanie Ward, *Unemployment and the State in Britain: The Means Test and Protest in 1930s South Wales and North-East England* (Manchester, 2013), p. 65.
10 David Vincent, *Poor Citizens: The State and the Poor in Twentieth-Century Britain* (London, 1991), pp. 70 and 224.
11 Norman McCord, *North East England: An Economic and Social History* (Batsford Academic, 1979) pp. 243–4.
12 Chapman Family Archive. The reference to 'Echo Thompson' was to the prominent councillor and PAC member, Edwin Thompson. 'Nine bob' was nine shillings, and 'a quid' was £1 (twenty shillings).

13 *Shields Daily Gazette*, 21 December 1931.
14 *Shields Daily Gazette*, 7 January 1932.
15 Ibid. William (Bill) Blyton later became a South Shields Labour Councillor from 1936-1945, and Labour MP for Houghton-le-Spring from 1945 to 1964 when he retired and was elevated to the House of Lords as Baron Blyton of South Shields.
16 Ward, op. cit., p. 125.
17 *Northern Echo*, 12 September 1932.
18 McCord, op. cit., pp. 255–6.
19 *Northern Echo*, 28 November 1932.
20 Ibid.
21 *Shields Daily Gazette*, 23 March 1932. The Sutton Dwellings Trust was eventually absorbed into one of the country's largest housing associations, the Clarion Housing Group. I am grateful to their Deeds department for kindly making available a copy of the conveyancing documentation.
22 *Shields Daily Gazette*, ibid.
23 *Shields Gazette*, 16 September 1932.
24 Ibid.
25 *Shields Daily Gazette*, 10 December 1931. (Note: from 20 April 1932, the newspaper became simply the *Shields Gazette*).
26 Ibid.
27 Ibid.
28 *Shields Gazette*, 27 April 1932.
29 *Shields Gazette*, 1 August 1932
30 Ibid.
31 *Shields Gazette*, 7 November 1932.
32 *Shields Gazette*, 9 November 1932.
33 *Shields Gazette*, 5 November 1932.

9 Parliament and the 'Special Areas'

1   Diane Urquhart, 'Edith Helen Vane-Tempest-Stewart, Marchioness of Londonderry', in H.C.G. Matthew and Brian Harrison, editors, *Oxford Dictionary of National Biography* (Oxford, 2004), vol.52, pp. 661–2.
2   *Newcastle Journal*, 19 April 1932.
3   Hansard, *HC Debate*, 18 April 1932, vol. 264, cc. 1259–319.
4   Hansard, op. cit.
5   Hansard, op. cit.
6   *Shields Daily Gazette*, 19 April 1932 (and Hansard, op. cit.).
7   *Shields Gazette*, 21 April 1932.
8   Hansard, *Housing HC Debate*, 7 December 1932, vol. 272, cc. 1625–92. There was a full report in the *Shields Gazette* on 8 December.
9   As reported in the *Shields Gazette*, 8 December 1932.
10 Hansard, *Ministry of Health Debate*, 7 July 1933, vol. 280, cc. 645-728.
11 Diane Spour, 'Housing and Social Conditions in South Shields in the 1930s', in Side Photographic Gallery, *Housing Clearance in the 1930s: James Henry Cleet, A South Shields Photographer* (Newcastle, 1979).
12 South Shields Borough Council, *The South Shields Centenary, 1850–1950*.

13 *Shields Gazette*, 28 January 1933. See also Norman L. Middlemiss, *British Shipbuilding Yards, Volume I: North-East Coast* (Newcastle upon Tyne, 1993), p. 107.

14 Ellen Wilkinson, *The Town That Was Murdered* (London, 1939), pp. 191–2.

15 Wilkinson, op. cit., p. 163.

16 *Newcastle Journal*, 7 December 1933.

17 Ibid.

18 *Shields Gazette*, 8 June 1934.

19 Capt. D. Euan Wallace, 'Durham and Tyneside', in Ministry of Labour, *Reports of Investigations into the Industrial Conditions in Certain Depressed Areas* (HMSO, cmd. 4728, 1934), pp. 76, 106 and 117.

20 *Shields Gazette*, 8 November 1934. For fuller details see Wallace, op. cit., pp. 106–110.

21 Ibid.

22 *Shields Gazette*, 4 January 1935.

23 *Northern Echo*, 1 October 1935.

24 *Sunderland Echo*, 15 December 1933. See also Hansard, *HC Debate, 5s*, 11–21 December 1933.

25 *Shields Gazette*, 13 November 1934.

26 Stephanie Ward, *Unemployment and the State in Britain* (Manchester, 2013), Chapter 5.

27 Paul Tutt Stafford, 'Unemployment Assistance in Great Britain', *The American Political Science Review*, vol. XXXI, 1937, p. 441.

28 *Shields Gazette*, 13 February 1935. See also Ward, op. cit., p. 178.

29 *Shields Gazette*, 7 May 1935.

30 Chapman Family Archive.

31 *News Chronicle*, 14 May 1935.

32 A.J.P. Taylor, *English History 1914–1945* (Oxford, 1965), p. 383.

33 Stuart Ball, *Parliament and Politics in the Age of Baldwin and MacDonald: The Headlam Diaries 1923–1935* (London, 1992), p. 228. Cuthbert Headlam's positive remarks about Robert were praise indeed, since he made numerous scathing comments about public figures in London and County Durham in his diaries.

34 *Shields Gazette*, 7 November 1935.

35 Ibid.

36 *Shields Gazette*, 8 November 1935.

37 *North Mail and Newcastle Chronicle*, 31 October 1935.

38 *Shields Gazette*, 31 October 1935.

39 *Northern Echo*, 2 November 1935.

40 *Shields Gazette*, 30 October 1935.

41 Norman McCord, *North East England: An Economic and Social History* (London, 1979), p. 217.

42 *Sunderland Echo*, 2 November 1935.

43 Ball, op. cit., p. 346.

44 Robert was not correct in saying that the Labour Government of 1929–31 had introduced the Means Test. It had, in October 1930, appointed a Royal Commission on Unemployment Insurance, whose Interim Report of June 1931 had proposed means-testing of 'transitional benefit' in the case of single adults, married women and those in receipt of fixed incomes other than savings. Furthermore, the Minister of Labour, Margaret Bondfield, echoed this recommendation by suggesting in August 1931 that 'transitional benefits' should indeed be subject to a means test. However, the Government imploded on the

issue of national expenditure cuts generally, and it fell on 22 August 1931, to be replaced by a new National Government on 24 August. It was this Government that introduced the Household Means Test in November. For a full account, from which the above summary is derived, see W.R. Garside, *British Unemployment 1919–1939* (Cambridge, 1990), pp. 51–65.

45 *North Mail*, 9 November 1935.
46 *Sunderland Echo*, 9 November 1935.
47 *North Mail*, 7 November 1935.
48 *Newcastle Journal*, 7 November 1935.
49 *Shields Gazette*, 11 November 1935.
50 *Northern Echo*, 16 November 1935.
51 *Shields Gazette*, December 1935.
52 Ibid.
53 *Shields Gazette*, 24 January 1936.
54 Mourners included Sir James Readhead, Shannon Stevenson of the Northern Press (publishers of the *Shields Gazette*), the chairman of the South Shields Gas Company (where Henry had been an auditor, a director for thirty-four years and latterly vice-chairman), and Councillor J.B. Potts, president of the South Shields Rotary Club. There were representatives from the South Shields Savings Bank (where Henry had been an auditor and manager), the North of England Steamship Owners Association and from his accountancy firm, Henry Chapman Son & Co. and the South Shields Commercial Permanent Building Society (which he had also founded). There were representatives of the South Shields Cricket and Westoe Rugby and Lawn Tennis Club (where he was president), Durham County Cricket Club and the South Shields Swimming Club (where he had been a founder member). The Ingham Infirmary (where Henry had been a life governor and chairman of the General Committee before the First World War), the Marine School (where Henry had been a governor for thirty-five years and latterly chairman), and the South Shields Boys' High School (where he had been a governor for decades) were all represented in strength.
55 Chapman Family Archive (Robert Chapman's Harton Ward Election Manifesto, 1 November 1933).
56 See 'New High School at Harton' in Mike Todd's comprehensive website, www.boyshighschool.co.uk.
57 *Newcastle Journal*, 13 March 1936.
58 *Sunday Sun*, 22 March 1936.
59 Ibid.
60 Wilkinson, op. cit., p. 209.
61 Borough of South Tyneside, *75 Years of Service, 1910–1985* (South Shields, 1985), p. 6. The publication was compiled by Denis Johnson, Local Studies Librarian.
62 Middlemiss, op. cit., pp. 106–7.
63 *Sunderland Echo*, 21 April 1938.
64 *Shields Gazette*, 20 September 1938
65 *Shields Gazette*, 11 October 1938.
66 *Shields Gazette*, 6 October 1938.
67 *Sunderland Echo*, 16 December 1938.
68 *Shields Gazette*, 22 February 1939.
69 Municipal clinics' 1939 brochure prepared for royal visit, Chapman Family Archive.

70 Chapman Family Archive.
71 *Shields Gazette*, 9 August 1939.
72 *Shields Gazette*, 19 May 1939.
73 *Shields Gazette*, 15 April 1939.
74 Ibid.
75 Ibid.

10 Undercliff

1 Nikolaus Pevsner, *The Buildings of England, County Durham*, second edition, revised by Elizabeth Williamson (New Haven and London, 1985), pp. 129–30.
2 I am grateful for commissioned research on Benjamin Ward's military records carried out by Chris Baker (www.fourteeneighteen.co.uk), from which this summary is derived.
3 Wancourt was captured by the 50th (Northumbrian) Division during the Battle of Arras, in the summer of 1917.
4 See Chapter 6 for extracts from Archie Shiel's War Diaries, quoted in C.H. Ommanney's *The War History of the 1st Northumbrian Brigade RFA (TF)*, in Everard Wyrall's *The Fiftieth Division, 1914–1919,* and in Brig. O.F.G. Hogg's *The History of the 3rd Durham Volunteer Artillery, 1860–1960*. Colonel Shiel himself had a distinguished First World War record, being awarded the DSO for displaying exceptional leadership and courage during heavy German artillery fire near Wancourt.
5 Their distant cousin, Charlotte Sebag-Montefiore, became a friend of the author at Cambridge University in the mid-1960s.
6 'A Shieldsman's Diary' by 'Odd Man Out', who recalled 'Tubby' Clayton's visit fourteen years later in the *Shields Gazette*, 9 December 1940.
7 Ibid.
8 Roger Pooley, 'The Pilgrim's Progress and the Line of Allegory', in Anne Dunan-Page, editor, *The Cambridge Companion to Bunyan* (Cambridge, 2010), p. 89.
9 John Bunyan, *The Pilgrim's Progress*, edited by James Blanton Wharey (second edition, revised by Roger Sharrock, Oxford, 1960), p. 37.
10 See Chapter 7.
11 See Hew Stevenson, *Jobs for the Boys* (London, 2009), pp. 309 and 342.
12 Frank Manders and Jill Brown, *The North East Coast Exhibition 1929 – A Photographic Celebration* (City of Newcastle upon Tyne Libraries and Arts, 1929).
13 Sir Arthur W. Lambert, *Northumbria's Spacious Year, 1929* (Newcastle, 1930), pp. 46–7. The author was Lord Mayor of Newcastle in 1929 and chairman of the exhibition.
14 I am grateful to Owen P. Elton, Head of Mathematics at Marlborough College, for providing a detailed explanation of Alan Robson's diagram, summarising it in correspondence as 'The forces acting on a motorcyclist riding the Wall of Death and consequent centripetal acceleration.'
15 Chapman Family Archive.
16 See Pevsner, op. cit., p. 130.
17 *Shields Gazette*, 11 July 1932.
18 Ibid.
19 *Shields Gazette*, 7 July 1932.

20 *Shields Gazette*, 19 September 1932.
21 Kathleen, one of the 'pretty daughters' of Mr and Mrs W.A. Armstrong, was Robert's god-daughter.
22 *Shields Gazette*, 19 September 1932.
23 *Shields Gazette*, 21 September 1932.
24 *Shields Gazette*, 21 September 1932.
25 *Shields Gazette*, 11 January 1934.
26 *Shields Gazette*, 2 August 1934.
27 *The Tatler*, 27 June 1934. The portrait was donated to the South Shields Museum and Art Gallery by the author's father, Sir Robin Chapman, Bt.
28 After his defeat by the British in Egypt, Napoleon returned for the last time to his family house in Ajaccio, Corsica, now the Musée national de la maison Bonaparte, whose 'conservateur général du Patrimoine' is M. Jean-Marc Olivesi. The author donated the manuscript to this museum in 2013.
29 Chapman Family Archive.
30 *Sunderland Echo*, 31 August 1939.

11 The Second World War, 1939–45

1   County Borough of South Shields, *Report of Emergency Committee to Town Council*, 6 December 1939, vol. 88, p. 853.
2   David Rissik, *The DLI At War: The History of the Durham Light Infantry 1939–1945* (Durham, 1953), p. 6.
3   Harry Moses, *For Your Tomorrow: A History of the 2nd Battalion, Durham Light Infantry 1919–1955* (Durham, 2012), p. 57.
4   Address by Maj. Gen. Robin Brims, Col The Light Infantry, at the Memorial Service for Capt. Richard Wallace Annand, VC, DL, Durham Cathedral, 7 February 2015, Chapman Family Archive.
5   Rissik, op. cit., pp. 14–15.
6   Address by Maj. Gen. Robin Brims, op. cit., Chapman Family Archive. Also quoted in *Newcastle Journal and North Mail*, 28 August 1940.
7   Address by Maj. Gen. Robin Brims, op. cit., Chapman Family Archive.
8   Chapman Family Archive.
9   *Daily Sketch*, 24 August 1940.
10 Gen. Sir Frederick Pile, *Ack-Ack: Britain's Defence Against Air Attack During the Second World War* (London, 1949), p. 140. Gen. Pile was the outstandingly effective General Officer Commanding-in-Chief of Anti-Aircraft Command throughout the war.
11 Amy C. Flagg published *Humanity and Courage: A Pictorial Record* (South Shields, 1944 or 1945). This quotation is from her unpublished accompanying text, *Detailed Account of All Raids* (Local Collections, *The Word*, South Tyneside Council, South Shields).
12 Letter to Barbara Tonks, his future wife, 20 October 1940, Chapman Family Archive.
13 Pile, op. cit., p. 177.
14 Colin Dobinson, *AA Command: Britain's Anti-Aircraft Defences of World War II* (London, 2001), pp. 158, 272.

15 For a full listing of all searchlight sites on Tyneside, and for a very comprehensive 'facts and figures' account of the war, see Roy Ripley and Brian Pears, *North-East Diary 1938–1945*, www.ne-diary.genuki.uk

16 Flagg, *Detailed Account of All Raids*, op. cit., pp. 20–1.

17 Ripley and Pears, op. cit., Background Information, Section 54, 'Women's Voluntary Service'.

18 Chapman Family Archive.

19 Forbes, *Two Small Ships* (London, 1957), p. 115. One of these 'small ships' was HMS *Pathfinder*, on which he served.

20 David Forbes, op. cit., p. 116.

21 R&W Hawthorn, Leslie & Co. Ltd, *Our Ships at War, 1939–1945* (Newcastle upon Tyne, no date), p. 26. The sailors who served on her were the lucky ones. *Pathfinder* herself was declared a total loss in February 1945 after bomb damage from Japanese aircraft off Ramree Island, Burma.

22 Chapman Family Archive.

23 Flagg, *Detailed Account of Air Raids*, op. cit., p. 27.

24 Flagg, op. cit., p. 29.

25 *Durham County Advertizer*, 5 July 1940.

26 Jeremy A. Crang, *The British Army and the People's War 1939–1945* (Manchester, 2000), p. 91.

27 Crang, op. cit., p. 63.

28 Crang, op. cit., p. 93.

29 Crang, op. cit., p. 93.

30 *Shields Gazette*, 18 November 1939.

31 Minutes of the National Councils of YMCA's North-Eastern Area War Emergency Committee, 12 June 1942 (YMCA Archive, Cadbury Research Library Special Collections, University of Birmingham).

32 Jeffrey Richards, *Dream Palace: Cinema and Society in Britain 1930–1939* (London, 1984), p. 51.

33 County Borough of South Shields, *Minutes of the Meeting of the Town Council*, 9 November 1933.

34 *Shields Gazette*, 8 March 1941.

35 *Shields Gazette*, 2 September 1943.

36 Pile, op. cit., p. 193.

37 Chapman Family Archive.

38 Flagg, *Detailed Account of Air Raids*, op. cit., p. 35.

39 *John Readhead & Sons Ltd, South Shields, 1865–1965* (published by the company, South Shields, undated), p. 39. 'E-boats' were fast attack 'Enemy' boats, whose 'Alley' was principally the Baltic Sea and English Channel.

40 Quoted in R&W Hawthorn, Leslie & Co. Ltd, op. cit.

41 *Shields Gazette*, 21 December 1939.

42 Jean Elliott of South Shields joined the Wrens at the same time as Elizabeth Brady, in 1940, and was interviewed in the Turk's Head Hotel in Newcastle upon Tyne. Her interesting recollections as 'Jenny Wren' were published in *Women's War Memories* by the West Park Community Centre, South Shields, 1987 (Local History Collection, *The Word*, South Tyneside Council, South Shields).

43 For this account of Elizabeth Brady's war service I am indebted to commissioned research carried out by Mary Ingham (www.womenhistoryco.uk), author of *Tracing Your Women Ancestors*.

44 Pile, op. cit., p. 326.

45 County Borough of South Shields, *Minutes of the Meeting of the Town Council*, 6 June 1945.

12 Royalty and Recognition

1   *The Times*, 22 June 1946.

2   *Durham County Advertiser*, 24 October 1947.

3   Ibid.

4   *Yorkshire Post*, 24 October 1947.

5   *Sunderland Echo*, 5 October 1949.

6   *Shields Gazette*, 24 February 1949.

7   Ibid. and Chapman Family Archive (for Robert Chapman's speech in full).

8   Ibid.

9   For a full account of the background to this Bill and its passage through Parliament, see Hugh Dalton, *The Fateful Years: Memoirs 1931–1945* (London, 1957), pp. 434–54.

10 *Shields Gazette*, 26 March 1945.

11 See Gavin McCrone, *Regional Policy in Britain* (London, 1969), pp. 106–19 for a detailed account and evaluation.

12 Chapman Family Archive.

13 W.H. Bevan, *The Team Valley Industrial Estate: A History* (1976, unpublished, Tyne and Wear Archives, Newcastle upon Tyne), pp. 9 and 10.

14 Board note to 25th and final AGM of North Eastern Trading Estate Ltd, 19 October 1960, before its amalgamation into the English Estates Corporation (Chapman Family Archive).

15 *Shields Gazette*, 1 March 1950.

16 *Sunderland Echo*, 8 March 1950.

17 *Shields Gazette*, 4 January 1952. BSM Dunn's recollection was not quite correct on one point. Robert was a Lieutenant-Colonel and Commanding Officer of 250 Brigade RFA when he was wounded on 4 April 1918, and he had acted in the role of Brigadier-General in January and February 1918, signing divisional artillery orders. However, he was not formally appointed an Acting Brigadier-General. I am grateful to Chris Baker of fourteeneighteenresearch for this clarification.

18 *The South Shields Centenary*, County Borough of South Shields (1950).

19 See *Evening Chronicle*, 11 April 1951.

20 See *Sunderland Echo*, *Northern Echo* and *Shields Gazette*, 20 July 1953.

21 Chapman Family Archive.

22 These and later quotations are from the *Newcastle Journal Modern Homes Supplement*, 6 April 1954.

23 *Durham County Advertiser*, 6 November 1953.

24 *Shields Gazette*, 5 March 1956.

25 *Shields Gazette*, 1 January 1958.

26 *The Journal*, 16 November 1959.

27 *Shields Gazette*, 22 May 1960.

28 'Foreword' to Brigadier O.F.G. Hogg, *The History of the 3rd Durham Volunteer Artillery, now part of the 274th (Northumbrian) Field Regiment, RA (TA) 1860–1960* (South Shields, 1961).

29 *Shields Gazette*, 16 February 1961.

30 Assizes were 'periodical sessions in each county of England and Wales for the administration of civil and criminal justice' (*Shorter Oxford English Dictionary*, 2007).

31 *Northern Echo*, 30 January 1961.

32 Naomi Eisenstadt, '50 years of family service units', *Social Work in Action*, vol. 10, 1998 – issue 4, pp. 37–46 (www.tandfonline.com/doi/abs/10.1080/09503159808411502).

33 This and the preceding quotations are from the *Evening Chronicle*, 25 May 1962.

34 *The Victor*, no. 49, 27 January 1962.

35 *Shields Gazette*, 29 March 1963.

36 *Sunderland Echo*, 24 July 1963.

37 *Shields Gazette*, 5 September 1963.

38 The hymn's words were taken from 'The Supreme Sacrifice', a poem by (Sir) John S. Arkwright, published in *The Supreme Sacrifice and Other Poems in Time of War* (London, 1919).

39 Robert had an almost bewildering number of qualifications, medals and awards. By the time he died he was Col Sir Robert Chapman, Bt, CB, CMG, CBE, DSO, TD, JP, DL, BA, FCA, OStJ, Croix de Chevalier de la Légion d'honneur. 'OStJ' was the abbreviation for an Officer of the Order of St John.

INDEX

Note: illustrations are indicated by *italicised* page references, and notes by the suffix 'n'